Introduction to and the Treatises of St. Jerome

Introduction to and the Treatises of St. Jerome

Introduction to and the Treatises of St. Jerome

© Lighthouse Publishing 2024

Written by: St. Jerome (Unknown – 326 or 328 AD)
Translated by: Rev. James B.H. Howkins (1879)
Updated into Modern U.S English: A.M. Overett (b.1960)

All rights reserved. Without limiting the rights under copyright reserved above, no part of this publication may be reproduced, stored in a retrieval system, or transmitted, in any form or by any means (electronic, mechanical, photocopying, recording or otherwise), without the prior written permission of the copyright owner of this book.

Published by
Lighthouse Publishing
SAN 257-4330
228 Freedom Parkway
Hoschton, GA 30548
United States of America

www.lighthousechristianpublishing.com

Prolegomena to Jerome.

I.—Introductory.

St. Jerome's importance lies in the facts: (1) That he was the author of the Vulgate Translation of the Bible into Latin, (2) That he bore the chief part in introducing the ascetic life into Western Europe, (3) That his writings more than those of any of the Fathers bring before us the general as well as the ecclesiastical life of his time. It was a time of special interest, the last age of the old Greco-Roman civilization, the beginning of an altered world. It included the reigns of Julian (361–63), Valens (364–78), Valentinian (364–75), Gratian (375–83), Theodosius (379–95) and his sons, the definitive establishment of orthodox Christianity in the Empire, and the sack of Rome by Alaric (410). It was the age of the great Fathers, of Ambrose and Augustine in the West, of Basil, the Gregories, and Chrysostom in the East. With several of these Jerome was brought into personal contact; of Ambrose he often speaks in his writings (Apol. i. 2, iii. 14, in this series Vol. iii., pp. 484 and 526; also this Vol., pp. 74 and 496, Pref. to Origen and S. Luke; and the Pref. to Didymus on the Holy Spirit, quoted in Rufinus' Apology, ii. 24, 43, Vol. iii. of this series, pp. 470 and 480; also On Illust. Men, c. 124, Vol. iii. 383; see also Index—Ambrose); with Augustin he carried on an important correspondence (see Table of Contents); he studied under Gregory Nazianzen (80, 93; see also Illust. Men, c. 117, Vol. iii. 382) at the time of the Council at Constantinople, 381; he was acquainted with Gregory of Nyssa (Illust. Men, c. 128, Vol. iii. 338); he translated the diatribe of Theophilus of Alexandria against Chrysostom

(214, 215). He ranks as one of the four Doctors of the Latin Church, and his influence was the most lasting; for, though he was not a great original thinker like Augustin, nor a champion like Ambrose, nor an organizer and spreader of Christianity like Gregory, his influence outlasted theirs. Their influence in the Middle Ages was confined to a comparatively small circle; but the monastic institutions which he introduced, the value for relics and sacred places which he defended, the deference which he showed for Episcopal authority, especially that of the Roman Pontiff, were the chief features of the Christian system for a thousand years; his Vulgate was the Bible of Western Christendom till the Reformation. To the theologian he is interesting rather for what he records than for any contribution of his own to the science; but to the historian his vivid descriptions of persons and things at an important though melancholy epoch of the world are of inestimable value.

II.—Contemporary History.

The references in this Section, where numbers alone are given, are to the date A. D.

It seems desirable to prefix to this Introduction some account of the times of St. Jerome. General and ecclesiastical history must not be kept too far apart.

Jerome was born in the troubled times which followed the death of Constantine (337), and before Constantius became sole Emperor (353). He was still a schoolboy during the reign of Julian (361–63), and when he heard of his death. During his student life at Rome, Jovian and Valentinian were Emperors, and at Treves, where he next sojourned, the latter Emperor held his court. His first letter refers to a scene in which Ambrose, then Prefect of Liguria, seems to have taken part (370), and his settlement at Aquileia synchronizes with the law of Valentinian restraining legacies to the clergy (370). He went to the East in the year of the death of Athanasius (373), and during his stay in the desert and at Antioch (374-80) occurred the death of Valentinian, the defeat and death of his brother Valens in the battle of Adrianople, the elevation of Theodosius to the purple, and the call of Gregory Nazianzen to Constantinople. He was ordained by Paulinus, one of the three Bishops of Antioch, and studied under Apollinaris, thus touching on both the chief points for which the Council of Constantinople was called (381). At that Council he was probably present, being, as stated above, a disciple of its president, Gregory Nazianzen. He was present also at the Western Council held the next year in Rome under Pope Damasus, whose trusted counsellor he became (pp. 233, 255). His later life, spent at Bethlehem (386–420), witnessed the division of the Empire between the sons of Theodosius, the fall of the Prefect Rufinus (p. 174), to whom Jerome had been denounced, the triumph of Stilicho and his death (at which he weakly rejoiced, p. 237), Alaric's sack of Rome (410) and his death, the revolt of Heraclian, the marriage of Alaric's successor, Adolphus, with the Emperor's sister, Galla Placidia, and the death of Arcadius (408); in ecclesiastical matters, it witnessed the rise of Chrysostom (398) and his exile (403) and death (407), the condemnation of Origenism (400), and the Pelagian controversy (415). It is of this period that we are now to give a sketch.

The Emperor Constantius "may be dismissed," says Gibbon, "with the remark that he inherited the defects without the abilities of his father." He died in Cilicia on November 3, 361; he had been stained in his youth by the blood of nine of his near relatives; he had fallen early under the dominion of the eunuchs of his palace; and he had done little for the defense of the empire. In ecclesiastical matters he had favored the Arian cause, and had banished the orthodox Bishops of the principal sees, and had visited Athanasius of Alexandria with his especial displeasure. His jealousy of his cousin Julian, who had risen to fame by his just and vigorous administration and by his victories over the Germans, led him into acts which provoked the legions of Gaul and caused them to hail Julian as their Emperor. His overtures of peace were rejected by Constantius; he marched rapidly toward Constantinople, and Constantius, leaving the Persian war in which he was engaged, turned westward to meet him. The death of Constantius saved the world from civil war.

Julian's accession was hailed by all who felt the need of a strong ruler; and his first measures were just and tolerant. He recalled from exile the Bishops whom Constantius had banished; his private life was virtuous, and his love of learning endeared him to some of the best of his subjects. But his contempt of Christianity made him first impatient and then a persecutor. He forbade Christians, or Galileans as he called them, to teach in the schools, or to follow the learned professions; he restored Paganism, though it was observed that the Paganism he introduced was in many ways modified by Christian influence; and he favored the Jews and wished them to rebuild their temple at Jerusalem. What the result of his retrogressive policy would have been it is hard to say. He died in a skirmish in the Persian war, on June 26, 363.

Jovian, who succeeded him, was a Christian; and his election showed that the anti-Christian policy of Julian had been without effect. He proclaimed a complete toleration, but died before reaching Constantinople, only six months after his election.

Valentinian, his successor, was an orthodox Christian, his brother Valens, whom he associated with himself, an Arian. Valentinian established his court at Treves, and successfully kept back the barbarians. Thither in 366 Jerome went for a time, and he describes the curious customs of the tribes whom he saw there (Against Jovinian, ii. 7, p. 394). The Emperors proclaimed toleration, which extended even to the celebration of the Eleusinian mysteries. But their inquisitorial and cruel treatment of all suspected of magic arts had a repressive effect upon learning. Their foundation of schools and endowment of physicians for the poorer citizens show that the hopes of social improvement were not extinguished. Yet the state of society in Rome and in other large cities, as given at this time by Ammianus Marcellinus (cxiv. 6, xxviii. 4. See Gibbon, iv. 77. Ed. Milman & Smith), reveals to us the causes of the fall of Rome.

In the reign of Valentinian many ecclesiastical events of great importance took place. The election of Damasus to the Popedom in 366, when the rival factions of Damasus and Ursinus filled the whole city with their conflict, and churches were stormed and strewed with the slain, showed how important the Bishopric of Rome had become. "If you would make me Pope, perhaps I might become a Christian," said Prætextatus, the worshipper of the old gods, to Damasus, who wished to convert him (see

p. 428). The law of Valentinian forbidding legacies to be made to the clergy shows also their wealth and deterioration (p. 92). But this reign produced some of the greatest Bishops and leaders whom the Church has known. Athanasius died in 373. Ambrose became Bishop of Milan in 374. Basil was Bishop of Cæsarea in Cappadocia from 370 to 379.

Meanwhile, the reign of Valens in the East was unsuccessful, and ended in a great disaster. The Visigoths, and Ostrogoths, or Gruthungi, pressed by the Huns, implored permission to cross the Danube from their settlements in Dacia and to be allowed to cultivate the waste lands of Thrace and Asia Minor. This was conceded to them; but they were ill-treated and cajoled, and at last asserted their rights by force; and the Emperor, who attacked them near Adrianople, was defeated and slain, and his army destroyed (378). The Goths were now a formidable force within the Empire. It was in the year before the death of Valens (377) that Stridon, the birthplace of Jerome, was destroyed.

Valentinian had died in 375, leaving two sons, Gratian, an accomplished youth of eighteen, who became Emperor of Gaul and the West, and Valentinian II., then a child, who was nominal Emperor of Italy and the central provinces, and who, with his mother Justina, had his residence at Milan. Gratian distinguished himself by his conduct of several expeditions against the German tribes beyond the Rhine, and, upon the death of his uncle Valens, nominated Theodosius to be Emperor of the East. But he afterwards yielded to idleness and frivolous pleasure, and in 383 was murdered by the agents of the usurper Maximus.

Theodosius, the son of the elder Theodosius, who had recovered Britain and Africa for the Empire, but had on a false accusation been put to death at Carthage, was called to the Empire from his retirement in Spain. He showed himself a great and capable ruler. He took the Goths in detail and gradually dispossessed them. He put down the usurper Maximus (383), and on the death of the young Valentinian (392) fought against the usurper Eugenius, and became sole Emperor (394) in the year before his death. He reformed the laws, enacting the Theodosian Code. In his reign Paganism was finally suppressed. He caused a vote to be taken in the Roman Senate for the establishment of Christian worship and the suppression of Paganism. He destroyed the temples—the destruction of the Serapeum at Alexandria in 389 being the most notable instance of this—and supported Ambrose in his vehement efforts for the suppression of Paganism. Though he loyally befriended the Empress Justina, who was an Arian, and her young son Valentinian II., he did not support their demand for the toleration of Arian worship at Milan which Ambrose had denied to them, and he suppressed Arianism throughout the Empire. To settle the doctrinal disputes raised by the teaching of Apollinaris, Bishop of the Syrian Laodicæa, who held that the Logos in Christ supplied the place of the human soul, and the disputed succession at Antioch, where the Episcopal throne was claimed by the Arian Vitalis, the Trinitarian but Arian-ordained Meletius, and Paulinus the champion of the uncompromising orthodoxy of the West, he summoned the Council of Constantinople, which met in 381. The President of the Council was Gregory Nazianzen, who had come to Constantinople in 379, and, partly through his own eloquence and other great powers, partly through the influence of Theodosius, had won his way from the position of minister of a single church, the Anastasis, to the Episcopal throne. The Egyptian Bishops opposed him and vainly endeavored to foist in the Cynic Maximus into his place. The Council did not succeed in settling the dispute at Antioch, but they maintained the Nicene creed, and added to it all the articles after "I believe in the Holy Ghost." The Council held at Rome in the following year (382), to which Jerome went with Epiphanius, Bishop of Cyprus, and Paulinus of Antioch (p. 255), contradicted that of Constantinople on the subject of the succession at Antioch, but agreed with it on the creed. Gregory Nazianzen soon after the Council resigned the Bishopric of Constantinople, and Damasus, Bishop of Rome, died in 384.

Theodosius was, like Henry II. of England, liable to violent accesses of passion. When the people of Antioch rose in insurrection in 387, and destroyed the busts of the Emperor, he gave an order that the city should be razed and reduced to the rank of a village, from which sentence he was only deterred by the entreaties of the Governor of the city and its Bishop, John Chrysostom. When a similar rising took place at Thessalonica in 390, he was not similarly appeased, but ordered that the people when summoned to the theatre should be massacred by his soldiers, and seven thousand men, women and children were thus put to death. Ambrose, on Theodosius' coming to Milan, refused to admit him to the communion of the Church till he had undergone five months of penance and showed his repentance for his crime.

On the death of the young Valentinian in 391, Eugenius the rhetorician usurped the throne of the West. Justina fled to the court of Theodosius, who, after long preparations, marched against Eugenius, and defeated him at Aquileia in 394. Theodosius, however, did not long survive his rival. After this last success he gave himself up to ease and self-indulgence, and died 395.

The Empire was divided between the sons of Theodosius. Arcadius, who became Emperor of the East, was eighteen years of age, and Honorius, fourteen. Both were weak characters, ill-suited to cope with the growing dangers of the Empire. Arcadius married Eudoxia, a woman of a worldly and violent disposition. Honorius married the daughter of Stilicho, the great semi-barbarian general, who was his cousin, having married Serena, the daughter of Honorius, brother to the great Theodosius. Arcadius' minister, Rufinus, became so unbearable in his rapacity (see Jerome's allusion to him, p. 447) that a tumult was raised against him and he was put to death (395). Honorius removed his court to Ravenna, among the pine forests of which he was more secure from invasion; and, so long as he was under the guidance of Stilicho, was able to live in security.

John Chrysostom became Bishop of Constantinople in 398, and by his sermons and ascetic discipline exerted a large influence. But intrigues were raised against him by Theophilus of Alexandria on account of his reception of the Long Monks, whom Theophilus had banished in his zeal against Origenism. And the Empress Eudoxia, whom his plain speaking had offended, endeavored to work his ruin. He was banished, after having been once brought back to the capital by the entreaties of the people, in 404, and died in 407, having continued to exercise his influence over the Church generally from his exile at Comana in Pontus. His remains were brought to Constantinople thirty years later, and were welcomed by Theodosius II. and his consort Eudocia with tears of repentance for the fault of their predecessors. Arcadius died in 408, leaving as his heir the young Theodosius, then but seven years old. His daughter Pulcheria and the Prefect Anthemius administered the Empire successfully; the Huns, who had entered the Roman territory and encamped in Thrace, were persuaded to withdraw, and the Eastern Empire enjoyed peace during the remainder of the reign of Theodosius II.

Turning to ecclesiastical affairs, we find a certain calm settling down upon the Church after the Council of Constantinople, and an unwillingness to reopen the subjects of strife. Men used the name of heretic rather as something to frighten their opponents, and sought to identify opinions which they disliked with the Arianism of the past, which all alike condemned. There were much fewer Councils of Bishops and no General Council for fifty years (Ephesus, 431). But other subjects of dispute arose, the Christian community being saturated with Greek contentiousness. The first of these related to Origenism. The works of the great and original church teacher of Alexandria of the third century (~254) had been little studied for above a hundred years, when a new interest in them arose both in the East and the West. The earnest study of Scripture which led to the formation of the Vulgate, or translation from the original into the vulgar tongue of the Latin world, led to a wish to consult the greatest textual writer and interpreter of Scripture who had as yet appeared; and those who learned from his Bible work to admire him were led also to study his doctrinal views. It happened to Origen, as to many modern teachers, that his name came to be identified with one or two prominent doctrines; and, as men speak of Calvinism or Erastianism or Hegelianism, so they spoke of Origenism. The doctrines which they connected with Origen were taken from his most important work, the Περὶ ’Αρχῶν, "on First Principles." They were mainly (1) his expressions relating to the subordination of the Son to the Father, and (2) his eschatology. As to the first of these, they took isolated expressions, such as, "The Son does not see the Father," or, "the Son is darkness in comparison with the Father," and they spoke of him as the father of Arius; as to the second, they fastened upon his speculative ideas, that the coming of men's souls into this world was a fall from a previous state of being; that men may rise into an angelic state; that the material body is destined to pass away; and that in the consummation of all things all spiritual beings, including the fallen angels, will be schooled into obedience, so that the universe may be brought back into harmony. Men were incapable of entering into the general system of Origen, and still more of understanding his historical position. The Pope Anastasius who condemned him in 404 says plainly that he knows neither who Origen was nor when he lived (see Vol. iii. 433); and they consequently took his tenets in an absolute sense, and thought of him as denying the divinity of Christ, or the condemnation of the wicked, or the resurrection of the body. His views were most widely spread in Egypt, where the contrary tendency of Anthropomorphism, that is, the conception of God as the subject of human properties and passions, was also widely prevalent. Theophilus, Bishop of Alexandria, at first was generally favorable to Origen, as was also Jerome; but, through various causes, not unmixed with personal feeling, he turned against Origenism in a fanatical and persecuting temper. He procured the condemnation of

Origenism by the Bishops of Egypt, Syria, and Cyprus, and also by those of Rome and Italy; and he pursued those who had fled from his persecution to Constantinople, and branded Chrysostom, who had receive them, as a heretic. In all this he was aided by Jerome, who translated his missives into Latin (see Letters 86 to 100, 113 and 114). But the whole matter was transacted without any Council being called; the Bishops were taken as speaking the general sentiment, and their decisions were reinforced by a decree of the Emperors (400).

The second controversy (which also was disposed of without any General Council) was that of Pelagianism. Pelagius and Cælestius, monks of Britain, had come to Rome in 409, and maintained the doctrine of Free Will and the possibility of a man living without sin, against the Augustinian doctrine of Grace, which asserted the helplessness of man and issued in absolute predestinarianism. They passed into Africa with the crowds who were escaping from Alaric's invasion, and there confronted the influence of Augustin. Condemned by a Council at Carthage in 413, they passed into Palestine, and procured recognition from Councils held at Jerusalem and Diospolis in 415, notwithstanding the presence of Orosius, Augustin's friend, and the accusations of the Gaulish Bishops, Heros and Lazarus. Jerome was invited to write against them (pp. 272, 279), and their followers rose against him and burnt his monasteries (p. 280, Augustin De Gest. Pel. c. 66), after which they visited Ephesus and Rome, and were at first received by the Pope Zosimus; and several Bishops, of whom the chief was Julian of Eclana, espoused their cause. But Augustin's influence prevailed in the West, while in the East little interest was taken in a controversy which was humanistic rather than strictly theological, and men's minds were being drawn to the questions of Christology, which led to the Nestorian controversy and the Council of Ephesus (431).

The forces of the barbarians, which in the reign of Valens had threatened Constantinople, were diverted to the West in the reign of the sons of Theodosius. Those who remained within the boundaries of the Empire imbibed something of Roman civilization, and, in many cases, became servants of Rome; and, as the subjects of the Empire withdrew through love of luxury from military duties, the power of the barbarians enlisted as mercenaries increased. Alaric, who now rose to power, occupied an ambiguous position. He marched with his Gothic army into Greece (396), and, being a Christian, thought himself justified in plundering the historic fanes of the old religion. He was attacked by Stilicho near the Isthmus of Corinth, and defeated, but he contrived to transport his army across the gulf and to take possession of Epiris (397), and the ministers of Arcadius thought it prudent to make peace with him. In 398 he became at once Master-General of Illyricum and King of the Visigoths; and, his rights not being respected by the Emperor of the West, he invaded the North of Italy. He was vanquished by Stilicho in the battles of Pollentia and Verona (403); but the conqueror, who well knew the increasing weakness of Rome, made peace with Alaric and acknowledged his official position. Alaric retreated for a time, but another barbarian invader, Radagaisus or Radaghast, with a mixed host of Vandals, Suevi, and Burgundians, forced his way to Florence. He was there met by Stilicho who gained over him his last great victory on the heights of Fiesole (406). The policy of conciliation adopted by Stilicho might have converted Alaric and his Goths into the guards of the Empire; but his action was disowned, and he was treated as a traitor and put to death in 408. Then Alaric advanced to the attack upon Rome. He was induced by fair promises to raise the siege; but, finding that no faith could be placed in the court of Ravenna, he renewed the siege, and took the city on August 26, 410. The only redeeming feature in the terrible destruction which ensued was the respect of the Goths for the Christian religion. They spared the clergy and the churches and those who had taken refuge in them; and even the rich plate and ornaments of divine worship were held sacred from their rapacity. But the knell of Roman greatness had been sounded, and the end of the Empire was near at hand. Alaric on leaving Rome ravaged Italy. He marched to Rhegium, the flames of which Rufinus saw from the opposite coast while he wrote his Commentary on the Book of Numbers (Vol. iii. p. 568); but his attempt to cross into Sicily was frustrated by a storm, and he himself died before the year of the sack of Rome had closed. His successor, Adolphus, made peace with Rome, and dared to ask for the hand of Galla Placidia, the sister of Honorius. The King of the Goths was accepted as the brother-in-law of the Roman Emperor.

  The Empire of the West might now be compared to a ship heaving to and fro in a troubled sea, encompassed by enemies and without captain or rudder. Britain revolted in 409. From 409 to 413 Gaul was a prey to revolutions, and the usurper Constantine was with difficulty overcome by the Roman General Constantius, only to be followed by fresh usurpers, Jovinus, Sebastian, and Attalus. The Count Heraclian dared to invade Rome itself in 413, though defeat and death were the penalty.

One by one the provinces of the Empire passed into the hands of the barbarians. The Goths settled in Aquitaine and in Spain; the Vandals turned down into Africa; the Burgundians settled in the East and North of France, and the Franks in the center. The ruin of the Empire of the West was practically consummated at the time of Jerome's death in 419, though sixty years of disaster and disgrace intervened before its final extinction.

Meanwhile the distressed condition of Italy had driven large numbers of persons, especially of the clergy and the upper classes of society, to take refuge in the East, so as almost to justify Thierry's designation of the movement as an emigration to the Holy Land. Jerome and his friends received this tide of fugitives at Bethlehem, and corresponded with those left behind; and thus the evils of the time made the Solitary of the East the chief Doctor of the West.

III.—Life of Jerome.

The figures in parentheses, when not otherwise indicated, refer to the pages in this volume.

For a full account of the Life, the translator must refer to an article (Hieronymus) written by him in Smith and Wace's *Dictionary of Christian Biography*. A shorter statement may suffice here, since the chief sources of information are contained in this volume, and to these reference will be continually made.

Childhood and Youth. A.D. 345. Jerome was born at Stridon, near Aquileia, but in Pannonia, a place which was partially destroyed in the Gothic invasion of 377 (On Illustrious Men, 135, Vol. iii. p. 304). Jerome's own property, however, remained, though in a ruinous state, in 397 (140). His father Eusebius (Ill. Men, as above) and his mother were Catholic Christians (492), but he was not baptized in infancy. The family was moderately wealthy, possessing houses (140) and slaves (Apol. i. 30, Vol. iii. p. 498), and was intimate with the richer family from which sprang Bonosus, Jerome's foster brother and friend (6). The parents were living in 373 when Jerome first went to the East (35), but probably died at the destruction of Stridon. He had a brother, Paulinian, twenty years his junior (140, 173), and we read of a sister (8, 9), and an aunt named Castorina (13).

He received a good education, but declares that he was an idle boy (Vol. iii. 498). He was at a grammar school when the Emperor Julian died (Comm. on Habakkuk iii. 14) and soon after went to Rome with his friend Bonosus (6), where he studied rhetoric (at that time the all-embracing pursuit) under Ælius Donatus (Vol. iii. 491), and frequented 363 the lawcourts (Comm. on Gal., ii. 13).

363–66. He fell into sin (9, 15, 78), but was drawn into the company of young Christians who on Sundays visited the tombs of the martyrs in the Catacombs (Com. on Ezek., ch. 40, v. 5), and is believed to have been baptized by the Pope Liberius in 366 (20). He was already a keen student, though as yet having little knowledge of Greek (Rufinus Apol. ii. 9, Vol. iii. p. 464), and had begun the acquisition of a library (35).

366–70. From Rome Jerome went with Bonosus to Gaul, passing, however, through Northern Italy, where they made acquaintance with Rufinus, probably at his native place, Concordia (Ep. v. 2, comp. with iii. 3, pp. 7, 11). He stayed at Treves (7), and travelled in its neighborhood (394), and copied mss., and wrote a mystical Commentary on Obadiah (401).

Aquileia. Returning probably by Vercellæ (1) to Italy he was for three years at Aquileia, where he entered definitively upon the twin pursuits of his life, Scriptural study and the fostering of asceticism.

370–73. A society of congenial minds gathered round him, comprising Rufinus, Bonosus, Heliodorus (afterwards Bishop of Altinum), Chromatius (afterwards Bishop of Aquileia), and his brother Eusebius, and the Archdeacon Jovinus, the monk Chrysogonus, the subdeacon Niceas, Innocentius, and Hylas, the freedman of the wealthy but ascetic Roman lady, Melania, together with Evagrius (afterwards Bishop of Antioch), who had come to Italy with Eusebius, Bishop of Vercellæ, on his return from exile. For the mention of these in various parts of Jerome's works, the Index must be consulted. These ascetics did not form a monastery. There were as yet no Orders or Rules. The vow was merely a "purpose" (*propositum*) which each privately took on himself and the terms of which each man freely prescribed. The Greek word *Monachus* (Monk) was used, but only implied living a single or separate life. Some were hermits (5, 9, 247), some lived in cities (121, 250). Jovinian was a monk, though antiascetic (378); Heliodorus (91) and John of Jerusalem (174) were monks, though Bishops. Some members of the ascetic society at Aquileia may have resided in the same house; but there was no cenobitic discipline. Jerome visited Stridon and the neighboring town of Æmona (12), and perhaps resided at his native place for a time, but he complains of the worldliness of the people of his native town and of the opposition of their Bishop, Lupicinus (8 n. 10). The friends at Aquileia were united in the closest friendship.

373. Rufinus' baptism (7, Ruf. Ap. i. 4, Vol. iii. 436) and the writing of Jerome's first letter on "the woman seven times struck with the axe" are the only incidents which have come down to us of this period. We only know that the society was broken up by some event which Jerome speaks of as "a sudden storm," and "a monstrous rending asunder" (5).

Jerome determined on going to the East with Evagrius and Heliodorus; Innocentius, Niceas, and Hylas accompanied him (1, 5, 6, 10). Chromatius, Eusebius, and Jovinus remained in Italy. Bonosus retired to an island in the Adriatic, where he lived the life of a hermit (5, 9). Rufinus went to Egypt and subsequently to Palestine in the company of Melania (6, 7). Jerome and his companions travelled through Thrace, Pontus, Bithynia, Galatia, at the capital of which (Ancyra) he appears to have stayed (497), Cappadocia, and Cilicia, to Antioch, their haven of rest (5). But they did not long remain together. Heliodorus made a journey to Jerusalem, where he was the guest of Florentius (6).

374. Jerome was in ill health, and at length, in the middle of Lent (36), fell into a fever of which he nearly died. To this illness belongs his anti-Ciceronian dream (36, Apol. ii. 6, Vol. iii. 462), which finally determined him to abandon secular learning and devote himself to sacred studies. The successive deaths of Innocentius and Hylas left Jerome alone with Evagrius, at whose country house he fell in with the ancient hermit Malchus (315), and was encouraged by him in the ascetic tendency. He hoped to see Rufinus, wrote to him through Florentius (4, 6), but he did not come; and he determined to embrace the

life of solitude. Heliodorus had some thought of accompanying him, but, to Jerome's great chagrin) felt the call to pastoral work to be the stronger, and returned to Italy (8, 13, 123).

The Desert. 374–379. Jerome spent the next five years in the Desert of Chalcis, to the east of Antioch (7). It was peopled by hermits who, though living apart for most purposes, were under some kind of authority (4, 21). Jerome wrote to their head, Theodosius, begging to be admitted into their company (4). His life while in the desert was one of rigorous penance, of tears and groans alternating with spiritual ecstasy, and of temptations from the haunting memories of Roman life (24, 25); he lived in a cell or cavern; he earned his daily bread, and was clad in sackcloth (21, 24), but he was not wholly cut off from converse with men. He saw Evagrius frequently (7, 8); he wrote and received letters and books (7, 11); he learned Hebrew from a converted Jew (Ep. xviii. 10), and copied and translated the Gospel according to the Hebrews (Ill. Men, 2, 3, Vol. iii. 362), and his brother solitaries he found only too accessible (Ep. xvii. 3). Towards the close of his sojourn he became involved in the controversies then agitating the Church at Antioch, where Arian Vitalis, the orthodox but Arian-ordained Meletius, and the Western Paulinus disputed the possession of the bishopric (20). Jerome found himself beset with demands for a confession of faith in terms strange to his Western education (19, 20). He appealed to Pope Damasus for advice (19, 20); but he and his friends found his position intolerable. They would rather, he says, live among wild beasts than among Christians such as those about them. In the autumn of 378 he wrote to Marcus, then head of the eremite community, to say that he only begged for the "hospitality of the desert" for a few months: in the spring he would be gone (21).

379. Accordingly, in the spring of 379 he came to Antioch and attached himself to the party of Paulinus, the Western and orthodox Bishop, who ordained him presbyter, though he then and always afterwards declined the active ministry (446). He pursued his studies under the celebrated Apollinarius of Laodicæa, though not accepting his views (176), and wrote his "Dialogue against the Luciferians" (319–334).

Constantinople. 380. The next year Jerome went, with his Bishop, Paulinus, to Constantinople, and was there during the Second General Council, at which the views of his teacher, Apollinarius, were condemned, and sentence was passed in the cause of his Bishop. He placed himself under the teaching of Gregory Nazianzen (80, 93, 357; Ill. Men, 117), and became acquainted with Gregory of Nyssa (Ill. Men, 128); he translated the Chronicle of Eusebius and dedicated it to Vincentius and Gallienus, the former of whom became henceforward his companion (483, 444–446); he imbibed his admiration for Origen, translating his Homilies on Jeremiah and Ezekiel, and writing to Damasus on the meaning given by Origen to the Seraphim in Is. vi. (22).

381. These literary labors were carried on under the disadvantage of a weakness of the eyes, from which he henceforward constantly suffered. But there is in his writings not a single reference to the Council of Constantinople, and only cursory references to that held the next year at Rome, in which he was certainly called to take part (233; Ruf. Epil. to Pamph., Vol. iii. 426, 513).

Rome. 382–5. He went to Rome with his Bishop, Paulinus, and with Epiphanius, Bishop of Salamis in

Cyprus. At the Council which was there held he was present as a learned man whose help the Pope required. There is no ground for the notion that he became his official secretary. But for the two main objects of Jerome's life his sojourn in Rome presented great opportunities. Damasus thoroughly appreciated his eminence as a biblical scholar. He constantly sent him questions, the replies to which form short exegetical treatises, such as those reckoned among Jerome's letters on the word Hosanna and the Prodigal Son. It was also for Pope Damasus that he undertook a revised version of the Psalms, a version which was used in the Roman Church for more than eleven centuries (492, 494), and also a revised version of the New Testament, the preface to which is of much critical value (487, 488; see also p. 357, where a whole clause in 1 Cor. vii. 35 is said to have been omitted in the old version because of the difficulty of translation). He further began the collation of the various texts of the LXX. and the other Greek versions of the Old Testament, and began to form the convictions which afterwards led to his translation direct from the Hebrew (484). These biblical studies made him acquainted with the works of Origen, and he conceived a great and almost passionate admiration for that "brazen-hearted" (Chalchenterus) worker and teacher of the Church (46), and he permitted himself to use expressions too indiscriminate in praise of him and too contemptuous towards his adversaries, which were afterwards thrown in his teeth (Ruf. Ap. ii. 14, Vol. iii. 467).

For the promotion of asceticism he found in Rome a congenial soil. Epiphanius, himself the pupil of the hermits Hesychias and Hilarion (Sozom. vi. 32, Vol. ii. 369, 370), was the guest of the noble and wealthy lady

Paula, the heiress of the Æmilian race (196), who was already disposed to the ascetic life. To the circle of her family and friends Jerome was soon admitted, and she became his devoted disciple and friend during the remainder of her life (Letter cviii.). Her son, Toxotius, and her daughters, Blesilla, the young widow (47–49), Paulina, the wife of Jerome's friend, the ascetic Senator Pammachius (135), and Julia Eustochium (196), each in special ways affected the life of Jerome. Her friends, Marcella and Principia (253), Asella (42, 58), Lea (42), Furia and Titiana, Marcellina and Felicitas (60) and Fabiola, all of them belonging to the highest Roman families, formed a circle of renuntiants who sought refuge in the ascetic life from the wastefulness and immorality of those of their own quality. Marcella's house on the Aventine was their meeting place (41, 58). There they prayed and sang psalms in the Hebrew, which they had learned for the purpose (210), and read the Scriptures under the guidance of their teacher (41, 255), who wrote for them many of his expository letters, whose ascetic writings they committed to memory, and whose private letters to them (Letters xxiii.–xlvi.) reveal the various phases of the new Roman and Christian life. These are concentrated in the Treatise on the Preservation of Virginity which he addressed to Eustochium (Letter xxii.). This period also produced the first of Jerome's controversial treatises, that against Helvidius on the perpetual virginity of Mary (334–346).

384–5. This congenial scene of activity and friendship was broken up by the death of Damasus. The new Pope, Siricius, to whom many had thought of Jerome as a rival (59), was without sympathy for him: he had offended almost every class of the community by his unrestrained satire (Letters xxii., xl., liv., etc.): he had awakened suspicion by his over praise of Origen (46); and at the funeral of Blesilla, whose end was believed to have been hastened by the hard life enjoined upon her, the fury of the people was excited against Jerome and the cry was raised "The monks to the Tiber!" (53). He felt that he was vainly trying to "sing the Lord's song in a strange land" (60) and he resolved to leave Rome forever and to seek a retreat in Palestine. His departure in August and the feelings excited by it are described in a passage in his Apology against Rufinus (Ap. iii. 22, Vol. iii. 530) and in his letter to Asella (Letter xlv.) written at the moment of his embarkation at Ostia.

385–6. Jerome sailed with Vincentius and with his brother Paulinian (Vol. iii. 530 as above) direct to Antioch. Paula and Eustochium, leaving the other members of their family, went to Cyprus to see Epiphanius; and the two parties united at Antioch (198). Thence they passed through Palestine and Jerusalem, on to Egypt, where they visited the abode of the monks of Nitria (202) and became acquainted with Didymus, "the blind seer" of Alexandria (176): and they returned to Palestine in the autumn of 386, and settled at Bethlehem for the remainder of their lives.

Bethlehem, First Period. Jerome's life at Bethlehem lasted thirty-four years. A monastery was built, of which he was the head, and a convent for women over which Paula and Eustochium successively presided (206), a church where all assembled (206, 292), and a hospice for pilgrims who came to visit the holy places from all parts of the world (140). These institutions were supported by the wealth of Paula until, through the profusion of her charities, she was so impoverished that she rather depended on Jerome and his brother, who sold the remains of their family property for their support (140). He lived in a cell, surrounded by his library, to which he constantly made additions (Ruf. Ap. ii. 8 (2), Vol. iii. 464). He lived on bread and vegetables (165), and speaks of his life as one of repentance and prayer (446), but no special austerities are mentioned in his writings, and he did not think piety increased by the absence of cleanliness (33, 34). He never officiated in the services (83), but was much absorbed in the cares (140) and discipline (Letter cxlvii.) of the monastery, and by the crowds of monks who came from all parts of the world (64, 65, 500). Sulpicius Severus (Dial. i. 8) tells us that when he was with him towards the close of his life, he had the charge of the parish of Bethlehem; and the presbyters associated with him certainly prepared candidates for baptism (446); but his call, as he often confesses, was not to the pastorate, but to the study (Letter cxii.). He had youths to whom he taught Latin classics (Ruf. Apol. ii. 8 (2), Vol. iii. 465); and he expounded the Scriptures daily to the brethren in the monastery (Apol. ii. 124, Vol. iii. 515). Sulpicius speaks of him as always reading or writing, never resting day or night. Translations, commentaries, controversial works, letters dealing with important subjects, flowed constantly from his pen, while the notes passing between him and Paula and Eustochium were without number (Ill. Men, 135, Vol. iii. 384), and everything that he wrote was caught up by friends or by enemies and published (79). He worked amidst great distractions, not merely from the cares of the monasteries and the hospice, but from the need of entertaining persons of distinction, like Fabiola (161), from all parts of the world (153, 287, 161); from the need of replying to the letters brought by messengers from the most distant countries for those who sought advice of the renowned teacher (Letters cxvi.–cxxx.); from prolonged illnesses (188, 215); at times from poverty; from the panic of barbarian invasions (161, 252), and from the attacks of his enemies, who in the year 417 burned his monasteries (281, 282).

He spared no pains nor expense in the production of his works. He perfected his knowledge of Hebrew by the aid of a Jew who came to him like Nicodemus by night (176); he also learned Chaldee (493); and for special parts of his Bible work he obtained special aid from a distance (491, 494), obtaining funds, when his own had failed, from his old friends Chromatius and Heliodorus (492).

386–92. The list of his works during the first six years of his residence at Bethlehem comprises the completion of the Commentary on Ecclesiastes, and the translation of Didymus on the Holy Spirit; the Commentaries on Ephesians and Galatians, Titus and Philemon (498); a revision of the version of the New Testament begun in Rome; a Treatise on Psalms x.–xvi., and Translation of Origen on St. Luke and the Psalms; the Book on the Names of Hebrew Places, mainly translated from Eusebius; the Book of Hebrew Proper Names and that of Hebrew Questions on Genesis; the revision of his translation of the LXX., involving a comparison of Origen's Hexapla; a considerable part of the Vulgate; the Lives of the hermits Malchus and Hilarion; and the Catalogue of Illustrious Church Writers. The only letter preserved to us of this period is that written in the name of Paula and Eustochium to invite Marcella to come to Palestine (60).

Bethlehem, Second Period. 392–405. The second period of Jerome's stay at Bethlehem is the period of his most conspicuous activity, which was partly employed in the salutary work of finishing the Vulgate and in writing letters which rank among the finest of his compositions, but largely also in controversies, in which the worst parts of his character and influence are brought into prominence.

395, 398 and 404–5, 394–97. There were also great external hindrances to his work: the panic arising from the invasion of the Huns, on account of which the inmates of the monasteries had to leave their homes and prepare to embark at Joppa (161); there were long periods of ill health; and there was the quarrel with the Bishop of Jerusalem which led to a kind of excommunication of the monks of Bethlehem (446, 447).

The letters of this second period are those numbered 47 to 116. They comprise those to Nepotianus, nephew of Heliodorus, on the duties of the pastorate (89–96); that to Heliodorus, on the death of his nephew (123–131); that to Paulinus, the Roman Senator, afterwards Bishop of Nola, on his poem in praise of Theodosius, and on the study of Scripture (96–102); that to Furia, on the maintenance of widowhood (102–109); that to the Spanish noble Lucinius, who had sent scribes to copy Jerome's works (151–154), and to his widow Theodora (154, 155); those to Abigaus, a blind Spanish presbyter (156, 157), and to Salvina, widow of Nebridius, and closely connected with the Emperor Theodosius (163–168); that to Amandus, the Roman presbyter, on a difficult case of conscience (149–151); the letter to Oceanus, defending the second marriage of a Spanish Bishop (141–146); the letter to Læta, wife of Toxotius, son of Paula, on the education of her infant daughter (189–195); and those gems of his writings, the sketches of the lives (Epitaphia) of Fabiola (157–163) and of Paula (195–212).

The Vulgate. 391–403. The work of Jerome's life, the Vulgate version of the Scriptures, was completed in this period. The version which bore the name of Vulgate, the popular or vernacular version, in his day (44, 487–488) was a loose translation of the LXX., of which almost every copy varied from every other. His first effort, therefore, was to translate, or to revise the existing translations, from a correct version of the LXX. And this revised version he used in his familiar expositions, in the monastery (Apol. ii. 24, Vol. iii. 515), though a great part of it was lost even in his lifetime (280), and all that now remains of it is Job, the Psalms, and the Preface to the Books of Solomon (494). But even the most correct text of the LXX., as he saw at once, was insufficient. In Origen's Hexapla the versions of Theodotion, Aquila, and Symmachus were given, together with two others called Quinta and Sexta, in parallel columns with the LXX. These constantly differed; and the only mode of deciding between them was by going back to the Hebrew—"Hebraica Veritas," as he constantly terms it (80, 486, 494).

392. Accordingly, he set himself at once, in his settlement at Bethlehem, to the preliminary labors required for this task; and in the sketch of his works in the Catalogue (Vol. iii. 384; On Ill. Men, 135) he says: The New Testament I have restored according to the Greek original; the Old I have translated in accordance with the Hebrew."

393. But no portion was as yet published. In the following year he published the prophets (80) and sent other portions of his Old Testament version to Marcella at Rome, keeping the rest shut up in his closet (80), and awaiting the judgment of his friends on the portions submitted to them. He purposed from the first to publish the whole, as we see from what he calls his "helmeted preface" to the Books of Samuel and of Kings (489). But it was published in fragments, according as he had leisure to give it a final revision, or according as other circumstances were favorable. The series of Prefaces (487–494) shows that some parts were written or revised in great haste (492, 494), some parts extorted from him by the importunity of his friends (488; see Apol. ii. 25, in Vol. iii. 515); that he was subjected to severe censures and misunderstanding, as to which he was extremely sensitive; that at times he so shrank from publicity that he wished his friends only to read it privately; that he was often, especially in the later portions, dependent on his friends for the provision of the copyists (492, 494). The order of publication can be traced. The Books of Samuel and of the Kings came first, then Job and the Prophets, Ezra and Nehemiah, and the Book of Genesis. Thus far he had proceeded in the year 393 when a break of three years occurred through external hindrances, of which the panic of the invasion of the Huns was the chief.

395. He then, at the entreaty of Chromatius and Heliodorus (492), completed the Books of Solomon, intending to proceed systematically to the end.

398. But illness intervened, after which he states that the first eight books were still wanting in the copies made for the Spaniard Lucinius (153);

403. nor was the publication resumed till five years later, when the remaining books from Exodus to Ruth and the Book of Esther were brought out (489, 491).

404. The whole was then collected, by others rather than by himself, and gradually superseded all other Latin versions, and, coupled with the version of the New Testament previously made, became the received, or Vulgate, edition of the Bible.

393–404. The second period of Jerome's stay at Bethlehem is the period of his great controversies. These are no less than six in number. (1) That with Jovinian on ascetic practices. (2) That with the Origenists, in which he worked with Theophilus of Alexandria and the Western Bishops. (3) That with John, Bishop of Jerusalem. (4) That with Rufinus. (5) That with Vigilantius. (6) That with Augustin. These may be described somewhat cursorily, the reader being referred for a more detailed statement of them to the Letters and Treatises themselves and to the notices prefixed to them.

(1) *Jovinian.* Jovinian was a Roman monk or, rather, solitary (for many took private monastic vows without entering any order or monastery) who had perceived the danger of degrading the ordinary Christian life which lurked in the profession of asceticism. He was not, to judge by Jerome's quotations from him (347), a man of superior ability; but there are no apparent grounds for the imputations which Jerome throws upon his character. He put off the monastic dress, and lived like other men; and, though he refused to marry, maintained his right as a Christian to do so. He argued that the conditions of virginity, marriage, and widowhood were equal in God's sight, provided men lived in faith and piety; and that eating and fasting were indifferent if men

gave God thanks. He seems to have had some influence, and it is stated that some who had made vows of virginity were led through his teaching to marry. Certainly his views were condemned by the Pope Siricius, by Ambrose, and by Augustin.

393. He published a book in Rome, maintaining these opinions, and others of a more speculative character, which was sent to Jerome, and was at once answered by him in his treatise "Against Jovinian" (346–416). The more speculative matters he deals with calmly; but the anti-ascetic views he treats with violence and contempt. "These are the hissings of the old serpent; by these the dragon expelled man from Paradise." His intemperateness, which threw contempt upon marriage, was severely blamed by his friends at Rome, who tried to stop the publication (79; see also Ruf. Apol. ii. 44, Vol. iii. 480); but he only replied by renewed expressions of derision, and, several years later, when he has occasion to refer to Jovinian, he says, "This man, after being condemned by the authority of the Roman Church, amidst his feasts of pheasants and swine's flesh, I will not say gave up, but belched out, his life" (417).

(2) *Origenism.* 393–403. The second great controversy in which Jerome was engaged at this period relates to Origenism, about which a great controversy had arisen at Alexandria, leading to its condemnation by the Bishops of Palestine and Cyprus in the East, and by the Pope and the Bishop of Milan and others in the West.

The great church teacher of Alexandria in the third century was but little known in the West. Anastasius the Pope, in the year 399, declared that he neither knew who he was nor what he had written (Vol. iii. 433). Jerome, who had made acquaintance with his writings during his first sojourn in the East, conceived a strong admiration for him; he did not, indeed, accept all his views, as may be seen from the first letter in which he alludes to him (22); but on his coming to Rome he did all in his power to make him known. He was invited by Damasus to translate some of his works (485); and when he found ignorant condemnations passed upon him he praised him with his usual vehemence and without discrimination, even eulogizing the Περὶ ’Αρχῶν on which the subsequent controversy mainly turned (46; Ruf. Ap. ii. 13, Vol. iii. 467). He had also quoted without blame in his Commentary on the Ephesians statements such as those relating to the pre-existence of human souls and possible restoration of Satan (Ruf. Apol. i. 448, 454). But it was rather a literary enthusiasm and an admiration of original genius than an express consent to Origen's system. His calm judgment in later years was, that his literary services to the Church were inestimable, but that his doctrinal views were to be read with the greatest caution, and that those specially impugned were heretical (176, 177, 238, 244). It must be allowed, however, that he appears in his earlier stage as the vehement panegyrist of Origen (46, 48), and in his later stage as his equally vehement condemner; and also that this change seems less the effect of conviction than of a fear of the imputation of heresy (Apol. iii. 33, Vol. iii. 535).

The monks in the deserts near Alexandria were divided, some holding Origenistic views, and some those of an opposite tendency and verging upon Anthropomorphism. Theophilus, the Bishop of Alexandria, at first sided with the Origenists, but afterwards turned against them, and became their relentless persecutor. During his former phase he was appealed to by John, Bishop of Jerusalem, in his controversy with Epiphanius and Jerome (427), and took his part so vehemently that he sent his confidant Isidore to Jerusalem, nominally to inquire, but really to crush out all opposition, as he stated in a letter to John (444). This letter fell into the hands of Jerome and his friends, and the intentions of Theophilus were frustrated. A period of suspicious silence followed (134); but when Theophilus had undergone his change he found a ready instrument in Jerome, who threw himself eagerly into the conflict (182–184), translated the encyclicals of Theophilus (185, 186, 189) which led to the condemnation of Origen in the East, and even his diatribe against St. John Chrysostom for receiving Isidore and his brethren, whom Theophilus now treated as his enemies (214). Jerome also, through his friends Pammachius, Marcella, and Eusebius (186, 256), procured the condemnation of Origen in the West.

(3) *John of Jerusalem.* The controversy with John of Jerusalem forms an episode in the more general controversy. John had been trained among the Origenistic ascetics, Epiphanius among the anti-Origenists. Jerome appears to have undergone no change in his sentiments as to Origen during the first period of his stay at Bethlehem [see his Preface to the Book of Hebrew Questions (486, 487) written in 388], and was on good terms with the Bishop of Jerusalem and with Rufinus, who was then living on the Mount of Olives.

393. But at the beginning of the second period a certain Aterbius came to Jerusalem and spread suspicion and alarm of heresy. Jerome, perhaps weakly, "gave him satisfaction" as to his faith (Apol. iii. 33, Vol. iii. 535), while by John and Rufinus he was treated as a busybody (*id.*). This produced the first estrangement, which was

greatly increased by the visit of Epiphanius in the following year. The scenes which followed may be read in Jerome's treatise, "Against John of Jerusalem" (430) and in Epiphanius' letter translated by Jerome (83–85). Epiphanius was popular at Jerusalem, and after a scene in the church, in which he preached against Origenism and John against Anthropomorphism, a breach was made between the two prelates. Epiphanius came to stay at Bethlehem, and spoke of John as well nigh a heretic. John spoke of Epiphanius as "that old tard" (430). The monks of Bethlehem took part with Epiphanius; and he, to prevent their being deprived of clerical ministration by Bishop John, ordained Jerome's brother Paulinian at his monastery of Ad in the diocese of Eleutheropolis. He was then only thirty years old, and was ordained against his will, and with the employment of force and even gagging (83). Epiphanius, returning to Cyprus, wrote to John a letter explaining his conduct (83–89) which was translated by Jerome, but which did little to allay the strife. John placed the monasteries, at least partially, under an interdict (446–447), and appealed to Rome and to Alexandria, and afterwards to Rufinus, the Pretorian Prefect at Constantinople (174, 447). Theophilus at first took John's side vehemently; but the mission of his confidant Isidore miscarried (444, 445), and after some time his views of the situation changed and he made peace with Jerome and his friends.

397 or 398. John also was appeased; and Jerome, who had written a long and bitter account of the controversy in his treatise to Pammachius "Against John of Jerusalem" (424–447), seems suddenly to have let the whole matter drop; the treatise was not finished and was not published, and we read of the strife no more.

(4) Rufinus. 398–404. The quarrel with Jerome's early friend Rufinus did not, like that with John pass away. Jerome had deeply loved Rufinus (4) and highly respected Melania in early days (5, 7, 53). He had spoken of Rufinus in his Chronicle for the year 378 as "insignis monachus" (Ruf. Ap. ii. 25, 26, Vol. iii. 471); we do not read of any estrangement till some years after his return to Palestine.

392. We do not, indeed, find the warm affection which we should expect in two intimate friends who meet after a long separation; and it is possible that Jerome's omission of Rufinus' name from his Catalogue of Church Writers may indicate a coolness on one side which was resented on the other. But they admit that their friendship remained (Ruf. Ap. ii. 8 (2), vol. iii. 465), and that there was frequent intercourse between the monks of Bethlehem and those of the Mount of Olives (*id.*).

393–394. The visit of Aterbius (Ap. iii. 33, Vol. iii. 535) and that of Epiphanius mark the time of estrangement. Rufinus was with Bishop John in the scenes in the Church of the Resurrection, and is mentioned in Epiphanius' letter as a presbyter as to whose views he is paternally anxious (84-87). In the quarrel between John and Jerome Rufinus took decidedly the Bishop's side (84, 430, compared with 250). Jerome's mind grew full of suspicion, so that he even imputed to him that he had bribed someone in the monastery at Bethlehem to steal from the lodgings of Fabiola his translation of the letter of Epiphanius to John (Ap. iii. 4, Vol. iii. 521).

397. But when Rufinus was leaving Palestine, friendship was restored. They partook together of the Eucharist, and joined hands (Ap. iii. 33, Vol. iii. 535), and

Jerome accompanied his friend some way upon his journey; but the reconciliation was short-lived. When in Rome, Rufinus prefixed to a translation of Origen's Περὶ 'Αρχῶν a preface (168–170) which referred in laudatory terms to Jerome as his forerunner in this work, thus seeming to expose Jerome to the suspicions and condemnation which might be expected to fall on one who undertook such a work. This work was sent to Jerome by his friends Pammachius and Oceanus (175), together with a Preface written by Rufinus to a translation of the Apology for Origen by Pamphilus the Martyr. They spoke of the alarm excited at Rome by the translation of the Περὶ 'Αρχῶν, and their suspicions that the translation was so made as to veil the heresies contained in the original work; they begged that Jerome would translate the work as it stood in the original, and pointed out that his own reputation for orthodoxy was at stake (175). Jerome at once complied. He sent to them a literal translation of Origen's work together with a letter describing the relation in which he had stood and still stood to Origen: he admired him as a biblical scholar, but had never accepted him as a dogmatic teacher (176, 177). He at the same time wrote a letter to Rufinus, couched in friendly terms, but remonstrating with him for the use he had made of his name (170). This letter, having been sent to Jerome's friends at Rome, was kept back by them (Ap. i. 12, Vol. iii. 489) and not delivered to Rufinus, and thus the quarrel, which might have been allayed, became irreparable.

401–404. The further progress of the dispute is described in the notice prefixed to the Apologies of Jerome and Rufinus (Vol. iii. 434–5, 482, 518). It may suffice here to say that this disgraceful and unseemly wrangle between two well-known Christian teachers, conducted publicly before the whole Church, and breeding a hatred which Jerome continued to express even after Rufinus' death (498, 500) has only one redeeming feature to the historian, namely, that it brings to our knowledge many instructive facts which would otherwise have lain hid.

396. (5) *Vigilantius.* The controversy with Vigilantius consists only of Jerome's letter to him (131–133) and the treatise "against Vigilantius" (417–423). He had been originally introduced to Jerome by Paulinus, Bishop of Nola, who spoke of him in high terms (123). No questions arose between them during his stay at Bethlehem. He even spoke of Jerome at times with extravagant praise (132). But he appears to have had some connection with Rufinus (Ap. iii. 19, Vol. iii. 529), and Jerome accused him afterwards of having conveyed some mss. into the monastery at Bethlehem, probably from that on the Mount of Olives (Apol. iii. 5, 19, Vol. iii. 521, 529). Jerome afterwards heard a report that Vigilantius had written and spoken against him in various places (131), and had accused him of Origenism. To this his letter is a reply. The anti-ascetic writings of Vigilantius to which Jerome's treatise is a reply have not come down to us. Gennadius (de Script. Eccl. 35) says that he was an ignorant man, but polished in words. But, whatever his ability or literary power, he was one of the few who were able to judge rightly of the ascetic and superstitious practices by which Christianity was being overlaid; and it is on this point that Jerome is most violent and contemptuous in his treatment of him. The notices prefixed to the Letter (131) and Treatise (417) will complete this statement.

394–404. (6) *Augustin*. The remaining controversy of this period is that with St. Augustin. The two men had at an earlier time had some friendly relations, and Alypius, Augustin's friend, had stayed with Jerome at Bethlehem. But Augustin, then coadjutor Bishop of Hippo, in a letter to Jerome (112), found fault with some of his statements in his Commentary on the Galatians, to which, no doubt, his attention had been called by Alypius. Jerome had maintained that the scene in Gal. ii. in which St. Paul rebukes St. Peter for inconsistent compliances with Judaism, was a merely feigned dispute, arranged between the two Apostles in order to make the truth clear to the members of the Church. Augustin objects that this is practically imputing falsehood to the Apostles. He touched upon other points, such as the translation of Scripture and the doctrine of marriage, in a manner savoring of assumption, considering the high position of Jerome, who was also eight years his senior. Through a strange series of misadventures, which illustrate the difficulty of communications at that epoch, this letter was never delivered to Jerome till nine years after it was written. It fell into the hands of persons who copied it, and became known in the West. Jerome heard casually that it had been seen among his works in an island in the Adriatic. It appeared as if Augustin had wished to gain credit by attacking a well-known man behind his back. And this suspicion was hardly allayed by a second letter from Augustin, which partially explained what had occurred (140), or by a third, in which, in answer to a letter from Jerome sending some of his works and warning his correspondent that, if it came to blows, the result might be like that described in Virgil, where the old Entellus strikes down young Dares, Augustin criticizes both severely and ignorantly Jerome's great work of translating the Hebrew Scriptures. Jerome's patience begins to fail (189). "Send me your original letter," he says, "signed by your own hand, or else cease to attack me." And he comments in his turn somewhat sharply on some of Augustin's interpretations of the Psalms. It was only on the receipt of Augustin's reply to this letter (214), couched in terms of deep respect, and deprecating any ill feeling between Christian friends, such as had arisen in the case of Rufinus, that Jerome finally answered the original letter, written ten years before, and received a letter which completely restored friendship. Henceforward they are at one. Letters pass freely between them; Augustin consults Jerome on the difficult question of the origin of souls (272, 283), and foregoes the expression of Traducianism, to which he is inclined, in deference to Jerome's objections; and he consults him on the Pelagian question, and sends Orosius to sit at his feet. Jerome recognizes that each has his proper gift, and gives a plenary adherence to all that Augustin teaches. Alypius, their original link, is joined with Augustin in the address of Jerome's last letter to him (282); Paula, the granddaughter of Jerome's chief friend, is called by him the granddaughter of Augustin; and through this unity the families of Paula and Melania, which had been severed by the adherence of the one to Jerome and the other to Rufinus, are reunited by the coming of Pinianus and his wife, the younger Melania, from the church of Hippo to the convent at Bethlehem. The letters from which this episode is drawn are incorporated into the volume containing works of Augustin, and are not reprinted here. But no life of Jerome, however limited or unpretending, would be satisfactory without some account of the relations of the two great doctors of Latin Christianity.

Bethlehem, Third Period. 405–420. The last period of Jerome's life was passed in the midst of privations, the loss of friends, and frequent illnesses. Paula had died. Jerome was poor (500, 214, 215) and often weak (498, 500). His eyesight failed (*id.*). He had enemies around him (261, 262) and in the high places of the Empire (237, 499). The barbarians were sweeping across the Empire (237, 500), some, like the Isaurians, threatening the North of Palestine (214) and even penetrating at one time to Southern Syria and Egypt (*id.*), while the mainstream, after devastating Jerome's native Dalmatia, passed on under Alaric to the sack of Rome.

410. Fugitives from Rome and Italy crowded to Bethlehem, adding greatly to Jerome's labors (499, 500). It seemed as if the end of the world were at hand (260). In the sack of Rome Pammachius and Marcella died (257, 500). Eustochium followed them eight years later. The controversy with the Pelagians led to the burning of the monasteries at Bethlehem, probably also to renewed estrangement of his Bishop, John of Jerusalem, and his successor Praylus.

417. But he continued his work with no abatement of ardor or vigor, as may be seen from the Prefaces to his later Commentaries (500, 501). He had still friends about him, Pinianus, Albina, Melania, and the younger Paula (Ep. cxliii.); a few survivors even in Rome, Oceanus and the younger Fabiola (252, 253); and men in many lands who honored and consulted him, as is seen by his letters; and, above all, the friendship of Augustin. The letters of this period take a wider range than those going before, Jerome's fame being now worldwide; their addresses

embrace Dalmatia (220), Gaul (215), Rome (252, 253), and Africa (260, 261). Their contents will be best estimated from the notices prefixed to them; but we may mark as specially important the ascetic letter to Rusticus, on the solitary life (244), to Ageruchia, and those on perseverance in widowhood (230), and to Demetrias on the preservation of virginity (260–272), which contain vivid pictures of the life (233) and events (236, 237) of the time, and of the sack of Rome (237, 257); the Memoir, addressed to Principia, of Marcella, who died from her ill treatment in that great day of doom (253); the letter to Evangelus (288) containing Jerome's view of the origin and mutual relations of the three orders of the Ministry; and that to Sabinianus, the lapsed Deacon, who had introduced disorder into the monasteries at Bethlehem (289–295).

Pelagianism. The only great controversy of this period is the Pelagian, in which Jerome seems to have engaged rather at the instance of others than on his own initiative. He shows some mildness in dealing with the Pelagians, and wishes more to win than to condemn them (449, 499); his temperament was not such as to incline him, like Augustin, to take an attitude of vehement hostility to the Pelagian tenets.

414–418. But Orosius came from North Africa, where the Council of Carthage had lately been held; and when, the next year, Pelagius and Cælestius came to Palestine, and Councils were held, first at Jerusalem under Bishop John, who was favorable to the reception of Pelagius, and subsequently at Diospolis, Palestine became the center of the controversy.

416. Augustin from Africa and Ctesiphon from Rome appealed to him (272, 280); both Orosius and

Pelagius quoted his words as making for them; and at length Jerome himself felt compelled to take the pen. He resorted in this his last controversial work, as in his first against the Luciferians, to the form of dialogue. The argument must be praised for its moderation, though it must be confessed that this is gained at the expense of liveliness; it was impossible for Jerome, as a "Synergist," or believer in the co-operation of the human will with the divine, to throw himself into the fray with the eagerness of a convinced Predestinarian. But he does not scruple to brand Pelagius as a heretic; and to a heretic he would show no mercy (449). His treatise, notwithstanding its fine-drawn argument, made him at once the leader of the orthodox party in the East, and the target for the enmity of their adversaries.

416–7. A crowd of Pelagian monks attacked the monasteries, slew some of their inmates, and burned or threw down the buildings, the tower in which Jerome had taken refuge alone escaping (Aug. de Gestis Pelag. 66). This violence, however, was checked by a strong letter from Pope Innocentius (280, 281) to Bishop John, who died soon after; and Jerome, to whom the Pope wrote at the same time (280), speaks of Augustin's cause as triumphant (282), and of Pelagius, like another Catiline, having left the country, though Jerusalem remains in the hands of some hostile power which he speaks of under the name of Nebuchadnezzar (282). It cannot be said, however, that Jerome's arguments produced much effect in the East. He was withstood by Theodore of Mopsuestia (see Migne's Jerome, ii. 807–14) as "saying that men sin by nature, not by will"; and from the West also a treatise opposing his views was sent to him (282) by Annianus, a deacon of Celeda, to which he was never able to reply.

His Bible work during these last fifteen years consisted entirely of Commentaries on the Prophets. Those on the Minor Prophets were finished in 406; that on Daniel in 407; that on Isaiah in 408–10; that on Ezekiel in 410–14. That on Jeremiah up to ch. xxxii. Occupied the remaining years. The Prefaces to these Commentaries {499–501) are full of interest, recording the sack of Rome (499, 500), the death of Rufinus (498, 500), and the rise of Pelagianism, while the Commentary on Ezekiel itself (Book ix.) speaks of the occupation of Rome by Heraclian. His failing health and eyesight (498, 500), the Pelagian Controversy, the other trials above mentioned (499) and the care of the monasteries and pilgrims (500, 501), increased by the death of Eustochium in 418, shortened his time for work, and his Commentary on Jeremiah was cut short at ch. xxxii. by his last illness. Yet his last work is full of energy and of his old controversial vigor.

The last year of his life is believed to have been occupied by a long illness, in which he was tended by the younger Paula and Melania. The Chronicle of Prosper of Aquitaine gives September 20, 420, as the day of his death. Many legends sprung up around his memory. His remains are said to have been transferred from the place where they were buried beside those of Paula and Eustochium, near the grotto of the Nativity, to the Church of Santa Maria Maggiore at Rome, and miracles to have been wrought at his tomb. His descriptions of hermit life in the desert no doubt gave rise to the tradition that he was always attended by a lion, as represented in painting and sculpture, especially in the well-known painting of Albert Dürer. With such traditions a historical work must not be burdened.

IV.—The Writings of Jerome.

The following is a list of the writings arranged under various heads, and showing the date of composition and the place held by each in the Edition of Vallarsi, the eleven volumes of which will be found in Migne's Patrologia, vols. xxii. to xxx. The references are to the volumes of Jerome's works (i.–xi.) in that edition.

I. Bible translations:

(1) From the Hebrew.—The Vulgate of the Old Testament, written at Bethlehem, begun 391, finished 404, vol. ix.

(2) From the Septuagint.—The Psalms as used at Rome, written in Rome, 383, and the Psalms as used in Gaul, written at Bethlehem about 388. These two are in parallel columns in vol. x. The Gallican Psaltery is collated with the Hebrew, and shows by obeli (†) the parts which are in the LXX. and not in the Hebrew, and by asterisks (*) the parts which are in the Hebrew and not in the Greek.

The Book of Job, forming a part of the translation of the LXX. made between 386 and 392 at Bethlehem, the rest of which was lost (Ep. 134), vol. x.

(3) From the Chaldee.—The Books of Tobit and Judith, Bethlehem, 398, vol. x.

(4) From the Greek.—The Vulgate version of the New Testament made at Rome between 382 and 385. The preface is only to the Gospels, but Jerome speaks of and quotes from his version of the other part also (De Vir. Ill. 135; Ep. 71 and 27), vol. x.

II. Commentaries:

(1) Original.—Ecclesiastes, vol. iii., Bethlehem, 388; Isaiah, vol. iv., Bethlehem, 410; Jeremiah i.–xxxii.,

41, vol. iv., Bethlehem, 419; Ezekiel, vol. v., Bethlehem, 410–14; Daniel, vol. v., Bethlehem, 407; the Minor Prophets, vol. vi., Bethlehem, at various times between 391 and 406; Matthew, vol. vii., Bethlehem, 398; Galatians, Ephesians, Titus, Philemon, vol. vii, Bethlehem, 388.

(2) Translated from Origen.—Homilies on Jeremiah and Ezekiel, vol. v., Bethlehem, 381; on Luke, vol. vii., Bethlehem, 389; Canticles, vol. iii., Rome and Bethlehem, 385–87.

There is also a Commentary on Job, and a specimen of one on the Psalms, attributed to Jerome, vol. vii., and the translation of Origen's Homilies on Isaiah, also attributed to him, vol. iv.

Books illustrative of Scripture:

(1) Book of Hebrew names, or Glossary of Proper Names in the Old Testament, Bethlehem, 388, vol. iii. 1.

(2) Book of Questions on Genesis, Bethlehem, 388, vol. iii. 301.

(3) A translation of Eusebius' book on the sites and names of Hebrew places, Bethlehem, 388, vol. iii. 321.

(4) Translation of Didymus on the Holy Spirit, Rome and Bethlehem, 385–87, vol. ii.105.

IV. Books on Church History and Controversy (all in vol. ii.):

(1) Book of Illustrious Men, or Catalogue of Ecclesiastical Writers, Bethlehem, 392.

(2) Dialogue with a Luciferian, Antioch, 379.

(3) Lives of the Hermits: Paulus, Desert, 374; Malchus and Hilarion, Bethlehem, 390.

(4) Translation of the Rule of Pachomius, Bethlehem, 404.

(5) Books of ascetic controversy, against Helvidius, Rome, 304; against Jovinian, Bethlehem, 393; against Vigilantius, Bethlehem, 406.

(6) Books of personal controversy, against John, Bishop of Jerusalem, Bethlehem, 397 or 398; against Rufinus, i. and ii. 402, iii. 404.

(7) Dialogue with a Pelagian, Bethlehem, 416.

V. General History:

Translation of the Chronicle of Eusebius, with Jerome's additions, vol. viii., Constantinople, 382.

VI. Personal:

The series of letters, vol. i. Ep. i., Aquileia, 311; 2–4, Antioch, 374; 5–17, Desert 374–79; 18, Constantinople, 381; 19–45, Rome, 382–85; 46–148, Bethlehem, 386–418.

The works attributed to Jerome, but not genuine, which are given in Vallarsi's edition are: A breviary, commentary, and preface on the Psalms, vol. vii.; some Greek fragment and a lexicon of Hebrew names; the names of places in the Acts; the ten names of God; the benedictions of the patriarchs; the ten temptations in the desert; a commentary on the Song of Deborah; Hebrew Questions in Kings and Chronicles; an exposition of Job, vol. iii.; three letters in vol. i., and fifty-one in vol. xi., together with several miscellaneous writings in vol. xi. most of which are by Pelagius.

Bibliography.—The writings of Jerome were, on the whole, well preserved, owing to the great honor in which he was held, in the Middle Ages. Considering the number of the mss., the variations are not numerous. The Editio Princeps of the Letters and a few of the Treatises appeared in Rome in 1470, and another almost contemporaneous with this in Maintz (Schöffer), after which they were reprinted in Venice (1476), Rome (1479), Parma (1480), Nürenberg (1485), and in several other places. The Editio Princeps of the Commentaries appeared in Nürenberg in 1477, and was several times reprinted in other places; that of the Translation of Origen's Homilies on St. Luke, etc., in Basle, 1475; that of the Lives of the Hermits in Nürenberg, 1476, and of the Chronicle at Milan in 1475. But the true Editio Princeps, containing Jerome's works as a whole, is that of Erasmus (Basle, 1516–20), who bestowed on it his great critical power, aided by his strong admiration for Jerome. He was assisted by OEcolampadius and other scholars. This held its ground till 1560, when an edition appeared by Marianus Victorius, afterwards Bishop of Rieti (Rome, Paulus Manutius), which enlarged the notes and corrected the text of Erasmus, but, like him, included many spurious writings. This edition was dedicated to Pius V. and Gregory XIII., and was the favorite edition of the Roman Church. In 1684 appeared the edition of Tribbechovius of Gotha (Frankfort and Leipzig) which embodied the emendations of critics up to that date, and was published at the expense of the Protestant Frederick, Duke of Saxony. In 1693 came the Benedictine edition of Martianay and Pouget (Paris), which gave the original text of the Vulgate and a new, though still very imperfect arrangement of the Letters and Treatises. But all previous editions were thrown into the shade by that of Dominic Vallarsi the learned priest of Verona (folio ed., Verona, 1734–42; quarto, Venice, 1766–72). In this edition the Treatises are separated from the Letters, and both Letters and Treatises are arranged in order of time, the dates and the process by which they are arrived at being clearly given. I have only in one or two instances found reason to alter Vallarsi's dates. The explanatory notes, however, are not as complete as might be wished, and the references are often wrong or imperfect. This edition is reprinted by Migne, who marks the pages of it in large print in the text, and most modern writers refer to it alone, as has been done in this volume.

Literature.—Three short Lives of Jerome, composed in the Middle Ages by unknown authors (one of which was falsely attributed to Gennadius), are given by Vallarsi in his Prolegomena (vol. i. 175–214); one of these is said by Zockler to be by Sebastian of Monte Cassino. Another, written in the fourteenth century by John Andreas of Bologna, was printed at Basle in 1514; and a work by Lasserré was published at Paris in 1530, with a curious title, "La Vie de Monseigneur Sainct Hierome," with "La Vie de Madame Saincte Paule"; and later works belonging to the uncritical region of thought were published later in Madrid by Bonadies in 1595, and by Cermellus in Ferrara (1648), the latter entirely made up of quotations from Jerome's writings.

Meanwhile the critical faculty had been aroused. Erasmus and Marianus Victorius prefixed Lives of Jerome to their editions of his works in 1516 and 1565; and Baronius in his Annals and Du Pin in his *Bibliotheque des Auteurs Ecclésiastiques* (1686) brought to light additional facts. Martianay at the close of his edition of Jerome's works published a *Life*, embodying many records of Jerome from the Fathers, but with many mistakes of chronology, some of which were rectified by Tillemont in his painstaking *Mémoires* (Paris, 1707) and by Ceillier in his *Histoire des Auteurs Ecclésiastiques* (Paris, 1742). The work of Sebastiano Dolci (Ancona, 1750) is entirely taken from Jerome's own writings.

But in reference to the Life as to the Writings of Jerome a new epoch was made by Vallarsi in the Preface and the Life prefixed to his Edition of Jerome. Though somewhat dry, it is thoroughly trustworthy, and in Migne's edition more accessible than any other to those who read Latin. The Bollandist Stilling (Acta Sanctorum, vol. viii., Antwerp, 1762), is less occupied with additions to our knowledge of the man and his works than with the honoring of the Saint. The work of the learned Dane, Engelstoft (1797), gives a more comprehensive estimate of Jerome's historical position than any of his predecessors. The account of Jerome in Schrökh's Ecclesiastical History (1786) and the articles of Cölln in Ersch and Grüber's Encyclopädie and of Hagenbach in Herzog's Real-Encyclopädie are excellent. In French we have the account of Jerome's ascetic influence in Montalembert's *Monks of the West* (Paris, 1861); and the *Histoire de St. Jérome* by Collombet (Paris, 1844) is useful in the appreciation of the personal and archaeological part of the subject, though accepting with uncritical partisanship the polemical attitude of Jerome. We may add for English readers the articles Hieronymus in the *Dictionaries of Greek and Roman Biography* and *of Christian Biography*.

Our own generation has produced two excellent works: that of Dr. Otto Zöckler, *Hieronymus, Sein Leben und Werken* (Gotha, Perthes, 1865), and that of Amédée Thierry, *Saint Jérome, la Société chrétienne à Rome et l'émigration romaine en terre sainte* (Paris, 1867, originally published in the *Revue des Deux Mondes*). The former is a lucid, impartial, and comprehensive account of Jerome's Life and Writings; the latter, a series of very vivid and interesting sketches of Jerome himself, his friends and his times, which, though generally accurate, is occasionally swayed from truth by imagination, and at times is betrayed by sympathy with the modern Roman Catholic system into mistakes of judgment. Both these writers give copious and enlightening extracts from Jerome's writings in the original; but the value of those of Thierry is lessened by the references being to the ill-arranged edition of Martianay instead of that of Vallarsi.

It will be sufficiently obvious why it has been impossible to include all the works of Jerome in the present translation, but a few explanations may be desirable.

An exact translation of the Vulgate would serve no good purpose; and, if made, would naturally form part of a series designed to illustrate the criticism of the Scriptures.

The Commentaries and works illustrative of the Scriptures would by themselves form two volumes of equal size with the present. Though they contain much that is interesting—the opinions of various writers, such as Origen, Apollinarius, Gregory Nazianzen, or Didymus, a few celebrated passages, such as that which caused the controversy between Jerome and Augustin, and a few remarkable allusions to historical events, such as the capture of Rome by Heraclian—the general tenor of them is hardly of sufficient importance to justify the labor of translation or the bulk and expense of the additional volumes. An exception might be made in favor of the Book on the Site and Names of Hebrew Places; but this is a work of Eusebius rather than Jerome (see pp. 485, 486 and Prolegomena to Eusebius, Vol. i. of this series); and it was necessary to confine the Translation of Jerome to a single volume, with the exception of the Book *On*

Illustrious Men and the *Apology against Rufinus*, which will be found in Vol. iii. of this Series.

The Chronicle of Eusebius would, if translated at all, find its place in the works of Eusebius.

The Books on Church History and Controversy are given in full.

Of the Letters, which, excepting the Vulgate, form the most important legacy of Jerome to posterity, all those which have a personal or a historical interest have been translated. The only omissions are (1) the exegetical letters, to which what has been said of the Commentaries applies; (2) the letters to Augustin, which will be found in Vol. i. of the first series of this Library, annexed to the letters of Augustin to which they are replies; and (3) the encyclicals and letters of Theophilus, which have been summarized.

For a separate statement of the works which are given in this volume the reader will naturally consult the table of contents; and, for a more detailed account of the books themselves, the introductions prefixed to each.

V.—Estimate of the Scope and Value of Jerome's Writings.

General. The writings of Jerome must be estimated not merely by their intrinsic merits, but by his historical position and influence. It has already been pointed out that he stands at the close of the old Greco-Roman civilization: the last Roman poet of any repute, Claudian, and the last Roman historian, Ammianus Marcellinus, died before him. Augustin survived him, but the other great Fathers, both in the East and in the West, had passed away before him. The sack of Rome by Alaric (410) and its capture by Heraclian (413) took place in his lifetime, and the Empire of the West fell in the next thirty years. Communication between East and West had become rarer and mutual knowledge less. Eusebius knew no Latin, Ambrose no Greek; Rufinus, though a second-rate scholar, was welcomed in Italy on his return from the East in 397 as capable of imparting to the Latins the treasures of the Greek Church writers. The general enfeeblement of the human mind, which remains one of the problems of history, had set in. The new age of Christendom which was struggling to the birth was subject to the influence of Jerome more than to that of any of the Fathers.

Secular Learning. As regards general learning, indeed, it was impossible that any legacy should descend from him. He had systematically disparaged it (35-36, 498), though making use and even a parade of it (101, 114, 149, 178); and had defended himself by disingenuous pleas from the charge of acquiring it after his mature convictions were formed (Apol. i. 30, 31, Vol. iii. 498–499). His influence, therefore, would but increase the deep ignorance of literature which now settled upon mankind till the times of the Renaissance. His style indeed, is excellent, correct, and well balanced, full of animation and of happy phrases (see Index— Proverbs), and passing from one subject to another with great versatility. It is contrasted by Erasmus with the barbarisms of the Schoolmen, as that of the Christian Cicero. But it has also Cicero's faults, especially his diffuseness. His Latinity is remarkably pure, and with the exception of the frequent use of the infinitive to express a purpose, and of a few words of late-Latin like *confortare*, we are hardly aware in reading him that we are 400 years away from the Augustan Age. His mastery of style is the more remarkable because he wrote nothing but a few letters and a very poor Commentary till about his thirty-fifth year.

Letters. His letters gain their special charm from being so personal. He himself, his correspondents, and the scenes in which they moved, are made to live before our eyes. See especially his descriptions of Roman life in the Epistles to Eustochium (Ep. xxii.), to Paula on the death of Blesilla (Ep. xxxix.), to Læta (Ep. cvii.) on the education of her child, and Ageruchia (Ep. cxxiii.); his account of the lives of Fabiola (Ep. lxxvii.), of Paula (Ep. cviii.), and of Marcella (Ep. cxxvii.); his description of the clerical life in his letter to Nepotian (Ep. lii.), and of the monastic life in his letters to Rusticus (Ep. cxxv.) and to Sabinian (Ep. cxlvii.); his letters of spiritual counsel to a mother and daughter (Ep. cxvii.), to Julianus (Ep. cxviii.), and to Rusticus (Ep. cxxii.), and of hermit life in his letter to Eustochium (Ep. xxii., pp. 24–25); his satirical description of Onasus (Ep. xl.), Rufinus (p. 250), and Vigilantius (p. 417); his enthusiastic delight in the Holy Land in the letter written by him to Paula and Eustochium inviting Marcella to join them (Ep. xlvi). Other characteristic and celebrated letters are those to Asella (xlv.) on his leaving Rome; to Pammachius (lvii.) on the best method of translation, which shows the liberties taken by translators in his time; to Oceanus (lxix.) in defense of a second marriage contracted by a Spanish Bishop, the first having been before baptism; to Magnus (lxx.), indicating his use of secular literature, and showing the great range of his knowledge; to Lucinius (lxxi.) on the copying of his works; to Avitus (cxxiv.) on the book of Origen, Περὶ Ἀρχῶν; to Demetrias (cxxx.) on the maintenance of virginity; to Ctesiphon (cxxxiii.) on the Pelagian controversy. (See also Index, words Stories and Pictures of Contemporary Life.)

Publication. Two circumstances conduced to the vividness and importance of this series of letters. One of these is the fact that no distinct line separated private documents from those designed for publication. In the Catalogue of his works (De Vir. Ill. 135)1 he says: "Of the Letters to Paula and Eustochium, the number is infinite: I write them every day." And, when he became celebrated, he says (79) that whatever he wrote was at once laid hold of and published, alike by friends and enemies. We have therefore frequently his most confidential utterances; while on the other hand his letters frequently pass into treatises, and he turns to address others than those to whom he is writing (59, 273, 274). But the process of publication was precarious; so that between Letters xlvi. and xlvii. there is a gap of seven years (386–93) without any letter. The other circumstance is the difficulty of communication, which made letters rare and induced greater care in their composition. Both these circumstances are well illustrated by the early correspondence of Jerome with Augustin. Augustin wrote from Hippo in Africa a long and important letter to Jerome (Ep. lvi.) in the year 394, which did not reach Jerome at Bethlehem for nearly ten years. It was committed to a presbyter named Profuturus to carry to Jerome; but he, being elected to a bishopric before he started, turned back, and soon afterwards died. The letter was neither forwarded to Jerome nor returned to Augustin; but it was copied by others and became known in the West, while its somewhat severe criticisms were unknown to Jerome himself. After a time Augustin became aware by a short letter of introduction written by Jerome to a friend that his first letter had miscarried, and he wrote a second (Ep. lxvii.) much in the same strain; but Paulus, to whom it was entrusted, alleging his fear of the sea, failed to go to Bethlehem; and a copy of the letter was found a year or two afterwards by a friend of Jerome's bound up with some of Augustin's treatises in an island of the Adriatic. Jerome on hearing of this was naturally incensed; and it was not till the year 404 that he received an authentic copy of both letters direct from Augustin, and was able to return an answer. His answer, however, and a knowledge of his views are fuller than they might have been had personal communication been easier.

Knowledge. His knowledge was vast and many-sided [See especially the enumeration of Christian writers who used Pagan literature (149–151), the curious stories about marriage gathered from all ages (383–386), the descriptions of various kinds of food and medicines (392–394) and the account of Pythagoras and his doctrines (Apol. iii., 39, 40, in this Series, Vol. iii. 538)], but it was rather the curiosity of the monks of a later day than the temper of the philosopher or the historian. He was well acquainted with the history and literature of Rome and of Greece; he translated the Chronicle of Eusebius; he speaks of the various routes to India (245), of the Brahmans (97, 193, 397), of the custom of Suttee (381), and of Buddha (380). But he is quite uncritical; he makes no correction of the faults of the Chronicle, and his own additions to it reveal his credulity. He was deeply affected by the sack of Rome, and recurs to it again and again; but his reflections upon this and similar events hardly go beyond those of a medieval chronicler. He is a recluse, and has no thought of the general interests of mankind.

Church History. This lack of criticism and of general interests combined with lack of time to prevent his making any considerable contribution to church history. That he had some faculties for this is shown by several passages in his Dialogue with a Luciferian (328–331) and his Catalogue of Ecclesiastical Writers (On Illustrious Men, Vol. iii. 361–384). But his conception of church history is shown by his declaration (315) that he intended the Lives of Malchus and Hilarion as part of a series, which when completed would have formed an ecclesiastical history. Such a history would have been nothing more than a prolix edition of Rufinus' History of the Monks. Jerome's value to the church historian is quite of another kind; it lies in the illustration of contemporary life furnished by his own life and letters and by the controversies in which he was engaged.

Theology. These controversies bring us to consider Jerome's position as a theologian. Here he is admittedly weak. He had no real interest in the subject. The first of his letters which deals with theology, that written from the Desert to Pope Damasus, points out clearly the difficulty raised by the difference of phraseology of East and West, the Eastern speaking of one Essence and three Substances, the Western, of one Substance and three Persons. But he makes no attempt to grasp the reality lying behind these expressions, and merely asks not to have the Eastern terms forced on his acceptance, while he professes in the most absolute terms his submission to the decision of the Bishop of Rome. This lack of genuine theological interest best explains his conduct in relation to Origen, his extravagant laudation of him at one time (46), his violent condemnation at another (187). He was carried away by Origen's genius and industry in the department of biblical criticism and exegesis in which he was himself absorbed, and though in his earlier discussion of the Vision of Isaiah (22), which touched the doctrine of the Trinity, he had put aside Origen's view that the Seraphim were the Son and the Spirit as wrongly expressing their relation to the Father, the doctrinal question was feebly present to his thoughts, and he repeated Origen's exposition without blame as to the pre-existence of souls and the restoration of Satan (Ruf. Apol. ii. 13, Vol. iii. 467). When the subject of Origen's orthodoxy was raised at a later time, he was unaware of any inconsistency when he fell in with the general condemnation of his doctrine. So with regard to Eusebius of Cæsarea. In the Preface to the translation of his Book on the Site and Names of Hebrew Places (485), he is "vir admirabilis"; in his controversy with Rufinus, Eusebius is nothing but a heretic. In his controversy with Augustin as to the quarrel between St. Peter and St. Paul in Gal. ii., which he interpreted as fictitious and pre-arranged with a view to bring out St. Paul's solution of the question about the Gentile converts, he was manifestly in the wrong, and eventually seems to have felt this, yet as one who was silenced rather than convinced. At a later period he says to Augustin (Ep. cxxxiv.), "If the heretics see that we hold divergent opinions they will say calumniously that this is a result of hatred, whereas it is my firm resolution to love you, to look up to you, to defer to you with admiration, and to defend your opinions as my own." His dread of heresy may be gathered from passage in the Anti-Pelagian Dialogue (i. 28) in which he expressly declares that, while sin can be forgiven, heresy, as being impiety, is subject to the threat: "They that forsake the Lord shall be consumed." It is true that in his Catalogue he shows wider sympathies, and defends himself in writing to Augustin for the admission into it of men like Philo Judæus and Seneca. But this, though it might have led him to the larger views of the heathen world held by Origen and Clement, did not prevent his condemning to eternal torments even the most virtuous of the heathen. He tells Marcella, a Roman lady (41–42), that one object he has in writing to her is to instruct her that the consul-elect Vettius Agorius Prætextatus, who was known as a model of public and domestic virtue, and who had then recently died, is in Tartarus, while their friend Lea, who had died the same day, is in heaven.

The lack of deep theological conviction is shown in his Dialogue against the Pelagians, where it is evident that he is far from that original and deep view of human corruption which Augustin maintained; indeed, he appears at times to be arguing against his own side, when he says (471) that, "Till the end we are subject to sin; not," (as the opponent falsely imputes to him) "through the fault of our nature and constitution, but through frailty and the mutability of the human will, which varies from moment to moment"—a sentence which might be taken as expressing the doctrine of Pelagius himself. It is evident that in these cases he is swayed not so much by the force of truth as by the authority of certain powerful Bishops and the wish to maintain his orthodox reputation. In his other controversies, with Helvidius, Jovinian, John, Bishop of Jerusalem, Vigilantius, and Rufinus, his method is take for granted the opinion current among the Christians of his day, and to support it by copious (sometimes excessive) quotations from Scripture, and by arguments sometimes well-chosen and acutely maintained, as in the book against Helvidius (339), sometimes of the most frivolous character, as in that against Vigilantius (422). In the three last of these controversies the opposition is embittered by personal feeling, and Jerome hardly places any restraint on the contempt and hatred which it engenders.

In his criticisms on Scripture, however, he has a freer judgment, as when he says (337): Whether you think that Moses wrote the Pentateuch, or that Ezra re-edited it, in either case I make no objection;" or (349) that it was the Book of Deuteronomy which was found in the Temple in the reign of Josiah; or contrasts "the flickering flame of the Apostles" with the brightness of the lamp of Christ" (468). There are three points especially on which Jerome reached an independent conviction, and maintained it courageously. (1) He made a clear distinction between the Old Testament Canon and the Apocrypha (194, 491, 492, 493) and this although he records the fact that the Nicene Council had placed the Book of Judith in the Canon (494). For this he is justly commemorated in the Articles of the Church of England (Art. 6). (2) He maintains the essential identity of Bishops and Presbyters (288) and the development of the Episcopal out of the Presbyteral office (288, 289), in the face of the rapid tendency to the extreme exaltation of the Episcopate (92). (3) In the great work of his life, the composition of the Vulgate, he showed a clear and matured conviction, and a noble tenacity, unshaken either by popular clamor (490) or authority like that Augustin (189).

A few words may here be said on the asceticism which Jerome so eagerly promoted. If we ask how it was that he embraced it so fervently as to read it into almost every line of the Scriptures, we can only answer that it was part of the spirit of the time. Jerome did not have the elevation of mind which might have enabled him to exercise a judgment upon the current, which was bearing him away, or the higher critical power which would distinguish between what was in the Scriptures and what he brought to them. His habit of mind was to accept his general principles from some kind of church authority, which was partly that of the Bishops, partly the general drift of the sentiment of the Christians of his day; and having accepted them, to advocate them vehemently and without discrimination. Jerome could indeed exercise a certain moderation, even in matters of asceticism (246, 267). But his general attitude is that which disdained the common joys of life, which thought of eating, drinking, clothing or lodging, and most of all marriage, as physical indulgences which should suppressed as far as possible, rather than as the means of a noble social intercourse; and dread of impurity haunts him to such an extent as to entirely vitiate his view of society, and to cause him to disparage, and all but forbid, the married relation (29, 384, etc.). His view of monasticism in its inner principles is seen in his treatises against Helvidius, Jovinian, and Vigilantius. The reader may be specially referred to a passage in the last-named treatise, p. 423. If we ask the further question, how the tendency arose which so completely swayed him, we can only attribute it to the state of Roman society in the fourth and fifth centuries, which laid earnest men open to influences already working in other parts of the world. Jerome knew of the Brahmans and the Gymnosophists of India (97, 193, 397), and he several times mentions Buddha (380) as an example of asceticism. But students of Buddhism have failed to trace any direct filiation between the asceticism of the East and the West.1 The existence of Essenes in Palestine and the Therapeutæ in Egypt, and the unquestionable fact that Christian asceticism originated in Egypt, make some connection with the East probable; and the system of Manes, though at once repudiated, may have exerted some subtle influence. Certain states of the human mind seem all-pervasive, like the causes of diseases which spring up at once in many different places; and principles like those of asceticism maybe communicated through chance conversations or commercial intercourse when the soil is prepared for their reception.

But it seems better to look to the social and political state of the world as the predisposing cause of monasticism. Even in the East it is thought that the miserable conditions of practical life have been the main cause of a religion of despair; and the decline and fall of the Roman Empire in the fourth and fifth centuries offered similar causes in abundance. The grace which is completely absent from the great Christian writers of that epoch is hope. Such hope as is found even in the Civitas Dei of Augustin is entirely that of the world to come. The world before them seemed hopelessly corrupt. The descriptions of private morals given by Jerome are borne out by Ammianus Marcellinus; the failure of public spirit and military valor was equally conspicuous; and Gratian and Stilicho appear on the scene only to be murdered. When the crash of Alaric's sack of Rome shook the existing world, no one realized that a new Christian world was coming, and the flight which Jerome witnessed of thousands of citizens from the sinking city to the mountains of Palestine was but one symptom of the despair which made them, to use Jerome's words, "quit the most frequented cities that in the fields and solitude they might mourn for sin and draw down on themselves the compassion of Christ" (446).

As an illustrator of Scripture, Jerome did much, and in some respects excellent work. The Book of Hebrew Names was no doubt of much use in the ages in which men were ignorant of Hebrew, although it has the clumsy arrangement of a separate glossary for each book of the Bible; it is very faulty and uncritical; there is no explanation, for instance, of Lehi in Judges, or of Engedi or Ichabod in 1 Samuel, or of Bethabara or Bethany in John, and the meanings given to words are extremely uncritical and sometimes absurd. Cherubim is said to mean a multitude of knowledge; Jezebel, "flowing with blood, a litter, a dung heap"; and Laodicæa, "the tribe beloved of the Lord, or, they have been in vomiting." It is worthless now except as showing the state of knowledge of the fourth century A.D., and that of the author of the Vulgate.

The Book of the Site and Names of Hebrew Places belongs rather to Eusebius than to Jerome, being translated from Eusebius, though with some additions. An account of it is given in the Prolegomena to Eusebius. The arrangement of this book is, like the former, very inconvenient, the names under each letter being placed in separate groups in the order of the books of Scripture in which they occur: for instance, under the letter A we have first the names in Genesis, then those in Exodus, and so on. But there is less room here for what is fanciful, and the testimony of men who lived in Palestine in the fourth and fifth centuries is of great value still to the student of sacred topography. When the places are outside the writer's knowledge, credulity is apt to creep in, as when the author tells us that in Ararat portions of the ark are still to be found.

The Book of Hebrew Questions on Genesis is simply a set of notes on passages where the reference to the Hebrew text gives a different reading from that of the LXX., which was received as authoritative up to Jerome's day. For instance, in Gen. xlvi. 26, the LXX. Says that Joseph's descendants born in Egypt were nine, the Hebrew, two. Jerome accounts for the discrepancy by the supposition that the LXX. added in the sons of Ephraim and Manasseh, who were subsequently born in Egypt, and who in the LXX. are enumerated just before. Jerome states in the preface his intention to compose a similar set of notes to each book of the Old Testament, but he was never able to go beyond Genesis. What he gives us is of considerable interest and value, so that it is a matter of regret that he could not go further.

As a commentator, Jerome's fault is a lack of independence; his merit lies in giving fully the opinions of others which we might otherwise not have known. This he considers, as seen in his controversy with Rufinus, the principal task of a commentator (Apol. i. 16, Vol. iii. 491). In the passages there at issue, he states the most incongruous interpretations without criticizing them, and Rufinus can hardly be blamed for suggesting that he is sometimes expressing his own opinion under that of "another." In matters of ordinary interpretation his judgment is good. But fanciful ideas are apt to intrude, as when, in the Commentary on Ecclesiastes, the city delivered by the poor wise man is made to mean the individual delivered from Satan by the better man within him, or the Church delivered from the hosts of darkness by Christ. When an occasion for the introduction of asceticism occurs, Jerome never hesitates at any process, however absurd, which will draw the passage to a sanction of his peculiar views (Against Jovin. i. 30, p. 368). We should have been glad, had space permitted, to have given a specimen of his better style of exposition, but it was found necessary to suppress this.

It is as a translator of Scripture that Jerome is best known. His Vulgate was made at the right moment and by the right man. The Latin language was still living, although Latin civilization was dying; and Jerome was a master of it. It is only to be regretted that he did not give fuller scope to his literary power in his translation of Scripture. In his letter to Pammachius on the best method of translation (114), he advocates great freedom of treatment, even such as amounts to paraphrase, and even to the insertion of sentences congruous to the sense of the author. He takes the fact that the quotations in the New Testament from the Old often present discrepancies in words and sense as justifying similar discrepancies in a translation. He does not, however, appear in dealing with ordinary books to have used this license in any extreme way; and his translations, without departing from correctness, read as good literary composition. But from the operation of his rules of translation he expressly excepts the Scriptures. "In other books," he says (113), "my effort is not to express word by word, but meaning by meaning; but in the Holy Scriptures even the order of the words has a secret meaning" (et ordo verborum mysterium est). He even says (80): "A version made for the use of the Church, even though it may possess a literary charm, ought to disguise and avoid it as far as possible." This belief in a secret meaning in the words and their order as apart from the sense goes far to injure the Vulgate translation. His principles, indeed, are excellent, namely, (1) never to swerve needlessly from the original; (2) to avoid solecisms; (3) even by the admission of solecisms, to give the true sense. But it is evident that they must be vitiated by the supposition of a hidden sense in the arrangement of the words; and the result is a style which frequently deprives a passage of its proper elegance, and the pleasure which it should give to the reader, and a too frequent introduction of solecisms and abandonment of the attempt to make sense of a passage. It also gives an air of saintly unreality to many parts of the Scriptures and thus to produce confusion. The merits of the translation are also very various, as was the time which Jerome bestowed on the different parts. The Books of Solomon, for instance, he translated very rapidly (492), the Book of Tobit in a single day (494). For some parts he trusted to his own knowledge, for others he obtained aid at great cost of money and trouble (Preface to Job and to Tobit, 491, 494). But, while we thus go behind the scenes, we must not fail to look at the completed work as a whole. It was wrought out with noble perseverance and unflinching purpose amidst many discouragements. It was highly prized even in Jerome's lifetime, so that he is able to record that a large part of the Old Testament was translated into Greek from his version by his friend Sophronius, and was read in the Eastern Churches (492). After his death it won its way to become the Vulgate or common version of Western Christendom; it was the Bible of the Middle Ages; and in the year 1546 (eleven centuries after its author's death) was pronounced by the Council of Trent to be the only true version, and alone authorized to be printed.

A few personal details must be given to illustrate his method of composition and his surroundings. Nothing is known of his personal appearance. His health was weak, and he had several long illnesses, especially in the years 398, 404, and in the last year of his life. His eyes began to fail during his stay at Constantinople in 380–382, and he usually employed an amanuensis; but he still wrote at times, and what he wrote was more polished than what he dictated. "In the one case I constantly turn the stylus; in the other, whatever words come into my mouth I heap together in my rapid utterance" (Ep. lxxiv. 6). He composed with great rapidity, and dictated at times as much as one thousand lines in a day (Comm. On Ephes., Book ii. Preface). He often, especially when in weak health, lay on a couch (Ep. lxxiv. 6), taking down one volume after another to aid in the composition of his Commentaries. And he often sat late into the night [his book against Vigilantius was "the lucubration of a single night" (423)], the days being occupied in business of various kinds, as stated above—the monasteries, the entertainment of strangers, the teaching of boys, the exposition of Scripture to his brethren in the monastery, and, according to Sulpicius Severus, the charge of the parish of Bethlehem. As has been mentioned above, he was interrupted again and again by illness, and on several occasions was in alarm from the threatened invasions of the Huns and Isaurians, and at the end of his life from the violent adherents of Pelagius. He also suffered from poverty, and his friends one by one were taken from him. But he persevered against all obstacles; and his latest works, the Anti-Pelagian Dialogue and the Commentary on Jeremiah, show little if any diminution of power.

VI.—Character and Influence of Jerome.

This Introduction must be concluded with a few words on the character and influence of Jerome, which are taken from the article upon him in the *Dictionary of Christian Biography*. He was vain and unable to bear rivals, extremely sensitive as to the estimation in which he was held by his contemporaries, and especially by the Bishops; passionate and resentful, but at times becoming suddenly placable; scornful and violent in controversy; kind to the weak and the poor; respectful in his dealings with women; entirely without avarice; extraordinarily diligent in work, and nobly tenacious of the main objects to which he devoted his life. There was, however, something of monkish cowardice in his asceticism, and his influence was not felt by the strong.

His influence grew through his life and increased after his death. If we may use a scriptural phrase which has sometimes been applied to such influence, "He lived and reigned for a thousand years." His writings contain the whole spirit of the Church of the Middle Ages, its monasticism, its contrast of sacred things with profane, its credulity and superstition, its value for relics, its subjection to hierarchical authority, its dread of heresy, its passion for pilgrimages. To the society which was thus in a great measure formed by him, his Bible was the greatest boon which could have been given. But he founded no school and had no inspiring power; there was no courage or width of view in his spiritual legacy such as could break through the fatal circle of bondage to received authority which was closing round mankind. As Thierry says in the last words of his work on St. Jerome, "There is no continuation of his work; a few more letters of Augustin and Paulinus, and night falls over the West."

The Life of Paulus the First Hermit.

The Life of Paulus was written in the year 374 or 375 during Jerome's stay in the desert of Syria, as is seen from c. 6, and was dedicated to Paulus of Concordia as stated in Jerome's

1. It has been a subject of wide-spread and frequent discussion what monk was the first to give a signal example of the hermit life. For some going back too far have found a beginning in those holy men Elias and John, of whom the former seems to have been more than a monk and the latter to have begun to prophesy before his birth. Others, and their opinion is that commonly received, maintain that Antony was the originator of this mode of life, which view is partly true. Partly I say, for the fact is not so much that he preceded the rest as that they all derived from him the necessary stimulus. But it is asserted even at the present day by Amathas and Macarius, two of Antony's disciples, the former of whom laid his master in the grave, that a certain Paul of Thebes was the leader in the movement, though not the first to bear the name, and this opinion has my approval also. Some as they think fit circulate stories such as this—that he was a man living in an underground cave with flowing hair down to his feet, and invent many incredible tales which it would be useless to detail. Nor does the opinion of men who lie without any sense of shame seem worthy of refutation. So then inasmuch as both Greek and Roman writers have handed down careful

accounts of Antony, I have determined to write a short history of Paul's early and latter days, more because the thing has been passed over than from confidence in my own ability. What his middle life was like, and what snares of Satan he experienced, no man, it is thought, has yet discovered.

2. During the persecutions of Decius and Valerian, when Cornelius at Rome and Cyprian at Carthage shed their blood in blessed martyrdom, many churches in Egypt and the Thebaid were laid waste by the fury of the storm. At that time the Christians would often pray that they might be smitten with the sword for the name of Christ. But the desire of the crafty foe was to slay the soul, not the body; and this he did by searching diligently for slow but deadly tortures. In the words of Cyprian himself who suffered at his hands: they who wished to die were not suffered to be slain. We give two illustrations, both as specially noteworthy and to make the cruelty of the enemy better known.

3. A martyr, steadfast in faith, who stood fast as a conqueror amidst the racks and burning plates, was ordered by him to be smeared with honey and to be made to lie under a blazing sun with his hands tied behind his back, so that he who had already surmounted the heat of the frying-pan might be vanquished by the stings of flies. Another who was in the bloom of youth was taken by his command to some delightful pleasure gardens, and there amid white lilies and blushing roses, close by a gently murmuring stream, while overhead the soft whisper of the wind played among the leaves of the trees, was laid upon a deep luxurious feather-bed, bound with fetters of sweet garlands to prevent his escape. When all had withdrawn from him a harlot of great beauty drew near and began

with voluptuous embrace to throw her arms around his neck, and, wicked even to relate! to handle his person, so that when once the lusts of the flesh were roused, she might accomplish her licentious purpose. What to do, and whither to turn, the soldier of Christ knew not. Unconquered by tortures he was being overcome by pleasure. At last, with an inspiration from heaven he bit off the end of his tongue and spat it in her face as she kissed him. Thus the sensations of lust were subdued by the intense pain which followed.

4. While such enormities were being perpetrated in the lower part of the Thebaid, Paul and his newly married sister were bereaved of both their parents, he being about sixteen years of age. He was heir to a rich inheritance, highly skilled in both Greek and Egyptian learning, gifted with a gentle disposition and a deep love for God. Amid the thunders of persecution he retired to a house at a considerable distance and in a more secluded spot. But to what crimes does not the "accursed thirst for gold" impel the human heart? His brother-in-law conceived the thought of betraying the youth whom he was bound to conceal. Neither a wife's tears which so often prevail, nor the ties of blood, nor the all-seeing eye of God above him could turn the traitor from his wickedness. "He came, he was urgent, he acted with cruelty while seeming only to press the claims of affection."

5. The young man had the tact to understand this, and, conforming his will to the necessity, fled to the mountain wilds to wait for the end of the persecution. He began with easy stages, and repeated halts, to advance into the desert. At length he found a rocky mountain, at the foot of which, closed by a stone, was a cave of no

great size. He removed the stone (so eager are men to learn what is hidden), made eager search, and saw within a large hall, open to the sky, but shaded by the widespread branches of an ancient palm. The tree, however, did not conceal a fountain of transparent clearness, the waters whereof no sooner gushed forth than the stream was swallowed up in a small opening of the same ground which gave it birth. There were besides in the mountain, which was full of cavities, many habitable places, in which were seen, now rough with rust, anvils and hammers for stamping money. The place, Egyptian writers relate, was a secret mint at the time of Antony's union with Cleopatra.

6. Accordingly, regarding his abode as a gift from God, he fell in love with it, and there in prayer and solitude spent all the rest of his life. The palm afforded him food and clothing. And, that no one may deem this impossible, I call to witness Jesus and His holy angels that I have seen and still see in that part of the desert which lies between Syria and the Saracens' country, monks of whom one was shut up for thirty years and lived on barley bread and muddy water, while another in an old cistern (called in the country dialect of Syria *Gubba*) kept himself alive on five dried figs a day. What I relate then is so strange that it will appear incredible to those who do not believe the words that "all things are possible to him that believeth."

7. But to return to the point at which I digressed. The blessed Paul had already lived on earth the life of heaven for a hundred and thirteen years, and Antony at the age of ninety was dwelling in another place of solitude (as he himself was wont to declare), when the thought occurred to the latter, that no monk more perfect than

himself had settled in the desert. However, in the stillness of the night it was revealed to him that there was farther in the desert a much better man than he, and that he ought to go and visit him. So then at break of day the venerable old man, supporting and guiding his weak limbs with a staff, started to go: but what direction to choose he knew not. Scorching noontide came, with a broiling sun overhead, but still he did not suffer himself to be turned from the journey he had begun. Said he, "I believe in my God: some time or other He will shew me the fellow servant whom He promised me." He said no more. All at once he beholds a creature of mingled shape, half horse half man, called by the poets Hippocentaur. At the sight of this he arms himself by making on his forehead the sign of salvation, and then exclaims, "Holloa! Where in these parts is a servant of God living?" The monster after gnashing out some kind of outlandish utterance, in words broken rather than spoken through his bristling lips, at length finds a friendly mode of communication, and extending his right hand points out the way desired. Then with swift flight he crosses the spreading plain and vanishes from the sight of his wondering companion. But whether the devil took this shape to terrify him, or whether it be that the desert which is known to abound in monstrous animals engenders that kind of creature also, we cannot decide.

8. Antony was amazed, and thinking over what he had seen went on his way. Before long in a small rocky valley shut in on all sides he sees a mannikin with hooked snout, horned forehead, and extremities like goats' feet. When he saw this, Antony like a good soldier seized the shield of faith and the helmet of hope: the creature none the less began to offer to him the fruit of the palm-trees to

support him on his journey and as it were pledges of peace. Antony perceiving this stopped and asked who he was. The answer he received from him was this: "I am a mortal being and one of those inhabitants of the desert whom the Gentiles deluded by various forms of error worship under the names of Fauns, Satyrs, and Incubi. I am sent to represent my tribe. We pray you in our behalf to entreat the favor of your Lord and ours, who, we have learnt, came once to save the world, and 'whose sound has gone forth into all the earth.'" As he uttered such words as these, the aged traveler's cheeks streamed with tears, the marks of his deep feeling, which he shed in the fulness of his joy. He rejoiced over the Glory of Christ and the destruction of Satan, and marveling all the while that he could understand the Satyr's language, and striking the ground with his staff, he said, "Woe to thee, Alexandria, who instead of God worshipped monsters! Woe to thee, harlot city, into which have flowed together the demons of the whole world! What will you say now? Beasts speak of Christ, and you instead of God worship monsters." He had not finished speaking when, as if on wings, the wild creature fled away. Let no one scruple to believe this incident; its truth is supported by what took place when Constantine was on the throne, a matter of which the whole world was witness. For a man of that kind was brought alive to Alexandria and shewn as a wonderful sight to the people. Afterwards his lifeless body, to prevent its decay through the summer heat, was preserved in salt and brought to Antioch that the Emperor might see it.

9. To pursue my proposed story. Antony traversed the region on which he had entered, seeing only the traces of wild beasts, and the wide waste of the desert. What to

do, whither to wend his way, he knew not. Another day had now passed. One thing alone was left him, his confident belief that he could not be forsaken by Christ. The darkness of the second night he wore away in prayer. While it was still twilight, he saw not far away a she-wolf gasping with parching thirst and creeping to the foot of the mountain. He followed it with his eyes; and after the beast had disappeared in a cave he drew near and began to look within. His curiosity profited nothing: the darkness hindered vision. But, as the Scripture saith, perfect love cast out fear. With halting step and bated breath he entered, carefully feeling his way; he advanced little by little and repeatedly listened for the sound. At length through the fearful midnight darkness a light appeared in the distance. In his eager haste he struck his foot against a stone and roused the echoes; whereupon the blessed Paul closed the open door and made it fast with a bar. Then Antony sank to the ground at the entrance and until the sixth hour or later craved admission, saying, "Who I am, whence, and why I have come, you know. I know I am not worthy to look upon you: yet unless I see you I will not go away. You welcome beasts: why not a man? I asked and I have found: I knock that it may be opened to me. But if I do not succeed, I will die here on your threshold. You will "Prayers like these do not mean threats; there is no trickery in tears. Are you surprised at my not welcoming you when you have come here to die?" Thus with smiles Paul gave him access, and, the door being opened, they threw themselves into each other's arms, greeted one another by name, and joined in thanksgiving to God.

10. After the sacred kiss Paul sat down and thus began to address Antony. "Behold the man whom you

have sought with so much toil, his limbs decayed with age, his gray hairs unkempt. You see before you a man who ere long will be dust. But love endures all things. Tell me therefore, I pray you, how fares the human race? Are new homes springing up in the ancient cities? What government directs the world? Are there still some remaining for the demons to carry away by their delusions?" Thus conversing they noticed with wonder a raven which had settled on the bough of a tree, and was then flying gently down till it came and laid a whole loaf of bread before them. They were astonished, and when it had gone, "See," said Paul, "the Lord truly loving, truly merciful, has sent us a meal. For the last sixty years I have always received half a loaf: but at your coming Christ has doubled his soldier's rations."

11. Accordingly, having returned thanks to the Lord, they sat down together on the brink of the glassy spring. At this point a dispute arose as to who should break the bread, and nearly the whole day until eventide was spent in the discussion. Paul urged in support of his view the rites of hospitality, Antony pleaded age. At length it was arranged that each should seize the loaf on the side nearest to himself, pull towards him, and keep for his own the part left in his hands. Then on hands and knees they drank a little water from the spring, and offering to God the sacrifice of praise passed the night in vigil. At the return of day the blessed Paul thus spoke to Antony: "I knew long since, brother, that you were dwelling in those parts: long ago God promised you to me for a fellow-servant; but the time of my falling asleep now draws nigh; I have always longed to be dissolved and to be with Christ; my course is finished, and there remains for me a crown of righteousness. Therefore you have been

sent by the Lord to lay my poor body in the ground, yea to return earth to earth."

12. On hearing this Antony with tears and groans began to pray that he would not desert him, but would take him for a companion on that journey. His friend replied: "You ought not to seek your own, but another man's good. It is expedient for you to lay aside the burden of the flesh and to follow the Lamb; but it is expedient for the rest of the brethren to be trained by your example. Wherefore be so good as to go and fetch the cloak Bishop Athanasius gave you, to wrap my poor body in." The blessed Paul asked this favor not because he cared much whether his corpse when it decayed were clothed or naked (why should he indeed, when he had so long worn a garment of palm-leaves stitched together?); but that he might soften his friend's regrets at his decease. Antony was astonished to find Paul had heard of Athanasius and his cloak; and, seeing as it were Christ Himself in him, he mentally worshipped God without venturing to add a single word; then silently weeping he once more kissed his eyes and hands, and set out on his return to the monastery which was afterwards seized by the Saracens. His steps lagged behind his will. Yet, exhausted as he was with fasting and broken by age, his courage proved victorious over his years.

13. At last wearied and panting for breath he completed his journey and reached his little dwelling. Here he was met by two disciples who had begun to wait upon him in his advanced age. Said they, "Where have you stayed so long, father?" He replied, "Woe to me a sinner! I do not deserve the name of monk. I have seen Elias, I have seen John in the desert, and I have really seen Paul in Paradise." He then closed his lips, beat upon

his breast, and brought out the cloak from his cell. When his disciples asked him to explain the matter somewhat more fully he said, "There is a time to keep silence, and a time to speak."

14. He then went out, and without taking so much as a morsel of food returned the same way he came, longing for him alone, thirsting to see him, having eyes and thought for none but him. For he was afraid, and the event proved his anticipations correct, that in his absence his friend might yield up his spirit to Christ. And now another day had dawned and a three hours' journey still remained, when he saw Paul in robes of snowy white ascending on high among the bands of angels, and the choirs of prophets and apostles. Immediately he fell on his face, and threw the coarse sand upon his head, weeping and wailing as he cried, "Why do you cast me from you, Paul? Why go without one farewell? Have you made yourself known so late only to depart so soon?"

15. The blessed Antony used afterwards to relate that he traversed the rest of the distance at such speed that he flew along like a bird; and not without reason: for on entering the cave he saw the lifeless body in a kneeling attitude, with head erect and hands uplifted. The first thing he did, supposing him to be alive, was to pray by his side. But when he did not hear the sighs which usually come from one in prayer, he fell to kisses and tears, and he then understood that even the dead body of the saint with duteous gestures was praying to God unto whom all things live.

16. Then having wrapped up the body and carried it forth, all the while chanting hymns and psalms according to the Christian tradition, Antony began to lament that he had no implement for digging the ground.

So in a surging sea of thought and pondering many plans he said: "If I return to the monastery, there is a four days' journey: if I stay here I shall do no good. I will die then, as is fitting, beside Thy warrior, O Christ, and will quickly breathe my last breath. While he turned these things over in his mind, behold, two lions from the recesses of the desert with manes flying on their necks came rushing along. At first he was horrified at the sight, but again turning his thoughts to God, he waited without alarm, as though they were doves that he saw. They came straight to the corpse of the blessed old man and there stopped, fawned upon it and lay down at its feet, roaring aloud as if to make it known that they were mourning in the only way possible to them. Then they began to paw the ground close by, and vie with one another in excavating the sand, until they dug out a place just large enough to hold a man. And immediately, as if demanding a reward for their work, pricking up their ears while they lowered their heads, they came to Antony and began to lick his hands and feet. He perceived that they were begging a blessing from him, and at once with an outburst of praise to Christ that even dumb animals felt His divinity, he said, "Lord, without whose command not a leaf drops from the tree, not a sparrow falls to the ground, grant them what thou knowest to be best." Then he waved his hand and bade them depart. When they were gone he bent his aged shoulders beneath the burden of the saint's body, laid it in the grave, covered it with the excavated soil, and raised over it the customary mound. Another day dawned, and then, that the affectionate heir might not be without something belonging to the intestate dead, he took for himself the tunic which after the manner of wicker-work the saint had woven out of palm-leaves. And so returning to the monastery he unfolded everything in order to his disciples, and on the feast-days of Easter and Pentecost he always wore Paul's tunic.

17. I may be permitted at the end of this little treatise to ask those who do not know the extent of their possessions, who adorn their homes with marble, who string house to house and field to field, what did this old man in his nakedness ever lack? Your drinking vessels are of precious stones; he satisfied his thirst with the hollow of his hand. Your tunics are of wrought gold; he had not the raiment of the meanest of your slaves. But on the other hand, poor though he was, Paradise is open to him; you with all your gold will be received into Gehenna. He though naked yet kept the robe of Christ; you, clad in your silks, have lost the vesture of Christ. Paul lies covered with worthless dust, but will rise again to glory; over you are raised costly tombs, but both you and your wealth are doomed to the burning. Have a care, I pray you, at least have a care for the riches you love. Why are even the grave-clothes of your dead made of gold? Why does not your vaunting cease even amid mourning and tears? Cannot the carcasses of rich men decay except in silk?

18. I beseech you, reader, whoever you may be, to remember Jerome the sinner. He, if God would give him his choice, would much sooner take Paul's tunic with his merits, than the purple of kings with their punishment.

Introduction to and the Treatises of St. Jerome

The Life of S. Hilarion.

The life of Hilarion was written by Jerome in 390 at Bethlehem. Its object was to further the ascetic life to which he was devoted. It contains, amidst much that is legendary, some statements which attach it to genuine history, and is in any case a curious record of the state of the human mind in the 4th century. A theory started in Germany, that it was a sort of religious romance, seems destitute of foundation. It may possibly have been, in Jerome's intention, a contribution to the church history the writing of which he proposed but never executed. (See the Life of Malchus, c. 1.)

1. Before I begin to write the life of the blessed Hilarion I invoke the aid of the Holy Spirit who dwelt in him, that He who bestowed upon the saint his virtues may grant me such power of speech to relate them that my words may be adequate to his deeds. For the virtue of those who have done great deeds is esteemed in proportion to the ability with which it has been praised by men of genius. Alexander the Great of Macedon who is spoken of by Daniel as the ram, or the panther, or the he-goat, on reaching the grave of Achilles exclaimed "Happy Youth! to have the privilege of a great herald of your worth," meaning, of course, Homer. I, however, have to tell the story of the life and conversation of a man so renowned that even Homer were he here would either envy me the theme or prove unequal to it. It is true that that holy man Epiphanius, bishop of Salamis in Cyprus, who had much intercourse with Hilarion, set forth his

praises in a short but widely circulated letter. Yet it is one thing to praise the dead in general terms, another to relate their characteristic virtues. And so we in taking up the work begun by him do him service rather than wrong: we despise the abuse of some who as they once disparaged my hero Paulus, will now perhaps disparage Hilarion; the former they censured for his solitary life; they may find fault with the latter for his intercourse with the world; the one was always out of sight, therefore they think he had no existence; the other was seen by many, therefore he is deemed of no account. It is just what their ancestors the Pharisees did of old! they were not pleased with John fasting in the desert, nor with our Lord and Savior in the busy throng, eating and drinking. But I will put my hand to the work on which I have resolved, and go on my way closing my ears to the barking of Scylla's hounds.

2. The birthplace of Hilarion was the village Thabatha, situate about five miles to the south of Gaza, a city of Palestine. His parents were idolaters, and therefore, as the saying is, the rose blossomed on the thorn. By them he was committed to the charge of a Grammarian at Alexandria, where, so far as his age allowed, he gave proofs of remarkable ability and character: and in a short time endeared himself to all and became an accomplished speaker. More important than all this, he was a believer in the Lord Jesus, and took no delight in the madness of the circus, the blood of the arena, the excesses of the theatre: his whole pleasure was in the assemblies of the Church.

3. At that time he heard of the famous name of Antony, which was in the mouth of all the races of Egypt. He was fired with a desire to see him, and set out for the desert. He no sooner saw him than he changed his former

mode of life and abode with him about two months, studying the method of his life and the gravity of his conduct: his assiduity in prayer, his humility in his dealings with the brethren, his severity in rebuke, his eagerness in exhortation. He noted too that the saint would never on account of bodily weakness break his rule of abstinence or deviate from the plainness of his food. At last, unable to endure any longer the crowds of those who visited the saint because of various afflictions or the assaults of demons, and deeming it a strange anomaly that he should have to bear in the desert the crowds of the cities, he thought it was better for him to begin as Antony had begun. Said he: "Antony is reaping the reward of victory like a hero who has proved his bravery. I have not entered on the soldier's career." He therefore returned with certain monks to his country, and, his parents being now dead, gave part of his property to his brothers, part to the poor, keeping nothing at all for himself, for he remembered with awe the passage in the Acts of the Apostles and dreaded the example and the punishment of Ananias and Sapphira; above all he was mindful of the Lord's words, "whosoever he be of you that renounces not all that he hath, he cannot be my disciple." At this time he was about fifteen years old. Accordingly, stripped bare and armed with the weapons of Christ, he entered the wilderness which stretches to the left seven miles from Majoma, the port of Gaza, as you go along the coast to Egypt. And although the locality had a record of robbery and of blood, and his relatives and friends warned him of the danger he was incurring, he despised death that he might escape death.

4. His courage and tender years would have been a marvel to all, were it not that his heart was on fire and his

eyes bright with the gleams and sparks of faith. His cheeks were smooth, his body thin and delicate, unfit to bear the slightest injury which cold or heat could inflict. What then? With no other covering for his limbs but a shirt of sackcloth, and a cloak of skins which the blessed Antony had given him when he set out, and a blanket of the coarsest sort, he found pleasure in the vast and terrible wilderness with the sea on one side and the marshland on the other. His food was only fifteen dried figs after sunset. And because the district was notorious for brigandage, it was his practice never to abide long in the same place. What was the devil to do? Whither could he turn? He who once boasted and said, "I will ascend into heaven, I will set my throne above the stars of the sky, I will be like the most High," saw himself conquered and trodden underfoot by a boy whose years did not allow of sin.

5. Satan therefore tickled his senses and, as is his wont, lighted in his maturing body the fires of lust. This mere beginner in Christ's school was forced to think of what he knew not, and to revolve whole trains of thought concerning that of which he had no experience. Angry with himself and beating his bosom (as if with the blow of his hand he could shut out his thoughts) "Ass!" he exclaimed, "I'll stop your kicking, I will not feed you with barley, but with chaff. I will weaken you with hunger and thirst, I will lade you with heavy burdens, I will drive you through heat and cold, that you may think more of food than wantonness." So for three or four days afterwards he sustained his sinking spirit with the juice of herbs and a few dried figs, praying frequently and singing, and hoeing the ground that the suffering of fasting might be doubled by the pain of toil. At the same time he wove baskets of rushes and emulated the

discipline of the Egyptian monks, and put into practice the Apostle's precept, "If any will not work, neither let him eat." By these practices, he became so enfeebled and his frame so wasted, that his bones scarcely held together.

6. One night he began to hear the wailing of infants, the bleating of flocks, the lowing of oxen, the lament of what seemed to be women, the roaring of lions, the noise of an army, and moreover various portentous cries which made him in alarm shrink from the sound ere he had the sight. He understood that the demons were disporting themselves, and falling on his knees he made the sign of the cross on his forehead. Thus armed as he lay he fought the more bravely, half longing to see those whom he shuddered to hear, and anxiously looking in every direction. Meanwhile all at once in the bright moonlight he saw a chariot with dashing steeds rushing upon him. He called upon Jesus, and suddenly before his eyes, the earth was opened and the whole array was swallowed up. Then he said, "The horse and his rider hath He thrown into the sea." And, "Some trust in chariots, and some in horses; but we will triumph in the name of the Lord our God."

7. So many were his temptations and so various the snares of demons night and day, that if I wished to relate them, a volume would not suffice. How often when he lay down did naked women appear to him, how often sumptuous feasts when he was hungry! Sometimes as he prayed a howling wolf sprang past or a snarling fox, and when he sang a gladiatorial show was before him, and a man newly slain would seem to fall at his feet and ask him for burial.

8. Once upon a time he was praying with his head upon the ground. As is the way with men, his attention

was withdrawn from his devotions, and he was thinking of something else, when a tormentor sprang upon his back and driving his heels into his sides and beating him across the neck with a horse-whip cried out "Come! why are you asleep?" Then with a loud laugh asked if he was tired and would like to have some barley.

9. From his sixteenth to his twentieth year he shielded himself from heat and rain in a little hut which he had constructed of reeds and sedge. Afterwards he built himself a small cell which remains to the present day, five feet in height, that is less than his own height, and only a little more in length. One might suppose it a tomb rather than a house.

10. He shaved his hair once a year on Easter Day, and until his death was accustomed to lie on the bare ground or on a bed of rushes. The sackcloth which he had once put on he never washed, and he used to say that it was going too far to look for cleanliness in goats' hair-cloth. Nor did he change his shirt unless the one he wore was almost in rags. He had committed the Sacred Writings to memory, and after prayer and singing was wont to recite them as if in the presence of God. It would be tedious to narrate singly the successive steps of his spiritual ascent; I will therefore set them in a summary way before my reader, and describe his mode of life at each stage, and will afterwards return to proper historical sequence.

11. From his twentieth to his twenty-seventh year, for three years his food was half a pint of lentils moistened with cold water, and for the next three dry bread with salt and water. From his twenty-seventh year onward to the thirtieth, he supported himself on wild herbs and the raw roots of certain shrubs. From his thirty-

first to his thirty-fifth year, he had for food six ounces of barley bread, and vegetables slightly cooked without oil. But finding his eyes growing dim and his whole body shriveled with a scabby eruption and dry mange, he added oil to his former food and up to the sixty-third year of his life followed this temperate course, tasting neither fruit nor pulse, nor anything whatsoever besides. Then when he saw that his bodily health was broken down, and thought death was near, from his sixty-fourth year to his eightieth he abstained from bread. The fervor of his spirit was so wonderful, that at times when others are wont to allow themselves some laxity of living he appeared to be entering like a novice on the service of the Lord. He made a sort of broth from meal and bruised herbs, food and drink together scarcely weighing six ounces, and, while obeying this rule of diet, he never broke his fast before sunset, not even on festivals nor in severe sickness. But it is now time to return to the course of event.

12. While still living in the hut, at the age of eighteen, robbers came to him by night, either supposing that he had something which they might carry off, or considering that they would be brought into contempt if a solitary boy felt no dread of their attacks. They searched up and down between the sea and the marsh from evening until daybreak without being able to find his resting place. Then, having discovered the boy by the light of day they asked him, half in jest, "What would you do if robbers came to you?" He replied, "He that has nothing does not fear robbers." Said they, "At all events, you might be killed." "I might," said he, "I might; and therefore I do not fear robbers because I am prepared to die." Then they marveled at his firmness and faith, confessed how they had wandered about in the night, and how their eyes had

been blinded, and promised to lead a stricter life in the future.

13. He had now spent twenty-two years in the wilderness and was the common theme in all the cities of Palestine, though everywhere known by repute only. The first person bold enough to break into the presence of the blessed Hilarion was a certain woman of Eleutheropolis who found that she was despised by her husband on account of her sterility (for in fifteen years she had borne no fruit of wedlock). He had no expectation of her coming when she suddenly threw herself at his feet. "Forgive my boldness," she said: "take pity on my necessity. Why do you turn away your eyes? Why shun my entreaties? Do not think of me as a woman, but as an object of compassion. It was my sex that bore the Savior. They that are whole have no need of a physician, but they that are sick." At length, after a long time he no longer turned away, but looked at the woman and asked the cause of her coming and of her tears. On learning this he raised his eyes to heaven and bade her have faith, then wept over her as she departed. Within a year he saw her with a son.

14. This his first miracle was succeeded by another still greater and more notable. Aristæneté the wife of Elpidius who was afterwards pretorian prefect, a woman well known among her own people, still better known among Christians, on her return with her husband, from visiting the blessed Antony, was delayed at Gaza by the sickness of her three children; for there, whether it was owing to the vitiated atmosphere, or whether it was, as afterwards became clear, for the glory of God's servant Hilarion, they were all alike seized by a semitertian ague and despaired of by the physicians. The mother lay wailing, or as one might say walked up and down

between the corpses of her three sons not knowing which she should first have to mourn for. When, however, she knew that there was a certain monk in the neighboring wilderness, forgetting her matronly state (she only remembered she was a mother) she set out accompanied by her handmaids and eunuchs, and was hardly persuaded by her husband to take an ass to ride upon. On reaching the saint she said, "I pray you by Jesus our most merciful God, I beseech you by His cross and blood, to restore to me my three sons, so that the name of our Lord and Savior may be glorified in the city of the Gentiles. Then shall his servants enter Gaza and the idol Marnas shall fall to the ground." At first he refused and said that he never left his cell and was not accustomed to enter a house, much less the city; but she threw herself upon the ground and cried repeatedly, "Hilarion, servant of Christ, give me back my children: Antony kept them safe in Egypt, do you save them in Syria." All present were weeping, and the saint himself wept as he denied her. What need to say more? the woman did not leave him till he promised that he would enter Gaza after sunset. On coming thither he made the sign of the cross over the bed and fevered limbs of each, and called upon the name of Jesus. Marvelous efficacy of the Name! As if from three fountains the sweat burst forth at the same time: in that very hour they took food, recognized their mourning mother, and, with thanks to God, warmly kissed the saint's hands. When the matter was noised abroad, and the fame of it spread far and wide, the people flocked to him from Syria and Egypt, so that many believed in Christ and professed themselves monks. For as yet there were no monasteries in Palestine, nor had anyone known a monk in Syria before the saintly Hilarion. It was he who originated this mode of life and devotion, and who first trained men to it in that province. The Lord Jesus had in Egypt the aged Antony: in Palestine He had the youthful Hilarion.

15. Facidia is a hamlet belonging to Rhino-Corura, a city of Egypt. From this village a woman who had been blind for ten years was brought to the blessed Hilarion, and on being presented to him by the brethren (for there were now many monks with him) affirmed that she had spent all her substance on physicians. The saint replied: "If you had given to the poor what you have wasted on physicians, the true physician Jesus would have cured you." But when she cried aloud and entreated pity, he spat into her eyes, in imitation of the Savior, and with similar instant effect.

16. A charioteer, also of Gaza, stricken by a demon in his chariot became perfectly stiff, so that he could neither move his hand nor bend his neck. He was brought on a litter, but could only signify his petition by moving his tongue; and was told that he could not be healed unless he first believed in Christ and promised to forsake his former occupation. He believed, he promised, and he was healed: and rejoiced more in the saving of the soul than in that of the body.

17. Again, a very powerful youth called Marsitas from the neighborhood of Jerusalem plumed himself so highly on his strength that he carried fifteen bushels of grain for a long time and over a considerable distance, and considered it as his highest glory that he could beat the asses in endurance. This man was afflicted with a grievous demon and could not endure chains, or fetters, but broke even the bolts and bars of the doors. He had bitten off the noses and ears of many: had broken the feet of some, the legs of others. He had struck such terror of

himself into everybody, that he was laden with chains and dragged by ropes on all sides like a wild bull to the monastery. As soon as the brethren saw him they were greatly alarmed (for the man was of gigantic size) and told the Father. He, seated as he was, commanded him to be brought to him and released. When he was free, "Bow your head," said he, "and come." The man began to tremble; he twisted his neck round and did not dare to look him in the face, but laid aside all his fierceness and began to lick his feet as he sat. At last the demon which had possessed the young man being tortured by the saint's adjurations came forth on the seventh day.

18. Nor must we omit to tell that Orion, a leading man and wealthy citizen of Aira, on the coast of the Red Sea, being possessed by a legion of demons was brought to him. Hands, neck, sides, feet were laden with iron, and his glaring eyes portended an access of raging madness. As the saint was walking with the brethren and expounding some passage of Scripture the man broke from the hands of his keepers, clasped him from behind and raised him aloft. There was a shout from all, for they feared lest he might crush his limbs wasted as they were with fasting. The saint smiled and said, "Be quiet, and let me have my rival in the wrestling match to myself." Then he bent back his hand over his shoulder till he touched the man's head, seized his hair and drew him round so as to be foot to foot with him; he then stretched both his hands in a straight line, and trod on his two feet with both his own, while he cried out again and again, "To torment with you! ye crowd of demons, to torment!" The sufferer shouted aloud and bent back his neck till his head touched the ground, while the saint said, "Lord Jesus, release this wretched man, release this captive. Thine it is to conquer

many, no less than one." What I now relate is unparalleled: from one man's lips were heard different voices and as it were the confused shouts of a multitude. Well, he too was cured, and not long after came with his wife and children to the monastery bringing many gifts expressive of his gratitude. The saint thus addressed him—"Have you not read what befell Gehazi and Simon, one of whom took a reward, the other offered it, the former in order to sell grace, the latter to buy it?" And when Orion said with tears, "Take it and give it to the poor," he replied, "You can best distribute your own gifts, for you tread the streets of the cities and know the poor. Why should I who have forsaken my own seek another man's? To many the name of the poor is a pretext for their avarice; but compassion knows no artifices. No one better spends than he who keeps nothing for himself." The man was sad and lay upon the ground. "Be not sad, my son," he said; "what I do for my own good I do also for yours. If I were to take these gifts I should myself offend God, and, moreover, the legion would return to you."

19. There is a story relating to Majomites of Gaza which it is impossible to pass over in silence. While quarrying building stones on the shore not far from the monastery he was helplessly paralyzed, and after being carried to the saint by his fellow-workman immediately returned to his work in perfect health. I ought to explain that the shore of Palestine and Egypt naturally consists of soft sand and gravel which gradually becomes consolidated and hardens into rock; and thus though to the eye it remains the same it is no longer the same to the touch.

20. Another story relates to Italicus, a citizen of the same town. He was a Christian and kept horses for the

circus to contend against those of the Duumvir of Gaza who was a votary of the idol god Marnas. This custom at least in Roman cities was as old as the days of Romulus, and was instituted in commemoration of the successful seizure of the Sabine women. The chariots raced seven times round the circus in honor of Consus in his character of the God of Counsel. Victory lay with the team which tired out the horses opposed to them. Now the rival of Italicus had in his pay a magician to incite his horses by certain demoniacal incantations, and keep back those of his opponent. Italicus therefore came to the blessed Hilarion and besought his aid not so much for the injury of his adversary as for protection for himself. It seemed absurd for the venerable old man to waste prayers on trifles of this sort. He therefore smiled and said, "Why do you not rather give the price of the horses to the poor for the salvation of your soul?" His visitor replied that his office was a public duty, and that he acted not so much from choice as from compulsion, that no Christian man could employ magic, but would rather seek aid from a servant of Christ, especially against the people of Gaza who were enemies of God, and who would exult over the Church of Christ more than over him. At the request therefore of the brethren who were present he ordered an earthenware cup out of which he was wont to drink to be filled with water and given to Italicus. The latter took it and sprinkled it over his stable and horses, his charioteers and his chariot, and the barriers of the course. The crowd was in a marvelous state of excitement, for the enemy in derision had published the news of what was going to be done, and the backers of Italicus were in high spirits at the victory which they promised themselves. The signal is given; the one team flies towards the goal, the other sticks fast: the wheels are glowing hot beneath the chariot of the one, while the other scarce catches a glimpse of their opponents' backs as they flit past. The shouts of the crowd swell to a roar, and the heathens themselves with one voice declare Marnas is conquered by Christ. After this the opponents in their rage demanded that Hilarion as a Christian magician should be dragged to execution. This decisive victory and several others which followed in successive games of the circus caused many to turn to the faith.

21. There was a youth in the neighborhood of the same market-town of Gaza who was desperately in love with one of God's virgins. After he had tried again and again those touches, jests, nods, and whispers which so commonly lead to the destruction of virginity, but had made no progress by these means, he went to a magician at Memphis to whom he proposed to make known his wretched state, and then, fortified with his arts, to return to his assault upon the virgin. Accordingly after a year's instruction by the priest of Æsculapius, who does not heal souls but destroys them, he came full of the lust which he had previously allowed his mind to entertain, and buried beneath the threshold of the girl's house certain magical formula and revolting figures engraven on a plate of Cyprian brass. Thereupon the maid began to show signs of insanity, to throw away the covering of her head, tear her hair, gnash her teeth, and loudly call the youth by name. Her intense affection had become a frenzy. Her parents therefore brought her to the monastery and delivered her to the aged saint. No sooner was this done than the devil began to howl and confess. "I was compelled, I was carried off against my will. How happy I was when I used to beguile the men of Memphis in their

dreams! What crosses, what torture I suffer! You force me to go out, and I am kept bound under the threshold. I cannot go out unless the young man who keeps me there lets me go." The old man answered, "Your strength must be great indeed, if a bit of thread and a plate can keep you bound. Tell me, how is it that you dared to enter into this maid who belongs to God?" "That I might preserve her as a virgin," said he. "You preserve her, betrayer of chastity! Why did you not rather enter into him who sent you?" "For what purpose," he answers, "should I enter into one who was in alliance with a comrade of my own, the demon of love?" But the saint would not command search to be made for either the young man or the charms till the maiden had undergone a process of purgation, for fear that it might be thought that the demon had been released by means of incantations, or that he himself had attached credit to what he said. He declared that demons are deceitful and well versed in dissimulation, and sharply rebuked the virgin when she had recovered her health for having by her conduct given an opportunity for the demon to enter.

22. It was not only in Palestine and the neighboring cities of Egypt or Syria that he was in high repute, but his fame had reached distant provinces. An officer of the Emperor Constantius whose golden hair and personal beauty revealed his country (it lay between the Saxons and the Alemanni, was of no great extent but powerful, and is known to historians as Germany, but is now called France), had long, that is to say from infancy, been pursued by a devil, who forced him in the night to howl, groan, and gnash his teeth. He therefore secretly asked the Emperor for a post-warrant, plainly telling him why he wanted it, and having also obtained letters to the

legate at Palestine came with great pomp and a large retinue to Gaza. On his inquiring of the local senators where Hilarion the monk dwelt, the people of Gaza were much alarmed, and supposing that he had been sent by the Emperor, brought him to the monastery, that they might show respect to one so highly accredited, and that, if any guilt had been incurred by them by injuries previously done by them to Hilarion it might be obliterated by their present dutifulness. The old man at the time was taking a walk on the soft sands and was humming some passage or other from the psalms. Seeing so great a company approaching he stopped, and having returned the salutes of all while he raised his hand and gave them his blessing, after an hour's interval he bade the rest withdraw, but would have his visitor together with servants and officers remain: for by the man's eyes and countenance he knew the cause of his coming. Immediately on being questioned by the servant of God the man sprang up on tiptoe, so as scarcely to touch the ground with his feet, and with a wild roar replied in Syriac in which language he had been interrogated. Pure Syriac was heard flowing from the lips of a barbarian who knew only French and Latin, and that without the absence of a sibilant, or an aspirate, or an idiom of the speech of Palestine. The demon then confessed by what means he had entered into him. Further, that his interpreters who knew only Greek and Latin might understand, Hilarion questioned him also in Greek, and when he gave the same answer in the same words and alleged in excuse many occasions on which spells had been laid upon him, and how he was bound to yield to magic arts, "I care not," said the saint, "how you came to enter, but I command you in the name of our Lord Jesus Christ to come out." The man, as soon as he was healed, with a rough simplicity offered him ten pounds of gold. But the saint took from him only bread, and told him that they who were nourished on such food regarded gold as mire.

23. It is not enough to speak of men; brute animals were also daily brought to him in a state of madness, and among them a Bactrian camel of enormous size amid the shouts of thirty men or more who held him tight with stout ropes. He had already injured many. His eyes were bloodshot, his mouth filled with foam, his rolling tongue swollen, and above every other source of terror was his loud and hideous roar. Well, the old man ordered him to be let go. At once those who brought him as well as the attendants of the saint fled away without exception. The saint went by himself to meet him, and addressing him in Syriac said, "You do not alarm me, devil, huge though your present body is. Whether in a fox or a camel you are just the same." Meanwhile he stood with outstretched hand. The brute raging and looking as if he would devour Hilarion came up to him, but immediately fell down, laid its head on the ground, and to the amazement of all present showed suddenly no less tameness than it had exhibited ferocity before. But the old man declared to them how the devil, for men's sake, seizes even beasts of burden; that he is inflamed by such intense hatred for men that he desires to destroy not only them but what belongs to them. As an illustration of this he added the fact that before he was permitted to try the saintly Job, he made an end of all his substance. Nor ought it to disturb anyone that by the Lord's command two thousand swine were slain by the agency of demons, since those who witnessed the miracle could not have believed that so great a multitude of demons had gone out of the man unless an

equally vast number of swine had rushed to ruin, showing that it was a legion that impelled them.

24. Time would fail me if I wished to relate all the miracles which were wrought by him. For to such a pitch of glory was he raised by the Lord that the blessed Antony among the rest hearing of his life wrote to him and gladly received his letters. And if ever the sick from Syria came to him he would say to them, "Why have you taken the trouble to come so far, when you have there my son Hilarion?" Following his example, however, innumerable monasteries sprang up throughout the whole of Palestine, and all the monks flocked to him. When he saw this he praised the Lord for His grace, and exhorted them individually to the profit of their souls, telling them that the fashion of this world passes away, and that the true life is that which is purchased by suffering in the present.

25. Wishing to set the monks an example of humility and of zeal he was accustomed on fixed days before the vintage to visit their cells. When the brethren knew this they would all come together to meet him, and in company with their distinguished leader go the round of the monasteries, taking with them provisions, because sometimes as many as two thousand men were assembled. But, as time went on, all the settlements round gladly gave food to the neighboring monks for the entertainment of the saints. Moreover, the care he took to prevent any brother however humble or poor being passed over is evidenced by the journey which he once took into the desert of Cades to visit one of his disciples. With a great company of monks he reached Elusa, as it happened on the day when the annual festival had brought all the people together to the temple of Venus. This, goddess is

worshipped on account of Lucifer to whom the Saracen nation is devoted. The very town too is to a great extent semi barbarous, owing to its situation. When therefore it was heard that Saint Hilarion was passing through (he had frequently healed many Saracens possessed by demons), they went to meet him in crowds with their wives and children, bending their heads and crying in the Syriac tongue *Barech*, that is, *Bless*. He received them with courtesy and humility, and prayed that they might worship God rather than stones; at the same time, weeping copiously, he looked up to heaven and promised that if they would believe in Christ he would visit them often. By the marvelous grace of God they did not suffer him to depart before he had drawn the outline of a church, and their priest with his garland upon his head had been signed with the sign of Christ.

26. Another year, again, when he was setting out to visit the monasteries and was drawing up a list of those with whom he must stay and whom he must see in passing, the monks knowing that one of their number was a niggard, and being at the same time desirous to cure his complaint, asked the saint to stay with him. He replied, "Do you wish me to inflict injury on you and annoyance on the brother?" The niggardly brother on hearing of this was ashamed, and with the strenuous support of all his brethren, at length obtained from the saint a reluctant promise to put his monastery on the roll of his resting places. Ten days after they came to him and found the keepers already on guard in the vineyard through which their course lay, to keep off all comers with stones and clods and slings. In the morning they all departed without having eaten a grape, while the old man smiled and pretended not to know what had happened.

27. Once when they were being entertained by another monk whose name was Sabus (we must not of course give the name of the niggard, we may tell that of this generous man), because it was the Lord's day, they were all invited by him into the vineyard so that before the hour for food came they might relieve the toil of the journey by a repast of grapes. Said the saint, "Cursed be he who looks for the refreshment of the body before that of the soul. Let us pray, let us sing, let us do our duty to God, and then we will hasten to the vineyard." When the service was over, he stood on an eminence and blessed the vineyard and let his own sheep go to their pasture. Now those who partook were not less than three thousand. And whereas the whole vineyard had been estimated at a hundred flagons, within thirty days he made it worth three hundred. The niggardly brother gathered much less than usual, and he was grieved to find that even what he had turned to vinegar. The old man had predicted this to many brethren before it happened. He particularly abhorred such monks as were led by their lack of faith to hoard for the future, and were careful about expense, or raiment, or some other of those things which pass away with the world.

28. Lastly he would not even look at one of the brethren who lived about five miles off because he ascertained that he very jealously guarded his bit of ground, and had a little money. The offender wishing to be reconciled to the old man often came to the brethren, and in particular to Hesychius who was specially dear to Hilarion. One day accordingly he brought a bundle of green chick-pea just as it had been gathered. Hesychius placed it on the table against the evening, whereupon the old man cried out that he could not bear the stench, and

asked where it came from. Hesychius replied that a certain brother had sent the brethren the first fruits of his ground. "Don't you notice," said he, "the horrid stench, and detect the foul odor of avarice in the peas? Send it to the cattle, send to the brute-beasts and see whether they can eat it." No sooner was it in obedience to his command laid in the manger than the cattle in the wildest alarm and bellowing loudly broke their fastenings and fled in different directions. For the old man was enabled by grace to tell from the odor of bodies and garments, and the things which any one had touched, by what demon or with what vice the individual was distressed.

29. His sixty-third year found the old man at the head of a grand monastery and a multitude of resident brethren. There were such crowds of persons constantly bringing those who suffered from various kinds of sickness or were possessed of unclean spirits, that the whole circuit of the wilderness was full of all sorts of people. And as the saint saw all this he wept daily and called to mind with incredible regret his former mode of life. When one of the brethren asked him why he was so dejected he replied, "I have returned again to the world and have received my reward in my lifetime. The people of Palestine and the adjoining province think me of some importance, and under pretense of a monastery for the well-ordering of the brethren I have all the apparatus of a paltry life about me." The brethren, however, kept watch over him and in particular Hesychius, who had a marvelously devoted affection and veneration for the old man. After he had spent two years in these lamentations Aristæneté the lady of whom we made mention before, as being then the wife of a prefect though without any of a prefect's ostentation, came to him intending to pay a visit

to Antony also. He said to her, "I should like to go myself too if I were not kept a prisoner in this monastery, and if my going could be fruitful. For it is now two days since mankind was bereaved of him who was so truly a father to them all." She believed his word and stayed where she was: and after a few days the news came that Antony had fallen asleep.

30. Some may wonder at the miracles he worked, or his incredible fasting, knowledge, and humility. Nothing so astonishes me as his power to tread underfoot honor and glory. Bishops, presbyters, crowds of clergymen and monks, of Christian matrons even (a great temptation), and a rabble from all quarters in town and country were congregating about him, and even judges and others holding high positions, that they might receive at his hands the bread or oil which he had blessed. But he thought of nothing but solitude, so much so that one day he determined to be gone, and having procured an ass (he was almost exhausted with fasting and could scarcely walk) endeavored to steal away. The news spread far and wide, and, just as if a public mourning for the desolation of Palestine were decreed, ten thousand people of various ages and both sexes came together to prevent his departure. He was unmoved by entreaties, and striking the sand with his stick kept saying: "I will not make my Lord a deceiver; I cannot look upon churches overthrown, Christ's altars trodden down, the blood of my sons poured out." All who were present began to understand that some secret had been revealed to him which he was unwilling to confess, but they none the less kept guard over him that he might not go. He therefore determined, and publicly called all to witness, that he would take neither food nor drink unless he were released. Only after seven days was

he relieved from his fasting; when having bidden farewell to numerous friends, he came to Betilium attended by a countless multitude. There he prevailed upon the crowd to return and chose as his companions forty monks who had resources for the journey and were capable of travelling during fasting-time, that is, after sunset. He then visited the brethren who were in the neighboring desert and sojourning at a place called Lychnos, and after three days came to the castle of Theubatus to see Dracontius, bishop and confessor, who was in exile there. The bishop was beyond measure cheered by the presence of so distinguished a man. At the end of another three days he set out for Babylon and arrived there after a hard journey. Then he visited Philo the bishop, who was also a confessor; for the Emperor Constantius who favored the Arian heresy had transported both of them to those parts. Departing thence he came in three days to the town Aphroditon. There he met with a deacon Baisanes who kept dromedaries which were hired, on account of the scarcity of water in the desert, to carry travelers who wished to visit Antony. He then made known to the brethren that the anniversary of the blessed Antony's decease was at hand, and that he must spend a whole night in vigil in the very place where the saint had died. So then after three days journey through the waste and terrible desert they at length came to a very high mountain, and there found two monks, Isaac and Pelusianus, the former of whom had been one of Antony's attendants.

31. The occasion seems a fitting one, since we are on the spot itself, to describe the abode of this great man. There is a high and rocky mountain extending for about a mile, with gushing springs amongst its spurs, the waters

of which are partly absorbed by the sand, partly flow towards the plain and gradually form a stream shaded on either side by countless palms which lend much pleasantness and charm to the place. Here the old man might be seen pacing to and fro with the disciples of blessed Antony. Here, so they said, Antony himself used to sing, pray, work, and rest when weary. Those vines and shrubs were planted by his own hand: that garden bed was his own design. This pool for watering the garden was made by him after much toil. That hoe was handled by him for many years. Hilarion would lie upon the saint's bed and as though it were still warm would affectionately kiss it. The cell was square, its sides measuring no more than the length of a sleeping man. Moreover on the lofty mountaintop, the ascent of which was by a zig-zag path very difficult, were to be seen two cells of the same dimensions, in which he stayed when he escaped from the crowds of visitors or the company of his disciples. These were cut out of the live rock and were only furnished with doors. When they came to the garden, "You see," said Isaac, "this garden with its shrubs and green vegetables; about three years ago it was ravaged by a troop of wild asses. One of their leaders was hidden by Antony to stand still while he thrashed the animal's sides with a stick and wanted to know why they devoured what they had not sown. And ever afterwards, excepting the water which they were accustomed to come and drink, they never touched anything, not a bush or a vegetable." The old man further asked to be shown his burial place, and they thereupon took him aside; but whether they showed him the tomb or not is unknown. It is related that the motive for secrecy was compliance with Antony's orders and to prevent Pergamius, a very wealthy man of the district, from removing the saint's body to his house and erecting a shrine to his memory.

32. Having returned to Aphroditon and keeping with him only two of the brethren, he stayed in the neighboring desert, and practiced such rigid abstinence and silence that he felt that then for the first time he had begun to serve Christ. Three years had now elapsed since the heavens had been closed and the land had suffered from drought, and it was commonly said that even the elements were lamenting the death of Antony. Hilarion did not remain unknown to the inhabitants of that place any more than to others, but men and women with ghastly faces and wasted by hunger earnestly entreated the servant of Christ, as being the blessed Antony's successor, to give them rain. Hilarion when he saw them was strangely affected with compassion and, raising his eyes to heaven and lifting up both his hands, he at once obtained their petition. But, strange to say, that parched and sandy district, after the rain had fallen, unexpectedly produced such vast numbers of serpents and poisonous animals that many who were bitten would have died at once if they had not run to Hilarion. He therefore blessed some oil with which all the husbandmen and shepherds touched their wounds, and found an infallible cure.

33. Seeing that even there surprising respect was paid to him, he went to Alexandria, intending to cross from thence to the farther oasis of the desert. And because he had never stayed in cities since he entered on the monk's life, he turned aside to some brethren at Bruchium, not far from Alexandria, whom he knew, and who welcomed the old man with the greatest pleasure. It was now night when all at once they heard his disciples saddling the ass and making ready for the journey. They

therefore threw themselves at his feet and besought him not to leave them; they fell prostrate before the door, and declared they would rather die than lose such a guest. He answered: "My reason for hastening away is that I may not give you trouble. You will no doubt afterwards discover that I have not suddenly left without good cause." Next day the authorities of Gaza with the lictors of the prefect having heard of his arrival on the previous day, entered the monastery, and when they failed to find him anywhere they began to say to one another: "What we heard is true. He is a magician and knows the future." The fact was that the city of Gaza on Julian's accession to the throne, after the departure of Hilarion from Palestine and the destruction of his monastery, had presented a petition to the Emperor requesting that both Hilarion and Hesychius might be put to death, and a proclamation had been published everywhere that search should be made for them.

34. Having then left Bruchium, he entered the oasis through the trackless desert, and there abode for a year, more or less. But, inasmuch as his fame had travelled thither also, he felt that he could not be hidden in the East, where he was known to many by report and by sight, and began to think of taking ship for some solitary island, so that having been exposed to public view by the land, he might at least find concealment in the sea. Just about that time Hadrian, his disciple, arrived from Palestine with information that Julian was slain and that a Christian emperor had commenced his reign; he ought therefore, it was said, to return to the relics of his monastery. But he, when he heard this, solemnly refused to return; and hiring a camel crossed the desert waste and reached Paretonium, a city on the coast of Libya. There

the ill-starred Hadrian wishing to return to Palestine and unwilling to part with the renown so long attaching to his master's name, heaped reproaches upon him, and at last having packed up the presents which he had brought him from the brethren, set out without the knowledge of Hilarion. As I shall have no further opportunity of referring to this man, I would only record, for the terror of those who despise their masters, that after a little while he was attacked by the king's-evil and turned to a mass of corruption.

35. The old man accompanied by Gazanus went on board a ship which was sailing to Sicily. Half way across the Adriatic he was preparing to pay his fare by selling a copy of the Gospels which he had written with his own hand in his youth, when the son of the master of the ship seized by a demon began to cry out and say: "Hilarion, servant of God, why is it that through you we cannot be safe even on the sea? Spare me a little until I reach land. Let me not be cast out here and thrown into the deep." The saint replied: "If my God permit you to remain, remain; but if He casts you out, why bring odium upon me a sinner and a beggar?" This he said that the sailors and merchants on board might not betray him on reaching shore. Not long after, the boy was cleansed, his father and the rest who were present having given their word that they would not reveal the name of the saint to anyone.

36. On approaching Pachynus, a promontory of Sicily, he offered the master the Gospel for the passage of himself and Gazanus. The man was unwilling to take it, all the more because he saw that excepting that volume and the clothes they wore they had nothing, and at last he swore he would not take it. But the aged saint, ardent and

confident in the consciousness of his poverty, rejoiced exceedingly that he had no worldly possessions and was accounted a beggar by the people of the place.

37. Once more, on thinking the matter over and fearing that merchants coming from the East might make him known, he fled to the interior, some twenty miles from the sea, and there on an abandoned piece of ground, every day tied up a bundle of firewood which he laid upon the back of his disciple, and sold at some neighboring mansion. They thus supported themselves and were able to purchase a morsel of bread for any chance visitors. But that came exactly to pass which is written: "a city set on a hill cannot be hid." It happened that one of the shields-men who was vexed by a demon was in the basilica of the blessed Peter at Rome, when the unclean spirit within him cried out, "A few days ago Christ's servant Hilarion entered Sicily and no one knew him, and he thinks he is hidden. I will go and betray him." Immediately he embarked with his attendants in a ship lying in harbor, sailed to Pachynus and, led by the demon to the old man's hut, there prostrated himself and was cured on the spot. This, his first miracle in Sicily, brought the sick to him in countless numbers (but it brought also a multitude of religious persons); insomuch that one of the leading men who was swollen with the dropsy was cured the same day that he came. He afterwards offered the saint gifts without end, but the saint replied to him in the words of the Savior to his disciples: "Freely ye received, freely give."

38. While this was going on in Sicily Hesychius his disciple was searching the world over for the old man, traversing the coast, penetrating deserts, clinging all the while to the belief that wherever he was he could not long

be hidden. At the end of three years he heard at Methona from a certain Jew, who dealt in old-clothes, that a Christian prophet had appeared in Sicily, and was working such miracles and signs, one might think him one of the ancient saints. So he asked about his dress, gait, and speech, and in particular his age, but could learn nothing. His informant merely declared that he had heard of the man by report. He therefore crossed the Adriatic and after a prosperous voyage came to Pachynus, where he took up his abode in a cottage on the shore of the bay, and, on inquiring for tidings of the old man, discovered by the tale which everyone told him where he was, and what he was doing. Nothing about him surprised them all so much as the fact that after such great signs and wonders he had not accepted even a crust of bread from anyone in the district. And, to cut my story short, the holy man Hesychius fell down at his master's knees and bedewed his feet with tears; at length he was gently raised by him, and when two or three days had been spent in talking over matters, he learned from Gazanus that Hilarion no longer felt himself able to live in those parts, but wanted to go to certain barbarous races where his name and fame were unknown.

39. He therefore brought him to Epidaurus, a town in Dalmatia, where he stayed for a few days in the country near, but could not be hid. An enormous serpent, of the sort which the people of those parts call *boas* because they are so large that they often swallow oxen, was ravaging the whole province far and wide, and was devouring not only flocks and herds, but husbandmen and shepherds who were drawn in by the force of its breathing. He ordered a pyre to be prepared for it, then sent up a prayer to Christ, called forth the reptile, bade it

climb the pile of wood, and then applied the fire. And so before all the people he burnt the savage beast to ashes. But now he began anxiously to ask what he was to do, whither to betake himself. Once more he prepared for flight, and in thought ranged through solitary lands, grieving that his miracles could speak of him though his tongue was silent.

40. At that time there was an earthquake over the whole world, following on the death of Julian, which caused the sea to burst its bounds, and left ships hanging on the edge of mountain steeps. It seemed as though God were threatening a second deluge, or all things were returning to original chaos. When the people of Epidaurus saw this, I mean the roaring waves and heaving waters and the swirling billows mountain-high dashing on the shore, fearing that what they saw had happened elsewhere might befall them and their town be utterly destroyed, they made their way to the old man, and as if preparing for a battle placed him on the shore. After making the sign of the cross three times on the sand, he faced the sea, stretched out his hands, and no one would believe to what a height the swelling sea stood like a wall before him. It roared for a long time as if indignant at the barrier, then little by little sank to its level. Epidaurus and all the region roundabout tell the story to this day, and mothers teach their children to hand down the remembrance of it to posterity. Verily, what was said to the Apostles, "If ye have faith, ye shall say to this mountain, Remove into the sea, and it shall be done," may be even literally fulfilled, provided one has such faith as the Lord commanded the Apostles to have. For what difference does it make whether a mountain descends into the sea, or huge

mountains of waters everywhere else fluid suddenly become hard as rock at the old man's feet?

41. The whole country marveled and the fame of the great miracle was in everyone's mouth, even at Salonæ. When the old man knew this was the case he escaped secretly by night in a small cutter, and finding a merchant ship after two days came to Cyprus. Between Malea and Cythera, the pirates, who had left on the shore that part of their fleet which is worked by poles instead of sails, bore down on them with two light vessels of considerable size; and besides this they were buffeted by the waves on every side. All the rowers began to be alarmed, to weep, to leave their places, to get out their poles, and, as though one message was not enough, again and again told the old man that pirates were at hand. Looking at them in the distance he gently smiled, then turned to his disciples and said, "O ye of little faith, wherefore do ye doubt? Are these more than the army of Pharaoh? Yet they were all drowned by the will of God." Thus he spoke, but none the less the enemy with foaming prows kept drawing nearer and were now only a stone's throw distant. He stood upon the prow of the vessel facing them with out-stretched hand, and said, "Thus far and no farther." Marvelous to relate, the boats at once bounded back, and though urged forward by the oars fell farther and farther astern. The pirates were astonished to find themselves going back, and labored with all their strength to reach the vessel, but were carried to the shore faster by far than they came.

42. I pass by the rest for fear I should seem in my history to be publishing a volume of miracles. I will only say this, that when sailing with a fair wind among the Cyclades he heard the voices of unclean spirits shouting

in all directions from towns and villages, and running in crowds to the shore. Having then entered Paphos, the city of Cyprus renowned in the songs of the poets, the ruins of whose temples after frequent earthquakes are the only evidences at the present day of its former grandeur, he began to live in obscurity about two miles from the city, and rejoiced in having a few days rest. But not quite twenty days passed before throughout the whole island whoever had unclean spirits began to cry out that Hilarion Christ's servant had come, and that they must go to him with all speed. Salamis, Curium, Lapetha, and the other cities joined in the cry, while many declared that they knew Hilarion and that he was indeed the servant of Christ, but where he was they could not tell. So within a trifle more than thirty days, about two hundred people, both men and women, came together to him. When he saw them he lamented that they would not suffer him to be quiet, and thirsting in a kind of manner to avenge himself, he lashed them with such urgency of prayer that some immediately, others after two or three days, all within a week, were cured.

43. Here he stayed two years, always thinking of flight, and in the meantime sent Hesychius, who was to return in the spring, to Palestine to salute the brethren and visit the ashes of his monastery. When the latter returned he found Hilarion longing to sail again to Egypt, that is to the locality called Bucolia; but he persuaded him that, since there were no Christians there, but only a fierce and barbarous people, he should rather go to a spot in Cyprus itself which was higher up and more retired. After a long and diligent search he found such a place twelve miles from the sea far off among the recesses of rugged mountains, the ascent to which could hardly be

accomplished by creeping on hands and knees. Thither he conducted him. The old man entered and gazed around. It was indeed a lonely and terrible place; for though surrounded by trees on every side, with water streaming from the brow of the hill, a delightful bit of garden, and fruit-trees in abundance (of which, however, he never ate), yet it had close by the ruins of an ancient temple from which, as he himself was wont to relate and his disciples testify, the voices of such countless demons re-echoed night and day, that you might have thought there was an army of them. He was highly pleased at the idea of having his opponents in the neighborhood, and abode there five years, cheered in these his last days by the frequent visits of Hesychius, for owing to the steep and rugged ascent, and the numerous ghosts (so the story ran), nobody or scarcely anybody either could or dared to go up to him. One day, however, as he was leaving his garden, he saw a man completely paralyzed lying in front of the gates. He asked Hesychius who he was, or how he had been brought. Hesychius replied that he was the agent at the country-house to which the garden belonged in which they were located. Weeping much and stretching out his hand to the prostrate man he said, "I bid you in the name of our Lord Jesus Christ arise and walk." The words were still on the lips of the speaker, when, with miraculous speed, the limbs were strengthened and the man arose and stood firm. Once this was noised abroad the need of many overcame even the pathless journey and the dangers of the place. The occupants of all the houses round about had nothing so much in their thoughts as to prevent the possibility of his escape, a rumor having spread concerning him to the effect that he could not stay long in the same place. This habit of his was not due to levity or childishness, but to the fact that he shunned the worry of publicity and praise, and always longed for silence and a life of obscurity.

44. In his eightieth year, during the absence of Hesychius, he wrote by way of a will a short letter with his own hand, and left him all his riches (that is to say, a copy of the gospels, and his sack-cloth tunic, cowl and cloak), for his servant had died a few days before. Many devout men therefore came to the invalid from Paphos, and especially because they had heard of his saying that he must soon migrate to the Lord and must be liberated from the bonds of the body. There came also Constantia a holy woman whose son-in-law and daughter he had anointed with oil and saved from death. He earnestly entreated them all not to let him be kept even a moment of time after death, but to bury him immediately in the same garden, just as he was, clad in his goat-hair tunic, cowl, and his peasant's cloak.

45. His body was now all but cold, and nought was left of life but reason. Yet with eyes wide open he kept repeating, "Go forth, what do you fear? Go forth, my soul, why do you hesitate? You have served Christ nearly seventy years, and do you fear death?" Thus saying he breathed his last. He was immediately buried before the city heard of his death.

46. When the holy man Hesychius heard of his decease, he went to Cyprus and, to lull the suspicions of the natives who were keeping strict guard, pretended that he wished to live in the same garden, and then in the course of about ten months, though at great peril to his life, stole the saint's body. He carried it to Majuma; and there all the monks and crowds of towns-folk going in procession laid it to rest in the ancient monastery. His

tunic, cowl and cloak, were uninjured; the whole body as perfect as if alive, and so fragrant with sweet odors that one might suppose it to have been embalmed.

47. In bringing my book to an end I think I ought not to omit to mention the devotion of the holy woman Constantia who, when a message was brought her that Hilarion's body was in Palestine, immediately died, proving even by death the sincerity of her love for the servant of God. For she was accustomed to spend whole nights in vigil at his tomb, and to converse with him as if he were present in order to stimulate her prayers. Even at the present day one may see a strange dispute between the people of Palestine and the Cypriotes, the one contending that they have the body, the other the spirit of Hilarion. And yet in both places great miracles are wrought daily, but to a greater extent in the garden of Cyprus, perhaps because that spot was dearest to him.

The Life of Malchus, the Captive Monk.

The life of Malchus was written at Bethlehem, a.d., 391. Its origin and purpose are sufficiently described in chapters 1 and 2.

1. They who have to fight a naval battle prepare for it in harbors and calm waters by adjusting the helm, plying the oars, and making ready the hooks and grappling irons. They draw up the soldiers on the decks and accustom them to stand steady with poised foot and on slippery ground; so that they may not shrink from all this when the real encounter comes, because they have had experience of it in the sham fight. And so it is in my case. I have long held my peace, because silence was

imposed on me by one to whom I give pain when I speak of him. But now, in preparing to write history on a wider scale I desire to practice myself by means of this little work and as it were to wipe the rust from my tongue. For I have purposed (if God grant me life, and if my censurers will at length cease to persecute me, now that I am a fugitive and shut up in a monastery) to write a history of the church of Christ from the advent of our Savior up to our own age, that is from the apostles to the dregs of time in which we live, and to show by what means and through what agents it received its birth, and how, as it gained strength, it grew by persecution and was crowned with martyrdom; and then, after reaching the Christian Emperors, how it increased in influence and in wealth but decreased in Christian virtues. But of this elsewhere. Now to the matter in hand.

2. Maronia is a little hamlet some thirty miles to the east of Antioch in Syria. After having many owners or landlords, at the time when I was staying as a young man in Syria it came into the possession of my intimate friend, the Bishop Evagrius, whose name I now give in order to show the source of my information. Well, there was at the place at that time an old man by name Malchus, which we might render "king," a Syrian by race and speech, in fact a genuine son of the soil. His companion was an old woman very decrepit who seemed to be at death's door, both of them so zealously pious and such constant frequenters of the Church, they might have been taken for Zacharias and Elizabeth in the Gospel but for the fact that there was no John to be seen. With some curiosity I asked the neighbors what was the link between them; was it marriage, or kindred, or the bond of the Spirit? All with one accord replied that they were holy people, well

pleasing to God, and gave me a strange account of them. Longing to know more I began to question the man with much eagerness about the truth of what I heard, and learnt as follows.

3. My son, said he, I used to farm a bit of ground at Nisibis and was an only son. My parents regarding me as the heir and the only survivor of their race, wished to force me into marriage, but I said I would rather be a monk. How my father threatened and my mother coaxed me to betray my chastity requires no other proof than the fact that I fled from home and parents. I could not go to the East because Persia was close by and the frontiers were guarded by the soldiers of Rome; I therefore turned my steps to the West, taking with me some little provision for the journey, but barely sufficient to ward off destitution. To be brief, I came at last to the desert of Chalcis which is situate between Immæ and Beroa farther south. There, finding some monks, I placed myself under their direction, earning my livelihood by the labor of my hands, and curbing the wantonness of the flesh by fasting. After many years the desire came over me to return to my country, and stay with my mother and cheer her widowhood while she lived (for my father, as I had already heard, was dead), and then to sell the little property and give part to the poor, settle part on the monasteries and (I blush to confess my faithlessness) keep some to spend in comforts for myself. My abbot began to cry out that it was a temptation of the devil, and that under fair pretexts some snare of the old enemy lay hid. It was, he declared, a case of the dog returning to his vomit. Many monks, he said, had been deceived by such suggestions, for the devil never showed himself openly. He set before me many examples from the Scriptures, and

told me that even Adam and Eve in the beginning had been overthrown by him through the hope of becoming gods. When he failed to convince me he fell upon his knees and besought me not to forsake him, nor ruin myself by looking back after putting my hand to the plough. Unhappily for myself I had the misfortune to conquer my adviser. I thought he was seeking not my salvation but his own comfort. So he followed me from the monastery as if he had been going to a funeral, and at last bade me farewell, saying, "I see that you bear the brand of a son of Satan. I do not ask your reasons nor take your excuses. The sheep which forsakes its fellows is at once exposed to the jaws of the wolf."

4. On the road from Beroa to Edessa adjoining the high-way is a waste over which the Saracens roam to and fro without having any fixed abode. Through fear of them travelers in those parts assemble in numbers, so that by mutual assistance they may escape impending danger. There were in my company men, women, old men, youths, children, altogether about seventy persons. All of a sudden the Ishmaelites on horses and camels made an assault upon us, with their flowing hair bound with fillets, their bodies half-naked, with their broad military boots, their cloaks streaming behind them, and their quivers slung upon the shoulders. They carried their bows unstrung and brandished their long spears; for they had come not to fight, but to plunder. We were seized, dispersed, and carried in different directions. I, meanwhile, repenting too late of the step I had taken, and far indeed from gaining possession of my inheritance, was assigned, along with another poor sufferer, a woman, to the service of one and the same owner. We were led, or rather carried, high upon the camel's back through a

desert waste, every moment expecting destruction, and suspended, I may say, rather than seated. Flesh half raw was our food, camel's milk our drink.

5. At length, after crossing a great river we came to the interior of the desert, where, being commanded after the custom of the people to pay reverence to the mistress and her children, we bowed our heads. Here, as if I were a prisoner, I changed my dress, that is, learnt to go naked, the heat being so excessive as to allow of no clothing beyond a covering for the loins. Some sheep were given to me to tend, and, comparatively speaking, I found this occupation a comfort, for I seldom saw my masters or fellow slaves. My fate seemed to be like that of Jacob in sacred history, and reminded me also of Moses; both of whom were once shepherds in the desert. I fed on fresh cheese and milk, prayed continually, and sang psalms which I had learnt in the monastery. I was delighted with my captivity, and thanked God because I had found in the desert the monk's estate which I was on the point of losing in my country.

6. But no condition can ever shut out the Devil. How manifold past expression are his snares! Hid though I was, his malice found me out. My master seeing his flock increasing and finding no dishonesty in me (I knew that the Apostle has given command that masters should be as faithfully served as God Himself), and wishing to reward me in order to secure my greater fidelity, gave me the woman who was once my fellow servant in captivity. On my refusing and saying I was a Christian, and that it was not lawful for me to take a woman to wife so long as her husband was alive (her husband had been captured with us, but carried off by another master), my owner was relentless in his rage, drew his sword and began to make

at me. If I had not without delay stretched out my hand and taken possession of the woman, he would have slain me on the spot. Well; by this time a darker night than usual had set in and, for me, all too soon. I led my bride into an old cave; sorrow was bride's-maid; we shrank from each other but did not confess it. Then I really felt my captivity; I threw myself down on the ground, and began to lament the monastic state which I had lost, and said: "Wretched man that I am! have I been preserved for this? has my wickedness brought me to this, that in my gray hairs I must lose my virgin state and become a married man? What is the good of having despised parents, country, property, for the Lord's sake, if I do the thing I wished to avoid doing when I despised them? And yet it may be perhaps the case that I am in this condition because I longed for home. What are we to do, my soul? are we to perish, or conquer? Are we to wait for the hand of the Lord, or pierce ourselves with our own sword? Turn your weapon against yourself; I must fear your death, my soul, more than the death of the body. Chastity preserved has its own martyrdom. Let the witness for Christ lie unburied in the desert; I will be at once the persecutor and the martyr." Thus speaking I drew my sword which glittered even in the dark, and turning its point towards me said: "Farewell, unhappy woman: receive me as a martyr not as a husband." She threw herself at my feet and exclaimed: "I pray you by Jesus Christ, and adjure you by this hour of trial, do not shed your blood and bring its guilt upon me. If you choose to die, first turn your sword against me. Let us rather be united upon these terms. Supposing my husband should return to me, I would preserve the chastity which I have learnt in captivity; I would even die rather than lose it.

Why should you die to prevent a union with me? I would die if you desired it. Take me then as the partner of your chastity; and love me more in this union of the spirit than you could in that of the body only. Let our master believe that you are my husband. Christ knows you are my brother. We shall easily convince them we are married when they see us so loving." I confess, I was astonished and, much as I had before admired the virtue of the woman, I now loved her as a wife still more. Yet I never gazed upon her naked person; I never touched her flesh, for I was afraid of losing in peace what I had preserved in the conflict. In this strange wedlock many days passed away. Marriage had made us more pleasing to our masters, and there was no suspicion of our flight; sometimes I was absent for even a whole month like a trusty shepherd traversing the wilderness.

7. After a long time as I sat one day by myself in the desert with nothing in sight save earth and sky, I began quickly to turn things over in my thoughts, and amongst others called to mind my friends the monks, and specially the look of the father who had instructed me, kept me, and lost me. While I was thus musing I saw a crowd of ants swarming over a narrow path. The loads they carried were clearly larger than their own bodies. Some with their forceps were dragging along the seeds of herbs: others were excavating the earth from pits and banking it up to keep out the water. One party, in view of approaching winter, and wishing to prevent their store from being converted into grass through the dampness of the ground, were cutting off the tips of the grains they had carried in; another with solemn lamentation were removing the dead. And, what is stranger still in such a host, those coming out did not hinder those going in; nay

rather, if they saw one fall beneath his burden they would put their shoulders to the load and give him assistance. In short that day afforded me a delightful entertainment. So, remembering how Solomon sends us to the shrewdness of the ant and quickens our sluggish faculties by setting before us such an example, I began to tire of captivity, and to regret the monk's cell, and long to imitate those ants and their doings, where toil is for the community, and, since nothing belongs to any one, all things belong to all.

8. When I returned to my chamber, my wife met me. My looks betrayed the sadness of my heart. She asked why I was so dispirited. I told her the reasons, and exhorted her to escape. She did not reject the idea. I begged her to be silent on the matter. She pledged her word. We constantly spoke to one another in whispers; and we floated in suspense betwixt hope and fear. I had in the flock two very fine he-goats: these I killed, made their skins into bottles, and from their flesh prepared food for the way. Then in the early evening when our masters thought we had retired to rest we began our journey, taking with us the bottles and part of the flesh. When we reached the river which was about ten miles off, having inflated the skins and got astride upon them, we entrusted ourselves to the water, slowly propelling ourselves with our feet, that we might be carried down by the stream to a point on the opposite bank much below that at which we embarked, and that thus the pursuers might lose the track. But meanwhile the flesh became sodden and partly lost, and we could not depend on it for more than three days' sustenance. We drank till we could drink no more by way of preparing for the thirst we expected to endure, then hastened away, constantly looking behind us, and

advanced more by night than day, on account both of the ambushes of the roaming Saracens, and of the excessive heat of the sun. I grow terrified even as I relate what happened; and, although my mind is perfectly at rest, yet my frame shudders from head to foot.

9. Three days after we saw in the dim distance two men riding on camels approaching with all speed. At once foreboding ill I began to think my master purposed putting us to death, and our sun seemed to grow dark again. In the midst of our fear, and just as we realized that our footsteps on the sand had betrayed us, we found on our right hand a cave which extended far underground. Well, we entered the cave: but we were afraid of venomous beasts such as vipers, basilisks, scorpions, and other creatures of the kind, which often resort to such shady places so as to avoid the heat of the sun. We therefore barely went inside, and took shelter in a pit on the left, not venturing a step farther, lest in fleeing from death we should run into death. We thought thus within ourselves: If the Lord helps us in our misery we have found safety: if He rejects us for our sins, we have found our grave. What do you suppose were our feelings? What was our terror, when in front of the cave, close by, there stood our master and fellow-servant, brought by the evidence of our footsteps to our hiding place? How much worse is death expected than death inflicted! Again my tongue stammers with distress and fear; it seems as if I heard my master's voice, and I hardly dare mutter a word. He sent his servant to drag us from the cavern while he himself held the camels and, sword in hand, waited for us to come. Meanwhile the servant entered about three or four cubits, and we in our hiding place saw his back though he could not see us, for the nature of the eye is

such that those who go into the shade out of the sunshine can see nothing. His voice echoed through the cave: "Come out, you felons; come out and die; why do you stay? Why do you delay? Come out, your master is calling and patiently waiting for you." He was still speaking when lo! through the gloom we saw a lioness seize the man, strangle him, and drag him, covered with blood, farther in. Good Jesus! how great was our terror now, how intense our joy! We beheld, though our master knew not of it, our enemy perish. He, when he saw that he was long in returning, supposed that the fugitives being two to one were offering resistance. Impatient in his rage, and sword still in hand, he came to the cavern, and shouted like a madman as he chided the slowness of his slave, but was seized upon by the wild beast before he reached our hiding place. Whoever would believe that before our eyes a brute would fight for us?

One cause of fear was removed, but there was the prospect of a similar death for ourselves, though the rage of the lion was not so bad to bear as the anger of the man. Our hearts failed for fear: without venturing to stir a step we awaited the issue, having no wall of defence in the midst of so great dangers save the consciousness of our chastity; when, early in the morning, the lioness, afraid of some snare and aware that she had been seen took up her cub in her teeth and carried it away, leaving us in possession of our retreat. Our confidence was not restored all at once. We did not rush out, but waited for a long time; for as often as we thought of coming out we pictured to ourselves the horror of falling in with her.

10. At last we got rid of our fright; and when that day was spent, we sallied forth towards evening, and saw the camels, on account of their great speed called

dromedaries, quietly chewing the cud. We mounted, and with the strength gained from the new supply of grain, after ten days travelling through the desert arrived at the Roman camp. After being presented to the tribune we told all, and from thence were sent to Sabianus, who commanded in Mesopotamia, where we sold our camels. My dear old abbot was now sleeping in the Lord; I betook myself therefore to this place, and returned to the monastic life, while I entrusted my companion here to the care of the virgins; for though I loved her as a sister, I did not commit myself to her as if she were my sister.

Malchus was an old man, I a youth, when he told me these things. I who have related them to you am now old, and I have set them forth as a history of chastity for the chaste. Virgins, I exhort you, guard your chastity. Tell the story to them that come after, that they may realize that in the midst of swords, and wild beasts of the desert, virtue is never a captive, and that he who is devoted to the service of Christ may die, but cannot be conquered.

The Dialogue Against the Luciferians.

Introduction.

This Dialogue was written about 379, seven years after the death of Lucifer, and very soon after Jerome's return from his hermit life in the desert of Chalcis. Though he received ordination from Paulinus, who had been consecrated by Lucifer, he had no sympathy with Lucifer's narrower views, as he shows plainly in this Dialogue. Lucifer, who was bishop of Cagliari in Sardinia, first came into prominent notice about a.d. 354, when great efforts were being made to procure a condemnation of S. Athanasius by the Western bishops. He energetically took up the cause of the saint, and at his own request was sent by Liberius, bishop of Rome, in company with the priest Pancratius and the deacon Hilarius, on a mission to the Emperor Constantius. The emperor granted a Council, which met at Milan in a.d. 354. Lucifer distinguished himself by resisting a proposition to condemn Athanasius, and did not hesitate to oppose the emperor with much violence. In consequence of this he was sent into exile from a.d. 355 to a.d. 361, the greater portion of which time was spent at Eleutheropolis in Palestine, though he afterwards removed to the Thebaid. It was at this time that his polemical writings appeared, the tone and temper of which is indicated by the mere titles *De Regibus Apostaticis* (of Apostate Kings), *De non Conveniendo cum Hæreticis, etc.* (of not holding communion with heretics). On the death of Constantius in 361, Julian permitted the exiled bishops to return; but Lucifer instead of going to Alexandria where a Council was to be held under the presidency of Athanasius for the healing of a schism in the Catholic party at Antioch (some of which held to Meletius, while others followed Eustathius), preferred to go straight to Antioch. There he ordained Paulinus, the leader of the latter section, as bishop of the Church. Eusebius of Vercellæ soon arrived with the synodal letters of the Council of Alexandria, but, finding himself thus anticipated, and shrinking from a collision with his friend, he retired immediately. Lucifer stayed, and "declared that he would not hold communion with Eusebius or any who adopted the moderate policy of the Alexandrian Council. By this Council it had been determined that actual Arians, if they renounced their heresy, should be pardoned, but not invested with ecclesiastical functions; and that those bishops who had merely consented to Arianism should remain undisturbed. It was this latter concession which offended Lucifer, and he became henceforth the champion of the principle that no one who had yielded to any compromise whatever with Arianism should be allowed to hold an ecclesiastical office." He was thus brought into antagonism with Athanasius himself, who, it has been seen, presided at Alexandria. Eventually he returned to his see in Sardinia where, according to Jerome's Chronicle, he died in 371. Luciferianism became extinct in the beginning of the following century, if not earlier. It hardly appears to have been formed into a separate organization, though an appeal was made to the emperor by some Luciferian presbyters about the year 384, and both Ambrose and Augustine speak of him as having fallen into the schism.

The argument of the Dialogue may be thus stated. It has been pointed out above that Lucifer of Cagliari, who had been banished from his see in the reign of Constantius because of his adherence to the cause of Athanasius, had, on the announcement of toleration at the accession of Julian (361), gone to Antioch and consecrated Paulinus a bishop. There were then three bishops of Antioch, Dorotheus the Arian (who had succeeded Euzoius in 376), Meletius who, though an Athanasian in opinion, had been consecrated by Arians or Semi-Arians, and Paulinus; besides Vitalis, bishop of a congregation of Apollinarians. Lucifer, in the earnestness of his anti-Arian opinion, refused to acknowledge as bishops those who had come over from Arianism, though he accepted the laymen who had been baptized by Arian bishops. This opinion led to the Luciferian schism, and forms the subject of the Dialogue.

The point urged by Orthodoxus throughout is that, since the Luciferian accepts as valid the baptism conferred by Arian bishops, it is inconsistent in him not to acknowledge the bishops who have repented of their Arian opinions. The Luciferian at first (2) in his eagerness, declares the Arians to be no better than heathen; but he sees that he has gone too far, and retracts this opinion. Still it is one thing, he says, (3) to admit a penitent neophyte, another to admit a man to be bishop and celebrate the Eucharist. We do not wish, he says (4) to preclude individuals who have fallen from repentance. And we, replies Orthodoxus, by admitting the bishops save not them only but their flocks also. "The salt," says the Luciferian (5), "which has lost its savor cannot be salted," and, "What communion has Christ with Belial?" But this, it is answered (6), would prove that Arians could not confer baptism at all. Yes, says the objector, they are like John the Baptist, whose baptism needed to be followed by that of Christ. But, it is replied, the bishop gives Christ's baptism and confers the Holy Spirit. The confirmation which follows (9) is rather a custom of the churches than the necessary means of grace.

The argument is felt to be approaching to a philosophical logomachy (10, 11), but it is resumed by the Luciferian. There is a real difference, he says (12), between the man who in his simplicity accepts baptism from an Arian bishop, and the bishop himself who understands the heresy. Yet both, it is replied (13), when they are penitent, should be received.

At this point (14) the Luciferian yields. But he wishes to be assured that what Orthodoxus recommends has been really the practice of the Church. This leads to a valuable chapter of Church history. Orthodoxus recalls the victories of the Church, which the Luciferians speak of as corrupt (15). The shame is that, though they have the true creed, they have too little faith. He then describes (17, 18) how the orthodox bishops were beguiled into accepting the creed of Ariminum, but afterwards saw their error (19). "The world groaned to find itself Arian." They did all that was possible to set things right. Why should they not be received, as all but the authors of heresy had been received at Nicæa? (20) Lucifer who was a good shepherd, and Hilary the Deacon, in separating their own small body into a sect have left the rest a prey to the wolf (20, 21). The wheat and tares must grow together (22). This has been the principle of the Church (23), as shown by Scripture (24) and Apostolic custom, and even Cyprian, when he wished penitent heretics to be re-baptized (25), could not prevail. Even Hilary by receiving baptism from the Church which always has re-admitted heretics in repentance (26, 27) acknowledges this principle. In that Church and its divisions and practice it is our duty to abide.

1. It happened not long ago that a follower of Lucifer had a dispute with a son of the Church. His loquacity was odious and the language he employed most abusive. For he declared that the world belonged to the devil, and, as is commonly said by them at the present day, that the Church was turned into a brothel. His opponent on the other hand, with reason indeed, but without due regard to time and place, urged that Christ did not die in vain, and that it was for something more than a Sardinian cloak of skins that the Son of God came

down from heaven. To be brief, the dispute was not settled when night interrupted the debate, and the lighting of the street-lamps gave the signal for the assembly to disperse. The combatants therefore withdrew, almost spitting in each other's faces, an arrangement having been previously made by the audience for a meeting in a quiet porch at daybreak. Thither, accordingly, they all came, and it was resolved that the words of both speakers should be taken down by reporters.

2. When all were seated, Helladius the Luciferian said, I want an answer first to my question. Are the Arians Christians or not?

Orthodoxus. I answer with another question, Are all heretics Christians?

L. If you call a man a heretic you deny that he is a Christian.

O. No heretics, then, are Christians.

L. I told you so before.

O. If they are not Christ's, they belong to the devil.

L. No one doubts that.

O. But if they belong to the devil, it makes no difference whether they are heretics or heathen.

L. I do not dispute the point.

O. We are then agreed that we must speak of a heretic as we would of a heathen.

L. Just so.

O. Now it is decided that heretics are heathen, put any question you please.

L. What I wanted to elicit by my question has been expressly stated, namely, that heretics are not Christians. Now comes the inference. If the Arians are heretics, and all heretics are heathen, the Arians are heathen too. But if the Arians are heathen and it is beyond dispute that the church has no communion with the Arians, that is with the heathen, it is clear that your church which welcomes bishops from the Arians, that is from the heathen, receives priests of the Capitol rather than bishops, and accordingly it ought more correctly to be called the synagogue of Anti-Christ than the Church of Christ.

O. Lo! what the prophet said is fulfilled: "They have digged a pit before me, they have fallen into the midst thereof themselves."

L. How so?

O. If the Arians are, as you say, heathen, and the assemblies of the Arians are the devil's camp, how is it that you receive a person who has been baptized in the devil's camp?

L. I do receive him, but as a penitent.

O. The fact is you don't know what you are saying. Does anyone receive a penitent heathen?

L. In my simplicity I replied when we began that all heretics are heathen. But the question was a captious one, and you shall have the full credit of victory in the first point. I will now proceed to the second and maintain that a layman coming from the Arians ought to be received if penitent, but not a cleric.

O. And yet, if you concede me the first point, the second is mine too.

L. Show me how it comes to be yours.

O. Don't you know that the clergy and laity have only one Christ, and that there is not one God of converts and another of bishops? Why then should not he who receives laymen receive clerics also?

L. There is a difference between shedding tears for sin, and handling the body of Christ; there is a difference between lying prostrate at the feet of the brethren, and from the high altar administering the Eucharist to the people. It is one thing to lament over the past, another to abandon sin and live the glorified life in the Church. You who yesterday impiously declared the Son of God to be a creature, you who every day, worse than a Jew, were wont to cast the stones of blasphemy at Christ, you whose hands are full of blood, whose pen was a soldier's spear, do you, the convert of a single hour, come into the Church as an adulterer might come to a virgin? If you repent of your sin, abandon your priestly functions: if you are shameless in your sin, remain what you were.

O. You are quite a rhetorician, and fly from the thicket of controversy to the open fields of declamation. But, I entreat you, refrain from common-places, and return to the ground and the lines marked out; afterwards, if you like, we will take a wider range.

L. There is no declamation in the case; my indignation is more than I can bear. Make what statements you please, argue as you please, you will never convince me that a penitent bishop should be treated like a penitent layman.

O. Since you put the whole thing in a nutshell and obstinately cling to your position, that the case of the bishop is different from that of the layman, I will do what you wish, and I shall not be sorry to avail myself of the opportunity you offer and come to close quarters. Explain why you receive a layman coming from the Arians, but do not receive a bishop.

L. I receive a layman who confesses that he has erred; and the Lord willed not the death of a sinner, but rather that he should repent.

O. Receive then also a bishop who, as well as the layman, confesses that he has erred, and it still holds good that the Lord willed not the death of a sinner, but rather that he should repent.

L. If he confesses his error why does he continue a bishop? Let him lay aside his episcopal functions, and I grant pardon to the penitent.

O. I will answer you in your own words. If a layman confesses his error, how is it he continues a layman? Let him lay aside his lay-priesthood, that is, his baptism, and I grant pardon to the penitent. For it is written "He made us to be a kingdom, to be priests unto his God and Father." And again, "A holy nation, a royal priesthood, an elect race." Everything which is forbidden to a Christian, is forbidden to both bishop and layman. He who does penance condemns his former life. If a penitent bishop may not continue what he was, neither may a penitent layman remain in that state on account of which he confesses himself a penitent.

L. We receive the laity, because no one will be induced to change, if he knows he must be baptized again. And then, if they are rejected, we become the cause of their destruction.

O. By receiving a layman you save a single soul: and I in receiving a bishop unite to the Church, I will not say the people of one city, but the whole province of which he is the head; if I drive him away, he will drag down many with him to ruin. Wherefore I beseech you to apply the same reason which you think you have for receiving the few to the salvation of the whole world. But if you are not satisfied with this, if you are so hard, or rather so unreasonably unmerciful as to think him who gave baptism an enemy of Christ, though you account him who received it a son, we do not so contradict ourselves: we either receive a bishop as well as the people which is constituted as a Christian people by him, or if we do not receive a bishop, we know that we must also reject his people.

5. L. Pray, have you not read what is said concerning the bishops, "Ye are the salt of the earth: but if the salt has lost its savor, wherewith shall it be salted? It is thenceforth good for nothing, but to be cast out and trodden under foot of man." And then there is the fact that the priest intercedes with God for the sinful people, while there is no one to entreat for the priest. Now these two passages of Scripture tend to the same conclusion. For as salt seasons all food and nothing is so pleasant as to please the palate without it: so the bishop is the seasoning of the whole world and of his own Church, and if he lose his savor through the denial of truth, or through heresy, or lust, or, to comprehend all in one word, through sin of any kind, by what other can he be seasoned, when he was the seasoning of all? The priest, we know, offers his oblation for the layman, lays his hand upon him when submissive, invokes the return of the Holy Spirit, and thus, after inviting the prayers of the people, reconciles to the altar him who had been delivered to Satan for the destruction of the flesh that the spirit might he saved; nor does he restore one member to health until all the members have wept together with him. For a father easily pardons his son, when the mother entreats for her offspring. If then it is by the priestly order that a penitent layman is restored to the Church, and pardon follows where sorrow has gone

before, it is clear that a priest who has been removed from his order cannot be restored to the place he has forfeited, because either he will be a penitent and then he cannot be a priest, or if he continues to hold office he cannot be brought back to the Church by penitential discipline. Will you dare to spoil the savor of the Church with the salt which has lost its savor? Will you replace at the altar the man who having been cast out ought to lie in the mire and be trodden under foot by all men? What then will become of the Apostle's command, "The bishop must be blameless as God's steward"? And again, "But let a man prove himself, and so let him come." What becomes of our Lord's intimation, "Neither cast your pearls before the swine"? But if you understand the words as a general admonition, how much more must care be exercised in the case of priests when so much precaution is taken where the laity are concerned? "Depart, I pray you," says the Lord by Moses, "from the tents of these wicked men, and touch nothing of theirs, lest ye be consumed in all their sins." And again in the Minor Prophets, "Their sacrifices shall be unto them as the bread of mourners; all that eat thereof shall be polluted." And in the Gospel the Lord says, "The lamp of the body is the eye: if therefore thine eye be single, thy whole body shall be full of light." For when the bishop preaches the true faith the darkness is scattered from the hearts of all. And he gives the reason, "Neither do men light a lamp, and put it under the bushel, but on the stand; and it shineth unto all that are in the house." That is, God's motive for lighting the fire of His knowledge in the bishop is that he may not shine for himself only, but for the common benefit. And in the next sentence "If," says he, "thine eye be evil, thy whole body shall be full of darkness. If therefore the light that is in thee be darkness, how great is the darkness!" And rightly; for since the bishop is appointed in the Church that he may restrain the people from error, how great will the error of the people be when he himself who teaches errs. How can he remit sins, who is himself a sinner? How can an impious man make a man holy? How shall the light enter into me, when my eye is blind? O misery! Antichrist's disciple governs the Church of Christ. And what are we to think of the words, "No man can serve two masters"? And that too "What communion hath light and darkness? And what concord hath Christ with Belial?" In the old testament we read, "No man that hath a blemish shall come nigh to offer the offerings of the Lord." And again, "Let the priests who come nigh to the Lord their God be clean, lest haply the Lord forsake them." And in the same place, "And when they draw nigh to minister in holy things, let them not bring sin upon themselves, lest they die." And there are many other passages which it would be an endless task to detail, and which I omit for the sake of brevity. For it is not the number of proofs that avails, but their weight. And all this proves that you with a little leaven have corrupted the whole lump of the Church, and receive the Eucharist to-day from the hand of one whom yesterday you loathed like an idol.

6. O. Your memory has served you, and you have certainly given us at great length many quotations from the sacred books: but after going all round the wood, you are caught in my hunting-nets. Let the case be as you would have it, that an Arian bishop is the enemy of Christ, let him be the salt that has lost its savor, let him be a lamp without flame, let him be an eye without a pupil: no doubt your argument will take you thus far—that he cannot salt another who himself has no salt: a blind man

cannot enlighten others, nor set them on fire when his own light has gone out. But why, when you swallow food which he has seasoned, do you reproach the seasoned with being saltless? Your Church is bright with his flame, and do you accuse his lamp of being extinguished? He gives you eyes, and are you blind? Wherefore, I pray you, either give him the power of sacrificing since you approve his baptism, or reject his baptism if you do not think him a priest. For it is impossible that he who is holy in baptism should be a sinner at the altar.

L. But when I receive a lay penitent, it is with laying on of hands, and invocation of the Holy Spirit, for I know that the Holy Spirit cannot be given by heretics.

O. All the paths of your propositions lead to the same meeting-point, and it is with you as with the frightened deer—while you fly from the feathers fluttering in the wind, you become entangled in the strongest of nets. For seeing that a man, baptized in the name of the Father and the Son and the Holy Ghost, becomes a temple of the Lord, and that while the old abode is destroyed a new shrine is built for the Trinity, how can you say that sins can be remitted among the Arians without the coming of the Holy Ghost? How is a soul purged from its former stains which has not the Holy Ghost? For it is not mere water which washes the soul, but it is itself first purified by the Spirit that it may be able to spiritually wash the souls of men. "The Spirit of the Lord," says Moses, "moved upon the face of the waters," from which it appears that there is no baptism without the Holy Ghost. Bethesda, the pool in Judea, could not cure the limbs of those who suffered from bodily weakness without the advent of an angel, and do you venture to bring me a soul washed with simple water, as though it had just come from the bath? Our Lord Jesus Christ Himself, of whom it is less correct to say that He was cleansed by washing than that by the washing of Himself He cleansed all waters, no sooner raised His head from the stream than He received the Holy Ghost. Not that He ever was without the Holy Ghost, inasmuch as He was born in the flesh through the Holy Ghost; but in order to prove that to be the true baptism by which the Holy Ghost comes. So then if an Arian cannot give the Holy Spirit, he cannot even baptize, because there is no baptism of the Church without the Holy Spirit. And you, when you receive a person baptized by an Arian and afterwards invoke the Holy Ghost, ought either to baptize him, because without the Holy Ghost he could not be baptized, or, if he was baptized in the Spirit, you must not invoke the Holy Ghost for your convert who received Him at the time of baptism.

7. L. Pray tell me, have you not read in the Acts of the Apostles that those who had already been baptized by John, on their saying in reply to the Apostle's question that they had not even heard what the Holy Ghost was, afterwards obtained the Holy Ghost? Whence it is clear that it is possible to be baptized, and yet not to have the Holy Ghost.

O. I do not think that those who form our audience are so ignorant of the sacred books that many words are needed to settle this little question. But before I say anything in support of my assertion, listen while I point out what confusion, upon your view, is introduced into Scripture. What do we mean by saying that John in his baptism could not give the Holy Spirit to others, yet gave him to Christ? And who is that John? "The voice of one crying in the wilderness, Make ye ready the way of the

Lord, make his paths straight." He who used to say, "Behold the Lamb of God, which taketh away the sins of the world": I say too little, he who from his mother's womb cried out, "And whence is this to me that the mother of my Lord should come unto me," did he not give the Holy Ghost? And did Ananias give him to Paul? It perhaps looks like boldness in me to prefer him to all other men. Hear then the words of our Lord, "Among them that are born of women there hath not arisen a greater than John the Baptist." For no prophet had the good fortune both to announce the coming of Christ, and to point Him out with the finger. And what necessity is there for me to dwell upon the praises of so illustrious a man when God the Father even calls him an angel? "Behold, I send my messenger (angel) before thy face, who shall prepare thy way before thee." He must have been an angel who after lodging in his mother's womb at once began to frequent the desert wilds, and while still an infant played with serpents; who, when his eyes had once gazed on Christ thought nothing else worth looking at; who exercised his voice, worthy of a messenger of God, in the words of the Lord, which are sweeter than honey and the honey-comb. And, to delay my question no further, thus it behooved the Forerunner of the Lord to grow up. Now is it possible that a man of such character and renown did not give the Holy Ghost, while Cornelius the centurion received Him before baptism? Tell me, pray, why could he not give Him? You don't know? Then listen to the teaching of Scripture: the baptism of John did not so much consist in the forgiveness of sins as in being a baptism of repentance for the remission of sins, that is, for a future remission, which was to follow through the sanctification of Christ. For it is written, "John came, who baptized in the wilderness, and preached the baptism of repentance unto remission of sins." And soon after, "And they were baptized of him in the river Jordan, confessing their sins." For as he himself preceded Christ as His forerunner, so also his baptism was the prelude to the Lord's baptism. "He that is of the earth," he said, "Speaks of the earth; he that cometh from heaven is above all." And again, "I indeed baptize you with water, he shall baptize you with the Holy Ghost." But if John, as he himself confessed, did not baptize with the Spirit, it follows that he did not forgive sins either, for no man has his sins remitted without the Holy Ghost. Or if you contentiously argue that, because the baptism of John was from heaven, therefore sins were forgiven by it, show me what more there is for us to get in Christ's baptism. Because it forgives sins, it releases from Gehenna. Because it releases from Gehenna, it is perfect. But no baptism can be called perfect except that which depends on the cross and resurrection of Christ. Thus, although John himself said, "He must increase, but I must decrease," in your perverse scrupulosity you give more than is due to the baptism of the servant, and destroy that of the master to which you leave no more than to the other. What is the drift of your assertion? Just this—it does not strike you as strange that those who had been baptized by John, should afterwards by the laying on of hands receive the Holy Ghost, although it is evident that they did not obtain even remission of sins apart from the faith which was to follow. But you who receive a person baptized by the Arians and allow him to have perfect baptism, after that admission do you invoke the Holy Ghost as if this were still some slight defect, whereas there is no baptism of Christ without the Holy Ghost? But

I have wandered too far, and when I might have met my opponent face to face and repelled his attack, I have only thrown a few light darts from a distance. The baptism of John was so far imperfect that it is plain they who had been baptized by him were afterwards baptized with the baptism of Christ. For thus the history relates, "And it came to pass that while Apollos was at Corinth, Paul having passed through the upper country came to Ephesus, and found certain disciples: and he said unto them, Did ye receive the Holy Ghost when ye believed? And they said unto him, Nay, we did not so much as hear whether the Holy Ghost was given. And he said, Into what then were ye baptized? And they said, Into John's baptism. And Paul said, John baptized with the baptism of repentance, saying unto the people, that they should believe on Him which should come after him, that is, on Jesus. And when they heard this, they were baptized into the name of the Lord Jesus: And when Paul had laid his hands upon them, immediately the Holy Ghost fell on them." If then they were baptized with the true and lawful baptism of the Church, and thus received the Holy Ghost: do you follow the apostles and baptize those who have not had Christian baptism, and you will be able to invoke the Holy Ghost.

8. L. Thirsty men in their dreams eagerly gulp down the water of the stream, and the more they drink the thirstier they are. In the same way you appear to me to have searched everywhere for arguments against the point I raised, and yet to be as far as ever from being satisfied. Don't you know that the laying on of hands after baptism and then the invocation of the Holy Spirit is a custom of the Churches? Do you demand Scripture proof? You may find it in the Acts of the Apostles. And even if it did not

rest on the authority of Scripture the consensus of the whole world in this respect would have the force of a command. For many other observances of the Churches, which are due to tradition, have acquired the authority of the written law, as for instance the practice of dipping the head three times in the laver, and then, after leaving the water, of tasting mingled milk and honey in representation of infancy; and, again, the practices of standing up in worship on the Lord's day, and ceasing from fasting every Pentecost; and there are many other unwritten practices which have won their place through reason and custom. So you see we follow the practice of the Church, although it may be clear that a person was baptized before the Spirit was invoked.

9. O. I do not deny that it is the practice of the Churches in the case of those who living far from the greater towns have been baptized by presbyters and deacons, for the bishop to visit them, and by the laying on of hands to invoke the Holy Ghost upon them. But how shall I describe your habit of applying the laws of the Church to heretics, and of exposing the virgin entrusted to you in the brothels of harlots? If a bishop lays his hands on men he lays them on those who have been baptized in the right faith, and who have believed that the Father, Son, and Holy Ghost, are three persons, but one essence. But an Arian has no faith but this (close your ears, my hearers, that you may not be defiled by words so grossly impious), that the Father alone is very God, and that Jesus Christ our Saviour is a creature, and the Holy Ghost the Servant of both. How can he then receive the Holy Ghost from the Church, who has not yet obtained remission of sins? For the Holy Ghost must have a clean abode: nor will He become a dweller in that temple which has not for

its chief priest the true faith. But if you now ask how it is that a person baptized in the Church does not receive the Holy Ghost, Whom we declare to be given in true baptism, except by the hands of the bishop, let me tell you that our authority for the rule is the fact that after our Lord's ascension the Holy Ghost descended upon the Apostles. And in many places we find it the practice, more by way of honoring the episcopate than from any compulsory law. Otherwise, if the Holy Ghost descends only at the bishop's prayer, they are greatly to be pitied who in isolated houses, or in forts, or retired places, after being baptized by the presbyters and deacons have fallen asleep before the bishop's visitation. The well-being of a Church depends upon the dignity of its chief-priest, and unless some extraordinary and unique functions be assigned to him, we shall have as many schisms in the Churches as there are priests. Hence it is that without ordination and the bishop's license neither presbyter nor deacon has the power to baptize. And yet, if necessity so be, we know that even laymen may, and frequently do, baptize. For as a man receives, so too he can give; for it will hardly be said that we must believe that the eunuch whom Philip baptized lacked the Holy Spirit. The Scripture thus speaks concerning him, "And they both went down into the water; and Philip baptized him." And on leaving the water, "The Holy Spirit fell upon the eunuch." You may perhaps think that we ought to set against this the passage in which we read, "Now when the apostles which were at Jerusalem heard that Samaria had received the word of God, they sent unto them Peter and John: who, when they were come down, prayed for them that they might receive the Holy Ghost: for as yet he was fallen upon none of them." But why this was, the context tells us,—"Only they had been baptized into the name of the Lord Jesus. Then laid they their hands on them, and they received the Holy Ghost." And if you here say that you do the same, because the heretics have not baptized into the Holy Spirit, I must remind you that Philip was not separated from the Apostles, but belonged to the same Church and preached the same Lord Jesus Christ: that he was without question a deacon of those who afterwards laid their hands on his converts. But when you say that the Arians have not a Church, but a synagogue, and that their clergy do not worship God but creatures and idols, how can you maintain that you ought to act upon the same principle in cases so totally different?

L. You repel my attack in front with vigor and firmness: but you are smitten in the rear and leave your back exposed to the darts. Let us even grant that the Arians have no baptism, and therefore that the Holy Ghost cannot be given by them, because they themselves have not yet received remission of sins; this altogether makes for victory on my side, and all your argumentative wrestling is but laborious toil to give me the conqueror's palm. An Arian has no baptism; how is it then that he has the episcopate? There is not even a layman among them, how can there be a bishop? I may not receive a beggar, do you receive a king? You surrender your camp to the enemy, and are we to reject one of their deserters?

11. O. If you remember what has been said you would know that you have been already answered; but in yielding to the love of contradiction you have wandered from the subject, like those persons who are talkative rather than eloquent, and who, when they cannot argue, still continue to wrangle. On the present occasion it is not my aim to either accuse or defend the Arians, but rather to

get safely past the turning-post of the race, and to maintain that we receive a bishop for the same reason that you receive a layman. If you grant forgiveness to the erring, I too pardon the penitent. If he that baptizes a person into our belief has had no injurious effect upon the person baptized, it follows that he who consecrates a bishop in the same faith causes no defilement to the person consecrated. Heresy is subtle, and therefore the simple-minded are easily deceived. To be deceived is the common lot of both layman and bishop. But you say, a bishop could not have been mistaken. The truth is, men are elected to the episcopate who come from the bosom of Plato and Aristophanes. How many can you find among them who are not fully instructed in these writers? Indeed all, whoever they may be, that are ordained at the present day from among the literate class make it their study not how to seek out the marrow of Scripture, but how to tickle the ears of the people with the flowers of rhetoric. We must further add that the Arian heresy goes hand in hand with the wisdom of the world, and borrows its streams of argument from the fountains of Aristotle. And so we will act like children when they try to outdo one another—whatever you say I will say: what you assert, I will assert: whatever you deny, I will deny. We allow that an Arian may baptize; then he must be a bishop. If we agree that Arian baptism is invalid, you must reject the layman, and I must not accept the bishop. I will follow you wherever you go; we shall either stick in the mud together, or shall get out together.

12. L. We pardon a layman because, when he was baptized, he had a sincere impression that he was joining the Church. He believed and was baptized in accordance with his faith.

O. That is something new for a man to be made a Christian by one who is not a Christian. When he joined the Arians into what faith was he baptized? Of course into that which the Arians held. If on the other hand we are to suppose that his own faith was correct, but that he was knowingly baptized by heretics, he does not deserve the indulgence we grant to the erring. But it is quite absurd to imagine that, going as a pupil to the master, he understands his art before he has been taught. Can you suppose that a man who has just turned from worshipping idols knows Christ better than his teacher does? If you say, he sincerely believed in the Father, and the Son, and the Holy Ghost, and therefore obtained baptism, what, let me ask, is the meaning of being sincerely ignorant of what one believes? He sincerely believed. What did he believe? Surely when he heard the three names, he believed in three Gods, and was an idolater; or by the three titles he was led to believe in a God with three names, and so fell into the Sabellian heresy. Or he was perhaps trained by the Arians to believe that there is one true God, the Father, but that the Son and the Holy Spirit are creatures. What else he may have believed, I know not: for we can hardly think that a man brought up in the Capitol would have learnt the doctrine of the co-essential Trinity. He would have known in that case that the Father, Son, and Holy Spirit are not divided in nature, but in person. He would have known also that the name of Son was implied in that of Father and the name of Father in that of Son. It is ridiculous to assert that anyone can dispute concerning the faith before he believes it; that he understands a mystery before he has been initiated; that the baptizer and the baptized hold different views respecting God. Besides, it is the custom at baptism to ask, after the confession of faith in the Trinity, do you believe in Holy Church? Do you believe in the remission of sins? What Church do you say he believed in? The Church of the Arians? But they have no Church. In ours? But the man was not baptized into it: he could not believe in that whereof he was ignorant.

  L. I see that you can prattle cleverly about each point that I raise; and when we let fly a dart you elude it by a harangue which serves you for a shield; I will therefore hurl a single spear which will be strong enough to pierce your defenses and the hail-storm of your words. I won't allow strength any longer to be overcome by artifice. Even a layman baptized without the Church, if he be baptized according to the faith, is received only as a penitent: but a bishop either does no penance and remains a bishop, or, if he does penance he ceases to be a bishop. Wherefore we do right both in welcoming the penitent layman, and in rejecting the bishop, if he wishes to continue in his office.

  O. An arrow which is discharged from the tight-drawn bow is not easy to avoid, for it reaches him at whom it was aimed before the shield can be raised to stop it. On the other hand your propositions are pointless and therefore cannot pierce an opponent. The spear then which you have hurled with all your might and about which you speak such threatening words, I turn aside, as the saying is, with my little finger. The point in dispute is not merely whether a bishop is incapable of penitence and a layman capable, but whether a heretic has received valid baptism. If he has not (and this follows from your position), how can he be a penitent, before he is a Christian? Show me that a layman coming from the Arians has valid baptism, and then I will not deny him penitence. But if he is not a Christian, if he had no priest to make him a Christian, how can he do penance when he is not yet a believer?

14. L. I beseech you lay aside the methods of the philosophers and let us talk with Christian simplicity; that is, if you are willing to follow not the logicians, but the Galilean fishermen. Does it seem right to you that an Arian should be a bishop?

O. You prove him a bishop because you receive those he has baptized. And it is here that you are to blame:—Why are there walls of separation between us when we are at one in faith and in receiving Arians?

L. I asked you before not to talk like a philosopher, but like a Christian.

O. Do you wish to learn, or to argue?

L. Of course I argue because I want to know the reason for what you do.

O. If you argue, you have already had an answer. I receive an Arian bishop for the same reason that you receive a person who is only baptized. If you wish to learn, come over to my side: for an opponent must be overcome, it is only a disciple who can be taught.

L. Before I can be a disciple, I must hear one preach whom I feel to be my master.

O. You are not dealing quite fairly: you wish me to be your teacher on the terms that you may treat me as an opponent whenever you please. I will teach you therefore in the same spirit. We agree in faith, we agree in receiving heretics, let us also be at one in our terms of communion.

L. That is not teaching, but arguing.

O. As you ask for peace with a shield in your hand, I also must carry my olive branch with a sword grafted in it.

L. I drop my hands in token of submission. You are conqueror. But in laying down my arms, I ask the meaning of the oath you force me to take.

O. Certainly, but first I congratulate you, and thank Christ my God for your good dispositions which have made you turn from the unsavory teaching of the Sardinians to that which the whole world approves as true; and no longer say as some do, "Help, Lord; for the godly man tease." By their impious words they make of none effect the cross of Christ, subject the Son of God to the devil, and would have us now understand the Lord's lamentation over sinners to apply to all men, "What profit is there in my blood, when I go down to the pit?" But God forbid that our Lord should have died in vain. The strong man is bound, and his goods are spoiled. What the Father says is fulfilled, "Ask of me, and I will give thee the nations for thine inheritance, and the uttermost parts of the earth for thy possession." "Then the channels of water appeared, and the foundations of the world were laid bare." "In them hath he set a tabernacle for the sun, and there is nothing hid from the heat thereof." The Psalmist fully possessed by God sings, "The swords of the enemy are come to an end, and the cities which thou hast overthrown."

15. And what is the position, I should like to know, of those excessively scrupulous, or rather excessively profane persons, who assert that there are more synagogues than Churches? How is it that the devil's kingdoms have been destroyed, and now at last in the consummation of the ages, the idols have fallen? If

Christ has no Church, or if he has one only, in Sardinia, he has grown very poor. And if Satan owns Britain, Gaul, the East, the races of India, barbarous nations, and the whole world at the same time, how is it that the trophies of the cross have been collected in a mere corner of the earth? Christ's powerful opponent, forsooth, gave over to him the serpent of Spain: he disdained to own a poor province and its half-starved inhabitants. If they flatter themselves that they have on their side that verse of the gospel, "Howbeit when the Son of man cometh, shall he find faith on the earth?" let me remind them that the faith in question is that of which the Lord himself said, "Thy faith hath made thee whole." And elsewhere, of the centurion, "I have not found so great faith, no, not in Israel." And again, to the Apostles, "Why are ye fearful, O ye of little faith?" In another place also, "If ye have faith as a grain of mustard seed, ye shall say unto this mountain, Remove hence to yonder place, and it shall remove." For neither the centurion nor that poor woman who for twelve years was wasting away with a bloody flux, had believed in the mysteries of the Trinity, for these were revealed to the Apostles after the resurrection of Christ; so that the faith of such as believe in the mystery of the Trinity might have its due preeminence: but it was her singleness of mind and her devotion to her God that met with our Lord's approval: "For she said within herself, If I do but touch his garment, I shall be made whole." This is the faith which our Lord said was seldom found. This is the faith which even in the case of those who believe aright is hard to find in perfection. "According to your faith, be it done unto you," says God. I do not, indeed, like the sound of those words. For if it be done unto me according to my faith, I shall perish. And yet I certainly believe in God the Father, I believe in God the Son, and I believe in God the Holy Ghost. I believe in one God; nevertheless, I would not have it done unto me according to my faith. For the enemy often comes, and sows tares in the Lord's harvest. I do not mean to imply that anything is greater than the purity of heart which believes that mystery; but undoubted faith towards God it is hard indeed to find. To make my meaning plain, let us suppose a case:—I stand to pray; I could not pray, if I did not believe; but if I really believed, I should cleanse that heart of mine with which God is seen, I should beat my hands upon my breast, the tears would stream down my cheeks, my body would shudder, my face grow pale, I should lie at my Lord's feet, weep over them, and wipe them with my hair, I should cling to the cross and not let go my hold until I obtained mercy. But, as it is, frequently in my prayers I am either walking in the arcades, or calculating my interest, or am carried away by base thoughts, so as to be occupied with things the mere mention of which makes me blush. Where is our faith? Are we to suppose that it was thus that Jonah prayed? or the three youths? or Daniel in the lion's den? or the robber on the cross? I have given these illustrations that you may understand my meaning. But let everyone commune with his own heart, and he will find throughout the whole of life how rare a thing it is to find a soul so faithful that it does nothing through the love of glory, nothing on account of the petty gossip of men. For he who fasts does not as an immediate consequence fast unto God, nor he who holds out his hand to a poor man, lend to the Lord. Vice is next-door neighbor to virtue. It is hard to rest content with God alone for judge.

16. L. I was reserving that passage until last, and you have anticipated my question about it. Almost all our party, or rather not mine anymore, use it as a sort of controversial battering ram: as such I am exceedingly glad to see it broken to pieces and pulverized. But will you be so good as to fully explain to me, not in the character of an opponent but of a disciple, why it is that the Church receives those who come from the Arians? The truth is I am unable to answer you a word, but I do not yet give a hearty assent to what you say.

17. O. When Constantius was on the throne and Eusebius and Hypatius were Consuls, there was composed, under the pretext of unity and faith, an unfaithful creed, as it is now acknowledged to have been. For at that time, nothing seemed so characteristic of piety, nothing so befitting a servant of God, as to follow after unity, and to shun separation from communion with the rest of the world. And all the more because the current profession of faith no longer exhibited on the face of it anything profane. "We believe," said they, "in one true God, the Father Almighty. This we also confess: We believe in the only begotten Son of God, who, before all worlds, and before all their origins, was born of God. The only begotten Son, moreover, we believe to be born alone of the Father alone, God of God, like to his Father who begot Him, according to the Scriptures; whose birth no one knows, but the Father alone who begot Him." Do we find any such words inserted here as "There was a time, when he was not?" Or "The Son of God is a creature though not made of things which exist." No. This is surely the perfection of faith to say we believe Him to be God of God. Moreover, they called Him the only begotten, "born alone of the Father." What is the meaning of *born?*

Surely, *not made*. His birth removed all suspicion of His being a creature. They added further, "Who came down from heaven, was conceived of the Holy Ghost, born of the Virgin Mary, crucified by Pontius Pilate, rose again the third day from the dead, ascended into heaven, sits at the right hand of the Father, who will come to judge the quick and the dead." There was the ring of piety in the words, and no one thought that poison was mingled with the honey of such a proclamation.

18. As regards the term *Usia*, it was not rejected without a show of reason for so doing. "Because it is not found in the Scriptures," they said, "and its novelty is a stumbling block to many, we have thought it best to dispense with it." The bishops were not anxious about the name, so long as that which it implied was secured. Lastly, at the very time when rumor was rife that there had been some insincerity in the statement of the faith, Valens, bishop of Mursa, who had drawn it up, in the presence of Taurus the pretorian prefect who attended the Synod by imperial command, declared that he was not an Arian, and that he utterly abhorred their blasphemies. However, the thing had been done in secret, and it had not extinguished the general feeling. So on another day, when crowds of bishops and laymen came together in the Church at Ariminum, Muzonius, bishop of the province of Byzacena, to whom by reason of seniority the first rank was assigned by all, spoke as follows: "One of our number has been authorized to read to you, reverend fathers, what reports are being spread and have reached us, so that the evil opinions which ought to grate upon our ears and be banished from our hearts may be condemned with one voice by us all." The whole body of bishops replied, Agreed. And so when Claudius, bishop of the

province of Picenum, at the request of all present, began to read the blasphemies attributed to Valens, Valens denied they were his and cried aloud, "If anyone denies Christ our Lord, the Son of God, begotten of the Father before the worlds, let him be anathema." There was a general chorus of approval, "Let him be anathema." "If anyone denies that the Son is like the Father according to the Scriptures, let him be anathema." All replied, "Let him be anathema." "If anyone does not say that the Son of God is co-eternal with the Father, let him be anathema." There was again a chorus of approval, "Let him be anathema." "If anyone says that the Son of God is a creature, like other creatures, let him be anathema." The answer was the same, "Let him be anathema." "If anyone says that the Son was of no existing things, yet not of God the Father, let him be anathema." All shouted together, "Let him be anathema." "If anyone says, There was a time when the Son was not, let him be anathema." At this point all the bishops and the whole Church together received the words of Valens with clapping of hands and stamping of feet. And if anyone thinks we have invented the story let him examine the public records. At all events the muniment-boxes of the Churches are full of it, and the circumstance is fresh in men's memory. Some of those who took part in the Synod are still alive, and the Arians themselves (a fact which may put the truth beyond dispute) do not deny the accuracy of our account. When, therefore, all extolled Valens to the sky and penitently condemned themselves for having suspected him, the same Claudius who before had begun to read, said "There are still a few points which have escaped the notice of my lord and brother Valens; if it seem good to you, let us, in order to remove all scruples, pass a general vote of censure upon them. If anyone says that the Son of God was indeed before all worlds but was by no means before all time, so that he puts some thing before Him, let him be anathema." And many other things which had a suspicious look were condemned by Valens when Claudius recited them. If anyone wishes to learn more about them he will find the account in the acts of the Synod of Ariminum, the source from which I have myself drawn them.

19. After these proceedings the Council was dissolved. All returned in gladness to their own provinces. For the Emperor and all good men had one and the same aim, that the East and West should be knit together by the bond of fellowship. But wickedness does not long lie hid, and the sore that is healed superficially before the bad humor has been worked off breaks out again. Valens and Ursacius and others associated with them in their wickedness, eminent Christian bishops of course, began to wave their palms, and to say they had not denied that He was a creature, but that He was like other creatures. At that moment the term *Usia* was abolished: the Nicene Faith stood condemned by acclamation. The whole world groaned, and was astonished to find itself Arian. Some, therefore, remained in their own communion, others began to send letters to those Confessors who as adherents of Athanasius were in exile; several despairingly bewailed the better relations into which they had entered. But a few, true to human nature, defended their mistake as an exhibition of wisdom. The ship of the Apostles was in peril, she was driven by the wind, her sides beaten with the waves: no hope was now left. But the Lord awoke and bade the tempest cease; the beast died, and there was a calm once again. To speak more

plainly, all the bishops who had been banished from their sees, by the clemency of the new emperor returned to their Churches. Then Egypt welcomed the triumphant Athanasius; then Hilary returned from the battle to the embrace of the Church of Gaul; then Eusebius returned and Italy laid aside her mourning weeds. The bishops who had been caught in the snare at Ariminum and had unwittingly come to be reported of as heretics, began to assemble, while they called the Body of our Lord and all that is holy in the Church to witness that they had not a suspicion of anything faulty in their own faith. We thought, said they, the words were to be taken in their natural meaning, and we had no suspicion that in the Church of God, the very home of simplicity and sincerity in the confession of truth, one thing could be kept secret in the heart, another uttered by the lips. We thought too well of bad men and were deceived. We did not suppose that the bishops of Christ were fighting against Christ. There was much besides which they said with tears, but I pass it over for brevity's sake. They were ready to condemn their former subscription as well as all the blasphemies of the Arians. Here I ask our excessively scrupulous friends what they think ought to have been done with those who made this Confession? Deprive the old bishops, they will say, and ordain new ones. The plan was tried. But how many whose conscience does not condemn them will allow themselves to be deprived. Particularly when all the people who loved their bishops flocked together, ready to stone and slay those who attempted to deprive them. The bishops should, it may be said, have kept to themselves within their own communion. That is to say, with senseless cruelty they would have surrendered the whole world to the devil.

Why condemn those who were not Arians? Why rend the Church when it was continuing in the harmony of the faith? Lastly, were they by obstinacy to make Arians of orthodox believers? We know that at the Council of Nicæa, which was assembled on account of the Arian perfidy, eight Arian bishops were welcomed, and there is not a bishop in the world at the present day whose ordination is not dependent on that Council. This being so, how could they act in opposition to it, when their loyalty to it had cost them the pain of exile?

20. L. Were Arians really then received after all? Pray tell me who they were.

O. Eusebius, bishop of Nicomedia, Theognis, bishop of Nicæa, Saras, at the time presbyter of Libya, Eusebius, bishop of Cæsarea in Palestine, and others whom it would be tedious to enumerate; Arius also, the presbyter, the original source of all the trouble; Euzoius the deacon, who succeeded Eudoxius as bishop of Antioch, and Achillas, the reader. These three who were clerics of the Church of Alexandria were the originators of the heresy.

L. Suppose a person were to deny that they were welcomed back, how is he to be refuted?

O. There are men still living who took part in that Council. And if that is not enough, because owing to the time that has elapsed they are but few, and it is impossible for witnesses to be everywhere, if we read the acts and names of the bishops of the Council of Nicæa, we find that those who we saw just now were welcomed back, did subscribe the *homoousion* along with the rest.

L. Will you point out how, after the Council of Nicæa, they relapsed into their unfaithfulness?

O. A good suggestion, for unbelievers are in the habit of shutting their eyes and denying that things which they dislike ever happened. But how could they afterwards do anything but relapse, when it was owing to them that the Council was convened, and their letters and impious treatises which were published before the Council, remain even to the present day? Seeing, therefore, that at that time three hundred bishops or more welcomed a few men whom they might have rejected without injury to the Church, I am surprised that certain persons, who are certainly upholders of the faith of Nicæa, are so harsh as to think that three Confessors returning from exile were not bound in the interests of the world's salvation to do what so many illustrious men did of their own accord. But, to go back to our starting point, on the return of the Confessors it was determined, in a synod afterwards held at Alexandria, that, the authors of the heresy excepted (who could not be excused on the ground of error), penitents should be admitted to communion with the Church: not that they who had been heretics could be bishops, but because it was clear that those who were received had not been heretics. The West assented to this decision, and it was through this conclusion, which the necessities of the times demanded, that the world was snatched from the jaws of Satan. I have reached a very difficult subject, where I am compelled against my wishes and my purpose, to think somewhat otherwise of that saintly man Lucifer than his merits demand, and my own courtesy requires. But what am I to do? Truth opens my mouth and urges my reluctant tongue to utter the thoughts of my heart. At such a crisis of the Church, when the wolves were wildly raging, he separated off a few sheep and abandoned the remnant of the flock. He himself was a good shepherd, but he was leaving a vast spoil to the beasts of prey. I take no notice of reports originating with certain evil speakers, though maintained by them to be authenticated facts; such as that he acted thus through the love of glory, and the desire of handing down his name to posterity; or again that he was influenced by the grudge he bore against Eusebius on account of the quarrel at Antioch. I believe none of these reports in the case of such a man; and this I will constantly affirm even now—that the difference between us and him is one of words, not of things, if he really does receive those who have been baptized by the Arians.

21. L. The account I used before to hear given of these things was widely different, and, as I now think, better calculated to promote error than hope. But I thank Christ my God for pouring into my heart the light of truth, that I might no longer profanely call the Church, which is His Virgin, the harlot of the devil. There is one other point I should like you to explain. What are we to say about Hilary who does not receive even those who have been baptized by the Arians?

O. Since Hilary when he left the Church was only a deacon, and since the Church is to him, though to him alone, a mere worldly multitude, he can neither duly celebrate the Eucharist, for he has no bishops or priests, nor can he give baptism without the Eucharist. And since the man is now dead, inasmuch as he was a deacon and could ordain no one to follow him, his sect died with him. For there is no such thing as a Church without bishops. But passing over a few very insignificant persons who are in their own esteem both laymen and bishops, let me point out to you what views we should hold respecting the Church at large.

L. You have settled a great question in three words, as the saying is, and indeed while you speak, I feel that I am on your side. But when you stop, some old misgivings arise as to why we receive those who have been baptized by heretics.

O. That is just what I had in mind when I said I would point out what views we ought to hold concerning the Church at large. For many are exercised by the misgivings you speak of. I shall perhaps be tedious in my explanation, but it is worthwhile if the truth gains.

22. Noah's ark was a type of the Church, as the Apostle Peter says—"In Noah's ark few, that is, eight souls, were saved through water: which also after a true likeness doth now save us, even baptism." As in the ark there were all kinds of animals, so also in the Church there are men of all races and characters. As in the one there was the leopard with the kids, the wolf with the lambs, so in the other there are found the righteous and sinners, that is, vessels of gold and silver with those of wood and of earth. The ark had its rooms: the Church has many mansions. Eight souls were saved in Noah's ark. And Ecclesiastes bids us "give a portion to seven yea, even unto eight," that is to believe both Testaments. This is why some psalms bear the inscription *for the octave*, and why the one hundred and nineteenth psalm is divided into portions of eight verses each beginning with its own letter for the instruction of the righteous. The beatitudes which our Lord spoke to his disciples on the mountain, thereby delineating the Church, are eight. And Ezekiel for the building of the temple employs the number eight. And you will find many other things expressed in the same way in the Scriptures. The raven also is sent forth from the ark but does not return, and afterwards the dove

announces peace to the earth. So also in the Church's baptism, that most unclean bird the devil is expelled, and the dove of the Holy Spirit announces peace to our earth. The construction of the ark was such that it began with being thirty cubits broad and gradually narrowed to one. Similarly the Church, consisting of many grades, ends in deacons, presbyters, and bishops. The ark was in peril in the flood, the Church is in peril in the world. When Noah left the ark he planted a vineyard, drank thereof, and was drunken. Christ also, born in the flesh, planted the Church and suffered. The elder son made sport of his father's nakedness, the younger covered it: and the Jews mocked God crucified, the Gentiles honored Him. The daylight would fail me if I were to explain all the mysteries of the ark and compare them with the Church. Who are the eagles amongst us? Who the doves and lions, who the stags, who the worms and serpents? So far as our subject requires I will briefly show you. It is not the sheep only who abide in the Church, nor do clean birds only fly to and fro there; but amid the grain other seed is sown, "amidst the neat corn-fields burrs and caltrops and barren oats lord it in the land." What is the husbandman to do? Root up the darnel? In that case the whole harvest is destroyed along with it. Every day the farmer diligently drives the birds away with strange noises, or frightens them with scarecrows: here he cracks a whip, there he spreads out some other object to terrify them. Nevertheless he suffers from the raids of nimble roes or the wantonness of the wild asses; here the mice convey the corn to their garners underground, there the ants crowd thickly in and ravage the corn-field. Thus the case stands. No one who has land is free from care. While the householder slept the enemy sowed tares among the wheat, and when the servants proposed to go and root them up the master forbade them, reserving for himself the separation of the chaff and the grain. There are vessels of wrath and of mercy which the Apostle speaks of in the house of God. The day then will come when the storehouses of the Church shall be opened and the Lord will bring forth the vessels of wrath; and, as they depart, the saints will say, "They went out from us, but they were not of us; for if they had been of us, they would no doubt have continued with us." No one can take to himself the prerogative of Christ, no one before the day of judgment can pass judgment upon men. If the Church is already cleansed, what shall we reserve for the Lord? "There is a way which seems right unto a man, but the end thereof are the ways of death." When our judgment is so prone to error, upon whose opinion can we rely?

23. Cyprian of blessed memory tried to avoid broken cisterns and not to drink of strange waters: and therefore, rejecting heretical baptism, he summoned his African synod in opposition to Stephen, who was the blessed Peter's twenty-second successor in the see of Rome. They met to discuss this matter; but the attempt failed. At last those very bishops who had together with him determined that heretics must be re-baptized, reverted to the old custom and published a fresh decree. Do you ask what course we must pursue? What we do our forefathers handed down to us as their forefathers to them. But why speak of later times? When the blood of Christ was but lately shed and the apostles were still in Judea, the Lord's body was asserted to be a phantom; the Galatians had been led away to the observance of the law, and the Apostle was a second time in travail with them; the Corinthians did not believe the resurrection of the flesh, and he endeavored by many arguments to bring them back to the right path. Then came Simon Magus and

his disciple Menander. They asserted themselves to be powers of God. Then Basilides invented the most high god *Abraxas* and the three hundred and sixty-five manifestations of him. Then Nicolas, one of the seven Deacons, and one whose lechery knew no rest by night or day, indulged in his filthy dreams. I say nothing of the Jewish heretics who before the coming of Christ destroyed the law delivered to them: of Dositheus, the leader of the Samaritans who rejected the prophets: of the Sadducees who sprang from his root and denied even the resurrection of the flesh: of the Pharisees who separated themselves from the Jews on account of certain superfluous observances, and took their name from the fact of their dissent: of the Herodians who accepted Herod as the Christ. I come to those heretics who have mangled the Gospels, Saturninus, and the Ophites, the Cainites and Sethites, and Carpocrates, and Cerinthus, and his successor Ebion, and the other pests, the most of which broke out while the apostle John was still alive, and yet we do not read that any of these men were re-baptized.

24. As we have made mention of that distinguished saint, let us show also from his Apocalypse that repentance unaccompanied by baptism ought to be allowed valid in the case of heretics. It is imputed (Rev. ii. 4) to the angel of Ephesus that he has forsaken his first love. In the angel of the Church of Pergamum the eating of idol-sacrifices is censured (Rev. ii. 14), and the doctrine of the Nicolaitans (ib. 15). Likewise the angel of Thyatira is rebuked (ib. 20) on account of Jezebel the prophetess, and the idol meats, and fornication. And yet the Lord encourages all these to repent, and adds a threat, moreover, of future punishment if they do not turn. Now he would not urge them to repent unless he intended to

grant pardon to the penitents. Is there any indication of his having said, Let them be rebaptized who have been baptized in the faith of the Nicolaitans? or let hands be laid upon those of the people of Pergamum who at that time believed, having held the doctrine of Balaam? Nay, rather, "Repent therefore," he says, "or else I come to thee quickly, and I will make war against them with the sword of my mouth."

25. If, however, those men who were ordained by Hilary, and who have lately become sheep without a shepherd, are disposed to allege Scripture in support of what the blessed Cyprian left in his letters advocating the re-baptization of heretics, I beg them to remember that he did not anathematize those who refused to follow him. At all events, he remained in communion with such as opposed his views. He was content with exhorting them, on account of Novatus and the numerous other heretics then springing up, to receive no one who did not condemn his previous error. In fact, he thus concludes the discussion of the subject with Stephen, the Roman Pontiff: "These things, dearest brother, I have brought to your knowledge on account of our mutual respect and love unfeigned, believing, as I do, that from the sincerity of your piety and your faith you will approve such things as are alike consonant with piety and true in themselves. But I know that some persons are unwilling to abandon views which they have once entertained, and are averse to a change of purpose; they would rather, without breaking the bond of peace and concord between colleagues, adhere to their own plans, when once they have been adopted. This is a matter in which we do not force anyone, or lay down a law for anyone; let each follow his own free choice in the administration of the Church: let

each be ruler in his own sphere since he must give account of his action to the Lord." In the letter also to Jubaianus on the re-baptization of heretics, towards the end, he says this: "I have written these few remarks, my dearest brother, to the best of my poor ability, without dictating to anyone, or prejudicing the case of anyone: I would not hinder a single bishop from doing what he thinks right with the full exercise of his own judgment. So far as is possible, we avoid disputes with colleagues and fellow-bishops about the heretics, and maintain with them a divine harmony and the Lord's peace, particularly since the Apostle says: 'But if any man seems to be contentious, we have no such custom, neither the churches of God.' With patience and gentleness we preserve charity at heart, the honor of our order, the bond of faith, the harmony of the episcopate."

26. There is another argument which I shall adduce, and against that not even Hilary, the modern Deucalion, will venture to mutter a syllable. If heretics are not baptized and must be re-baptized because they were not in the Church, Hilary himself also is not a Christian. For he was baptized in that Church which always allowed heretical baptism. Before the Synod of Ariminum was held, before Lucifer went into exile, Hilary when a deacon of the Roman Church welcomed those who came over from the heretics on account of the baptism which they had previously received. It can hardly be that Arians are the only heretics, and that we are to accept all but those whom they have baptized. You were a deacon, Hilary (the Church may say), and received those whom the Manicheans had baptized. You were a deacon, and acknowledged Ebion's baptism. All at once after Arius arose you began to be quite out of conceit with yourself.

You and your household separated from us, and opened a new laver of your own. If some angel or apostle has re-baptized you, I will not disparage your procedure. But since you who raise your sword against me are the son of my womb, and nourished on the milk of my breasts, return to me what I gave you, and be, if you can, a Christian in some other way. Suppose I am a harlot, still I am your mother. You say, I do not keep the marriage bed undefiled: still what I am now I was when you were conceived. If I commit adultery with Arius, I did the same before with Praxias, with Ebion, with Cerinthus, and Novatus. You think much of them and welcome them, adulterers as they are, to your mother's home. I don't know why one adulterer more than others should offend you.

27. But if anyone thinks it open to question whether heretics were always welcomed by our ancestors, let him read the letters of the blessed Cyprian in which he applies the lash to Stephen, bishop of Rome, and his errors which had grown inveterate by usage. Let him also read the pamphlets of Hilary on the re-baptization of heretics which he published against us, and he will there find Hilary himself confessing that Julius, Marcus, Sylvester, and the other bishops of old alike welcomed all heretics to repentance; and, further, to shew that he could not justly claim possession of the true custom; the Council of Nicæa also, to which we referred not long ago, welcomed all heretics with the exception of the disciples of Paul of Samosata. And, what is more, it allows a Novatian bishop on conversion to have the rank of presbyter, a decision which condemns both Lucifer and Hilary, since the same person who is ordained is also baptized.

28. I might spend the day in speaking to the same effect, and dry up all the streams of argument with the single Sun of the Church. But as we have already had a long discussion and the protracted controversy has wearied out the attention of our audience, I will tell you my opinion briefly and without reserve. We ought to remain in that Church which was founded by the Apostles and continues to this day. If ever you hear of any that are called Christians taking their name not from the Lord Jesus Christ, but from some other, for instance, Marcionites, Valentinians, Men of the mountain or the plain, you may be sure that you have there not the Church of Christ, but the synagogue of Antichrist. For the fact that they took their rise after the foundation of the Church is proof that they are those whose coming the Apostle foretold. And let them not flatter themselves if they think they have Scripture authority for their assertions, since the devil himself quoted Scripture, and the essence of the Scriptures is not the letter, but the meaning. Otherwise, if we follow the letter, we too can concoct a new dogma and assert that such persons as wear shoes and have two coats must not be received into the Church.

L. You must not suppose that victory rests with you only. We are both conquerors, and each of us carries off the palm,—you are victorious over me, and I over my error. May I always when I argue be so fortunate as to exchange wrong opinions for better ones. I must, however, make a confession, because I best know the character of my party, and own that they are more easily conquered than convinced.

The Perpetual Virginity of Blessed Mary.

Against Helvidius.

This tract appeared about a.d. 383. The question which gave occasion to it was whether the Mother of our Lord remained a Virgin after His birth. Helvidius maintained that the mention in the Gospels of the "sisters" and "brethren" of our Lord was proof that the Blessed Virgin had subsequent issue, and he supported his opinion by the writings of Tertullian and Victorinus. The outcome of his views was that virginity was ranked below matrimony. Jerome vigorously takes the other side, and tries to prove that the "sisters" and "brethren" spoken of, were either children of Joseph by a former marriage, or first cousins, children of the sister of the Virgin. A detailed account of the controversy will be found in Farrar's "Early Days of Christianity," pp. 124 sq. When Jerome wrote this treatise both he and Helvidius were at Rome, and Damasus was Pope. The only contemporary notice preserved of Helvidius is that by Jerome in the following pages.

Jerome maintains against Helvidius three propositions:—

1st. That Joseph was only putatively, not really, the husband of Mary.

2d. That the "brethren" of the Lord were his cousins, not his own brethren.

3d. That virginity is better than the married state.

1. The first of these occupies ch. 3–8. It turns upon the record in Matt. i. 18–25, and especially on the words,

"Before they came together" (c. 4), "knew her not till, &c." (5–8).

2. The second (c. 9–17) turns upon the words "first-born son" (9, 10), which, Jerome argues, are applicable not only to the eldest of several, but also to an only son: and the mention of brothers and sisters, whom Jerome asserts to have been children of Mary the wife of Cleophas or Clopas (11–16); he appeals to many Church writers in support of this view (17).

3. In support of his preference of virginity to marriage, Jerome argues that not only Mary but Joseph also remained in the virgin state (19); that, though marriage may sometimes be a holy estate, it presents great hindrances to prayer (20), and the teaching of Scripture is that the states of virginity and continency are more accordant with God's will than that of marriage (21, 22).

1. I was requested by certain of the brethren not long ago to reply to a pamphlet written by one Helvidius. I have deferred doing so, not because it is a difficult matter to maintain the truth and refute an ignorant boor who has scarce known the first glimmer of learning, but because I was afraid my reply might make him appear worth defeating. There was the further consideration that a turbulent fellow, the only individual in the world who thinks himself both priest and layman, one who, as has been said, thinks that eloquence consists in loquacity and considers speaking ill of anyone to be the witness of a good conscience, would begin to blaspheme worse than ever if opportunity of discussion were afforded him. He would stand as it were on a pedestal, and would publish his views far and wide. There was reason also to fear that when truth failed him he would assail his opponents with

the weapon of abuse. But all these motives for silence, though just, have more justly ceased to influence me, because of the scandal caused to the brethren who were disgusted at his ravings. The axe of the Gospel must therefore be now laid to the root of the barren tree, and both it and its fruitless foliage cast into the fire, so that Helvidius who has never learnt to speak, may at length learn to hold his tongue.

2. I must call upon the Holy Spirit to express His meaning by my mouth and defend the virginity of the Blessed Mary. I must call upon the Lord Jesus to guard the sacred lodging of the womb in which He abode for ten months from all suspicion of sexual intercourse. And I must also entreat God the Father to show that the mother of His Son, who was a mother before she was a bride, continued a Virgin after her son was born. We have no desire to career over the fields of eloquence, we do not resort to the snares of the logicians or the thickets of Aristotle. We shall adduce the actual words of Scripture. Let him be refuted by the same proofs which he employed against us, so that he may see that it was possible for him to read what is written, and yet to be unable to discern the established conclusion of a sound faith.

3. His first statement was: "Matthew says, Now the birth of Jesus Christ was on this wise: When his mother Mary had been betrothed to Joseph, before they came together she was found with child of the Holy Ghost. And Joseph her husband, being a righteous man, and not willing to make her a public example, was minded to put her away privately. But when he thought on these things, behold, an angel of the Lord appeared unto him in a dream, saying, Joseph, thou son of David, fear not to take unto thee Mary thy wife: for that which is

conceived in her is of the Holy Ghost." Notice, he says, that the word used is *betrothed*, not *entrusted* as you say, and of course the only reason why she was betrothed was that she might one day be married. And the Evangelist would not have said *before they came together* if they were not to come together, for no one would use the phrase *before he dined* of a man who was not going to dine. Then, again, the angel calls her *wife* and speaks of her as *united* to Joseph. We are next invited to listen to the declaration of Scripture: "And Joseph arose from his sleep, and did as the angel of the Lord commanded him, and took unto him his wife; and knew her not till she had brought forth her son."

4. Let us take the points one by one, and follow the tracks of this impiety that we may show that he has contradicted himself. He admits that she was betrothed, and in the next breath will have her to be a man's wife whom he has admitted to be his betrothed. Again, he calls her wife, and then says the only reason why she was betrothed was that she might one day be married. And, for fear we might not think that enough, "the word used," he says, "is *betrothed* and not *entrusted,* that is to say, not yet a wife, not yet united by the bond of wedlock." But when he continues, "the Evangelist would never have applied the words, *before they came together* to persons who were not to come together, any more than one says, before he dined, when the man is not going to dine," I know not whether to grieve or laugh. Shall I convict him of ignorance, or accuse him of rashness? Just as if, supposing a person to say, "Before dining in harbor I sailed to Africa," his words could not hold good unless he were compelled someday to dine in harbor. If I choose to say, "the apostle Paul before he went to Spain was put in

fetters at Rome," or (as I certainly might) "Helvidius, before he repented, was cut off by death," must Paul on being released at once go to Spain, or must Helvidius repent after death, although the Scripture says "In sheol who shall give thee thanks?" Must we not rather understand that the preposition *before,* although it frequently denotes order in time, yet sometimes refers only to order in thought? So that there is no necessity, if sufficient cause intervened to prevent it, for our thoughts to be realized. When, then, the Evangelist says *before they came together*, he indicates the time immediately preceding marriage, and shows that matters were so far advanced that she who had been betrothed was on the point of becoming a wife. As though he said, before they kissed and embraced, before the consummation of marriage, she was found to be with child. And she was found to be so by none other than Joseph, who watched the swelling womb of his betrothed with the anxious glances, and, at this time, almost the privilege, of a husband. Yet it does not follow, as the previous examples showed, that he had intercourse with Mary after her delivery, when his desires had been quenched by the fact that she had already conceived. And although we find it said to Joseph in a dream, "Fear not to take Mary thy wife"; and again, "Joseph arose from his sleep, and did as the angel of the Lord commanded him, and took unto him his wife," no one ought to be disturbed by this, as though, inasmuch as she is called *wife,* she ceases to be *betrothed,* for we know it is usual in Scripture to give the title to those who are betrothed. The following evidence from Deuteronomy establishes the point. "If the man," says the writer, "find the damsel that is betrothed in the field, and the man force her, and lie with her, he shall surely die, because he hath humbled his neighbor's wife." And in another place, "If there be a damsel that is a virgin betrothed unto an husband, and a man find her in the city, and lie with her; then ye shall bring them both out unto the gate of that city, and ye shall stone them with stones that they die; the damsel, because she cried not, being in the city; and the man, because he hath humbled his neighbor's wife: so thou shalt put away the evil from the midst of thee." Elsewhere also, "And what man is there that hath betrothed a wife, and hath not taken her? let him go and return unto his house, lest he die in the battle, and another man take her." But if anyone feels a doubt as to why the Virgin conceived after she was betrothed rather than when she had no one betrothed to her, or, to use the Scripture phrase, no husband, let me explain that there were three reasons. First, that by the genealogy of Joseph, whose kinswoman Mary was, Mary's origin might also be shown. Secondly, that she might not in accordance with the law of Moses be stoned as an adulteress. Thirdly, that in her flight to Egypt she might have some solace, though it was that of a guardian rather than a husband. For who at that time would have believed the Virgin's word that she had conceived of the Holy Ghost, and that the angel Gabriel had come and announced the purpose of God? and would not all have given their opinion against her as an adulteress, like Susanna? for at the present day, now that the whole world has embraced the faith, the Jews argue that when Isaiah says, "Behold, a virgin shall conceive and bear a son," the Hebrew word denotes a young woman, not a virgin, that is to say, the word is Almah, not Bethulah, a position which, farther on, we shall dispute more in detail. Lastly, excepting Joseph, and Elizabeth, and Mary herself, and some few others who, we may suppose, heard the truth from them, all considered Jesus to be the son of Joseph. And so far was this the case that even the Evangelists, expressing the prevailing opinion, which is the correct rule for a historian, call him the father of the Savior, as, for instance, "And he (that is, Simeon) came in the Spirit into the temple: and when the parents brought in the child Jesus, that they might do concerning him after the custom of the law;" and elsewhere, "And his parents went every year to Jerusalem at the feast of the Passover." And afterwards, "And when they had fulfilled the days, as they were returning, the boy Jesus tarried behind in Jerusalem; and his parents knew not of it." Observe also what Mary herself, who had replied to Gabriel with the words, "How shall this be, seeing I know not a man?" says concerning Joseph, "Son, why hast thou thus dealt with us? behold, thy father and I sought thee sorrowing." We have not here, as many maintain, the utterance of Jews or of mockers. The Evangelists call Joseph father: Mary confesses he was father. Not (as I said before) that Joseph was really the father of the Savior: but that, to preserve the reputation of Mary, he was regarded by all as his father, although, before he heard the admonition of the angel, "Joseph, thou son of David, fear not to take unto thee Mary thy wife: for that which is conceived in her is of the Holy Ghost," he had thoughts of putting her away privily; which shows that he well knew that the child conceived was not his. But we have said enough, more with the aim of imparting instruction than of answering an opponent, to show why Joseph is called the father of our Lord, and why Mary is called Joseph's wife. This also at once answers the question why certain persons are called his brethren.

5. This, however, is a point which will find its proper place further on. We must now hasten to other matters. The passage for discussion now is, "And Joseph arose from his sleep, and did as the angel of the Lord commanded him, and took unto him his wife and knew her not till she had brought forth a son, and he called his name Jesus." Here, first of all, it is quite needless for our opponent to show so elaborately that the word *know* has reference to coition, rather than to intellectual apprehension: as though anyone denied it, or any person in his senses could ever imagine the folly which Helvidius takes pains to refute. Then he would teach us that the adverb *till* implies a fixed and definite time, and when that is fulfilled, he says the event takes place which previously did not take place, as in the case before us, "and knew her not till she had brought forth a son." It is clear, says he, that she was known after she brought forth, and that that knowledge was only delayed by her engendering a son. To defend his position he piles up text upon text, waves his sword like a blindfolded gladiator, rattles his noisy tongue, and ends with wounding no one but himself.

6. Our reply is briefly this,—the words *knew* and *till* in the language of Holy Scripture are capable of a double meaning. As to the former, he himself gave us a dissertation to show that it must be referred to sexual intercourse, and no one doubts that it is often used of the knowledge of the understanding, as, for instance, "the boy Jesus tarried behind in Jerusalem, and his parents knew it not." Now we have to prove that just as in the one case he has followed the usage of Scripture, so with regard to the word *till* he is utterly refuted by the authority of the same Scripture, which often denotes by its use a fixed time (he

himself told us so), frequently time without limitation, as when God by the mouth of the prophet says to certain persons, "Even to old age I am he." Will He cease to be God when they have grown old? And the Savior in the Gospel tells the Apostles, "Lo, I am with you always, even unto the end of the world." Will the Lord then after the end of the world has come forsake His disciples, and at the very time when seated on twelve thrones they are to judge the twelve tribes of Israel will they be bereft of the company of their Lord? Again Paul the Apostle writing to the Corinthians says, "Christ the first-fruits, afterward they that are Christ's, at his coming. Then cometh the end, when he shall have delivered up the kingdom to God, even the Father, when he shall have put down all rule, and all authority and power. For he must reign, till he hath put all enemies under his feet." Granted that the passage relates to our Lord's human nature, we do not deny that the words are spoken of Him who endured the cross and is commanded to sit afterwards on the right hand. What does he mean then by saying, "for he must reign, till he hath put all enemies under his feet"? Is the Lord to reign only until His enemies begin to be under His feet, and once they are under His feet will He cease to reign? Of course His reign will then commence in its fulness when His enemies begin to be under His feet. David also in the fourth Song of Ascents speaks thus, "Behold, as the eyes of servants look unto the hand of their master, as the eyes of a maiden unto the hand of her mistress, so our eyes look unto the Lord our God, until he has mercy upon us." Will the prophet, then, look unto the Lord until he obtains mercy, and when mercy is obtained will he turn his eyes down to the ground? although elsewhere he says, "Mine eyes fail for thy salvation, and for the word of thy righteousness." I could accumulate countless instances of this usage, and cover the verbosity of our assailant with a cloud of proofs; I shall, however, add only a few, and leave the reader to discover like ones for himself.

7. The word of God says in Genesis, "And they gave unto Jacob all the strange gods which were in their hand, and the rings which were in their ears; and Jacob hid them under the oak which was by Shechem, and lost them until this day." Likewise at the end of Deuteronomy, "So Moses the servant of the Lord died there in the land of Moab, according to the word of the Lord. And he buried him in the valley, in the land of Moab over against Beth-peor: but no man knows of his sepulcher unto this day." We must certainly understand by *this day* the time of the composition of the history, whether you prefer the view that Moses was the author of the Pentateuch or that Ezra re-edited it. In either case I make no objection. The question now is whether the words *unto this day* are to be referred to the time of publishing or writing the books, and if so it is for him to show, now that so many years have rolled away since that day, that either the idols hidden beneath the oak have been found, or the grave of Moses discovered; for he obstinately maintains that what does not happen so long as the point of time indicated by *until* and *unto* has not been attained, begins to be when that point has been reached. He would do well to pay heed to the idiom of Holy Scripture, and understand with us, (it was here he stuck in the mud) that some things which might seem ambiguous if not expressed are plainly intimated, while others are left to the exercise of our intellect. For if, while the event was still fresh in memory and men were living who had seen Moses, it was possible for his grave to be unknown, much more may this be the

case after the lapse of so many ages. And in the same way must we interpret what we are told concerning Joseph. The Evangelist pointed out a circumstance which might have given rise to some scandal, namely, that Mary was not known by her husband until she was delivered, and he did so that we might be the more certain that she from whom Joseph refrained while there was room to doubt the import of the vision was not known after her delivery.

8. In short, what I want to know is why Joseph refrained until the day of her delivery? Helvidius will of course reply, because he heard the angel say, "that which is conceived in her is of the Holy Ghost." And in turn we rejoin that he had certainly heard him say, "Joseph, thou son of David, fear not to take unto thee Mary thy wife." The reason why he was forbidden to forsake his wife was that he might not think her an adulteress. Is it true then, that he was ordered not to have intercourse with his wife? Is it not plain that the warning was given him that he might not be separated from her? And could the just man dare, he says, to think of approaching her, when he heard that the Son of God was in her womb? Excellent! We are to believe then that the same man who gave so much credit to a dream that he did not dare to touch his wife, yet afterwards, when he had learnt from the shepherds that the angel of the Lord had come from heaven and said to them, "Be not afraid: for behold I bring you good tidings of great joy which shall be to all people, for there is born to you this day in the city of David a Savior, which is Christ the Lord;" and when the heavenly host had joined with him in the chorus "Glory to God in the highest, and on earth peace among men of good will;" and when he had seen just Simeon embrace the infant and exclaim, "Now let thou thy servant depart, O Lord, according to

thy word in peace: for mine eyes have seen thy salvation;" and when he had seen Anna the prophetess, the Magi, the Star, Herod, the angels; Helvidius, I say, would have us believe that Joseph, though well acquainted with such surprising wonders, dared to touch the temple of God, the abode of the Holy Ghost, the mother of his Lord? Mary at all events "kept all these sayings in her heart." You cannot for shame say Joseph did not know of them, for Luke tells us, "His father and mother were marveling at the things which were spoken concerning Him." And yet you with marvelous effrontery contend that the reading of the Greek manuscripts is corrupt, although it is that which nearly all the Greek writers have left us in their books, and not only so, but several of the Latin writers have taken the words the same way. Nor need we now consider the variations in the copies, since the whole record both of the Old and New Testament has since that time been translated into Latin, and we must believe that the water of the fountain flows purer than that of the stream.

9. Helvidius will answer, "What you say, is in my opinion mere trifling. Your arguments are so much waste of time, and the discussion shows more subtlety than truth. Why could not Scripture say, as it said of Thamar and Judah, 'And he took his wife, and knew her again no more'? Could not Matthew find words to express his meaning? 'He knew her not,' he says, 'until she brought forth a son.' He did then, after her delivery, know her, whom he had refrained from knowing until she was delivered."

10. If you are so contentious, your own thoughts shall now prove your master. You must not allow any time to intervene between delivery and intercourse. You must not say, "If a woman conceive seed and bear a man

child, then she shall be unclean seven days; as in the days of the separation of her sickness shall she be unclean. And in the eighth day the flesh of his foreskin shall be circumcised. And she shall continue in the blood of her purifying three and thirty days. She shall touch no hallowed thing," and so forth. On your showing, Joseph must at once approach, her, and be subject to Jeremiah's reproof, "They were as mad horses in respect of women: everyone neighed after his neighbor's wife." Otherwise, how can the words stand good, "he knew her not, till she had brought forth a son," if he waits after the time of another purifying has expired, if his lust must brook another long delay of forty days? The mother must go unpurged from her child-bed taint, and the wailing infant be attended to by the midwives, while the husband clasps his exhausted wife. Thus forsooth must their married life begin so that the Evangelist may not be convicted of falsehood. But God forbid that we should think thus of the Savior's mother and of a just man. No midwife assisted at His birth; no women's officiousness intervened. With her own hands she wrapped Him in the swaddling clothes, herself both mother and midwife, "and laid Him," we are told, "in a manger, because there was no room for them in the inn"; a statement which, on the one hand, refutes the ravings of the apocryphal accounts, for Mary herself wrapped Him in the swaddling clothes, and on the other makes the voluptuous notion of Helvidius impossible, since there was no place suitable for married intercourse in the inn.

    11. An ample reply has now been given to what he advanced respecting the words *before they came together,* and *he knew her not till she had brought forth a son.* I must now proceed, if my reply is to follow the order of

his argument, to the third point. He will have it that Mary bore other sons, and he quotes the passage, "And Joseph also went up to the city of David to enroll himself with Mary, who was betrothed to him, being great with child. And it came to pass, while they were there, the days were fulfilled that she should be delivered, and she brought forth her first-born son." From this he endeavors to show that the term *first-born* is inapplicable except to a person who has brothers, just as he is called *only begotten* who is the only son of his parents.

12. Our position is this: Every only begotten son is a first-born son, but not every firstborn is an only begotten. By first-born we understand not only one who is succeeded by others, but one who has had no predecessor. "Everything," says the Lord to Aaron, "that opened the womb of all flesh which they offer unto the Lord, both of man and beast, shall be thine: nevertheless the first born of man shalt thou surely redeem, and the firstling of unclean beasts shalt thou redeem." The word of God defines *first-born* as everything that opened the womb. Otherwise, if the title belongs to such only as have younger brothers, the priests cannot claim the firstlings until their successors have been begotten, lest, perchance, in case there were no subsequent delivery it should prove to be the first-born but not merely the only begotten. "And those that are to be redeemed of them from a month old shalt thou redeem, according to thine estimation for the money of five shekels, after the shekel of the sanctuary (the same is twenty gerahs). But the firstling of an ox, or the firstling of a sheep, or the firstling of a goat, thou shalt not redeem; they are holy." The word of God compels me to dedicate to God everything that opened the womb if it be the firstling of clean beasts: if of unclean

beasts, I must redeem it, and give the value to the priest. I might reply and say, Why do you tie me down to the short space of a month? Why do you speak of the first-born, when I cannot tell whether there are brothers to follow? Wait until the second is born. I owe nothing to the priest, unless the birth of a second should make the one I previously had the first-born. Will not the very points of the letters cry out against me and convict me of my folly, and declare that first-born is a title of him who opens the womb, and is not to be restricted to him who has brothers? And, then, to take the case of John: we are agreed that he was an only begotten son: I want to know if he was not also a first-born son, and whether he was not absolutely amenable to the law. There can be no doubt in the matter. At all events Scripture thus speaks of the Savior, "And when the days of her purification according to the law of Moses were fulfilled, they brought him up to Jerusalem, to present him to the Lord (as it is written in the law of the Lord, every male that opened the womb shall be called holy to the Lord) and to offer a sacrifice according to that which is said in the law of the Lord, a pair of turtle-doves, or two young pigeons." If this law relates only to the first-born, and there can be no first-born unless there are successors, no one ought to be bound by the law of the first-born who cannot tell whether there will be successors. But inasmuch as he who has no younger brothers is bound by the law of the firstborn, we gather that he is called the first-born who opens the womb and who has been preceded by none, not he whose birth is followed by that of a younger brother. Moses writes in Exodus, "And it came to pass at midnight, that the Lord smote all the first-born in the land of Egypt, from the first-born of Pharaoh that sat on his throne unto the first-born of the captive that was in the dungeon: And all the first-born of cattle." Tell me, were they who then perished by the destroyer, only your first-born, or, something more, did they include the only begotten? If only they who have brothers are called first-born, the only begotten were saved from death. And if it be the fact that the only begotten were slain, it was contrary to the sentence pronounced, for the only begotten to die as well as the first-born. You must either release the only begotten from the penalty, and in that case you become ridiculous: or, if you allow that they were slain, we gain our point, though we have not to thank you for it, that only begotten sons also are called first-born.

13. The last proposition of Helvidius was this, and it is what he wished to show when he treated of the first-born, that brethren of the Lord are mentioned in the Gospels. For example, "Behold, his mother and his brethren stood without, seeking to speak to him." And elsewhere, "After this he went down to Capernaum, he, and his mother, and his brethren." And again, "His brethren therefore said unto him, Depart hence, and go into Judea, that thy disciples also may behold the works which thou does. For no man doeth anything in secret, and himself seeks to be known openly. If thou does these things, manifest thyself to the world." And John adds, "For even his brethren did not believe on him." Mark also and Matthew, "And coming into his own country he taught them in their synagogues, insomuch that they were astonished, and said, Whence hath this man this wisdom, and mighty works? Is not this the carpenter's son? is not his mother called Mary? and his brethren James, and Joseph, and Simon, and Judas? And his sisters, are they not all with us?" Luke also in the Acts of the Apostles

relates, "These all with one accord continued steadfastly in prayer, with the women and Mary the mother of Jesus, and with his brethren." Paul the Apostle also is at one with them, and witnesses to their historical accuracy, "And I went up by revelation, but other of the apostles saw I none, save Peter and James the Lord's brother." And again in another place, "Have we no right to eat and drink? Have we no right to lead about wives even as the rest of the Apostles, and the brethren of the Lord, and Cephas?" And for fear any one should not allow the evidence of the Jews, since it was they from whose mouth we hear the name of His brothers, but should maintain that His countrymen were deceived by the same error in respect of the brothers into which they fell in their belief about the father, Helvidius utters a sharp note of warning and cries, "The same names are repeated by the Evangelists in another place, and the same persons are there brethren of the Lord and sons of Mary." Matthew says, "And many women were there (doubtless at the Lord's cross) beholding from afar, which had followed Jesus from Galilee, ministering unto him: among whom was Mary Magdalene, and Mary the mother of James and Joses, and the mother of the sons of Zebedee." Mark also, "And there were also women beholding from afar, among whom were both Mary Magdalene, and Mary the mother of James the less and of Joses, and Salome"; and in the same place shortly after, "And many other women which came up with him unto Jerusalem." Luke too, "Now there were Mary Magdalene, and Joanna, and Mary the mother of James, and the other women with them."

14. My reason for repeating the same thing again and again is to prevent him from raising a false issue and crying out that I have withheld such passages as make for

him, and that his view has been torn to shreds not by evidence of Scripture, but by evasive arguments. Observe, he says, James and Joses are sons of Mary, and the same persons who were called brethren by the Jews. Observe, Mary is the mother of James the less and of Joses. And James is called the less to distinguish him from James the greater, who was the son of Zebedee, as Mark elsewhere states, "And Mary Magdalene and Mary the mother of Joses beheld where he was laid. And when the sabbath was past, they bought spices, that they might come and anoint him." And, as might be expected, he says: "What a poor and impious view we take of Mary, if we hold that when other women were concerned about the burial of Jesus, she His mother was absent; or if we invent some kind of a second Mary; and all the more because the Gospel of S. John testifies that she was there present, when the Lord upon the cross commended her, as His mother and now a widow, to the care of John. Or must we suppose that the Evangelists were so far mistaken and so far mislead us as to call Mary the mother of those who were known to the Jews as brethren of Jesus?"

15. What darkness, what raging madness rushing to its own destruction! You say that the mother of the Lord was present at the cross, you say that she was entrusted to the disciple John on account of her widowhood and solitary condition: as if upon your own showing, she had not four sons, and numerous daughters, with whose solace she might comfort herself? You also apply to her the name of widow which is not found in Scripture. And although you quote all instances in the Gospels, the words of John alone displease you. You say in passing that she was present at the cross, that you may not appear to have omitted it on purpose, and yet not a

word about the women who were with her. I could pardon you if you were ignorant, but I see you have a reason for your silence. Let me point out then what John says, "But there were standing by the cross of Jesus his mother, and his mother's sister, Mary the wife of Clopas, and Mary Magdalene." No one doubts that there were two apostles called by the name James, James the son of Zebedee, and James the son of Alphæus. Do you intend the comparatively unknown James the less, who is called in Scripture the son of Mary, not however of Mary the mother of our Lord, to be an apostle, or not? If he is an apostle, he must be the son of Alphæus and a believer in Jesus, "For neither did his brethren believe in him." If he is not an apostle, but a third James (who he can be I cannot tell), how can he be regarded as the Lord's brother, and how, being a third, can he be called *less* to distinguish him from *greater*, when *greater* and *less* are used to denote the relations existing, not between three, but between two? Notice, moreover, that the Lord's brother is an apostle, since Paul says, "Then after three years I went up to Jerusalem to visit Cephas, and tarried with him fifteen days. But other of the Apostles saw I none, save James the Lord's brother." And in the same Epistle, "And when they perceived the grace that was given unto me, James and Cephas and John, who were reputed to be pillars," etc. And that you may not suppose this James to be the son of Zebedee, you have only to read the Acts of the Apostles, and you will find that the latter had already been slain by Herod. The only conclusion is that the Mary who is described as the mother of James the less was the wife of Alphæus and sister of Mary the Lord's mother, the one who is called by John the Evangelist "Mary of Clopas," whether after her father, or kindred, or for some other reason. But if you think they are two persons because elsewhere we read, "Mary the mother of James the less," and here, "Mary of Clopas," you have still to learn that it is customary in Scripture for the same individual to bear different names. Raguel, Moses' father-in-law, is also called Jethro. Gedeon, without any apparent reason for the change, all at once becomes Jerubbaal. Ozias, king of Judah, has an alternative, Azarias. Mount Tabor is called Itabyrium. Again Hermon is called by the Phenicians Sanior, and by the Amorites Sanir. The same tract of country is known by three names, Negebh, Teman, and Darom in Ezekiel. Peter is also called Simon and Cephas. Judas the zealot in another Gospel is called Thaddaeus. And there are numerous other examples which the reader will be able to collect for himself from every part of Scripture.

16. Now here we have the explanation of what I am endeavoring to show, how it is that the sons of Mary, the sister of our Lord's mother, who though not formerly believers afterwards did believe, can be called brethren of the Lord. Possibly the case might be that one of the brethren believed immediately while the others did not believe until long after, and that one Mary was the mother of James and Joses, namely, "Mary of Clopas," who is the same as the wife of Alphæus, the other, the mother of James the less. In any case, if she (the latter) had been the Lord's mother S. John would have allowed her the title, as everywhere else, and would not by calling her the mother of other sons have given a wrong impression. But at this stage I do not wish to argue for or against the supposition that Mary the wife of Clopas and Mary the mother of James and Joses were different women, provided it is clearly understood that Mary the mother of James and

Joses was not the same person as the Lord's mother. How then, says Helvidius, do you make out that they were called the Lord's brethren who were not his brethren? I will show how that is. In Holy Scripture there are four kinds of brethren—by nature, race, kindred, love. Instances of brethren by nature are Esau and Jacob, the twelve patriarchs, Andrew and Peter, James and John. As to race, all Jews are called brethren of one another, as in Deuteronomy, "If thy brother, a Hebrew man, or a Hebrew woman, be sold unto thee, and serve thee six years; then in the seventh year thou shalt let him go free from thee." And in the same book, "Thou shalt in anywise set him king over thee, whom the Lord thy God shall choose: one from among thy brethren shalt thou set king over thee; thou mayest not put a foreigner over thee, which is not thy brother." And again, "Thou shalt not see thy brother's ox or his sheep go astray, and hide thyself from them: thou shalt surely bring them again unto thy brother. And if thy brother be not nigh unto thee, or if thou know him not, then thou shalt bring it home to thine house, and it shall be with thee until thy brother seek after it, and thou shalt restore it to him again." And the Apostle Paul says, "I could wish that I myself were anathema from Christ for my brethren's sake, my kinsmen according to the flesh: who are Israelites." Moreover they are called brethren by kindred who are of one family, that is πατρία, which corresponds to the Latin *paternitas*, because from a single root a numerous progeny proceeds. In Genesis we read, "And Abram said unto Lot, Let there be no strife, I pray thee, between me and thee, and between my herdsmen and thy herdsmen; for we are brethren." And again, "So Lot chose him all the plain of Jordan, and Lot journeyed east: and they separated each from his brother." Certainly Lot was not Abraham's brother, but the son of Abraham's brother Aram. For Terah begat Abraham and Nahor and Aram: and Aram begat Lot. Again we read, "And Abram was seventy and five years old when he departed out of Haran. And Abram took Sarai his wife, and Lot his brother's son." But if you still doubt whether a nephew can be called a son, let me give you an instance. "And when Abram heard that his brother was taken captive, he led forth his trained men, born in his house, three hundred and eighteen." And after describing the night attack and the slaughter, he adds, "And he brought back all the goods, and also brought again his brother Lot." Let this suffice by way of proof of my assertion. But for fear you may make some caviling objection, and wriggle out of your difficulty like a snake, I must bind you fast with the bonds of proof to stop your hissing and complaining, for I know you would like to say you have been overcome not so much by Scripture truth as by intricate arguments. Jacob, the son of Isaac and Rebecca, when in fear of his brother's treachery he had gone to Mesopotamia, drew nigh and rolled away the stone from the mouth of the well, and watered the flocks of Laban, his mother's brother. "And Jacob kissed Rachel, and lifted up his voice, and wept. And Jacob told Rachel that he was her father's brother, and that he was Rebekah's son." Here is an example of the rule already referred to, by which a nephew is called a brother. And again, "Laban said unto Jacob. Because thou art my brother, shouldest thou therefore serve me for nought? Tell me what shall thy wages be." And so, when, at the end of twenty years, without the knowledge of his father-in-law and accompanied by his wives and sons he was returning to his country, on Laban overtaking him in the mountain of Gilead and failing to find the idols which Rachel hid among the baggage, Jacob answered and said to Laban, "What is my trespass? What is my sin, that thou hast so hotly pursued after me? Whereas thou hast felt all about my stuff, what hast thou found of all thy household stuff? Set it here before my brethren and thy brethren, that they may judge betwixt us two." Tell me who are those brothers of Jacob and Laban who were present there? Esau, Jacob's brother, was certainly not there, and Laban, the son of Bethuel, had no brothers although he had a sister Rebecca.

17. Innumerable instances of the same kind are to be found in the sacred books. But, to be brief, I will return to the last of the four classes of brethren, those, namely, who are brethren by affection, and these again fall into two divisions, those of the spiritual and those of the general relationship. I say *spiritual* because all of us Christians are called brethren, as in the verse, "Behold, how good and how pleasant it is for brethren to dwell together in unity." And in another psalm the Savior says, "I will declare thy name unto my brethren." And elsewhere, "Go unto my brethren and say to them." I say also *general*, because we are all children of one Father, there is a like bond of brotherhood between us all. "Tell these who hate you," says the prophet, "ye are our brethren." And the Apostle writing to the Corinthians: "If any man that is named brother be a fornicator, or covetous, or an idolater, or a reviler, or a drunkard, or an extortioner: with such a one no, not to eat." I now ask to which class you consider the Lord's brethren in the Gospel must be assigned. They are brethren by nature, you say. But Scripture does not say so; it calls them neither sons of Mary, nor of Joseph. Shall we say they are

brethren by race? But it is absurd to suppose that a few Jews were called His brethren when all Jews of the time might upon this principle have borne the title. Were they brethren by virtue of close intimacy and the union of heart and mind? If that were so, who were more truly His brethren than the apostles who received His private instruction and were called by Him His mother and His brethren? Again, if all men, as such, were His brethren, it would have been foolish to deliver a special message, "Behold, thy brethren seek thee," for all men alike were entitled to the name. The only alternative is to adopt the previous explanation and understand them to be called brethren in virtue of the bond of kindred, not of love and sympathy, nor by prerogative of race, nor yet by nature. Just as Lot was called Abraham's brother, and Jacob Laban's, just as the daughters of Zelophehad received a lot among their brethren, just as Abraham himself had to wife Sarah his sister, for he says, "She is indeed my sister, on the father's side, not on the mother's," that is to say, she was the daughter of his brother, not of his sister. Otherwise, what are we to say of Abraham, a just man, taking to wife the daughter of his own father? Scripture, in relating the history of the men of early times, does not outrage our ears by speaking of the enormity in express terms, but prefers to leave it to be inferred by the reader: and God afterwards gives to the prohibition the sanction of the law, and threatens, "He who takes his sister, born of his father, or of his mother, and beholds her nakedness, hath committed abomination, he shall be utterly destroyed. He hath uncovered his sister's nakedness, he shall bear his sin."

18. There are things which, in your extreme ignorance, you had never read, and therefore you

neglected the whole range of Scripture and employed your madness in outraging the Virgin, like the man in the story who being unknown to everybody and finding that he could devise no good deed by which to gain renown, burned the temple of Diana: and when no one revealed the sacrilegious act, it is said that he himself went up and down proclaiming that he was the man who had applied the fire. The rulers of Ephesus were curious to know what made him do this thing, whereupon he replied that if he could not have fame for good deeds, all men should give him credit for bad ones. Grecian history relates the incident. But you do worse. You have set on fire the temple of the Lord's body, you have defiled the sanctuary of the Holy Spirit from which you are determined to make a team of four brethren and a heap of sisters come forth. In a word, joining in the chorus of the Jews, you say, "Is not this the carpenter's son? is not his mother called Mary? and his brethren James, and Joseph, and Simon, and Judas? and his sisters, are they not all with us? The word *all* would not be used if there were not a crowd of them." Pray tell me, who, before you appeared, was acquainted with this blasphemy? who thought the theory worth two-pence? You have gained your desire, and are become notorious by crime. For myself who am your opponent, although we live in the same city, I don't know, as the saying is, whether you are white or black. I pass over faults of diction which abound in every book you write. I say not a word about your absurd introduction. Good heavens! I do not ask for eloquence, since, having none yourself, you applied for a supply of it to your brother Craterius. I do not ask for grace of style, I look for purity of soul: for with Christians it is the greatest of solecisms and of vices of style to introduce anything base either in word or action. I am come to the conclusion of my argument. I will deal with you as though I had as yet prevailed nothing; and you will find yourself on the horns of a dilemma. It is clear that our Lord's brethren bore the name in the same way that Joseph was called his father: "I and thy father sought thee sorrowing." It was His mother who said this, not the Jews. The Evangelist himself relates that His father and His mother were marveling at the things which were spoken concerning Him, and there are similar passages which we have already quoted in which Joseph and Mary are called his parents. Seeing that you have been foolish enough to persuade yourself that the Greek manuscripts are corrupt, you will perhaps plead the diversity of readings. I therefore come to the Gospel of John, and there it is plainly written, "Philip finds Nathanael, and says to him, We have found him of whom Moses in the law, and the prophets did write, Jesus of Nazareth, the son of Joseph." You will certainly find this in your manuscript. Now tell me, how is Jesus the son of Joseph when it is clear that He was begotten of the Holy Ghost? Was Joseph His true father? Dull as you are, you will not venture to say that. Was he His reputed father? If so, let the same rule be applied to them when they are called brethren, that you apply to Joseph when he is called father.

19. Now that I have cleared the rocks and shoals I must spread sail and make all speed to reach his epilogue. Feeling himself to be a smatterer, he there produces Tertullian as a witness and quotes the words of Victorinus bishop of Petavium. Of Tertullian I say no more than that he did not belong to the Church. But as regards Victorinus, I assert what has already been proved from the Gospel—that he spoke of the brethren of the Lord not as

being sons of Mary, but brethren in the sense I have explained, that is to say, brethren in point of kinship not by nature. We are, however, spending our strength on trifles, and, leaving the fountain of truth, are following the tiny streams of opinion. Might I not array against you the whole series of ancient writers? Ignatius, Polycarp, Irenaeus, Justin Martyr, and many other apostolic and eloquent men, who against Ebion, Theodotus of Byzantium, and Valentinus, held these same views, and wrote volumes replete with wisdom. If you had ever read what they wrote, you would be a wiser man. But I think it better to reply briefly to each point than to linger any longer and extend my book to an undue length.

20. I now direct the attack against the passage in which, wishing to show your cleverness, you institute a comparison between virginity and marriage. I could not forbear smiling, and I thought of the proverb, *did you ever see a camel dance?* "Are virgins better," you ask, "than Abraham, Isaac, and Jacob, who were married men? Are not infants daily fashioned by the hands of God in the wombs of their mothers? And if so, are we bound to blush at the thought of Mary having a husband after she was delivered? If they find any disgrace in this, they ought not consistently even to believe that God was born of the Virgin by natural delivery. For according to them there is more dishonor in a virgin giving birth to God by the organs of generation, than in a virgin being joined to her own husband after she has been delivered." Add, if you like, Helvidius, the other humiliations of nature, the womb for nine months growing larger, the sickness, the delivery, the blood, the swaddling-clothes. Picture to yourself the infant in the enveloping membranes. Introduce into your picture the hard manger, the wailing

of the infant, the circumcision on the eighth day, the time of purification, so that he may be proved to be unclean. We do not blush, we are not put to silence. The greater the humiliations He endured for me, the more I owe Him. And when you have given every detail, you will be able to produce nothing more shameful than the cross, which we confess, in which we believe, and by which we triumph over our enemies.

21. But as we do not deny what is written, so we do reject what is not written. We believe that God was born of the Virgin, because we read it. That Mary was married after she brought forth, we do not believe, because we do not read it. Nor do we say this to condemn marriage, for virginity itself is the fruit of marriage; but because when we are dealing with saints we must not judge rashly. If we adopt possibility as the standard of judgment, we might maintain that Joseph had several wives because Abraham had, and so had Jacob, and that the Lord's brethren were the issue of those wives, an invention which some hold with a rashness which springs from audacity not from piety. You say that Mary did not continue a virgin: I claim still more, that Joseph himself on account of Mary was a virgin, so that from a virgin wedlock a virgin son was born. For if as a holy man he does not come under the imputation of fornication, and it is nowhere written that he had another wife, but was the guardian of Mary whom he was supposed to have to wife rather than her husband, the conclusion is that he who was thought worthy to be called father of the Lord, remained a virgin.

22. And now that I am about to institute a comparison between virginity and marriage, I beseech my readers not to suppose that in praising virginity I have in

the least disparaged marriage, and separated the saints of the Old Testament from those of the New, that is to say, those who had wives and those who altogether refrained from the embraces of women: I rather think that in accordance with the difference in time and circumstance one rule applied to the former, another to us upon whom the ends of the world have come. So long as that law remained, "Be fruitful, and multiply and replenish the earth"; and "Cursed is the barren woman that bears not seed in Israel," they all married and were given in marriage, left father and mother, and became one flesh. But once in tones of thunder the words were heard, "The time is shortened, that henceforth those that have wives may be as though they had none": cleaving to the Lord, we are made one spirit with Him. And why? Because "He that is unmarried is careful for the things of the Lord, how he may please the Lord: but he that is married is careful for the things of the world, how he may please his wife. And there is a difference also between the wife and the virgin. She that is unmarried is careful for the things of the Lord, that she may be holy both in body and in spirit: but she that is married is careful for the things of the world, how she may please her husband." Why do you cavil? Why do you resist? The vessel of election says this; he tells us that there is a difference between the wife and the virgin. Observe what the happiness of that state must be in which even the distinction of sex is lost. The virgin is no longer called a woman. "She that is unmarried is careful for the things of the Lord, that she may be holy both in body and in spirit." A virgin is defined as she that is holy in body and in spirit, for it is no good to have virgin flesh if a woman be married in mind.

"But she that is married is careful for the things of the world, how she may please her husband." Do you think there is no difference between one who spends her time in prayer and fasting, and one who must, at her husband's approach, make up her countenance, walk with mincing gait, and feign a shew of endearment? The virgin's aim is to appear less comely; she will wrong herself so as to hide her natural attractions. The married woman has the paint laid on before her mirror, and, to the insult of her Maker, strives to acquire something more than her natural beauty. Then come the prattling of infants, the noisy household, children watching for her word and waiting for her kiss, the reckoning up of expenses, the preparation to meet the outlay. On one side you will see a company of cooks, girded for the onslaught and attacking the meat: there you may hear the hum of a multitude of weavers. Meanwhile a message is delivered that the husband and his friends have arrived. The wife, like a swallow, flies all over the house. "She has to see to everything. Is the sofa smooth? Is the pavement swept? Are the flowers in the cups? Is dinner ready?" Tell me, pray, where amid all this is there room for the thought of God? Are these happy homes? Where there is the beating of drums, the noise and clatter of pipe and lute, the clanging of cymbals, can any fear of God be found? The parasite is snubbed and feels proud of the honor. Enter next the half-naked victims of the passions, a mark for every lustful eye. The unhappy wife must either take pleasure in them, and perish, or be displeased, and provoke her husband. Hence arises discord, the seed-plot of divorce. Or suppose you find me a house where these things are unknown, which is a *rara avis* indeed! yet even there the very management of the household, the education of the children, the wants of the husband, the correction of the servants, cannot fail to call away the mind from the thought of God. "It had ceased to be with Sarah after the manner of women": so the Scripture says, and afterwards Abraham received the command, "In all that Sarah saith unto thee, hearken unto her voice." She who is not subject to the anxiety and pain of child-bearing and having passed the change of life has ceased to perform the functions of a woman, is freed from the curse of God: nor is her desire to her husband, but on the contrary her husband becomes subject to her, and the voice of the Lord commands him, "In all that Sarah saith unto thee, hearken unto her voice." Thus they begin to have time for prayer. For so long as the debt of marriage is paid, earnest prayer is neglected.

23. I do not deny that holy women are found both among widows and those who have husbands; but they are such as have ceased to be wives, or such as, even in the close bond of marriage, imitate virgin chastity. The Apostle, Christ speaking in him, briefly bore witness to this when he said, "She that is unmarried is careful for the things of the Lord, how she may please the Lord: but she that is married is careful for the things of the world, how she may please her husband." He leaves us the free exercise of our reason in the matter. He lays no necessity upon anyone nor leads anyone into a snare: he only persuades to that which is proper when he wishes all men to be as himself. He had not, it is true, a commandment from the Lord respecting virginity, for that grace surpasses the unassisted power of man, and it would have worn an air of immodesty to force men to fly in the face of nature, and to say in other words, I want you to be what the angels are. It is this angelic purity which secures to

virginity its highest reward, and the Apostle might have seemed to despise a course of life which involves no guilt. Nevertheless in the immediate context he adds, "But I give my judgment, as one that hath obtained mercy of the Lord to be faithful. I think therefore that this is good by reason of the present distress, namely, that it is good for a man to be as he is." What is meant by *present distress?* "Woe unto them that are with child and to them that give suck in those days!" The reason why the wood grows up is that it may be cut down. The field is sown that it may be reaped. The world is already full, and the population is too large for the soil. Every day we are being cut down by war, snatched away by disease, swallowed up by shipwreck, although we go to law with one another about the fences of our property. It is only one addition to the general rule which is made by those who follow the Lamb, and who have not defiled their garments, for they have continued in their virgin state. Notice the meaning of *defiling.* I shall not venture to explain it, for fear Helvidius may be abusive. I agree with you, when you say, that some virgins are nothing but tavern women; I say still more, that even adulteresses may be found among them, and, you will no doubt be still more surprised to hear, that some of the clergy are inn-keepers and some monks unchaste. Who does not at once understand that a tavern woman cannot be a virgin, nor an adulterer a monk, nor a clergy-man a tavern-keeper? Are we to blame virginity if its counterfeit is at fault? For my part, to pass over other persons and come to the virgin, I maintain that she who is engaged in huckstering, though for anything I know she may be a virgin in body, is no longer one in spirit.

24. I have become rhetorical, and have disported myself a little like a platform orator. You compelled me, Helvidius; for, brightly as the Gospel shines at the present day, you will have it that equal glory attaches to virginity and to the marriage state. And because I think that, finding the truth too strong for you, you will turn to disparaging my life and abusing my character (it is the way of weak women to talk tittle-tattle in corners when they have been put down by their masters), I shall anticipate you. I assure you that I shall regard your railing as a high distinction, since the same lips that assail me have disparaged Mary, and I, a servant of the Lord, am favored with the same barking eloquence as His mother.

Against Jovinianus.

Book I.

Jovinianus, concerning whom we know little more than is to be found in the two following books, had published at Rome a Latin treatise containing all, or part of the opinions here controverted, viz. (1) "That a virgin is no better as such than a wife in the sight of God. (2) Abstinence is no better than a thankful partaking of food. (3) A person baptized with the Spirit as well as with water cannot sin. (4) All sins are equal. (5) There is but one grade of punishment and one of reward in the future state." In addition to this he held the birth of our Lord to have been by a "true parturition," and was thus at issue with the orthodoxy of the time, according to which the infant Jesus passed through the walls of the womb as His Resurrection body afterwards did out of the tomb or through the closed doors. Pammachius, Jerome's friend, brought Jovinian's book under the notice of Siricius, bishop of Rome, and it was shortly afterwards condemned in synods at that city and at Milan (about a.d. 390). He subsequently sent Jovinian's books to Jerome, who answered them in the present treatise in the year 393. Nothing more is known of Jovinian, but it has been conjectured from Jerome's remark in the treatise against Vigilantius, where Jovinian is said to have "amidst pheasants and pork rather belched out than breathed out his life," and by a kind of transmigration to have transmitted his opinions into Vigilantius, that he had died before 409, the date of that work.

The first book is wholly on the first proposition of Jovinianus, that relating to marriage and virginity. The first three chapters are introductory. The rest may be divided into three parts:

 1 (ch. 4–13). An exposition, in Jerome's sense, of St. Paul's teaching in 1 Cor. vii.
 2 (ch. 14–39). A statement of the teaching which Jerome derives from the various books of both the Old and the New Testaments.
 3. A denunciation of Jovinianus (c. 40), and the praises of virginity and of single marriages derived from examples in the heathen world.

The treatise gives a remarkable specimen of Jerome's system of interpreting Scripture, and also of the methods by which asceticism was introduced into the Church, and marriage brought into disesteem.

St. Jerome

1. Very few days have elapsed since the holy brethren of Rome sent to me the treatises of a certain Jovinian with the request that I would reply to the follies contained in them, and would crush with evangelical and apostolic vigor the Epicurus of Christianity. I read but could not in the least comprehend them. I began therefore to give them closer attention, and to thoroughly sift not only words and sentences, but almost every single syllable; for I wished first to ascertain his meaning, and then to approve, or refute what he had said. But the style is so barbarous, and the language so vile and such a heap of blunders, that I could neither understand what he was talking about, nor by what arguments he was trying to prove his points. At one moment he is all bombast, at another he grovels: from time to time he lifts himself up, and then like a wounded snake finds his own effort too much for him. Not satisfied with the language of men, he attempts something loftier.

"The mountains labor; a poor mouse is born."
"That he's gone mad ev'n mad Orestes swears."

Moreover he involves everything in such inextricable confusion that the saying of Plautus might be applied to him:—"This is what none but a Sibyl will ever read."

To understand him we must be prophets. We read Apollo's raving prophetesses. We remember, too, what Virgil says of senseless noise. Heraclitus, also, surnamed the Obscure, the philosophers find hard to understand even with their utmost toil. But what are they compared with our riddle-maker, whose books are much more difficult to comprehend than to refute? Although (we must confess) the task of refuting them is no easy one. For how can you overcome a man when you are quite in the dark as to his meaning? But, not to be tedious to my reader, the introduction to his second book, of which he has discharged himself like a sot after a night's debauch, will show the character of his eloquence, and through what bright flowers of rhetoric he takes his stately course.

2. "I respond to your invitation, not that I may go through life with a high reputation, but may live free from idle rumour. I beseech the ground, the young shoots of our plantations, the plants and trees of tenderness snatched from the whirlpool of vice, to grant me audience and the support of many listeners. We know that the Church through hope, faith, charity, is inaccessible and impregnable. In it no one is immature: all are apt to learn: none can force a way into it by violence, or deceive it by craft."

3. What, I ask, is the meaning of these portentous words and of this grotesque description? Would you not think he was in a feverish dream, or that he was seized with madness and ought to be put into the strait jacket which Hippocrates prescribed? However often I read him, even till my heart sinks within me, I am still in uncertainty of his meaning. Everything starts from, everything depends upon, something else. It is impossible to make out any connection; and, excepting the proofs from Scripture which he has not dared to exchange for his own lovely flowers of rhetoric, his words suit all matter equally well, because they suit no matter at all. This circumstance led me shrewdly to suspect that his object in proclaiming the excellence of marriage was only to disparage virginity. For when the less is put upon a level with the greater, the lower profits by comparison, but the

St. Jerome

higher suffers wrong. For ourselves, we do not follow the views of Marcion and Manichæus, and disparage marriage; nor, deceived by the error of Tatian, the leader of the Encratites, do we think all intercourse impure; he condemns and rejects not only marriage but also food which God created for the use of man. We know that in a great house, there are not only vessels of gold and silver, but also of wood and earthenware. And that upon the foundation, Christ, which Paul the master-builder laid, some build gold, silver, precious stones: others, on the contrary, hay, wood, straw. We are not ignorant of the words, "Marriage is honorable among all, and the bed undefiled." We have read God's first command, "Be fruitful, and multiply, and replenish the earth"; but while we honor marriage we prefer virginity which is the offspring of marriage. Will silver cease to be silver, if gold is more precious than silver? Or is despite done to tree and corn, if we prefer the fruit to root and foliage, or the grain to stalk and ear? Virginity is to marriage what fruit is to the tree, or grain to the straw. Although the hundred-fold, the sixty-fold, and the thirty-fold spring from one earth and from one sowing, yet there is a great difference in respect of number. The thirty-fold has reference to marriage. The very way the 4266 fingers are combined—see how they seem to embrace, tenderly kiss, and pledge their troth either to other—is a picture of husband and wife. The sixty-fold applies to widows, because they are placed in a position of difficulty and distress. Hence the upper finger signifies their depression, and the greater the difficulty in resisting the allurements of pleasure once experienced, the greater the reward. Moreover (give good heed, my reader), to denote a hundred, the right hand is used instead of the left: a circle is made with the same fingers which on the left-hand represented widowhood, and thus the crown of virginity is expressed. In saying this I have followed my own impatient spirit rather than the course of the argument. For I had scarcely left harbor, and had barely hoisted sail, when a swelling tide of words suddenly swept me into the depths of the discussion. I must stay my course, and take in canvas for a little while; nor will I indulge my sword, anxious as it is to strike a blow for virginity. The farther back the catapult is drawn, the greater the force of the missile. To linger is not to lose, if by lingering victory is better assured. I will briefly set forth our adversary's views, and will drag them out from his books like snakes from the holes where they hide, and will separate the venomous head from the writhing body. What is baneful shall be discovered, that, when we have the power, it may be crushed.

He says that "virgins, widows, and married women, who have been once passed through the laver of Christ, if they are on a par in other respects, are of equal merit."

He endeavors to show that "they who with full assurance of faith have been born again in baptism, cannot be overthrown by the devil."

His third point is "that there is no difference between abstinence from food, and its reception with thanksgiving."

The fourth and last is "that there is one reward in the kingdom of heaven for all who have kept their baptismal vow."

4. This is the hissing of the old serpent; by counsel such as this the dragon drove man from Paradise. For he promised that if they would prefer fulness to fasting they should be immortal, as though it were an impossibility for them to fall; and while he promises they shall be as Gods, he drives them from Paradise, with the result that they who, while naked and unhampered, and as virgins unspotted enjoyed the fellowship of the Lord were cast down into the vale of tears, and sewed skins together to clothe themselves withal. But, not to detain the reader any longer, I will keep to the division given above and taking his propositions one by one will rely chiefly on the evidence of Scripture to refute them, for fear he may chatter and complain that he was overcome by rhetorical skill

rather than by force of truth. If I succeed in this and with the aid of a cloud of witnesses from both Testaments prove too strong for him, I will then accept his challenge, and adduce illustrations from secular literature. I will show that even among philosophers and distinguished statesmen, the virtuous are wont to be preferred by all to the voluptuous, that is to say men like Pythagoras, Plato and Aristides, to Aristippus, Epicurus and Alcibiades. I entreat virgins of both sexes and all such as are continent, the married also and the twice married, to assist my efforts with their prayers. Jovinian is the common enemy. For he who maintains all to be of equal merit, does no less injury to virginity in comparing it with marriage than he does to marriage, when he allows it to be lawful, but to the same extent as second and third marriages. But to digamists and trigamists also he does wrong, for he places on a level with them whoremongers and the most licentious persons as soon as they have repented; but perhaps those who have been married twice or thrice ought not to complain, for the same whoremonger if penitent is made equal in the kingdom of heaven even to virgins. I will therefore explain more clearly and in proper sequence the arguments he employs and the illustrations he adduces respecting marriage, and will treat them in the order in which he states them. And I beg the reader not to be disturbed if he is compelled to read Jovinian's nauseating trash. He will all the more gladly drink Christ's antidote after the devil's poisonous concoction. Listen with patience, ye virgins; listen, I pray you, to the voice of the most voluptuous of preachers; nay rather close your ears, as you would to the Syren's fabled songs, and pass on. For a little while endure the wrongs you suffer: think you are crucified with Christ, and are listening to the blasphemies of the Pharisees.

5. First of all, he says, God declares that "therefore shall a man leave his father and his mother, and shall cleave unto his wife: and they shall be one flesh." And lest we should say that this is a quotation from the Old Testament, he asserts that it has been confirmed by the Lord in the Gospel—"What God hath joined together, let not man put asunder": and he immediately adds, "Be fruitful, and multiply, and replenish the earth." He next repeats the names of Seth, Enos, Cainan, Mahalalel, Jared, Enoch, Methuselah, Lamech, Noah, and tells us that they all had wives and in accordance with the will of God begot sons, as though there could be any table of descent or any history of mankind without wives and children. "There," says he, "is Enoch, who walked with God and was carried up to heaven. There is Noah, the only person who, except his wife, and his sons and their wives, was saved at the deluge, although there must have been many persons not of marriageable age, and therefore presumably virgins. Again, after the deluge, when the human race started as it were anew, men and women were paired together and a fresh blessing was pronounced on procreation, "Be fruitful, and multiply, and replenish the earth." Moreover, free permission was given to eat flesh, "Every moving thing that lives shall be food for you; as the green herb have I given you all." He then flies off to Abraham, Isaac, and Jacob, of whom the first had three wives, the second one, the third four, Leah, Rachel, Billah, and Zilpah, and he declares that Abraham by his faith merited the blessing which he received in begetting his son. Sarah, typifying the Church, when it had ceased to be with her after the manner of women, exchanged the

curse of barrenness for the blessing of child-bearing. We are informed that Rebekah went like a prophet to inquire of the Lord, and was told, "Two nations and two peoples are in thy womb," that Jacob served for his wife, and that when Rachel, thinking it was in the power of her husband to give her children, said, "Give me children, or else I die," he replied, "Am I in God's stead, who hath withheld from thee the fruit of the womb?" so well aware was he that the fruit of marriage cometh from the Lord and not from the husband. We next learn that Joseph, a holy man of spotless chastity, and all the patriarchs, had wives, and that God blessed them all alike through the lips of Moses. Judah also and Thamar are brought upon the scene, and he censures Onan, slain by the Lord, because he, grudging to raise up seed to his brother, marred the marriage rite. He refers to Moses and the leprosy of Miriam, who, because she chided her brother on account of his wife, was stricken by the avenging hand of God. He praises Samson, I may even say extravagantly panegyrizes the uxorious Nazarite. Deborah also and Barak are mentioned, because, although they had not the benefit of virginity, they were victorious over the iron chariots of Sisera and Jabin. He brings forward Jael, the wife of Heber the Kenite, and extols her for arming herself with the stake. He says there was no difference between Jephthah and his virgin daughter, who was sacrificed to the Lord: nay, of the two, he prefers the faith of the father to that of the daughter who met death with grief and tears. He then comes to Samuel, another Nazarite of the Lord, who from infancy was brought up in the tabernacle and was clad in a linen ephod, or, as the words are rendered, *in linen vestments:* he, too, we are told, begot sons without a stain upon his priestly purity. He places Boaz and his wife Ruth side by side in his repository, and traces the descent of Jesse and David from them. He then points out how David himself, for the price of two hundred foreskins and at the peril of his life, was bedded with the king's daughter. What shall I say of Solomon, whom he includes in the list of husbands, and represents as a type of the Savior, maintaining that of him it was written, "Give the king thy judgments, O God, and thy righteousness unto the king's son"? And "To him shall be given of the gold of Sheba, and men shall pray for him continually." Then all at once he makes a jump to Elijah and Elisha, and tells us as a great secret that the spirit of Elijah rested on Elisha. Why he mentioned this he does not say. It can hardly be that he thinks Elijah and Elisha, like the rest, were married men. The next step is to Hezekiah, upon whose praises he dwells, and yet (I wonder why) forgets to mention that he said, "Henceforth I will beget children." He relates that Josiah, a righteous man, in whose time the book of Deuteronomy was found in the temple, was instructed by Huldah, wife of Shallum. Daniel also and the three youths are classed by him with the married. Suddenly he betakes himself to the Gospel, and adduces Zachariah and Elizabeth, Peter and his father-in-law, and the rest of the Apostles. His inference is thus expressed: "If they idly urge in defence of themselves the plea that the world in its early stage needed to be replenished, let them listen to the words of Paul, 'I desire therefore that the younger widows marry, bear children.' And 'Marriage is honorable and the bed undefiled.' And 'A wife is bound for so long time as her husband lives; but if the husband be dead, she is free to be married to whom she will; only in the Lord.' And 'Adam was not beguiled, but the woman being beguiled hath fallen into transgression: but she shall be saved through the child-bearing, if they continue in faith and love and sanctification with sobriety.' Surely we shall hear no more of the famous Apostolic utterance, 'And they who have wives as though they had them not.' It can hardly be that you will say the reason why he wished them to be married was that some widows had already turned back after Satan: as though virgins never fell and their fall was not more ruinous. All this makes it clear that in forbidding to marry, and to eat food which God created for use, you have consciences seared as with a hot iron, and are followers of the Manicheans." Then comes much more which it would be unprofitable to discuss. At last he dashes into rhetoric and apostrophizes virginity thus: "I do you no wrong, Virgin: you have chosen a life of chastity on account of the present distress: you determined on the course in order to be holy in body and spirit: be not proud: you and your married sisters are members of the same Church."

6. I have perhaps explained his position at too great a length, and become tedious to my reader; but I thought it best to draw up in full array against myself all his efforts, and to muster all the forces of the enemy with their squadrons and generals, lest after an early victory there should spring up a series of other engagements. I will not therefore do battle with single foes, nor will I be satisfied with skirmishes in which I meet small detachments of my opponents. The battle must be fought with the whole army of the enemy, and the disorderly rabble, fighting more like brigands than soldiers, must be repulsed by the skill and method of regular warfare. In the front rank I will set the Apostle Paul, and, since he is the bravest of generals, will arm him with his own weapons,

that is to say, his own statements. For the Corinthians asked many questions about this matter, and the doctor of the Gentiles and master of the Church gave full replies. What he decreed we may regard as the law of Christ speaking in him. At the same time, when we begin to refute the several arguments, I trust the reader will give me his attention even before the Apostle speaks, and will not, in his eagerness to discuss the most weighty points, neglect the premises, and rush at once to the conclusion.

7. Among other things the Corinthians asked in their letter whether after embracing the faith of Christ they ought to be unmarried, and for the sake of continence put away their wives, and whether believing virgins were at liberty to marry. And again, supposing that one of two Gentiles believed on Christ, whether the one that believed should leave the one that believed not? And in case it were allowable to take wives, would the Apostle direct that only Christian wives, or Gentiles also, should be taken? Let us then consider Paul's replies to these inquiries. "Now concerning the things whereof ye wrote: It is good for a man not to touch a woman. But, because of fornications, let each man have his own wife, and let each woman have her own husband. Let the husband render unto the wife her due: and likewise also the wife unto the husband. The wife hath not power over her own body, but the husband: And likewise also the husband hath not power over his own body, but the wife. Defraud ye not one the other, except it be by consent for a season, that ye may give yourselves unto prayer, and may be together again, that Satan tempt you not because of your incontinency. But this I say by way of permission not of commandment. Yet I would that all men were even as I myself. Howbeit each man hath his own gift from God,

one after this manner, and another after that. But I say to the unmarried and to widows, it is good for them if they abide even as I. But if they have not continency, let them marry: for it is better to marry than to burn." Let us turn back to the chief point of the evidence: "It is good," he says, "for a man not to touch a woman." If it is good not to touch a woman, it is bad to touch one: for there is no opposite to goodness but badness. But if it be bad and the evil is pardoned, the reason for the concession is to prevent worse evil. But surely a thing which is only allowed because there may be something worse has only a slight degree of goodness. He would never have added "let each man have his own wife," unless he had previously used the words "but, because of fornications." Do away with fornication, and he will not say "let each man have his own wife." Just as though one were to lay it down: "It is good to feed on wheaten bread, and to eat the finest wheat flour," and yet to prevent a person pressed by hunger from devouring cow-dung, I may allow him to eat barley. Does it follow that the wheat will not have its peculiar purity, because such a one prefers barley to excrement? That is naturally good which does not admit of comparison with what is bad, and is not eclipsed because something else is preferred. At the same time we must notice the Apostle's prudence. He did not say, it is good not to have a wife: but, it is good not to touch a woman: as though there were danger even in the touch: as though he who touched her, would not escape from her who "hunted for the precious life," who caused the young man's understanding to fly away. "Can a man take fire in his bosom, and his clothes not be burned? Or can one walk upon hot coals, and his feet not be scorched?" As then he who touches fire is instantly burned, so by the mere touch the peculiar nature of man and woman is perceived, and the difference of sex is understood. Heathen fables relate how Mithras and Ericthonius were begotten of the soil, in stone or earth, by raging lust. Hence it was that our Joseph, because the Egyptian woman wished to touch him, fled from her hands, and, as if he had been bitten by a mad dog and feared the spreading poison, threw away the cloak which she had touched. "But, because of fornications let each man have his own wife, and let each woman have her own husband." He did not say, because of fornication let each man marry a wife: otherwise by this excuse he would have thrown the reins to lust, and whenever a man's wife died, he would have to marry another to prevent fornication, but "have his own wife." Let him he says have and use his own wife, whom he had before he became a believer, and whom it would have been good not to touch, and, when once he became a follower of Christ, to know only as a sister, not as a wife unless fornication should make it excusable to touch her. "The wife hath not power over her own body, but the husband: and likewise also the husband hath not power over his own body, but the wife." The whole question here concerns those who are married men. Is it lawful for them to do what our Lord forbade in the Gospel, and to put away their wives? Whence it is that the Apostle says, "It is good for a man not to touch a woman." But inasmuch as he who is once married has no power to abstain except by mutual consent, and may not reject an unoffending partner, let the husband render unto the wife her due. He bound himself voluntarily that he might be under compulsion to render it. "Defraud ye not one the other, except it be by consent for a season, that ye may give yourselves unto prayer." What, I pray you, is the quality of that good thing which hinders prayer? which does not allow the body of Christ to be received? So long as I do the husband's part, I fail in continency. The same Apostle in another place commands us to pray always. If we are to pray always, it follows that we must never be in the bondage of wedlock, for as often as I render my wife her due, I cannot pray. The Apostle Peter had experience of the bonds of marriage. See how he fashions the Church, and what lesson he teaches Christians: "Ye husbands in like manner dwell with your wives according to knowledge, giving honor unto the woman, as unto the weaker vessel, as being also joint-heirs of the grace of life; to the end that your prayers be not hindered." Observe that, as S. Paul before, because in both cases the spirit is the same, so S. Peter now, says that prayers are hindered by the performance of marriage duty. When he says "likewise," he challenges the husbands to imitate their wives, because he has already given them commandment: "beholding your chaste conversation coupled with fear. Whose adorning let it not be the outward adorning of plaiting the hair, and of wearing jewels of gold, or of putting on apparel: but let it be the hidden man of the heart, in the incorruptible apparel of a meek and quiet spirit, which is in the sight of God of great price." You see what kind of wedlock he enjoins. Husbands and wives are to dwell together according to knowledge, so that they may know what God wishes and desires, and give honor to the weak vessel, woman. If we abstain from intercourse, we give honor to our wives: if we do not abstain, it is clear that insult is the opposite of honor. He also tells the wives to let their husbands "see their chaste behavior, and the hidden man of the heart, in the incorruptible apparel of a meek and quiet spirit." Words truly worthy of an apostle, and of Christ's rock! He lays down the law for husbands and wives, condemns outward ornament, while he praises continence, which is the ornament of the inner man, as seen in the incorruptible apparel of a meek and quiet spirit. In effect he says this: Since your outer man is corrupt, and you have ceased to possess the blessing of incorruption characteristic of virgins, at least imitate the incorruption of the spirit by subsequent abstinence, and what you cannot show in the body exhibit in the mind. For these are the riches, and these the ornaments of your union, which Christ seeks.

8. The words which follow, "that ye may give yourselves unto prayer, and may be together again," might lead one to suppose that the Apostle was expressing a wish and not making a concession because of the danger of a greater fall. He therefore at once adds, "lest Satan tempt you for your incontinency." It is a fine permission which is conveyed in the words "be together again." What it was that he blushed to call by its own name, and thought only better than a temptation of Satan and the effect of incontinence, we take trouble to discuss as if it were obscure, although he has explained his meaning by saying, "this I say by way of permission, not by way of command." And do we still hesitate to speak of marriage as a concession to weakness, not a thing commanded, as though second and third marriages were not allowed on the same ground, as though the doors of the Church were not opened by repentance even to fornicators, and what is more, to the incestuous? Take the case of the man who outraged his step-mother. Does not the Apostle, after delivering him, in his first Epistle to the Corinthians, to Satan for the destruction of the flesh that his spirit might

be saved, in the second Epistle take the offender back and strive to prevent a brother from being swallowed up by overmuch grief. The Apostle's wish is one thing, his pardon another. If a wish be expressed, it confers a right; if a thing is only called pardonable, we are wrong in using it. If you wish to know the Apostle's real mind, you must take in what follows: "but I would that all men were as I am." Happy is the man who is like Paul! Fortunate is he who attends to the Apostle's command, not to his concession. This, says he, I wish, this I desire that ye be imitators of me, as I also am of Christ, who was a Virgin born of a Virgin, uncorrupt of her who was uncorrupt. We, because we are men, cannot imitate our Lord's nativity; but we may at least imitate His life. The former was the blessed prerogative of divinity, the latter belongs to our human condition and is part of human effort. I would that all men were like me, that while they are like me, they may also become like Christ, to whom I am like. For "he that believeth in Christ ought himself also to walk even as He walked." "Howbeit each man hath his own gift from God, one after this manner, and another after that." What I wish, he says, is clear. But since in the Church there is a diversity of gifts, I acquiesce in marriage, lest I should seem to condemn nature. At the same time consider, that the gift of virginity is one, that of marriage, another. For were the reward the same for the married and for virgins, he would never after enjoining continence have said: "Each man hath his own gift from God, one after this manner, and another after that." Where there is a distinction in one particular, there is a diversity also in other points. I grant that even marriage is a gift of God, but between gift and gift there is great diversity. In fact the Apostle himself speaking of the same person who had repented of his incestuous conduct, says: "so that contrariwise ye should rather forgive him and comfort him, and to whom ye forgive anything, I forgive also." And that we might not think a man's gift contemptible, he added, "for what I also have forgiven, if I have forgiven anything, for your sakes have I forgiven it, in the presence of Christ." There is diversity in the gifts of Christ. Hence it is that by way of type Joseph has a coat of many colors. And in the forty fifth psalm we read, "at thy right hand doth stand the queen in a vesture of gold wrought about with divers colors." And the Apostle Peter says, "as heirs together of the manifold grace of God," where the more expressive Greek word ποικίλης, i.e., *varied*, is used.

9. Then come the words "But I say to the unmarried and to widows, it is good for them if they abide even as I. But if they have not continency, let them marry: for it is better to marry than to burn." Having conceded to married persons the enjoyment of wedlock and pointed out his own wishes, he passes on to the unmarried and to widows, sets before them his own practice for imitation, and calls them happy if they so abide. "But if they have not continency, let them marry," just as he said before "But because of fornications," and "Lest Satan tempt you, because of your incontinency." And he gives a reason for saying "If they have not continency, let them marry," viz. "It is better to marry than to burn." The reason why it is better to marry is that it is worse to burn. Let burning lust be absent, and he will not say it is better to marry. The word *better* always implies a comparison with something worse, not a thing absolutely good and incapable of comparison. It is as though he said, it is better to have one eye than neither, it is better to stand on one foot and to support the rest of the body with a stick, than to crawl

with broken legs. What do you say, Apostle? I do not believe you when you say, "Though I be rude in speech, yet am I not in knowledge." As humility is the source of the sayings "For I am not worthy to be called an Apostle," and "To me who am the least of the Apostles," and "As to one born out of due time," so here also we have an utterance of humility. You know the meaning of language, or you would not quote Epimenides, Menander, and Aratus. When you are discussing continence and virginity you say, "It is good for a man not to touch a woman." And, "It is good for them if they abide even as I." And, "I think that this is good by reason of the present distress." And, "That it is good for a man so to be." When you come to marriage, you do not say it is good to marry, because you cannot then add *"than to burn;"* but you say, "It is better to marry than to burn." If marriage in itself be good, do not compare it with fire, but simply say "It is good to marry." I suspect the goodness of that thing which is forced into the position of being only the lesser of two evils. What I want is not a smaller evil, but a thing absolutely good.

10. So far the first section has been explained. Let us now come to those which follow. "But unto the married I give charge, yea not I, but the Lord. That the wife depart not from her husband (but and if she depart, let her remain unmarried, or else be reconciled to her husband): and that the husband leave not his wife. But to the rest say I, not the Lord: If any brother hath an unbelieving wife, and she is content to dwell with him, let him not leave her," and so on to the words "As God hath called each, so let him walk. And so ordain I in all the churches." This passage has no bearing on our present controversy. For he ordains, according to the mind of the

Lord, that excepting the cause of fornication, a wife must not be put away, and that a wife who has been put away, may not, so long as her husband lives, be married to another, or at all events that her duty is to be reconciled to her husband. But in the case of those who are already married at the time of conversion, that is to say, supposing one of the two were a believer, he enjoins that the believer shall not put away the unbeliever. And after stating his reason, *viz.,* that the unbeliever who is unwilling to leave the believer becomes thereby a candidate for the faith, he commands, on the other hand, that if the unbeliever reject the faithful one on account of the faith of Christ, the believer ought to depart, lest husband or wife be preferred to Christ, in comparison with Whom we must hold even life itself cheap. Yet at the present day many women despising the Apostle's command, are joined to heathen husbands, and prostitute the temples of Christ to idols. They do not understand that they are part of His body though indeed they are His ribs. The Apostle is lenient to the union of unbelievers, who having (believing) husbands, afterwards come to believe in Christ. He does not extend his indulgence to those women who, although Christians, have been married to heathen husbands. To these he elsewhere says, "Be not unequally yoked with unbelievers: for what fellowship have righteousness and iniquity? or what communion hath light with darkness? And what concord hath Christ with Belial? or what portion hath a believer with an unbeliever? And what agreement hath a temple of God with idols? For we are a temple of the living God." Although I know that crowds of matrons will be furious against me: although I know that just as they have shamelessly despised the Lord, so they will rave at me who am but a flea and the least of

Christians: yet I will speak out what I think. I will say what the Apostle has taught me, that they are not on the side of righteousness, but of iniquity: not of light, but of darkness: that they do not belong to Christ, but to Belial: that they are not temples of the living God, but shrines and idols of the dead. And, if you wish to see more clearly how utterly unlawful it is for a Christian woman to marry a Gentile, consider what the same Apostle says, "A wife is bound for so long time as her husband lives: but if the husband be dead, she is free to be married to whom she will; only in the Lord," that is, to a Christian. He who allows second and third marriages in the Lord, forbids first marriages with a Gentile. Whence Abraham also makes his servant swear upon his thigh, that is, on Christ, Who was to spring from his seed, that he would not bring an alien-born as a wife for his son Isaac. And Ezra checked an offence of this kind against God by making his countrymen put away their wives. And the prophet Malachi thus speaks, "Judah hath dealt treacherously, and an abomination is committed in Israel and in Jerusalem; for Judah hath profaned the holiness of the Lord which he loveth, and hath married the daughter of a strange god. The Lord will cut off the man that doeth this, him that teaches and him that learns, out of the tents of Jacob, and him that offers an offering unto the Lord of hosts." I have said this that they who compare marriage with virginity, may at least know that such marriages as these are on a lower level than digamy and trigamy.

11. In the above discussion the Apostle has taught that the believer ought not to depart from the unbeliever, but remain in marriage as the faith found them, and that each man whether married or single should continue as he was when baptized into Christ; and then he suddenly

introduces the metaphors of circumcision and uncircumcision, of bond and free, and under those metaphors treats of the married and unmarried. "Was any man called being circumcised? let him not become uncircumcised. Circumcision is nothing, and uncircumcision is nothing: but the keeping of the commandments of God. Let each man abide in that calling wherein he was called. Wast thou called being a bondservant? Care not for it: but even if thou canst become free, use it rather. For he that was called in the Lord being a bondservant, is the Lord's freedman; likewise he that was called, being free, is Christ's bondservant. Ye were bought with a price; become not bondservants of men. Brethren, let each man, wherein he was called, therein abide with God." Some, I suppose, will find fault with the Apostle's way of reasoning. I would therefore ask first, What we are to infer from his suddenly passing in a discussion concerning husbands and wives to a comparison of Jew and Gentile, bond and free, and then returning, when this point is settled, to the question about virgins, and telling us "Concerning virgins I have no commandment from the Lord"; what has a comparison of Jew and Gentile, bond and free, to do with wedlock and virginity? In the next place, how are we to understand the words "Hath any been called in uncircumcision, let him not be circumcised"? Can a man who has lost his foreskin restore it again at his pleasure? Then, in what sense are we to explain "For he that was called in the Lord, being a bondservant, is the Lord's freedman: likewise he that was called, being free, is Christ's bondservant." Fourthly, how is it that he who commanded servants to obey their masters according to the flesh, now says, "Become not bondservants of men."

Lastly, how are we to connect with slavery, or with circumcision, his saying "Brethren, let each man, wherein he was called, therein abide with God," which even contradicts his previous opinion. We heard him say "Become not bondservants of men." How can we then possibly abide in that vocation wherein we were called, when many at the time they became believers had masters according to the flesh, whose bondservants they are now forbidden to be? Moreover, what has the argument about our abiding in the vocation wherein we were called, to do with circumcision? for in another place the same Apostle cries aloud "Behold I Paul tell you that, if ye be circumcised, Christ shall profit you nothing"? We must conclude, therefore, that a higher meaning should be given to circumcision and uncircumcision, bond and free, and that these words must be taken in close connection with what has gone before. "Was anyone called being circumcised? let him not become uncircumcised." If, he says, at the time you were called and became a believer in Christ, if I say, you were called being circumcised from a wife, that is, unmarried, do not marry a wife, that is, do not become uncircumcised, lest you lay upon the freedom of circumcision and chastity the burden of marriage. Again, if anyone was called in uncircumcision, let him not be circumcised. You had a wife, he says, when you believed: do not think the faith of Christ a reason for disagreement, because God called us in peace. "Circumcision is nothing, and uncircumcision is nothing; but the keeping of the commandments of God." For neither celibacy nor marriage availed anything without works, since even faith, which is specially characteristic of Christians, if it have not works, is said to be dead, and vestal virgins and Juno's widows might upon these terms be numbered with the saints. "Let each man in the vocation wherein he was called, therein abide." Whether he had, or had not, a wife when he believed, let him remain in that condition in which he was when called. Accordingly he does not so strongly urge virgins to be married, as forbid divorce. And as he debars those who have wives from putting them away, so he cuts off from virgins the power of being married. "Thou was called being a slave, heed it not; but even if thou canst become free, use it rather." Even if you have, he says, a wife, and are bound to her, and pay her due, and have not power over your own body; or if, to speak more clearly, you are the bondservant of your wife, be not sad upon that account, nor sigh for the loss of your virginity. But even if you can find some causes of discord, do not, for the sake of thoroughly enjoying the liberty of chastity, seek your own welfare by destroying another. Keep your wife awhile, and do not go too fast for her lagging footsteps: wait till she follows. If you are patient, your spouse will become a sister, "For he that was called in the Lord, being a bondservant, is the Lord's freedman: likewise, he that was called being free, is Christ's bondservant." He gives his reasons for not wishing wives to be forsaken. He therefore says, I command that Gentiles who believe on Christ do not abandon the married state in which they were before embracing the faith: for he who had a wife when he became a believer, is not so strictly devoted to the service of God as virgins and unmarried persons. But, in a manner, he has more freedom, and the reins of his bondage are relaxed; and, while he is the bondservant of a wife, he is, so to speak, the freedman of the Lord. Moreover, he who when called by the Lord had not a wife and was free from the bondage of wedlock, he is truly

Christ's bondservant. What happiness to be the bondservant, not of a wife but of Christ, to serve not the flesh, but the spirit! "For he who is joined unto the Lord is one spirit." There was some fear that by saying "Wast thou called being a bondservant? Care not for it: but, even if thou canst become free, use it rather," he might seem to have flouted continence, and to have given us up to the slavery of marriage. He therefore makes a remark which removes all cavil: "Ye were bought with a price, become not servants of men." We have been redeemed with the most precious blood of Christ: the Lamb was slain for us, and having been sprinkled with hyssop and the warm drops of His blood, we have rejected poisonous pleasure. Why do we at whose baptism Pharaoh died and all his host was drowned, again turn back in our hearts to Egypt, and after the manna, angels' food, sigh for the garlic and the onions and the cucumbers, and Pharaoh's meat?

12. Having discussed marriage and continency he at length comes to virginity and says "Now concerning virgins I have no commandment of the Lord: but I give my judgement, as one that hath obtained mercy of the Lord to be faithful. I think therefore that this is good by reason of the present distress, namely, that it is good for a man to be as he is." Here our opponent goes utterly wild with exultation: this is his strongest battering-ram with which he shakes the wall of virginity. "See," says he, "the Apostle confesses that as regards virgins he has no commandment of the Lord, and he who had with authority laid down the law respecting husbands and wives, does not dare to command what the Lord has not enjoined. And rightly too. For what is enjoined is commanded, what is commanded must be done, and that which must be done implies punishment if it be not done. For it is useless to

order a thing to be done and yet leave the individual free to do it or not do it. If the Lord had commanded virginity He would have seemed to condemn marriage, and to do away with the seed-plot of mankind, of which virginity itself is a growth. If He had cut off the root, how was He to expect fruit? If the foundations were not first laid, how was He to build the edifice, and put on the roof to cover all! Excavators toil hard to remove mountains; the bowels of the earth are pierced in the search for gold. And, when the tiny particles, first by the blast of the furnace, then by the hand of the cunning workman have been fashioned into an ornament, men do not call him blessed who has separated the gold from the dross, but him who wears the beautiful gold. Do not marvel then if, placed as we are, amid temptations of the flesh and incentives to vice, the angelic life be not exacted of us, but merely recommended. If advice be given, a man is free to proffer obedience; if there be a command, he is a servant bound to compliance. "I have no commandment," he says, "of the Lord: but I give my judgement, as one that hath obtained mercy of the Lord to be faithful." If you have no commandment of the Lord, how dare you give judgement without orders? The Apostle will reply: Do you wish me to give orders where the Lord has offered a favor rather than laid down a law? The great Creator and Fashioner, knowing the weakness of the vessel which he made, left virginity open to those whom He addressed; and shall I, the teacher of the Gentiles, who have become all things to all men that I might gain all, shall I lay upon the necks of weak believers from the very first the burden of perpetual chastity? Let them begin with short periods of release from the marriage bond, and give themselves unto prayer, that when they have tasted the sweets of chastity they may desire the perpetual possession of that wherewith they were temporarily delighted. The Lord, when tempted by the Pharisees, and asked whether according to the law of Moses it was permitted to put away a wife, forbade the practice altogether. After weighing His words the disciples said to Him: "If the case of the man is so with his wife, it is not expedient to marry. But He said unto them, all men cannot receive this saying, but they to whom it is given. For there are eunuchs, which were so born from their mother's womb: and there are eunuchs, which were made eunuchs by men: and there are eunuchs, which made themselves eunuchs for the kingdom of heaven's sake. He that is able to receive it, let him receive it." The reason is plain why the Apostle said, "concerning virgins I have no commandment of the Lord." Surely; because the Lord had previously said "All men cannot receive the word, but they to whom it is given," and "He that is able to receive it, let him receive it." The Master of the Christian race offers the reward, invites candidates to the course, holds in His hand the prize of virginity, points to the fountain of purity, and cries aloud "If any man thirst, let him come unto me and drink." "He that is able to receive it, let him receive it." He does not say, you must drink, you must run, willing or unwilling: but whoever is willing and able to run and to drink, he shall conquer, he shall be satisfied. And therefore Christ loves virgins more than others, because they willingly give what was not commanded them. And it indicates greater grace to offer what you are not bound to give, than to render what is exacted of you. The apostles, contemplating the burden of a wife, exclaimed, "If the case of the man is so with his wife, it is not expedient to marry." Our Lord thought well of their view. You rightly think, said He, that it is not expedient for a man who is hastening to the kingdom of heaven to take a wife: but it is a hard matter, and all men do not receive the saying, but they to whom it has been given. Some are eunuchs by nature, others by the violence of men. Those eunuchs please Me who are such not of necessity, but of free choice. Willingly do I take them into my bosom who have made themselves eunuchs for the kingdom of heaven's sake, and in order to worship Me have renounced the condition of their birth. We must now explain the words, "Those who have made themselves eunuchs for the kingdom of heaven's sake." If they who have made themselves eunuchs have the reward of the kingdom of heaven, it follows that they who have not made themselves such cannot be placed with those who have. He who is able, he says, to receive it, let him receive it. It is a mark of great faith and of great virtue, to be the pure temple of God, to offer oneself a whole burnt-offering, and, according to the same apostle, to be holy both in body and in spirit. These are the eunuchs, who thinking themselves dry trees because of their impotence, hear by the mouth of Isaiah that they have a place prepared in heaven for sons and daughters. Their type is Ebedmelech the eunuch in Jeremiah, and the eunuch of Queen Candace in the Acts of the Apostles, who on account of the strength of his faith gained the name of a *man*. These are they to whom Clement, who was the successor of the Apostle Peter, and of whom the Apostle Paul makes mention, wrote letters, directing almost the whole of his discourse to the subject of virgin purity. After them there is a long series of apostolic men, martyrs, and men illustrious no less for holiness than for eloquence, with whom we may very easily become acquainted through their own writings. "I think, therefore," he says, "that this is good for the present distress." What is this distress which, in contempt of the marriage tie, longs for the liberty of virginity? "Woe unto them that are with child and to them that give suck in those days." We have not here a condemnation of harlots and brothels, of whose damnation there is no doubt, but of the swelling womb, and wailing infancy, the fruit as well as the work of marriage. "For it is good for a man so to be." If it is good for a man so to be, it is bad for a man not so to be. "Art thou bound unto a wife? Seek not to be loosed. Art thou loosed from a wife? Seek not a wife." Each one of us has his appointed bounds; let me have what is mine, and keep your own. If thou art bound to a wife, give her not a bill of divorce. If I am loosed from a wife, I will not seek a wife. As I do not dissolve marriages once contracted: so you should not bind what is loosed. And at the same time the meaning of the words must be taken into account. He who has a wife is regarded as a debtor, and is said to be uncircumcised, to be the servant of his wife, and like bad servants to be *bound*. But he who has no wife, in the first place owes no man anything, then is circumcised, thirdly is free, lastly, is loosed.

13. Let us run through the remaining points, for our author is so voluminous that we cannot linger over every detail. "But and if thou marry, thou hast not sinned." It is one thing not to sin, another to do good. "And if a virgin marry, she hath not sinned." Not that virgin who has once for all dedicated herself to the service of God: for, should one of these marry, she will have damnation, because she has made of no account her first faith. But, if our adversary objects that this saying relates to widows, we reply that it applies with still greater force

to virgins, since marriage is forbidden even to widows whose previous marriage had been lawful. For virgins who marry after consecration are rather incestuous than adulterous. And, for fear he should by saying, "And if a virgin marry, she hath not sinned," again stimulate the unmarried to be married, he immediately checks himself, and by introducing another consideration, invalidates his previous concession. "Yet," says he, "such shall have tribulation in the flesh." Who are they who shall have tribulation in the flesh? They to whom he had before indulgently said "But and if thou marry, thou hast not sinned; and if a virgin marry, she hath not sinned. Yet such shall have tribulation in the flesh." We in our inexperience thought that marriage had at least the joys of the flesh. But if they who are married have tribulation even in the flesh, which is imagined to be the sole source of their pleasure, what else is there to marry for, when in the spirit, and in the mind, and in the flesh itself there is tribulation. "But I would spare you." Thus, he says, I allege tribulation as a motive, as though there were not greater obligations to refrain. "But this I say, brethren, the time is shortened, that henceforth both those that have wives may be as though they had none." I am by no means now discussing virgins, of whose happiness no one entertains a doubt. I am coming to the married. The time is short, the Lord is at hand. Even though we lived nine hundred years, as did men of old, yet we ought to think that short which must one day have an end, and cease to be. But, as things are, and it is not so much the joy as the tribulation of marriage that is short, why do we take wives whom we shall soon be compelled to lose? "And those that weep, and those that rejoice, and those that buy, and those that use the world, as though they wept not, as though they rejoiced not, as though they bought not, as though they did not use the world: for the fashion of this world passes away." If the world, which comprehends all things, passes away, yea if the fashion and intercourse of the world vanishes like the clouds, amongst the other works of the world, marriage too will vanish away. For after the resurrection there will be no wedlock. But if death be the end of marriage, why do we not voluntarily embrace the inevitable? And why do we not, encouraged by the hope of the reward, offer to God that which must be wrung from us against our will. "He that is unmarried is careful for the things of the Lord, how he may please the Lord: but he that is married is careful for the things of the world, how he may please his wife, and is divided." Let us look at the difference between the cares of the virgin, and those of the married man. The virgin longs to please the Lord, the husband to please his wife, and that he may please her he is careful for the things of the world, which will of course pass away with the world. "And he is divided," that is to say, is distracted with manifold cares and miseries. This is not the place to describe the difficulties of marriage, and to revel in rhetorical commonplaces. I think I delivered myself fully as regards this point in my argument against Helvidius, and in the book which I addressed to Eustochium. At all events Tertullian, while still a young man, gave himself full play with this subject. And my teacher, Gregory of Nazianzus, discussed virginity and marriage in some Greek verses. I now briefly beg my reader to note that in the Latin manuscripts we have the reading "there is a difference also between the virgin and the wife." The words, it is true, have a meaning of their own, and have by me, as well as by others, been so explained as showing the bearing of the passage. Yet they lack apostolic authority, since the Apostle's words are as we have translated them—"He is careful for the things of the world, how he may please his wife, and he is divided." Having laid down this, he passes to the virgins and the continent, and says "The woman that is unmarried and a virgin thinks of the things of the Lord, that she may be holy in body and in spirit." Not every unmarried woman is also a virgin. But every virgin is of course unmarried. It may be, that regard for elegance of expression led him to repeat the same idea by means of another word and speak of "a woman unmarried and a virgin"; or at least he may have wished to give to "unmarried" the definite meaning of "virgin," so that we might not suppose him to include harlots, united to no one by the fixed bonds of wedlock, among the "unmarried." Of what, then, does she that is unmarried and a virgin think? "The things of the Lord, that she may be holy both in body and in spirit." Supposing there were nothing else, and that no greater reward followed virginity, this would be motive enough for her choice, to think of the things of the Lord. But he immediately points out the contents of her thought—that she may be holy both in body and spirit. For there are virgins in the flesh, not in the spirit, whose body is intact, their soul corrupt. But that virgin is a sacrifice to Christ, whose mind has not been defiled by thought, nor her flesh by lust. On the other hand, she who is married thinks of the things of the world, how she may please her husband. Just as the man who has a wife is anxious for the things of the world, how he may please his wife, so the married woman thinks of the things of the world, how she may please her husband. But we are not of this world, which lieth in wickedness, the fashion of which passes away, and concerning which the Lord said to the Apostles, "If ye were of the world, the world would love its own." And lest perchance someone might suppose that he was laying the heavy burden of chastity on unwilling shoulders, he at once adds his reasons for persuading to it, and says: "And this I say for your profit; not that I may cast a snare upon you, but for that which is seemly, and that ye may attend upon the Lord without distraction." The Latin words do not convey the meaning of the Greek. What words shall we use to render Πρὸς τὸ εὔσχημον καὶ εὐπρόσεδρον τῷ Κυρί& 251· ἀπερισπάστως The difficulty of translation accounts for the fact that the clause is completely wanting in Latin manuscripts. Let us, however, use the passage as we have translated it. The Apostle does not lay a snare upon us, nor does he compel us to be what we do not wish to be; but he gives his advice as to what is fair and seemly, he would have us attend upon the Lord and ever be anxious about that service, and await the Lord's will, so that like active and well-armed soldiers we may obey orders, and may do so without distraction, which, according to Ecclesiastes, is given to the men of this world that they may be exercised thereby. But if anyone considers that his virgin, that is, his flesh, is wanton and boiling with lust, and cannot be bridled, and he must do one of two things, either take a wife or fall, let him do what he will, he does not sin if he marry. Let him do, he says, what he will, not what he ought. He does not sin if he marry a wife; yet, he does not well if he marry: "But he that stands steadfast in his heart, having no necessity, but hath power as touching his own will, and hath determined this in his own heart, to keep his own virgin, shall do well. So then both he that giveth his own virgin in marriage doeth well; and he that giveth her not in marriage shall do better." With marked propriety he had previously said "He who marries a wife does not sin": here he tells us "He that kept his own virgin doeth well." But it is one thing not to sin, another to do well. "Depart from evil," he says, "and do good." The former we forsake, the latter we follow. In this last lies perfection. But whereas he says "and he that giveth his virgin in marriage doeth well," it might be supposed that our remark does not hold good; he therefore forthwith detracts from this seeming good and puts it in the shade by comparing it with another, and saying, "and he that giveth her not in marriage shall do better." If he had not intended to draw the inference of doing better, he would never have previously referred to doing well. But where there is something good and something better, the reward is not in both cases the same, and where the reward is not one and the same, there of course the gifts are different. The difference, then, between marriage and virginity is as great as that between not sinning and doing well; nay rather, to speak less harshly, as great as between good and better.

14. He has ended his discussion of wedlock and virginity, and has carefully steered between the two precepts without turning to the right hand or to the left. He has followed the royal road and fulfilled the command not to be righteous over much. Now again he compares monogamy with digamy, and as he had subordinated marriage to virginity, so he makes second marriages inferior to first, and says, "A wife is bound for so long time as her husband lives; but if the husband be dead, she is free to be married to whom she will; only in the Lord. But she is happier if she abide as she is, after my judgement: and I think that I also have the Spirit of God." He allows second marriages, but to such persons as wish

for them and are not able to contain; lest, having "waxed wanton against Christ," they desire to marry, "having condemnation, because they have rejected their first faith;" and he makes the concession because many had already turned aside after Satan. "But," says he, "they will be happier if they abide as they are," and he immediately adds the weight of Apostolic authority, "after my judgement." And that an Apostle's authority might not, like that of an ordinary man, be without weight, he added, "and I think that I also have the Spirit of God." When he incites to continence, it is not by the judgement or spirit of man, but by the judgement and Spirit of God; when, however, he grants the indulgence of marriage, he does not mention the Spirit of God, but weighs his judgement with wisdom, and adapts the severity of the strain to the weakness of the individual. In this sense we must take the whole of the following passage: "For the woman that hath a husband is bound by law to the husband while he lives; but if the husband die, she is discharged from the law of the husband. So then if, while the husband lives, she be joined to another man, she shall be called an adulteress: but if the husband die, she is free from the law, so that she is no adulteress, though she be joined to another man." And similarly the words to Timothy, "I desire therefore that the younger widows marry, bear children, rule the household, give none occasion to the adversary for reviling: for already some are turned aside after Satan," and so on. For as on account of the danger of fornication he allows virgins to marry, and makes that excusable which in itself is not desirable, so to avoid this same fornication, he allows second marriages to widows. For it is better to know a single husband, though he be a second or third, than to have many paramours: that is, it is more tolerable for a woman to prostitute herself to one man than to many. At all events this is so if the Samaritan woman in John's Gospel who said she had her sixth husband was reproved by the Lord because he was not her husband. For where there are more husbands than one the proper idea of a husband, who is a single person, is destroyed. At the beginning one rib was turned into one wife. "And they two," he says, "shall be one flesh": not three, or four; otherwise, how can they be any longer two, if they are several. Lamech, a man of blood and a murderer, was the first who divided one flesh between two wives. Fratricide and digamy were abolished by the same punishment—that of the deluge. The one was avenged seven times, the other seventy times seven. The guilt is as widely different as are the numbers. What the holiness of second marriage is, appears from this—that a person twice married cannot be enrolled in the ranks of the clergy, and so the Apostle tells Timothy, "Let none be enrolled as a widow under threescore years old, having been the wife of one man." The whole command concerns those widows who are supported on the alms of the Church. The age is therefore limited, so that those only may receive the food of the poor who can no longer work. And at the same time, consider that she who has had two husbands, even though she be a widow, decrepit, and in want, is not a worthy recipient of the Church's funds. But if she be deprived of the bread of charity, how much more is she deprived of that bread which cometh down from heaven, and of which if a man eat unworthily, he shall be guilty of outrage offered to the body and the blood of Christ?

15. The passages, however, which I have adduced in support of my position and in which it is permitted to

widows, if they so desire, to marry again, are interpreted by some concerning those widows who had lost their husbands and were found in that condition when they became Christians. For, supposing a person baptized and her husband dead, it would not be consistent if the Apostle were to bid her marry another, when he enjoins even those who have wives to be as though they had them not. And this is why the number of wives which a man may take is not defined, because when Christian baptism has been received, even though a third or a fourth wife has been taken, she is reckoned as the first. Otherwise, if, after baptism and after the death of a first husband, a second is taken why should not a sixth after the death of the second, third, fourth, and fifth, and so on? For it is possible, that through some strange misfortune, or by the judgement of God cutting short repeated marriages, a young woman may have several husbands, while an old woman may be left a widow by her first husband in extreme age. The first Adam was married once: the second was unmarried. Let the supporters of second marriages shew us as their leader a third Adam who was twice married. But granted that Paul allowed second marriages: upon the same grounds it follows that he allows even third and fourth marriages, or a woman may marry as often as her husband dies. The Apostle was forced to choose many things which he did not like. He circumcised Timothy, and shaved his own head, practiced going barefoot, let his hair grow long, and cut it at Cenchrea. And he had certainly chastised the Galatians, and blamed Peter because for the sake of Jewish observances he separated himself from the Gentiles. As then in other points connected with the discipline of the Church he was a Jew to Jews, a Gentile to Gentiles, and was made all things to all men, that he might gain all: so too he allowed second marriages to incontinent persons, and did not limit the number of marriages, in order that women, although they saw themselves permitted to take a second husband, in the same way as a third or a fourth was allowed, might blush to take a second, lest they should be compared to those who were three or four times married. If more than one husband be allowed, it makes no difference whether he be a second or a third, because there is no longer a question of single marriage. "All things are lawful, but not all things are expedient." I do not condemn second, nor third, nor pardon the expression, eighth marriages: I will go still further and say that I welcome even a penitent whoremonger. Things that are equally lawful must be weighed in an even balance.

16. But he takes us to the Old Testament, and beginning with Adam goes on to Zacharias and Elizabeth. He next confronts us with Peter and the rest of the Apostles. We are therefore bound to traverse the same course of argument and show that chastity was always preferred to the condition of marriage. And as regards Adam and Eve we must maintain that before the fall they were virgins in Paradise: but after they sinned, and were cast out of Paradise, they were immediately married. Then we have the passage, "For this cause shall a man leave his father and mother, and shall cleave to his wife, and the twain shall become one flesh," in explanation of which the Apostle straightway adds, "This mystery is great, but I speak in regard of Christ, and of the Church." Christ in the flesh is a virgin, in the spirit he is once married. For he has one Church, concerning which the same Apostle says, "Husbands, love your wives, even as Christ also loved the Church." If Christ loves the Church holily,

chastely, and without spot, let husbands also love their wives in chastity. And let everyone know how to possess his vessel in sanctification and honor, not in the lust of concupiscence, as the Gentiles who know not God: "For God called us not for uncleanness, but in sanctification: seeing that ye have put off the old man with his doings, and have put on the new man, which is being renewed unto knowledge after the image of him that created him: where there cannot be male and female, Greek and Jew, circumcision and uncircumcision, barbarian, Scythian, bondman, freeman: but Christ is all, and in all." The link of marriage is not found in the image of the Creator. When difference of sex is done away, and we are putting off the old man, and putting on the new, then we are being born again into Christ a virgin, who was both born of a virgin, and is born again through virginity. And whereas he says, "Be fruitful, and multiply, and replenish the earth," it was necessary first to plant the wood and to let it grow, so that there might be an after-growth for cutting down. And at the same time we must bear in mind the meaning of the phrase, "replenish the earth." Marriage replenishes the earth, virginity fills Paradise. This too we must observe, at least if we would faithfully follow the Hebrew, that while Scripture on the first, third, fourth, fifth, and sixth days relates that, having finished the works of each, "God saw that it was good," on the second day it omitted this altogether, leaving us to understand that two is not a good number because it destroys unity, and prefigures the marriage compact. Hence it was that all the animals which Noah took into the ark by pairs were unclean. Odd numbers denote cleanness. And yet by the double number is represented another mystery: that not even in beasts and unclean birds is second marriage approved. For unclean animals went in two and two, and clean ones by sevens, so that Noah after the flood might be able to immediately offer to God sacrifices from the latter.

17. But if Enoch was translated, and Noah was preserved at the deluge, I do not think that Enoch was translated because he had a wife, but because he was the first to call upon God and to believe in the Creator; and the Apostle Paul fully instructs us concerning him in the Epistle to the Hebrews. Noah, moreover, who was preserved as a kind of second root for the human race, must of course be preserved together with his wife and sons, although in this there is a Scripture mystery. The ark, according to the Apostle Peter, was a type of the Church, in which eight souls were saved. When Noah entered into it, both he and his sons were separated from their wives; but when he landed from it, they united in pairs, and what had been separated in the ark, that is, in the Church, was joined together in the intercourse of the world. And at the same time if the ark had many compartments and little chambers, and was made with second and third stories, and was filled with different beasts, and was furnished with dwellings, great or small, according to the kind of animal, I think all this diversity in the compartments was a figure of the manifold character of the Church.

18. He raises the objection that when God gave his second blessing, permission was granted to eat flesh, which had not in the first benediction been allowed. He should know that just as divorce according to the Savior's word was not permitted from the beginning, but on account of the hardness of our heart was a concession of Moses to the human race, so too the eating of flesh was

unknown until the deluge. But after the deluge, like the quails given in the desert to the murmuring people, the poison of flesh-meat was offered to our teeth. The Apostle writing to the Ephesians teaches that God had purposed in the fullness of time to sum up and renew in Christ Jesus all things which are in heaven and in earth. Whence also the Savior himself in the Revelation of John says, "I am Alpha and Omega, the beginning and the ending." At the beginning of the human race we neither ate flesh, nor gave bills of divorce, nor suffered circumcision for a sign. Thus we reached the deluge. But after the deluge, together with the giving of the law which no one could fulfil, flesh was given for food, and divorce was allowed to hardhearted men, and the knife of circumcision was applied, as though the hand of God had fashioned us with something superfluous. But once Christ has come in the end of time, and Omega passed into Alpha and turned the end into the beginning, we are no longer allowed divorce, nor are we circumcised, nor do we eat flesh, for the Apostle says, "It is good not to eat flesh, nor to drink wine." For wine as well as flesh was consecrated after the deluge.

19. What shall I say of Abraham who had three wives, as Jovinianus says, and received circumcision as a sign of his faith? If we follow him in the number of his wives, let us also follow him in circumcision. We must not partly follow, partly reject him. Isaac, moreover, the husband of one wife, Rebecca, prefigures the Church of Christ, and reproves the wantonness of second marriage. And if Jacob had two pairs of wives and concubines, and our opponent will not admit that blear-eyed Leah, ugly and prolific, was a type of the synagogue, but that Rachel, beautiful and long barren, indicated the mystery of the

Church, let me remind him that when Jacob did this thing he was among the Assyrians, and in Mesopotamia in bondage to a hard master. But when he wished to enter the holy land, he raised on Mount Galeed the heap of witness, in token that the lord of Mesopotamia had failed to find anything among his baggage, and there swore that he would never return to the place of his bondage; and when, after wrestling with the angel at the brook Jabbok, he began to limp, because the great muscle of his thigh was withered, he at once gained the name of Israel. Then the wife whom he once loved, and for whom he had served, was slain by the son of sorrow near Bethlehem which was destined to be the birthplace of our Lord, the herald of virginity: and the intimacies of Mesopotamia died in the land of the Gospel.

20. But I wonder why he set Judah and Tamar before us for an example, unless perchance even harlots give him pleasure; or Onan who was slain because he grudged his brother seed. Does he imagine that we approve of any sexual intercourse except for the procreation of children? As regards Moses, it is clear that he would have been in peril at the inn, if Sephora which is by interpretation *a bird,* had not circumcised her son, and cut off the foreskin of marriage with the knife which prefigured the Gospel. This is that Moses who when he saw a great vision and heard an angel, or the Lord speaking in the bush, could not by any means approach to him without first loosing the latchet of his shoe, that is, putting off the bonds of marriage. And we need not be surprised at this in the case of one who was a prophet, lawgiver, and the friend of God, seeing that all the people when about to draw nigh to Mount Sinai, and to hear the voice speaking to them, were commanded to sanctify

themselves in three days, and keep themselves from their wives. I am out of order in violating historical sequence, but I may point out that the same thing was said by Ahimelech the priest to David when he fled to Nob: "If only the young men have kept themselves from women." And David answered, "of a truth about these three days." For the shew-bread, like the body of Christ, might not be eaten by those who rose from the marriage bed. And in passing we ought to consider the words "if only the young men have kept themselves from women." The truth is that, in view of the purity of the body of Christ, all sexual intercourse is unclean. In the law also it is enjoined that the high priest must not marry any but a virgin, nor must he take to wife a widow. If a virgin and a widow are on the same level, how is it that one is taken, the other rejected? And the widow of a priest is bidden abide in the house of her father, and not to contract a second marriage. If the sister of a priest dies in virginity, just as the priest is commanded to go to the funeral of his father and mother, so must he go to hers. But if she be married, she is despised as though she belonged not to him. He who has married a wife, and he who has planted a vineyard, an image of the propagation of children, is forbidden to go to the battle. For he who is the slave of his wife cannot be the Lord's soldier. And the laver in the tabernacle was cast from the mirrors of the women who fasted, signifying the bodies of pure virgins: And within, in the sanctuary, both cherubim, and mercy-seat, and the ark of the covenant, and the table of shew-bread, and the candlestick, and the censer, were made of the purest gold. For silver might not be brought into the holy of holies.

21. I must not linger over Moses when my purpose is at full speed to lightly touch on each topic and to sketch

the outline of a proper knowledge of my subject. I will pass to Joshua the son of Nun, who was previously called *Ause,* or better, as in the Hebrew, *Osee,* that is, *Savior.* For he, according to the epistle of Jude, saved the people of Israel and led them forth out of Egypt, and brought them into the land of promise. As soon as this Joshua reached the Jordan, the waters of marriage, which had ever flowed in the land, dried up and stood in one heap; and the whole people, barefooted and on dry ground, crossed over, and came to Gilgal, and there was a second time circumcised. If we take this literally, it cannot possibly stand. For if we had two foreskins, or if another could grow after the first was cut off, there would be room for speaking of a second circumcision. But the meaning is that Joshua circumcised the people who had crossed the desert, with the Gospel knife, and he circumcised them with a stone knife, that what in the case of Moses' son was prefigured in a few might under Joshua be fulfilled in all. Moreover, the very foreskins were heaped together and buried, and covered with earth, and the fact that the reproach of Egypt was taken away, and the name of the place, *Gilgal,* which is by interpretation *revelation,* show that while the people wandered in the desert uncircumcised their eyes were blinded. Let us see what follows. After this Gospel circumcision and the consecration of twelve stones at the place of revelation, the Passover was immediately celebrated, a lamb was slain for them, and they ate the food of the Holy Land. Joshua went forth, and was met by the Prince of the host, sword in hand, that is either to shew that he was ready to fight for the circumcised people, or to sever the tie of marriage. And in the same way that Moses was commanded, so was he: "loose thy shoe, for the place whereon thou stands is holy ground." For if the armed host of the Lord was represented by the trumpets of the priests, we may see in Jericho a type of the overthrow of the world by the preaching of the Gospel. And to pass over endless details (for it is not my purpose now to unfold all the mysteries of the Old Testament), five kings who previously reigned in the land of promise, and opposed the Gospel army, were overcome in battle with Joshua. I think it is clearly to be understood that before the Lord led his people from Egypt and circumcised them, sight, smell, taste, hearing, and touch had the dominion, and that to these, as to five princes, everything was subject. And when they took refuge in the cave of the body and in a place of darkness, Jesus entered the body itself and slew them, that the source of their power might be the instrument of their death.

22. But it is now time for us to raise the standard of Joshua's chastity. It is written that Moses had a wife. Now Moses is interpreted both by our Lord and by the Apostle to mean the law: "They have Moses and the prophets." And "Death reigned from Adam until Moses, even over them that had not sinned after the likeness of Adam's transgression." And no one doubts that in both passages Moses signifies the law. We read that Moses, that is the law, had a wife: shew me then in the same way that Joshua the son of Nun had either wife or children, and if you can do so, I will confess that I am beaten. He certainly received the fairest spot in the division of the land of Judah, and died, not in the *twenties*, which are ever unlucky in Scripture—by them are reckoned the years of Jacob's service, the price of Joseph, and sundry presents which Esau who was fond of them received—but in the *tens,* whose praises we have often sung; and he was

buried in *Thamnath Sare,* that is, *most perfect sovereignty,* or among those *of a new covering,* to signify the crowds of virgins, covered by the Savior's aid on Mount Ephraim, that is, the *fruitful mountain;* on the north of the Mountain of Gaash, which is, being interpreted, *disturbance:* for "Mount Sion is on the sides of the north, the city of the Great King," is ever exposed to hatred, and in every trial says "But my feet had well nigh slipped." The book which bears the name of Joshua ends with his burial. Again in the book of Judges we read of him as though he had risen and come to life again, and by way of summary his works are extolled. We read too "So Joshua sent the people away, every man unto his inheritance, that they might possess the land." And "Israel served the Lord all the days of Joshua," and so on. There immediately follows: "And Joshua the son of Nun, the servant of the Lord, died, being a hundred and ten years old." Moses, moreover, only saw the land of promise; he could not enter: and "he died in the land of Moab, and the Lord buried him in the valley in the land of Moab over against Beth-peor: but no man knows of his sepulcher unto this day." Let us compare the burial of the two: Moses died in the land of Moab, Joshua in the land of Judea. The former was buried in a valley over against the house of Phogor, which is, being interpreted, *reproach* (for the Hebrew Phogor corresponds to Priapus); the latter in Mount Ephraim on the north of Mount Gaash. And in the simple expressions of the sacred Scriptures there is always a more subtle meaning. The Jews gloried in children and child-bearing; and the barren woman, who had not offspring in Israel, was accursed; but blessed was he whose seed was in Sion, and his family in Jerusalem; and part of the highest blessing was, "Thy wife shall be as a fruitful vine, in the innermost parts of thy house, thy children like olive plants, round about thy table." Therefore his grave is described as placed in a valley over against the house of an idol which was in a special sense consecrated to lust. But we who fight under Joshua our leader, even to the present day know not where Moses was buried. For we despise Phogor, and all his shame, knowing that they who are in the flesh cannot please God. And the Lord before the flood had said "My spirit shall not abide in man forever, for that he also is flesh." Wherefore, when Moses died, the people of Israel mourned for him; but Joshua like one on his way to victory was unmourned. For marriage ends at death; virginity thereafter begins to wear the crown.

23. Next he brings forward Samson, and does not consider that the Lord's Nazarite was once shaven bald by a woman. And although Samson continues to be a type of the Savior because he loved a harlot from among the Gentiles, which harlot corresponds to the Church, and because he slew more enemies in his death than he did in his life, yet he does not set an example of conjugal chastity. And he surely reminds us of Jacob's prophecy—he was shaken by his runaway steed, bitten by an adder and fell backwards. But why he enumerated Deborah, and Barak, and the wife of Heber the Kenite, I am at a loss to understand. For it is one thing to draw up a list of military commanders in historical sequence, another to indicate certain figures of marriage which cannot be found in them. And whereas he prefers the fidelity of the father Jephthah to the tears of the virgin daughter, that makes for us. For we are not commending virgins of the world so much as those who are virgins for Christ's sake, and most Hebrews blame the father for the rash vow he made, "If

thou wilt indeed deliver the children of Ammon into mine hand, then it shall be, that whatsoever cometh forth of the doors of my house to meet me, when I return in peace from the children of Ammon, it shall be for the Lord's, and I will offer it up for a burnt offering." Supposing (they say) a dog or an ass had met him, what would he have done? Their meaning is that God so ordered events that he who had improvidently made a vow, should learn his error by the death of his daughter. And if Samuel who was brought up in the tabernacle married a wife, how does that prejudice virginity? As if at the present day also there were not many married priests, and as though the Apostle did not describe a bishop as the husband of one wife, having children with all purity. At the same time we must not forget that Samuel was a Levite, not a priest or high-priest. Hence it was that his mother made for him a linen ephod, that is, a linen garment to go over the shoulders, which was the proper dress of the Levites and of the inferior order. And so he is not named in the Psalms among the priests, but among those who call upon the name of the Lord: "Moses and Aaron among his priests, and Samuel among those who call upon his name." For[4] Levi begat Kohath, Kohath begat Amminadab, Amminadab begat Korah, Korah begat Assir, Assir begat Elkanah, Elkanah begat Zuph, Zuph begat Tahath, Tahath begat Eliel, Eliel begat Jeroham, Jeroham begat Elkanah, Elkanah begat Samuel. And no one doubts that the priests sprang from the stock of Aaron, Eleazar, and Phinees. And seeing that they had wives, they would be rightly brought against us, if, led away by the error of the Encratites, we were to maintain that marriage deserved censure, and our high priest were not after the order of Melchizedek, without father, without mother, Ἀ'γενεαλόγητος, that is, unmarried. And much fruit truly did Samuel reap from his children! he himself pleased God, but begat such children as displeased the Lord. But if in support of second marriage, he urges the instance of Boaz and Ruth, let him know that in the Gospel (S. Matt. i. 6) to typify the Church even Rahab the harlot is reckoned among our Lord's ancestors.

24. He boasts that David bought his wife for two hundred foreskins. But he should remember that David had numerous other wives, and afterwards received Michal, Saul's daughter, whom her father had delivered to another, and when he was old got heat from the embrace of the Shunammite maiden. And I do not say this because I am bold enough to disparage holy men, but because it is one thing to live under the law, another to live under the Gospel. David slew Uriah the Hittite and committed adultery with Bathsheba. And because he was a man of blood—the reference is not, as some think, to his wars, but to the murder—he was not permitted to build a temple of the Lord. But as for us, if we cause one of the least to stumble, and if we say to a brother *Raca,* or use our eyes improperly, it were good that a millstone were hanged about our neck, we shall be in danger of Gehenna, and a mere glance will be reckoned to us for adultery. He passes on to Solomon, through whom wisdom itself sang its own praises. Seeing that not content with dwelling upon his praises, he calls him uxorious, I am surprised that he did not add the words of the Canticles: "There are threescore queens, and fourscore concubines, and maidens without number," and those of the First Book of Kings; And he had seven hundred wives, princesses, and three hundred concubines, and others without number." These are they who turned away his heart from the Lord: and yet before

he had many wives, and fell into sins of the flesh, at the beginning of his reign and in his early years he built a temple to the Lord. For everyone is judged not for what he will be, but for what he is. But if Jovinianus approves the example of Solomon, he will no longer be in favor of second and third marriages only, but unless he has seven hundred wives and three hundred concubines, he cannot be the king's antitype or attain to his merit. I earnestly again and again remind you, my reader, that I am compelled to speak as I do, and that I do not disparage our predecessors under the law, but am well aware that they served their generation according to their circumstances, and fulfilled the Lord's command to increase, and multiply, and replenish the earth. And what is more they were figures of those that were to come. But we to whom it is said, "The time is shortened, that henceforth those that have wives may be as though they had none," have a different command, and for us virginity is consecrated by the Virgin Savior.

25. What folly it was to include Elijah and Elisha in a list of married men, is plain without a word from me. For, since John Baptist came in the spirit and power of Elijah, and John was a virgin, it is clear that he came not only in Elijah's spirit, but also in his bodily chastity. Then the passage relating to Hezekiah might be adduced (though Jovinianus with his wonted stupidity did not notice it), in which after his recovery and the addition of fifteen years to his life he said, "Now will I beget children." It must be remembered, however, that in the Hebrew texts the passage is not so, but runs thus: "The father to the children shall make known thy faithfulness." Nor need we wonder that Huldah, the prophetess, and wife of Shallum, was consulted by Josiah, King of Judah,

when the captivity was approaching and the wrath of the Lord was falling upon Jerusalem: since it is the rule of Scripture when holy men fail, to praise women to the reproach of men. And it is superfluous to speak of Daniel, for the Hebrews to the present day affirm that the three youths were eunuchs, in accordance with the declaration of God which Isaiah utters to Hezekiah: "And of thy sons that shall issue from thee, which thou shalt beget, shall they take away: and they shall be eunuchs in the palace of the King of Babylon." And again in Daniel we read: "And the king spoke unto Ashpenaz the master of his eunuchs, that he should bring in certain of the children of Israel, even of the seed royal and of the nobles: youth in whom was no blemish, but well favored, and skillful in all wisdom, and cunning in knowledge, and understanding science." The conclusion is that if Daniel and the three youths were chosen from the seed royal, and if Scripture foretold that that there should be eunuchs of the seed royal, these men were those who were made eunuchs. If he meets us with the argument that in Ezekiel it is said that Noah, Daniel and Job in a sinful land could not free their sons and daughters, we reply that the words are used hypothetically. Noah and Job were not in existence at that time: we know that they lived many ages before. And the meaning is this: if there were such and such men in a sinful land, they shall not be able to save their own sons and daughters: because the righteousness of the father shall not save the son, nor shall the sin of one be imputed to another. "For the soul that sinned, it shall die." This, too, must be said, that Daniel, as the history of his book shows, was taken captive with King Jehoiakim at the same time that Ezekiel was also led into captivity. How then could he have sons who was still a youth? And only three years had elapsed when he was brought in to wait upon the king. Let no one suppose that Ezekiel at this time remembers Daniel as a man, not as a youth; for "It came to pass," he says, "in the sixth year," that is of King Jehoiakim, "in the sixth month, in the fifth day of the month:" and, "as I sat in my house, and the elders of Judah sat before me." Yet on that same day it was said to him, "Though these three men, Noah, Daniel, and Job were in it." Daniel was therefore a youth, and known to the people, either on account of his interpretation of the king's dreams, or on account of the release of Susannah, and the slaying of the elders. And it is clearly proved that at the time these things were spoken of Noah, Daniel, and Job, Daniel was still a youth and could not have had sons and daughters, whom he might save by his righteousness. So far concerning the Law.

26. Coming to the Gospel he sets before us Zacharias and Elizabeth, Peter and his mother-in-law, and, with a shamelessness to which we have now grown accustomed, fails to understand that they, too, ought to have been reckoned among those who served the Law. For the Gospel had no being before the crucifixion of Christ—it was consecrated by His passion and by His blood. In accordance with this rule Peter and the other Apostles (I must give Jovinianus something now and then out of my abundance) had indeed wives, but those which they had taken before they knew the Gospel. But once they were received into the Apostolate, they forsook the offices of marriage. For when Peter, representing the Apostles, says to the Lord: "Lo we have left all and followed thee," the Lord answered him, "Verily I say unto you, there is no man that hath left house or wife, or brethren, or parents, or children for the kingdom of God's

sake, who shall not receive manifold more in this time, and in the world to come eternal life." But if, in order to show that all the Apostles had wives, he meets us with the words "Have we no right to lead about women or wives" (for γυνή in Greek has both meanings) "even as the rest of the apostles, and Cephas, and the brethren of the Lord?" let him add what is found in the Greek copies, "Have we no right to lead about women that are sisters, or wives?" This makes it clear that the writer referred to other holy women, who, in accordance with Jewish custom, ministered to their teachers of their substance, as we read was the practice with even our Lord himself. Where there is a previous reference to eating and drinking, and the outlay of money, and mention is afterwards made of women that are sisters, it is quite clear, as we have said, that we must understand, not wives, but those women who ministered of their substance. And we read the same account in the Old Testament of the Shunammite who was wont to welcome Elisha, and to put for him a table, and bread, and a candlestick, and the rest. At all events if we take γυναίκας to mean *wives*, not *women*, the addition of the word *sisters* destroys the effect of the word *wives*, and shews that they were related in spirit, not by wedlock. Nevertheless, with the exception of the Apostle Peter, it is not openly stated that the Apostles had wives; and since the statement is made of one while nothing is said about the rest, we must understand that those of whom Scripture gives no such description had no wives. Yet Jovinianus, who has arrayed against us Zacharias and Elizabeth, Peter and his wife's mother, should know, that John was the son of Zacharias and Elizabeth, that is, a virgin was the offspring of marriage, the Gospel of the law, chastity of matrimony; so that by a virgin prophet the virgin Lord might be both announced and baptized. But we might say concerning Peter, that he had a mother-in-law when he believed, and no longer had a wife, although in the "Sentences" we read of both his wife and daughter. But for the present our argument must be based wholly on Scripture. He has made his appeal to the Apostles, because he thinks that they, who hold the chief authority in our moral system and are the typical Christian teachers, were not virgins. If, then, we allow that they were not virgins (and, with the exception of Peter, the point cannot be proved), yet I must tell him that it is to the Apostles that the words of Isaiah relate: "Except the Lord of hosts had left unto us a small remnant, we should have been as Sodom, we should have been like unto Gomorrah." So, then, they who were by birth Jews could not under the Gospel recover the virginity which they had lost in Judaism. And yet John, one of the disciples, who is related to have been the youngest of the Apostles, and who was a virgin when he embraced Christianity, remained a virgin, and on that account was more beloved by our Lord, and lay upon the breast of Jesus. And what Peter, who had had a wife, did not dare ask, he requested John to ask. And after the resurrection, when Mary Magdalene told them that the Lord had risen, they both ran to the sepulcher, but John outran Peter. And when they were fishing in the ship on the lake of Gennesaret, Jesus stood upon the shore, and the Apostles knew not who it was they saw; the virgin alone recognized a virgin, and said to Peter, "It is the Lord." Again, after hearing the prediction that he must be bound by another, and led whither he would not, and must suffer on the cross, Peter said, "Lord what shall this man do?" being unwilling to desert John, with whom he had always been united. Our

Lord said to him, "What is that to thee if I wish him so to be?" Whence the saying went abroad among the brethren that that disciple should not die. Here we have a proof that virginity does not die, and that the defilement of marriage is not washed away by the blood of martyrdom, but virginity abides with Christ, and its sleep is not death but a passing to another state. If, however, Jovinianus should obstinately contend that John was not a virgin, (whereas we have maintained that his virginity was the cause of the special love our Lord bore to him), let him explain, if he was not a virgin, why it was that he was loved more than the other Apostles. But you say, the Church was founded upon Peter: although elsewhere the same is attributed to all the Apostles, and they all receive the keys of the kingdom of heaven, and the strength of the Church depends upon them all alike, yet one among the twelve is chosen so that when a head has been appointed, there may be no occasion for schism. But why was not John chosen, who was a virgin? Deference was paid to age, because Peter was the elder: one who was a youth, I may say almost a boy, could not be set over men of advanced age; and a good master who was bound to remove every occasion of strife among his disciples, and who had said to them, "Peace I leave with you, my peace I give unto you," and, "He that is the greater among you, let him be the least of all," would not be thought to afford cause of envy against the youth whom he had loved. We maybe sure that John was then a boy because ecclesiastical history most clearly proves that he lived to the reign of Trajan, that is, he fell asleep in the sixty-eighth year after our Lord's passion, as I have briefly noted in my treatise on *Illustrious Men*. Peter is an Apostle, and John is an Apostle—the one a married man, the other a virgin; but

Peter is an Apostle only, John is both an Apostle and an Evangelist, and a prophet. An Apostle, because he wrote to the Churches as a master; an Evangelist, because he composed a Gospel, a thing which no other of the Apostles, excepting Matthew, did; a prophet, for he saw in the island of Patmos, to which he had been banished by the Emperor Domitian as a martyr for the Lord, an Apocalypse containing the boundless mysteries of the future. Tertullian, moreover, relates that he was sent to Rome, and that having been plunged into a jar of boiling oil he came out fresher and more active than when he went in. But his very Gospel is widely different from the rest. Matthew as though he were writing of a man begins thus: "The book of the Generation of Jesus Christ, the son of David, the son of Abraham;" Luke begins with the priesthood of Zacharias; Mark with a prophecy of the prophets Malachi and Isaiah. The first has the face of a man, on account of the genealogical table; the second, the face of a calf, on account of the priesthood; the third, the face of a lion, on account of the voice of one crying in the desert, "Prepare ye the way of the Lord, make His paths straight." But John like an eagle soars aloft, and reaches the Father Himself, and says, "In the beginning was the Word, and the Word was with God, and the Word was God. The same was in the beginning with God," and so on. The virgin writer expounded mysteries which the married could not, and to briefly sum up all and show how great was the privilege of John, or rather of virginity in John, the Virgin Mother was entrusted by the Virgin Lord to the Virgin disciple.

  27. But we toil to no purpose. For our opponent urges against us the Apostolic sentence and says, "Adam was first formed, then Eve; and Adam was not beguiled,

but the woman being beguiled hath fallen into transgression: but she shall be saved through the childbearing, if they continue in faith and love and sanctification with sobriety." Let us consider what led the Apostle to make this declaration: "I desire therefore that the men pray in every place, lifting up holy hands, without wrath and disputing." So in due course he lays down rules of life for the women and says "In like manner that women adorn themselves in modest apparel, with shamefacedness and sobriety; not with braided hair, and gold or pearls or costly raiment; but (which becometh women professing godliness) through good works. Let a woman learn in quietness with all subjection. But I permit not a woman to teach, nor to have dominion over a man, but to be in quietness." And that the lot of a woman might not seem a hard one, reducing her to the condition of a slave to her husband, the Apostle recalls the ancient law and goes back to the first example: that Adam was first made, then the woman out of his rib; and that the Devil could not seduce Adam, but did seduce Eve; and that after displeasing God she was immediately subjected to the man, and began to turn to her husband; and he points out that she who was once tied with the bonds of marriage and was reduced to the condition of Eve, might blot out the old transgression by the procreation of children: provided, however, that she bring up the children themselves in the faith and love of Christ, and in sanctification and chastity; for we must not adopt the faulty reading of the Latin texts, *sobrietas*, but *castitas*, that is, σωφροσύνη. You see how you are mastered by the witness of this passage also, and cannot but be driven to admit that what you thought was on the side of marriage tells in favor of virginity. For if the woman is saved in child-bearing, and the more the children the greater the safety of the mothers, why did he add "if they continue in faith and love and sanctification with chastity"? The woman will then be saved, if she bears not children who will remain virgins: if what she has herself lost, she attains in her children, and makes up for the loss and decay, of the root by the excellence of the flower and fruit.

28. Above, in passing, when our opponent adduced Solomon, who, although he had many wives, nevertheless built the temple, I briefly replied that it was my intention to run over the remaining points. Now that he may not cry out that both Solomon and others under the law, prophets and holy men, have been dishonored by us, let us show what this very man with his many wives and concubines thought of marriage. For no one can know better than he who suffered through them, what a wife or woman is. Well then, he says in the Proverbs: "The foolish and bold woman comes to want bread." What bread? Surely that bread which cometh down from heaven: and he immediately adds "The earth-born perish in her house, rush into the depths of hell." Who are the earth-born that perish in her house? They of course who follow the first Adam, who is of the earth, and not the second, who is from heaven. And again in another place: "Like a worm in wood, so a wicked woman destroyed her husband." But if you assert that this was spoken of bad wives, I shall briefly answer: What necessity rests upon me to run the risk of the wife I marry proving good or bad? "It is better," he says, "to dwell in a desert land, than with a contentious and passionate woman in a wide house." How seldom we find a wife without these faults, he knows who is married. Hence that sublime orator,

Varius Geminus says well "The man who does not quarrel is a bachelor." "It is better to dwell in the corner of the housetop, than with a contentious woman in a house in common." If a house common to husband and wife makes a wife proud and breeds contempt for the husband: how much more if the wife be the richer of the two, and the husband but a lodger in her house! She begins to be not a wife, but mistress of the house; and if she offends her husband, they must part. "A continual dropping on a wintry day" turns a man out of doors, and so will a contentious woman drive a man from his own house. She floods his house with her constant nagging and daily chatter, and ousts him from his own home, that is the Church. Hence the same Solomon previously commands: "My son flows forth beyond." And the Apostle, writing to the Hebrews, says "Therefore we ought to give the more earnest heed to the things spoken, lest haply we flow forth beyond." But who can hide from himself what is thus enigmatically expressed? "The horseleech had three daughters, dearly loved, but they satisfied her not, and a fourth is not satisfied when you say Enough; the grave, and woman's love, and the earth that is not satisfied with water, and the fire that saith not, Enough." The horseleech is the devil, the daughters of the devil are dearly loved, and they cannot be satisfied with the blood of the slain: *the grave, and woman's love, and the earth dry and scorched with heat.* It is not the harlot, or the adulteress who is spoken of; but woman's love in general is accused of ever being insatiable; put it out, it bursts into flame; give it plenty, it is again in need; it enervates a man's mind, and engrosses all thought except for the passion which it feeds. What we read in the parable which follows is to the same effect: "For three things the earth doth tremble, and for four which it cannot bear: for a servant when he is king: and a fool when he is filled with meat: for an odious woman when she is married to a good husband: and an handmaid that is heir to her mistress." See how a wife is classed with the greatest evils. But if you reply that it is an *odious* wife, I will give you the same answer as before—the mere possibility of such danger is in itself no light matter. For he who marries a wife is uncertain whether he is marrying an odious woman or one worthy of his love. If she be odious, she is intolerable. If worthy of love, her love is compared to the grave, to the parched earth, and to fire.

29. Let us come to Ecclesiastes and adduce a few corroborative passages from him also. "To everything there is a season, and a time to every purpose under the heaven: a time to be born, and a time to die: a time to plant, and a time to pluck up that which is planted." We brought forth young under the law with Moses, let us die under the Gospel with Christ. We planted in marriage, let us by chastity pluck up that which was planted. "A time to embrace, and a time to refrain from embracing: a time to love, and a time to hate: a time for war, and a time for peace." And at the same time he warns us not to prefer the law to the Gospel; nor to think that virgin purity is to be placed on a level with marriage: "Better," he says, "is the end of a thing than the beginning thereof." And he immediately adds: "Say not thou, what is the cause that the former days were better than these? for thou dost not inquire wisely concerning this." And he gives the reason why the latter days are better than the former: "For wisdom with an inheritance is good." Under the law carnal wisdom was followed by the sword of death; under the Gospel an eternal inheritance awaits spiritual wisdom.

"Behold, this have I found, saith the Preacher, one man among a thousand have I found; but a woman among all those have I not found. Behold this only have I found, that God made man upright; but they have sought out many inventions." He says that he had found man upright. Consider the force of the words. The word *man* comprehends both male and female. "But a woman," he says, "among all these have I not found." Let us read the beginning of Genesis, and we shall find Adam, that is *man*, called both male and female. Having then been created by God good and upright, by our own fault we have fallen to a worse condition; and that which in Paradise had been upright, when we left Paradise was corrupt. If you object that before they sinned there was a distinction in sex between male and female, and that they could without sin have come together, it is uncertain what might have happened. For we cannot know the judgements of God, and anticipate his sentence as we choose. What really happened is plain enough,—that they who in Paradise remained in perpetual virginity, when they were expelled from Paradise were joined together. Or if Paradise admits of marriage, and there is no difference between marriage and virginity, what prevented their previous intercourse even in Paradise? They are driven out of Paradise; and what they did not there, they do on earth; so that from the very earliest days of humanity virginity was consecrated by Paradise, and marriage by earth. "Let thy garments be always white." The eternal whiteness of our garments is the purity of virginity. In the morning we sowed our seed, and in the evening let us not cease. Let us who served marriage under the law, serve virginity under the Gospel.

30. I pass to the Song of Songs, and whereas our opponent thinks it makes altogether for marriage, I shall show that it contains the mysteries of virginity. Let us hear what the bride says before that the bridegroom comes to earth, suffers, descends to the lower world, and rises again. "We will make for thee likenesses of gold with ornaments of silver while the king sits at his table." Before the Lord rose again, and the Gospel shone, the bride had not gold, but likenesses of gold. As for the silver, however, which she professes to have at the marriage, she not only had silver ornaments, but she had them in variety—in widows, in the continent, and in the married. Then the bridegroom makes answer to the bride, and teaches her that the shadow of the old law has passed away, and the truth of the Gospel has come. "Rise up, my love, my fair one, and come away, for lo, the winter is past, the rain is over and gone." This relates to the Old Testament. Once more he speaks of the Gospel and of virginity: "The flowers appear on the earth, the time of the pruning of vines has come." Does he not seem to you to say the very same thing that the Apostle says: "The time is shortened that henceforth both those that have wives may be as though they had none"? And more plainly does he herald chastity: "The voice," he says, "of the turtle is heard in our land." The turtle, the chaste of birds, always dwelling in lofty places, is a type of the Savior. Let us read the works of naturalists and we shall find that it is the nature of the turtle-dove, if it loses its mate, not to take another; and we shall understand that second marriage is repudiated even by dumb birds. And immediately the turtle says to its fellow: "The fig tree hath put forth its green figs," that is, the commandments of the old law have fallen, and the blossoming vines of the

Gospel give forth their fragrance. Whence the Apostle also says, "We are a sweet savor of Christ." "Arise, my love, my fair one, and come away. O my dove, thou art in the clefts of the rock, in the covert of the steep place. Let me see thy countenance, let me hear thy voice; for sweet is thy voice, and thy countenance is comely." Whilst thou covered thy countenance like Moses and the veil of the law remained, I neither saw thy face, nor did I condescend to hear thy voice. I said, "Yea, when ye make many prayers, I will not hear." But now with unveiled face behold my glory, and shelter thyself in the cleft and steep places of the solid rock. On hearing this the bride disclosed the mysteries of chastity: "My beloved is mine, and I am his: he feeds his flock among the lilies," that is among the pure virgin bands. Would you know what sort of a throne our true Solomon, the Prince of Peace, has, and what his attendants are like? "Behold," he says, "it is the litter of Solomon: threescore mighty men are about it, of the mighty men of Israel. They all handle the sword, and are expert in war: every man hath his sword upon his thigh." They who are about Solomon have their sword upon their thigh, like Ehud, the left-handed judge, who slew the fattest of foes, a man devoted to the flesh, and cut short all his pleasures. "I will get me," he says, "to the mountain of myrrh;" to those, that is, who have mortified their bodies; "and to the hill of frankincense," to the crowds of pure virgins; "and I will say to my bride, thou art all fair, my love, and there is no spot in thee." Whence too the Apostle: "That he might present the church to himself a glorious church, not having spot or wrinkle, or any such thing." "Come with me from Lebanon, my bride, with me from Lebanon. Thou shalt come and pass on from the beginning of faith, from the top of Sanir and

Hermon, from the lions' dens, from the mountains of the leopards." Lebanon is, being interpreted, *whiteness*. Come then, fairest bride, concerning whom it is elsewhere said "Who is she that cometh up, all in white?" and pass on by way of this world, from the beginning of faith, and from Sanir, which is by interpretation, *God of light*, as we read in the psalm: "Thy word is a lantern unto my feet, and light unto my path;" and "from Hermon," that is, *consecration*: and "flee from the lions' dens, and the mountains of the leopards who cannot change their spots." Flee, he says, from the lions' dens, flee from the pride of devils, that when thou hast been consecrated to me, I may be able to say unto thee: "Thou hast ravished my heart, my sister, my bride, thou hast ravished mine heart with one of thine eyes, with one chain of thy neck." What he says is something like this—I do not reject marriage: you have a second eye, the left, which I have given to you on account of the weakness of those who cannot see the right. But I am pleased with the right eye of virginity, and if it be blinded the whole body is in darkness. And that we might not think he had in view carnal love and bodily marriage, he at once excludes this meaning by saying "Thou hast ravished my heart, my bride, my sister." The name sister excludes all suspicion of unhallowed love. "How fair are thy breasts with wine," those breasts concerning which he had said above, My beloved is mine, and I am his: "betwixt my breasts shall he lie," that is in the princely portion of the heart where the Word of God has its lodging. What wine is that which gives beauty to the breasts of the bride, and fills them with the milk of chastity? That, forsooth, of which the bridegroom goes on to speak: "I have drunk my wine with my milk. Eat, O friends: yea, drink and be drunken, my brethren." Hence the Apostles also were said to be filled with new wine; with *new*, he says, not with *old* wine; because new wine is put into fresh wine-skins, and they did not walk in oldness of the letter, but in newness of the Spirit. This is wine wherewith when youths and maidens are intoxicated, they at once thirst for virginity; they are filled with the spirit of chastity, and the prophecy of Zechariah comes to pass, at least if we follow the Hebrew literally, for he prophesied concerning virgins: "And the streets of the city shall be full of boys and girls playing in the streets thereof. For what is his goodness, and what is his beauty, but the corn of the elect, and wine that giveth birth to virgins?" They are virgins of whom it is written in the forty-fifth psalm: "The virgins her companions that follow her shall be brought unto thee. With gladness and rejoicing shall they be led: they shall enter into the King's palace."

31. Then follows: "A garden shut up is my sister, my bride: a garden shut up, a fountain sealed." That which is shut up and sealed reminds us of the mother of our Lord who was a mother and a Virgin. Hence it was that no one before or after our Savior was laid in his new tomb, hewn in the solid rock. And yet she that was ever a Virgin is the mother of many virgins. For next we read: "Thy shoots are an orchard of pomegranates with precious fruits." By pomegranates and fruits is signified the blending of all virtues in virginity. "My beloved is white and ruddy"; white in virginity, ruddy in martyrdom. And because He is white and ruddy, therefore it is immediately added "His mouth is most sweet, yea, he is altogether lovely." The virgin bridegroom having been praised by the virgin bride, in turn praises the virgin bride, and says to her: "How beautiful are thy feet in sandals, O daughter

of Aminadab," which is, being interpreted, *a people that offered itself willingly.* For virginity is voluntary, and therefore the steps of the Church in the beauty of chastity are praised. This is not the time for me like a commentator to explain all the mysteries of virginity from the Song of Songs; I have no doubt that the fastidious reader will turn up his nose at what has already been said.

32. Isaiah tells of the mystery of our faith and hope: "Behold a virgin shall conceive, and bear a son, and shall call his name Emmanuel." I know that the Jews are accustomed to meet us with the objection that in Hebrew the word *Almah* does not mean a virgin, but *a young woman.* And, to speak truth, a virgin is properly called *Bethulah,* but a young woman, or a girl, is not *Almah,* but *Naarah!* What then is the meaning of *Almah?* A hidden virgin, that is, not merely virgin, but a virgin and something more, because not every virgin is hidden, shut off from the occasional sight of men. Then again, Rebecca, on account of her extreme purity, and because she was a type of the Church which she represented in her own virginity, is described in Genesis as *Almah,* not *Bethulah,* as may clearly be proved from the words of Abraham's servant, spoken by him in Mesopotamia: "And he said, O Lord, the God of my master Abraham, if now thou do prosper my way which I go: behold I stand by the fountain of water; and let it come to pass, that the maiden which cometh forth to draw, to whom I shall say, Give me, I pray thee, a little water of this pitcher to drink; and she shall say to me, Both drink thou, and I will also draw for thy camels: let the same be the woman whom the Lord hath appointed for my master's son." Where he speaks of the maiden coming forth to draw water, the Hebrew word is *Almah,* that is, a *virgin secluded,* and guarded by her

parents with extreme care. Or, if this be not so, let them at least show me where the word is applied to married women as well, and I will confess my ignorance. "Behold a virgin shall conceive and bear a son." If virginity be not preferred to marriage, why did not the Holy Spirit choose a married woman, or a widow? For at that time Anna the daughter of Phanuel, of the tribe of Aser, was alive, distinguished for purity, and always free to devote herself to prayers and fasting in the temple of God. If the life, and good works, and fasting without virginity can merit the advent of the Holy Spirit, she might well have been the mother of our Lord. Let us hasten to the rest: "The virgin daughter of Zion hath despised thee and laughed thee to scorn." To her whom he called daughter the prophet also gave the title virgin, for fear that if he spoke only of a daughter, it might be supposed that she was married. This is the virgin daughter whom elsewhere he thus addresses: "Sing, O barren, thou that dost not bear; break forth into singing, and cry aloud, thou that didst not travail with child: for more are the children of the desolate, than the children of the married wife, saith the Lord." This is she of whom God by the mouth of Jeremiah speaks, saying: "Can a maid forget her ornaments, or a bride her attire." Concerning her we read of a great miracle in the same prophecy—that a woman should compass a man, and that the Father of all things should be contained in a virgin's womb.

33. "Granted," says Jovinianus, "that there is a difference between marriage and virginity, what have you to say to this,—Suppose a virgin and a widow were baptized, and continued as they were, what difference will there be between them?" What we have already said concerning Peter and John, Anna and Mary, may be of

service here. For if there is no difference between a virgin and a widow, both being baptized, because baptism makes a new man, upon the same principle harlots and prostitutes, if they are baptized, will be equal to virgins. If previous marriage is no prejudice to a baptized widow, and past pleasures and the exposure of their bodies to public lust are no detriment in the case of harlots, once they have approached the laver they will gain the rewards of virginity. It is one thing to unite with God a mind pure and free from any stain of memory, another to remember the foul and forced embraces of a man, and in recollection to act a part which you do not in person. Jeremiah, who was sanctified in the womb, and was known in his mother's belly, enjoyed the high privilege because he was predestined to the blessing of virginity. And when all were captured, and even the vessels of the temple were plundered by the King of Babylon, he alone was liberated by the enemy, knew not the insults of captivity, and was supported by the conquerors; and Nebuchadnezzar, though he gave Nebuzaradan no charge concerning the Holy of Holies, did give him charge concerning Jeremiah. For that is the true temple of God, and that is the Holy of Holies, which is consecrated to the Lord by pure virginity. On the other hand, Ezekiel, who was kept captive in Babylon, who saw the storm approaching from the north, and the whirlwind sweeping all before it, says, "My wife died in the evening and I did in the morning as I was commanded." For the Lord had previously told him that in that day he should open his mouth, and speak, and no longer keep silence. Mark well, that while his wife was living he was not at liberty to admonish the people. His wife died, the bond of wedlock was broken, and without the least hesitation he constantly devoted himself to the prophetic office. For he who was called being free, is truly the Lord's bondservant. I do not deny the blessedness of widows who remain such after their baptism; nor do I disparage those wives who maintain their chastity in wedlock; but as they attain a greater reward with God than married women who pay the marriage due, let widows themselves be content to give the preference to virginity. For if a chastity which comes too late, when the glow of bodily pleasure is no longer felt, makes them feel superior to married women, why should they not acknowledge themselves inferior to perpetual virginity.

34. All that goes for nothing, says Jovinianus, because even bishops, priests, and deacons, husbands of one wife, and having children, were appointed by the Apostle. Just as the Apostle says he has no commandment respecting virgins, and yet gives his advice, as one who had obtained mercy from the Lord, and is anxious throughout the whole discussion to give virginity the preference over marriage, and advises what he does not venture to command, lest he seem to lay a snare, and to put a heavier burden upon man's nature than it can bear; so also in establishing the constitution of the Church, inasmuch as the elements of the early Church were drawn from the Gentiles, he made the rules for fresh believers somewhat lighter that they might not in alarm shrink from keeping them. Then, again, the Apostles and elders wrote letters from Jerusalem that no heavier burden should be laid on Gentile believers than that they should keep themselves from idolatry, and from fornication, and from things strangled. As though they were providing for infant children, they gave them milk to drink, not solid food. Nor did they lay down rules for continence, nor hint at

virginity, nor urge to fasting, nor repeat the directions given in the Gospel to the Apostles, not to have two tunics, nor scrip, nor money in their girdles, nor staff in their hand, nor shoes on their feet. And they certainly did not bid them, if they wished to be perfect, go and sell all that they had and give to the poor, and "come follow me." For if the young man who boasted of having done all that the law enjoins, when he heard this went away sorrowful, because he had great possessions, and the Pharisees derided an utterance such as this from our Lord's lips: how much more would the vast multitude of Gentiles, whose highest virtue consisted in not plundering another's goods, have repudiated the obligation of perpetual chastity and continence, when they were told in the letter to keep themselves from idols, and from fornication, seeing that fornication was heard of among them, and such fornication as was not "even among the Gentiles." But the very choice of a bishop makes for me. For he does not say: Let a bishop be chosen who marries one wife and begets children; but who marries one wife, and has his children in subjection and well disciplined. You surely admit that he is no bishop who during his episcopate begets children. The reverse is the case—if he be discovered, he will not be bound by the ordinary obligations of a husband, but will be condemned as an adulterer. Either permit priests to perform the work of marriage with the result that virginity and marriage are on a par: or if it is unlawful for priests to touch their wives, they are so far holy in that they imitate virgin chastity. But something more follows. A layman, or any believer, cannot pray unless he abstains from sexual intercourse. Now a priest must always offer sacrifices for the people: he must therefore always pray. And if he must always pray, he must always be released from the duties of marriage. For even under the old law they who used to offer sacrifices for the people not only remained in their houses, but purified themselves for the occasion by separating from their wives, nor would they drink wine or strong drink which are wont to stimulate lust. That married men are elected to the priesthood, I do not deny: the number of virgins is not so great as that of the priests required. Does it follow that because all the strongest men are chosen for the army, weaker men should not be taken as well? All cannot be strong. If an army were constituted of strength only, and numbers went for nothing, the feebler men might be rejected. As it is, men of second or third-rate strength are chosen, that the army may have its full numerical complement. How is it, then, you will say, that frequently at the ordination of priests a virgin is passed over, and a married man taken? Perhaps because he lacks other qualifications in keeping with virginity, or it may be that he is thought a virgin, and is not: or there may be a stigma on his virginity, or at all events virginity itself makes him proud, and while he plumes himself on mere bodily chastity, he neglects other virtues; he does not cherish the poor: he is too fond of money. It sometimes happens that a man has a gloomy visage, a frowning brow, a walk as though he were in a solemn procession, and so offends the people, who, because they have no fault to find with his life, hate his mere dress and gait. Many are chosen not out of affection for themselves, but out of hatred for another. In most cases the election is won by mere simplicity, while the shrewdness and discretion of another candidate elicit opposition as though they were evils. Sometimes the judgement of the commoner people is at fault, and in testing the qualities of the priesthood, the individual inclines to his own character, with the result that he looks not so much for a good candidate as for one like himself. Not unfrequently it happens that married men, who form the larger portion of the people, in approving married candidates seem to approve themselves, and it does not occur to them that the mere fact that they prefer a married person to a virgin is evidence of their inferiority to virgins. What I am going to say will perhaps offend many. Yet I will say it, and good men will not be angry with me, because they will not feel the sting of conscience. Sometimes it is the fault of the bishops, who choose into the ranks of the clergy not the best, but the cleverest, men, and think the more simple as well as innocent ones incapable; or, as though they were distributing the offices of an earthly service, they give posts to their kindred and relations; or they listen to the dictates of wealth. And, worse than all, they give promotion to the clergy who besmear them with flattery. To take the other view, if the Apostle's meaning be that marriage is necessary in a bishop, the Apostle himself ought not to have been a bishop, for he said, "Yet I would that all men were even as I myself." And John will be thought unworthy of this rank, and all the virgins, and the continent, the fairest gems that give grace and ornament to the Church. Bishop, priest, and deacon, are not honorable distinctions, but names of offices. And we do not read: "If a man seeks the office of a bishop, he desires a good degree," but, "he desires a good work," because by being placed in the higher order an opportunity is afforded him, if he chooses to avail himself of it, for the practice of virtue.

35. "The bishop, then, must be without reproach, so that he is the slave of no vice: "the husband of one

wife," that is, in the past, not in the present; "sober," or better, as it is in the Greek, "vigilant," that is νηφάλεον; "chaste," for that is the meaning of σώφρονα; "distinguished," both by chastity and conduct: "hospitable," so that he imitates Abraham, and with strangers, nay rather *in* strangers, entertains Christ; "apt to teach," for it profits nothing to enjoy the consciousness of virtue, unless a man be able to instruct the people entrusted to him, so that he can exhort in doctrine, and refute the gainsayers; "not a drunkard," for he who is constantly in the Holy of Holies and offers sacrifices, will not drink wine and strong drink, since wine is a luxury. If a bishop drink at all, let it be in such a way that no one will know whether he has drunk or not. "No striker," that is, a striker of men's consciences, for the Apostle is not pointing out what a boxer, but a pontiff ought not to do. He directly teaches what he ought to do: "but gentle, not contentious, no lover of money, one that rules well his own house, having his children in subjection with all chastity." See what chastity is required in a bishop! If his child be unchaste, he himself cannot be a bishop, and he offends God in the same way as did Eli the priest, who had indeed rebuked his sons, but because he had not put away the offenders, fell backwards and died before the lamp of God went out. "Women in like manner must be chaste," and so on. In every grade, and in both sexes, chastity has the chief place. You see then that the blessedness of a bishop, priest, or deacon, does not lie in the fact that they are bishops, priests, or deacons, but in their having the virtues which their names and offices imply. Otherwise, if a deacon be holier than his bishop, his lower grade will not give him a worse standing with Christ. If it were so, Stephen the deacon, the first to wear the martyr's crown, would be less in the kingdom of heaven than many bishops, and than Timothy and Titus, whom I venture to make neither inferior nor yet superior to him. Just as in the legions of the army there are generals, tribunes, centurions, javelin-men, and light-armed troops, common soldiers, and companies, but once the battle begins, all distinctions of rank are dropped, and the one thing looked for is valor: so too in this camp and in this battle, in which we contend against devils, not names but deeds are needed: and under the true commander, Christ, not the man who has the highest title has the greatest fame, but he who is the bravest warrior.

36. But you will say: "If everybody were a virgin, what would become of the human race"? Like shall here beget like. If everyone were a widow, or continent in marriage, how will mortal men be propagated? Upon this principle there will be nothing at all for fear that something else may cease to exist. To put a case: if all men were philosophers, there would be no husbandmen. Why speak of husbandmen? there would be no orators, no lawyers, no teachers of the other professions. If all men were leaders, what would become of the soldiers? If all were the head, whose head would they be called, when there were no other members? You are afraid that if the desire for virginity were general there would be no prostitutes, no adulteresses, no wailing infants in town or country. Every day the blood of adulterers is shed, adulterers are condemned, and lust is raging and rampant in the very presence of the laws and the symbols of authority and the courts of justice. Be not afraid that all will become virgins: virginity is a hard matter, and therefore rare, because it is hard: "Many are called, few chosen." Many begin, few persevere. And so the reward is

great for those who have persevered. If all were able to be virgins, our Lord would never have said: "He that is able to receive it, let him receive it:" and the Apostle would not have hesitated to give his advice,—"Now concerning virgins I have no commandment of the Lord." Why then, you will say, were the organs of generation created, and why were we so fashioned by the all-wise creator, that we burn for one another, and long for natural intercourse? To reply is to endanger our modesty: we are, as it were, between two rocks, the Symplegades of necessity and virtue, on either side; and must make shipwreck of either our sense of shame, or of the cause we defend: If we reply to your suggestions, shame covers our face. If shame secures silence, in a manner we seem to desert our post, and to leave the ground clear to the raging foe. Yet it is better, as the story goes, to shut our eyes and fight like the blindfold gladiators, than not to repel with the shield of truth the darts aimed at us. I can indeed say: "Our hinder parts which are banished from sight, and the lower portions of the abdomen, which perform the functions of nature, are the Creator's work." But inasmuch as the physical conformation of the organs of generation testifies to difference of sex, I shall briefly reply: Are we never then to forego lust, for fear that we may have members of this kind for nothing? Why then should a husband keep himself from his wife? Why should a widow persevere in chastity, if we were only born to live like beasts? Or what harm does it do me if another man lies with my wife? For as the teeth were made for chewing, and the food masticated passes into the stomach, and a man is not blamed for giving my wife bread: similarly if it was intended that the organs of generation should always be performing their office, when my vigor is spent let another take my place, and, if I may so speak, let my wife quench her burning lust where she can. But what does the Apostle mean by exhorting to continence, if continence be contrary to nature? What does our Lord mean when He instructs us in the various kinds of eunuchs. Surely the Apostle who bids us emulate his own chastity, must be asked, if we are to be consistent, Why are you like other men, Paul? Why are you distinguished from the female sex by a beard, hair, and other peculiarities of person? How is it that you have not swelling bosoms, and are not broad at the hips, narrow at the chest? Your voice is rugged, your speech rough, your eyebrows more shaggy. To no purpose you have all these manly qualities, if you forego the embraces of women. I am compelled to say something and become a fool: but you have forced me to dare to speak. Our Lord and Savior, Who though He was in the form of God, condescended to take the form of a servant, and became obedient to the Father even unto death, yea the death of the cross—what necessity was there for Him to be born with members which He was not going to use? He certainly was circumcised to manifest His sex. Why did he cause John the Apostle and John the Baptist to make themselves eunuchs through love of Him, after causing them to be born men? Let us then who believe in Christ follow His example. And if we knew Him after the flesh, let us no longer know Him according to the flesh. The substance of our resurrection bodies will certainly be the same as now, though of higher glory. For the Savior after His descent into hell had so far the selfsame body in which He was crucified, that He showed the disciples the marks of the nails in His hands and the wound in His side. Moreover, if we deny the identity of His body because He entered though the doors were shut, and this is not a property of human bodies, we must deny also that Peter and the Lord had real bodies because they walked upon the water, which is contrary to nature. "In the resurrection of the dead they will neither marry nor be given in marriage, but will be like the angels." What others will hereafter be in heaven, that virgins begin to be on earth. If likeness to the angels is promised us (and there is no difference of sex among the angels), we shall either be of no sex as are the angels, or at all events which is clearly proved, though we rise from the dead in our own sex, we shall not perform the functions of sex.

37. But why do we argue, and why are we eager to frame a clever and victorious reply to our opponent? "Old things have passed away, behold all things have become new." I will run through the utterances of the Apostles, and as to the instances afforded by Solomon I added short expositions to facilitate their being understood, so now I will go over the passages bearing on Christian purity and continence, and will make of many proofs a connected series. By this method I shall succeed in omitting nothing relating to chastity, and shall avoid being tediously long. Amongst other passages, Paul the Apostle writes to the Romans: "What fruit then had ye at that time in the things whereof ye are now ashamed? for the end of those things is death. But now being made free from sin, and become servants to God, ye have your fruit unto sanctification, and the end eternal life." I suppose too that the end of marriage is death. But the compensating fruit of sanctification, fruit belonging either to virginity or to continence, is eternal life. And afterwards: "Wherefore, my brethren, ye also were made dead to the law through the body of Christ; that ye should be joined to another, even to him who was raised from the dead, that we might

bring forth fruit unto God. For when we were in the flesh, the sinful passions, which were through the law, wrought in our members to bring forth fruit unto death. But now we have been discharged from the law, having died to that wherein we were holden; so that we serve in newness of the Spirit, and not in oldness of the letter." "When," he says, "we were in the flesh, and not in the newness of the Spirit but in the oldness of the letter," we did those things which pertained to the flesh, and bore fruit unto death. But now because we are dead to the law, through the body of Christ, let us bear fruit to God, that we may belong to Him who rose from the dead. And elsewhere, having previously said, "I know that the law is spiritual," and having discussed at some length the violence of the flesh which frequently drives us to do what we would not, he at last continues: "O wretched man that I am! Who shall deliver me out of the body of this death? I thank God through Jesus Christ our Lord." And again, "So then I myself with the mind serve the law of God; but with the flesh the law of sin." And, "There is therefore now no condemnation to them that are in Christ Jesus, who walk not after the flesh. For the law of the Spirit of life in Christ Jesus made me free from the law of sin and death." And more clearly in what follows he teaches that Christians do not walk according to the flesh but according to the Spirit: "For they that are after the flesh do mind the things of the flesh; but they that are after the spirit the things of the spirit. For the mind of the flesh is death; but the mind of the spirit is life and peace: because the mind of the flesh is enmity against God; for it is not subject to the law of God, neither indeed can it be: and they that are in the flesh cannot please God. But ye are not in the flesh, but in the Spirit, if so be that the Spirit of

God dwelleth in you," and so on to where he says, "So then, brethren, we are debtors, not to the flesh, to live after the flesh: for if ye live after the flesh, ye must die; but if by the spirit ye mortify the deeds of the body, ye shall live. For as many as are led by the Spirit of God, these are sons of God." If the wisdom of the flesh is enmity against God, and they who are in the flesh cannot please God, I think that they who perform the functions of marriage love the wisdom of the flesh, and therefore are in the flesh. The Apostle being desirous to withdraw us from the flesh and to join us to the Spirit, says afterwards: "I beseech you therefore, brethren, by the mercies of God, to present your bodies a living sacrifice, holy, acceptable to God, which is your reasonable service. And be not fashioned according to this world: but be ye transformed by the renewing of your mind, that ye may prove what is the good and acceptable and perfect will of God. For I say, through the grace that was given me, to every man that is among you, not to think of himself more highly than he ought to think; but to think according to chastity" (not *soberly* as the Latin versions badly render), but "think," he says, "according to chastity," for the Greek words are ἐις τὸ σωφρονεῖν. Let us consider what the Apostle says: "Be ye transformed by the renewing of your mind, that ye may prove what is the good and acceptable and perfect will of God." What he says is something like this—God indeed permits marriage, He permits second marriages, and if necessary, prefers even third marriages to fornication and adultery. But we who ought to present our bodies a living sacrifice, holy, acceptable to God, which is our reasonable service, should consider, not what God permits, but what He wishes: that we may prove what is the good and acceptable and perfect will of God.

It follows that what He merely permits is neither good, nor acceptable, nor perfect. And he gives his reasons for this advice: "Knowing the season, that now it is high time for you to awake out of sleep: for now is salvation nearer to us than when we first believed. The night is far spent, and the day is at hand." And lastly: "Put ye on the Lord Jesus Christ, and make not provision for the flesh, to fulfil the lusts thereof." God's will is one thing, His indulgence another. Whence, writing to the Corinthians, he says, "I, brethren, could not speak unto you as unto spiritual, but as unto carnal, even as unto babes in Christ. I have fed you with milk, and not with meat: for hitherto ye were not able to bear it, neither yet now are ye able. For ye are yet carnal." He who is in the merely animal state, and does not receive the things pertaining to the Spirit of God (for he is foolish, and cannot understand them, because they are spiritually discerned), he is not fed with the food of perfect chastity, but with the coarse milk of marriage. As through man came death, so also through man came the resurrection of the dead. As in Adam we all die, so in Christ we shall all be made alive. Under the law we served the old Adam, under the Gospel let us serve the new Adam. For the first man Adam was made a living soul, the last Adam was made a quickening spirit. "The first man is of the earth, earthy: the second man is of heaven. As is the earthy, such are they also that are earthy: and as is the heavenly, such are they also that are heavenly. And as we have borne the image of the earthy, we shall also bear the image of the heavenly. Now this I say, brethren, that flesh and blood cannot inherit the Kingdom of God; neither doth corruption inherit incorruption." This is so clear that no explanation can make it clearer: "Flesh and blood," he says, "cannot inherit the Kingdom of God, neither doth corruption inherit incorruption." If corruption attaches to all intercourse, and incorruption is characteristic of chastity, the rewards of chastity cannot belong to marriage. "For we know that if the earthly house of this tabernacle be dissolved, we have a building from God, a house not made with hands, eternal, in the heavens. For verily in this we groan, longing to be clothed upon with our habitation which is from heaven. We are willing to be absent from the body, and to be at home with the Lord. Wherefore also we make it our aim, whether in the body, or out of the body, to be well-pleasing unto God." And by way of more fully explaining what he did not wish them to be he says elsewhere: "I espoused you to one husband, that I might present you as a pure virgin to Christ." But if you choose to apply the words to the whole Assembly of believers, and in this betrothal to Christ include both married women, and the twice-married, and widows, and virgins, that also makes for us. For whilst he invites all to chastity and to the reward of virginity, he shows that virginity is more excellent than all these conditions. And again writing to the Galatians he says: "Because by the works of the law shall no flesh be justified." Among the works of the law is marriage, and accordingly under it they are cursed who have no children. And if under the Gospel it is permitted to have children, it is one thing to make a concession to weakness, another to hold out rewards to virtue.

38. Something else I will say to my friends who marry and after long chastity and continence begin to burn and are as wanton as the brutes: "Are ye so foolish? having begun in the Spirit, are ye now perfected in the flesh? Did ye suffer so many things in vain?" If the

Apostle in the case of some persons loosens the cords of continence, and lets them have a slack rein, he does so on account of the infirmity of the flesh. This is the enemy he has in view when he once more says: "Walk by the Spirit, and ye shall not fulfill the lust of the flesh. For the flesh lusted against the Spirit, and the Spirit against the flesh." It is unnecessary now to speak of the works of the flesh: it would be tedious, and he who chooses can easily gather them from the letter of the Apostle. I will only speak of the Spirit and its fruits, love, joy, peace, long suffering, kindness, goodness, faithfulness, meekness, continence. All the virtues of the Spirit are supported and protected by continence, which is as it were their solid foundation and crowning point. Against such there is no law. "And they that are of Christ have crucified their flesh with the passions and the lusts thereof. If we live by the Spirit, by the Spirit let us also walk." Why do we who with Christ have crucified our flesh and its passions and desires again desire to do the things of the flesh? "Whatsoever a man soweth, that shall he also reap. For he that soweth unto his own flesh, shall of the flesh reap corruption; but he that soweth unto the Spirit shall of the Spirit reap eternal life." I think that he who has a wife, so long as he reverts to the practice in question, that Satan may not tempt him, is sowing to the flesh and not to the Spirit. And he who sows to the flesh (the words are not mine, but the Apostle's) reaps corruption. God the Father chose us in Christ before the foundation of the world, that we might be holy and without spot before Him. We walked in the lusts of the flesh, doing the desires of the flesh and of the thoughts, and were children of wrath, even as the rest. But now He has raised us up with Him, and made us to sit with Him in the heavenly places in Christ Jesus, that we may put away according to our former manner of life the old man, which is corrupt according to the lusts of deceit, and that blessing may be applied to us which so finely concludes the mystical Epistle to the Ephesians: "Grace be with all them that love our Lord Jesus Christ in uncorruptness." "For our citizenship is in heaven; from whence also we wait for a Savior, the Lord Jesus Christ: who shall fashion anew the body of our humiliation, that it may be conformed to the body of his glory. Whatsoever things then are true, whatsoever are chaste, whatsoever things are just, whatsoever things pertain to purity, let us join ourselves to these, let us follow these. Christ hath reconciled us in his body to God the Father through his death, and has presented us holy and without spot, and without blame before himself: in whom we have been also circumcised, not with the circumcision made with hands, to the spoiling of the body of the flesh, but with the circumcision of Christ, having been buried with him in baptism, wherein also we rose with him. If then we have risen with Christ, let us seek those things which are above, where Christ sits on the right hand of God; let us set our affections on things above, not upon the things that are upon the earth. For we are dead, and our life is hid with Christ in God. When Christ our life shall appear, then we also shall appear with him in glory. No soldier on service entangles himself in the affairs of this life; that he may please him who enrolled him as a soldier. For the grace of God hath appeared, bringing salvation to all men, instructing us, to the intent that, denying ungodliness and worldly lusts, we should live purely and righteously and godly in this present world."

39. The day would not be long enough were I to attempt to relate all that the Apostle enjoins concerning

purity. These things are those concerning which our Lord said to the Apostles: "I have yet many things to say unto you, but ye cannot bear them now. Howbeit, when he, the Spirit of truth, is come, he shall guide you into all the truth." After the crucifixion of Christ, we find in the Acts of the Apostles that one house, that of Philip the Evangelist, produced four virgin daughters, to the end that Cæsarea, where the Gentile Church had been consecrated in the person of Cornelius the centurion, might afford an illustration of virginity. And whereas our Lord said in the Gospel: "The law and the prophets were until John," they because they were virgins are related to have prophesied even after John. For they could not be bound by the law of the Old Testament, who had shone with the brightness of virginity. Let us pass on to James, who was called the brother of the Lord, a man of such sanctity and righteousness, and distinguished by so rigid and perpetual a virginity, that even Josephus, the Jewish historian, relates that the overthrow of Jerusalem was due to his death. He, the first bishop of the Church at Jerusalem, which was composed of Jewish believers, to whom Paul went, accompanied by Titus and Barnabas, says in his Epistle: "Be not deceived, my beloved brethren. Every good gift and every perfect boon is from above, coming down from the Father of lights, with whom there is no difference, neither shadow that is cast by turning. Of his own will he brought us forth by the word of truth, that we should be a kind of first-fruits of his creatures." Himself a virgin, he teaches virginity in a mystery. Every perfect gift cometh down from above, where marriage is unknown; and it cometh down, not from any one you please, but from the Father of lights, Who says to the apostles, "Ye are the light of the world;" with Whom there is no difference of Jew, or Gentile, nor does that shadow which was the companion of the law, trouble those who have believed from among the nations; but with His word He begat us, and with the word of truth, because some shadow, image, and likeness of truth went before in the law, that we might be the first-fruits of His creatures. And as He who was Himself the first begotten from the dead has raised all that have died in Him: so He who was a virgin, consecrated the first-fruits of His virgins in His own virgin self. Let us also consider what Peter thinks of the calling of the Gentiles: "Blessed be the God and Father of our Lord Jesus Christ, who according to his great mercy begat us again unto a living hope by the resurrection of Jesus Christ from the dead, unto an inheritance incorruptible, and undefiled, and that fades not away, reserved in heaven for you, who by the power of God are guarded through faith unto a salvation ready to be revealed in the last time." Where we read of an inheritance incorruptible, and undefiled, and that fades not away, prepared in heaven and reserved for the last time, and of the hope of eternal life when they will neither marry, nor be given in marriage, there, in other words, the privileges of virginity are described. For he shows as much in what follows: "Wherefore girding up the loins of your mind, be sober and set your hope perfectly on the grace that is to be brought unto you at the revelation of Jesus Christ; as children of obedience, not fashioning yourselves according to your former lusts in the time of your ignorance; but like as he which called you is holy, be ye yourselves also holy in all manner of living; because it is written, ye shall be holy; for I am holy. For we were not redeemed with contemptible things, with silver or gold; but with the precious blood of a lamb without spot, Jesus

Christ, that we might purify our souls in obedience to the truth, having been begotten again not of corruptible seed, but of incorruptible, through the word of God, who lives and abides. And as living stones let us be built up a spiritual house, a holy priesthood offering up spiritual sacrifices through Christ our Lord. For we are an elect race, a royal priesthood, a holy nation, a people for God's own possession. Christ died for us in the flesh. Let us arm ourselves with the same conversation as did Christ; for he that hath suffered in the flesh hath ceased from sin; that we should no longer live the rest of our time in the flesh to the lusts of men, but to the will of God. For the time past is sufficient for us when we walked in lasciviousness, lusts, and other vices. Great and precious are the promises attaching to virginity which He has given us, that through it we may become partakers of the divine nature, having escaped from the corruption that is in the world through lust. The Lord knows how to deliver the godly out of temptation, and to keep the unrighteous under punishment unto the day of judgement, but chiefly them that walk after the flesh in the lust of defilement, and despise dominion, daring, self-willed. For they, as beasts of burden, without reason, think only of their belly and their lusts, railers who shall in their corruption be destroyed, and shall receive the reward of iniquity: men that count unrighteousness delight, spots and blemishes, thinking of nothing but their pleasures; having eyes full of adultery and insatiable lust, deceiving souls not yet strengthened by the love of Christ. For they utter swelling words and easily snare the unlearned with the seduction of the flesh; promising them liberty while they themselves are the slaves of vice, luxury, and corruption. For of what a man is overcome, of the same is he also brought into bondage.

But if, after they had escaped the defilements of the world through the knowledge of our Savior Jesus Christ, they are again overcome by that which they before overcame, the last state is become worse with them than the first. And it were better for them not to have known the way of righteousness, than, after knowing it, to turn back and forsake the holy commandment delivered unto them. And it has happened unto them according to the true proverb, the dog hath turned to his own vomit again, and the sow that had washed to wallowing in the mire." I have hesitated, for fear of being tedious, to quote the whole passage of the second Epistle of Peter, and have merely shown that the Holy Spirit in prophecy foretold the teachers of this time and their heresy. Lastly, he more clearly denotes them, saying, "In the last days seducing mockers shall come, walking after their own lusts."

40. The Apostle has described Jovinianus speaking with swelling cheeks and nicely balancing his inflated utterances, promising heavenly liberty, when he himself is the slave of vice and self-indulgence, a dog returning to his vomit. For although he boasts of being a monk, he has exchanged his dirty tunic, bare feet, common bread, and drink of water, for a snowy dress, sleek skin, honey-wine and dainty dishes, for the sauces of Apicius and Paxamus, for baths and rubbings, and for the cook-shops. Is it not clear that he prefers his belly to Christ, and thinks his ruddy complexion worth the kingdom of heaven? And yet that handsome monk so fat and sleek, and of bright appearance, who always walks with the air of a bridegroom, must either marry a wife if he is to show that virginity and marriage are equal: or if he does not marry one, it is useless for him to bandy words with us when his acts are on our side. And John

agrees with this almost to the letter: "Love not the world, neither the things that are in the world. If any man loves the world, the love of the Father is not in him. For all that is in the world is the lust of the flesh, and the lust of the eyes, and the pride of this life, which is not of the Father, but is of the world." And, "The world passes away, and the lust thereof: but he that doeth the will of God abides forever. A new commandment have I written unto you, which thing is true both in Christ and in you; because the darkness is passing away, and the true light already shineth." And again, "Beloved, now are we the children of God, and it is not yet made manifest what we shall be. But we know that, if he shall be manifested, we shall be like him: for we shall see him even as he is. And everyone that hath this hope purifies himself, even as he is pure. Herein is our love made perfect, if we have boldness in the day of judgement: that as he is, even so may we be in this world." The Epistle of Jude also expresses nearly the same: "Hating even the garment spotted by the flesh." Let us read the Apocalypse of John, and we shall there find the Lamb upon Mount Sion, and with Him "a hundred and forty-four thousand of them that were sealed, having His name and the name of His Father written in their foreheads, who sing a new song, and no one can sing that song save they who have been redeemed out of the earth. These are they who have not defiled themselves with women, for they continued virgins. These follow the Lamb whithersoever He goes for they were redeemed from among men, first-fruits to God and to the Lamb, and in their mouth was found no guile, and they are without spot." Out of each tribe, the tribe of Dan excepted, the place of which is taken by the tribe of Levi, twelve thousand virgins who have been sealed are spoken of as future believers, who have not defiled themselves with women. And that we may not suppose the reference to be to those who know not harlots, he immediately added: "For they continued virgins." Whereby he shows that all who have not preserved their virginity, in comparison of pure and angelic chastity and of our Lord Jesus Christ Himself, are defiled. "These are they who sing a new song which no man can sing except him that is a virgin. These are first-fruits unto God and unto the Lamb, and are without blemish." If virgins are first-fruits, it follows that widows and the continent in marriage, come after the first-fruits, that is, are in the second and third rank: nor can a lost people be saved unless it offers such sacrifices of chastity to God, and with pure victims reconcile the spotless Lamb. It would be endless work to explain the Gospel mystery of the ten virgins, five of whom were wise and five foolish. All I say now is, that as mere virginity without other works does not save, so all works without virginity, purity, continence, chastity, are imperfect. And we shall not be hindered in the least from taking this view by the objection of our opponent that our Lord was at Cana of Galilee, and joined in the marriage festivities when He turned water into wine. I shall very briefly reply, that He Who was circumcised on the eighth day, and for Whom a pair of turtle-doves and two young pigeons were offered on the day of purification, like others before He suffered, shewed His approval of Jewish custom, that He might not seem to give His enemies just cause for putting Him to death on the pretext that He destroyed the law and condemned nature. And even this was done for our sakes. For by going once to a marriage, He taught that men should marry only once. Moreover, at that time it was possible to injure virginity if marriage were not placed next to it, and the purity of widowhood in the third rank. But now when heretics are condemning wedlock, and despise the ordinance of God, we gladly hear anything he may say in praise of marriage. For the Church does not condemn marriage, but makes it subordinate; nor does she reject it, but regulates it; for she knows, as was said before, that in a great house there are not only vessels of gold and silver, but also of wood and earthenware; and that some are to honor, some to dishonor; and that whoever cleanses himself will be a vessel of honor, necessary, prepared for every good work.

41. I have given enough and more than enough illustrations from the divine writings of Christian chastity and angelic virginity. But as I understand that our opponent in his commentaries summons us to the tribunal of worldly wisdom, and we are told that views of this kind are never accepted in the world, and that our religion has invented a dogma against nature, I will quickly run through Greek and Roman and Foreign History, and will show that virginity ever took the lead of chastity. Fable relates that Atalanta, the virgin of Calydonian fame, lived for the chase and dwelt always in the woods; in other words that she did not set her heart on marriage with its troubles of pregnancy and of sickness, but upon the nobler life of freedom and chastity. Harpalyce too, a Thracian virgin, is described by the famous poet; and so is Camilia, queen of the Volsci, on whom, when she came to his assistance, Turnus had no higher praise which he could bestow than to call her a virgin. "O Virgin, Glory of Italy!" And that famous daughter of Leos, the lady of the brazen house, ever a virgin, is related to have freed her country from pestilence by her voluntary death: and the blood of the virgin Iphigenia is said to have calmed the

stormy winds. What need to tell of the Sibyls of Erythræ and Cumæ, and the eight others? Varro asserts there were ten whose ornament was virginity, and divination the reward of their virginity. But if in the Æolian dialect "Sibyl" is represented by Θεοβούλη, we must understand that a knowledge of the *Counsel of God* is rightly attributed to virginity alone. We read, too, that Cassandra and Chryseis, prophetesses of Apollo and Juno, were virgins. And there were innumerable priestesses of the Taurian Diana, and of Vesta. One of these, Munitia, being suspected of unchastity was buried alive, which would be in my opinion an unjust punishment, unless the violation of virginity were considered a serious crime. At all events how highly the Romans always esteemed virgins is clear from the fact that consuls and generals even in their triumphal chariots and bringing home the spoils of conquered nations, were wont to make way for them to pass. And so did men of all ranks. When Claudia, a Vestal Virgin, was suspected of unchastity, and a vessel containing the image of Cybele was aground in the Tiber, it is related that she, to prove her chastity, with her girdle drew the ship which a thousand men could not move. Yet, as the uncle of Lucan the poet says, it would have been better if this circumstance had decorated a chastity tried and proved, and had not pleaded in defence of a chastity equivocal. No wonder that we read such things of human beings, when heathen error also invented the virgin goddesses Minerva and Diana, and placed the Virgin among the twelve signs of the Zodiac, by means of which, as they suppose, the world revolves. It is a proof of the little esteem in which they held marriage that they did not even among the scorpions, centaurs, crabs, fishes, and Capricorn, thrust in a husband and wife. When the thirty tyrants of Athens had slain Phidon at the banquet, they commanded his virgin daughters to come to them, naked like harlots, and there upon the ground, red with their father's blood, to act the wanton. For a little while they hid their grief, and then when they saw the revelers were intoxicated, going out on the plea of easing nature, they embraced one another and threw themselves into a well, that by death they might save their virginity. The virgin daughter of Demotion, chief of the Areopagites, having heard of the death of her betrothed, Leosthenes, who had originated the Lamian war, slew herself, for she declared that although in body she was a virgin, yet if she were compelled to accept another, she should regard him as her second husband, when she had given her heart to Leosthenes. So close a friendship long existed between Sparta and Messene that for the furtherance of certain religious rites they even exchanged virgins. Well, on one occasion when the men of Messene attempted to outrage fifty Lacedæmonian virgins, out of so many not one consented, but they all most gladly died in defence of their chastity. Whence there arose a long and grievous war, and in the long run Mamertina was destroyed. Aristoclides, tyrant of Orchomenos, fell in love with a virgin of Stymphalus, and when after the death of her father she took refuge in the temple of Diana, and embraced the image of the goddess and could not be dragged thence by force, she was slain on the spot. Her death caused such intense grief throughout Arcadia that the people took up arms and avenged the virgin's death. Aristomenes of Messene, a just man, at a time when the Lacedæmonians, whom he had conquered, were celebrating by night the festival called the Hyacinthia, carried off from the sportive bands fifteen virgins, and fleeing all night at full speed got away from the Spartan territory. His companions wished to outrage them, but he admonished them to the best of his power not to do so, and when certain refused to obey, he slew them, and restrained the rest by fear. The maidens were afterwards ransomed by their kinsmen, and on seeing Aristomenes condemned for murder would not return to their country until clasping the knees of the judges they beheld the protector of their chastity acquitted. How shall we sufficiently praise the daughters of Scedasus at Leuctra in Boeotia? It is related that in the absence of their father they hospitably entertained two youths who were passing by, and who having drunk to excess violated the virgins in the course of the night. Being unwilling to survive the loss of their virginity, the maidens inflicted deadly wounds on one another. Nor would it be right to omit mention of the Locrian virgins. They were sent to Ilium according to custom which had lasted for nearly a thousand years, and yet not one gave occasion to any idle tale or filthy rumour of virginity defiled. Could any one pass over in silence the seven virgins of Miletus who, when the Gauls spread desolation far and wide, that they might suffer no indignity at the hands of the enemy, escaped disgrace by death, and left to all virgins the lesson of their example—that noble minds care more for chastity than life? Nicanor having conquered and overthrown Thebes was himself overcome by a passion for one captive virgin, whose voluntary self-surrender he longed for. A captive maid, he thought, must be only too glad. But he found that virginity is dearer to the pure in heart than a kingdom, when with tears and grief he held her in his arms slain by her own hand. Greek writers tell also of another Theban virgin who had been deflowered by a Macedonian foe, and who, hiding her grief for a while, slew the violator of her virginity as he slept, and then killed herself with the sword, so that she would neither live when her chastity was lost, nor die before she had avenged herself.

42. To come to the Gymnosophists of India, the opinion is authoritatively handed down that Budda, the founder of their religion, had his birth through the side of a virgin. And we need not wonder at this in the case of Barbarians when cultured Greece supposed that Minerva at her birth sprang from the head of Jove, and Father Bacchus from his thigh. Speusippus also, Plato's nephew, and Clearchus in his eulogy of Plato, and Anaxelides in the second book of his philosophy, relates that Perictione, the mother of Plato, was violated by an apparition of Apollo, and they agree in thinking that the prince of wisdom was born of a virgin. Timæus writes that the virgin daughter of Pythagoras was at the head of a band of virgins, and instructed them in chastity. Diodorus, the disciple of Socrates, is said to have had five daughters skilled in dialectics and distinguished for chastity, of whom a full account is given by Philo the master of Carneades. And mighty Rome cannot taunt us as though we had invented the story of the birth of our Lord and Savior from a virgin; for the Romans believe that the founders of their city and race were the offspring of the virgin Ilia and of Mars.

43. Let these allusions to the virgins of the world, brief and hastily gathered from many histories, now suffice. I will proceed to married women who were reluctant to survive the decease or violent death of their husbands for fear they might be forced into a second marriage, and who entertained a marvelous affection for

the only husbands they had. This may teach us that second marriage was repudiated among the heathen. Dido, the sister of Pygmalion, having collected a vast amount of gold and silver, sailed to Africa, and there built Carthage. And when her hand was sought in marriage by Iarbas, king of Libya, she deferred the marriage for a while until her country was settled. Not long after, having raised a funeral pyre to the memory of her former husband Sichæus, she preferred to "burn rather than to marry." Carthage was built by a woman of chastity, and its end was a tribute to the excellence of the virtue. For the wife of Hasdrubal, when the city was captured and set on fire, and she saw that she could not herself escape capture by the Romans, took her little children in either hand and leaped into the burning ruins of her house.

44. What need to tell of the wife of Niceratus, who, not enduring to wrong her husband, inflicted death upon herself rather than subject herself to the lust of the thirty tyrants whom Lysander had set over conquered Athens? Artemisia, also, wife of Mausolus, is related to have been distinguished for chastity. Though she was queen of Caria, and is extolled by great poets and historians, no higher praise is bestowed upon her than that when her husband was dead she loved him as much as when he was alive, and built a tomb so great that even to the present day all costly sepulchers are called after his name, *mausoleums*. Teuta, queen of the Illyrians, owed her long sway over brave warriors, and her frequent victories over Rome, to her marvelous chastity. The Indians and almost all the Barbarians have a plurality of wives. It is a law with them that the favorite wife must be burned with her dead husband. The wives therefore vie with one another for the husband's love, and the highest

ambition of the rivals, and the proof of chastity, is to be considered worthy of death. So then she that is victorious, having put on her former dress and ornaments, lies down beside the corpse, embracing and kissing it, and to the glory of chastity despises the flames which are burning beneath her. I suppose that she who dies thus, wants no second marriage. The famous Alcibiades, the friend of Socrates, when Athens was conquered, fled to Pharnabazus, who took a bribe from Lysander the Lacedæmonian leader and ordered him to be slain. He was strangled, and when his head had been cut off it was sent to Lysander as proof of the murder, but the rest of his body lay unburied. His concubine, therefore, all alone, in defiance of the command of the cruel enemy, in the midst of strangers, and in the face of peril, gave him due burial, for she was ready to die for the dead man whom she had loved when living. Let matrons, Christian matrons at all events, imitate the fidelity of concubines, and exhibit in their freedom what she in her captivity preserved.

45. Strato, ruler of Sidon, thought of dying by his own hand, that he might not be the sport of the Persians, who were close by and whose alliance he had discarded for the friendship of the king of Egypt. But he drew back in terror, and eying the sword which he had seized, awaited in alarm the approach of the enemy. His wife, knowing that he must be immediately taken, wrested the weapon from his hand, and pierced his side. When the body was properly laid out she lay down upon it in the agony of death, that she might not violate her virgin troth in the embraces of another. Xenophon, in describing the early years of the elder Cyrus, relates that when her husband Abradatas was slain, Panthea who had loved him intensely, placed herself beside the mangled body, then

stabbed herself, and let her blood run into her husband's wounds. The queen whom the king her husband had shewn naked and without her knowledge to his friend, thought she had good cause for slaying the king. She judged that she was not beloved if it was possible for her to be exhibited to another. Rhodogune, daughter of Darius, after the death of her husband, put to death the nurse who was trying to persuade her to marry again. Alcestis is related in story to have voluntarily died for Admetus, and Penelope's chastity is the theme of Homer's song. Laodamia's praises are also sung by the poets, because, when Protesilaus was slain at Troy, she refused to survive him.

46. I may pass on to Roman women; and the first that I shall mention is Lucretia, who would not survive her violated chastity, but blotted out the stain upon her person with her own blood. Duilius, the first Roman who won a naval triumph, took to wife a virgin, Bilia, of such extraordinary chastity that she was an example even to an age which held unchastity to be not merely vicious but monstrous. When he was grown old and feeble he was once in the course of a quarrel taunted with having bad breath. In dudgeon he betook himself home, and on complaining to his wife that she had never told him of it so that he might remedy the fault, he received the reply that she would have done so, but she thought that all men had foul breath as he had. In either case this chaste and noble woman deserves praise, whether she was not aware there was anything wrong with her husband, or if she patiently endured, and her husband discovered his unfortunate condition not by the disgust of a wife, but by the abuse of an enemy. At all events the woman who marries a second time cannot say this. Marcia, Cato's

younger daughter, on being asked after the loss of her husband why she did not marry again, replied that she could not find a man who wanted her more than her money. Her words teach us that men in choosing their wives look for riches rather than for chastity, and that many in marrying use not their eyes but their fingers. That *must* be an excellent thing which is won by avarice! When the same lady was mourning the loss of her husband, and the matrons asked what day would terminate her grief, she replied, "The same that terminates my life." I imagine that a woman who thus followed her husband in heart and mind had no thought of marrying again. Porcia, whom Brutus took to wife, was a virgin; Cato's wife, Marcia, was not a virgin; but Marcia went to and fro between Hortensius and Cato, and was quite content to live without Cato; while Porcia could not live without Brutus; for women attach themselves closely to particular men, and to keep to one is a strong link in the chain of affection. When a relative urged Annia to marry again (she was of full age and a goodly person), she answered, "I shall certainly not do so. For, if I find a good man, I have no wish to be in fear of losing him: if a bad one, why must I put up with a bad husband after having had a good one?" Porcia the younger, on hearing a certain lady of good character, who had a second husband, praised in her house, replied, "A chaste and happy matron never marries more than once." Marcella the elder, on being asked by her mother if she was glad she was married, answered, "So much so that I want nothing more." Valeria, sister of the Messalas, when she lost her husband Servius, would marry no one else. On being asked why not, she said that to her, her husband Servius was ever alive.

47. I feel that in giving this list of women I have said far more than is customary in illustrating a point, and that I might be justly censured by my learned reader. But what am I to do when the women of our time press me with apostolic authority, and before the first husband is buried, repeat from morning to night the precepts which allow a second marriage? Seeing they despise the fidelity which Christian purity dictates, let them at least learn chastity from the heathen. A book *On Marriage*, worth its weight in gold, passes under the name of Theophrastus. In it the author asks whether a wise man marries. And after laying down the conditions—that the wife must be fair, of good character, and honest parentage, the husband in good health and of ample means, and after saying that under these circumstances a wise man sometimes enters the state of matrimony, he immediately proceeds thus: "But all these conditions are seldom satisfied in marriage. A wise man therefore must not take a wife. For in the first place his study of philosophy will be hindered, and it is impossible for anyone to attend to his books and his wife. Matrons want many things, costly dresses, gold, jewels, great outlay, maid-servants, all kinds of furniture, litters and gilded coaches. Then come curtain-lectures the livelong night: she complains that one lady goes out better dressed than she: that another is looked up to by all: 'I am a poor despised nobody at the ladies' assemblies.' 'Why did you ogle that creature next door?' 'Why were you talking to the maid?' 'What did you bring from the market?' 'I am not allowed to have a single friend, or companion.' She suspects that her husband's love goes the same way as her hate. There may be in some neighbouring city the wisest of teachers; but if we have a wife we can neither leave her behind, nor take the burden

with us. To support a poor wife, is hard: to put up with a rich one, is torture. Notice, too, that in the case of a wife you cannot pick and choose: you must take her as you find her. If she has a bad temper, or is a fool, if she has a blemish, or is proud, or has bad breath, whatever her fault may be—all this we learn after marriage. Horses, asses, cattle, even slaves of the smallest worth, clothes, kettles, wooden seats, cups, and earthenware pitchers, are first tried and then bought: a wife is the only thing that is not shown before she is married, for fear she may not give satisfaction. Our gaze must always be directed to her face, and we must always praise her beauty: if you look at another woman, she thinks that she is out of favour. She must be called my lady, her birth-day must be kept, we must swear by her health and wish that she may survive us, respect must be paid to the nurse, to the nursemaid, to the father's slave, to the foster-child, to the handsome hangeron, to the curled darling who manages her affairs, and to the eunuch who ministers to the safe indulgence of her lust: names which are only a cloak for adultery. Upon whomsoever she sets her heart, they must have her love though they want her not. If you give her the management of the whole house, you must yourself be her slave. If you reserve something for yourself, she will not think you are loyal to her; but she will turn to strife and hatred, and unless you quickly take care, she will have the poison ready. If you introduce old women, and soothsayers, and prophets, and vendors of jewels and silken clothing, you imperil her chastity; if you shut the door upon them, she is injured and fancies you suspect her. But what is the good of even a careful guardian, when an unchaste wife cannot be watched, and a chaste one ought not to be? For necessity is but a faithless keeper of chastity, and she alone really deserves to be called pure, who is free to sin if she chooses. If a woman be fair, she soon finds lovers; if she be ugly, it is easy to be wanton. It is difficult to guard what many long for. It is annoying to have what no one thinks worth possessing. But the misery of having an ugly wife is less than that of watching a comely one. Nothing is safe, for which a whole people sighs and longs. One man entices with his figure, another with his brains, another with his wit, another with his open hand. Somehow, or sometime, the fortress is captured which is attacked on all sides. Men marry, indeed, so as to get a manager for the house, to solace weariness, to banish solitude; but a faithful slave is a far better manager, more submissive to the master, more observant of his ways, than a wife who thinks she proves herself mistress if she acts in opposition to her husband, that is, if she does what pleases her, not what she is commanded. But friends, and servants who are under the obligation of benefits received, are better able to wait upon us in sickness than a wife who makes us responsible for her tears (she will sell you enough to make a deluge for the hope of a legacy), boasts of her anxiety, but drives her sick husband to the distraction of despair. But if she herself is poorly, we must fall sick with her and never leave her bedside. Or if she be a good and agreeable wife (how rare a bird she is!), we have to share her groans in childbirth, and suffer torture when she is in danger. A wise man can never be alone. He has with him the good men of all time, and turns his mind freely wherever he chooses. What is inaccessible to him in person he can embrace in thought. And, if men are scarce, he converses with God. He is never less alone than when alone. Then again, to marry for the sake of children, so that our name may not perish, or that we may have support in old age, and leave our property without dispute, is the height of stupidity. For what is it to us when we are leaving the world if another bears our name, when even a son does not all at once take his father's title, and there are countless others who are called by the same name. Or what support in old age is he whom you bring up, and who may die before you, or turn out a reprobate? Or at all events when he reaches mature age, you may seem to him long in dying. Friends and relatives whom you can judiciously love are better and safer heirs than those whom you must make your heirs whether you like it or not. Indeed, the surest way of having a good heir is to ruin your fortune in a good cause while you live, not to leave the fruit of your labor to be used you know not how."

48. When Theophrastus thus discourses, are there any of us, Christians, whose conversation is in heaven and who daily say, "I long to be dissolved, and to be with Christ," whom he does not put to the blush? Shall a joint-heir of Christ really long for human heirs? And shall he desire children and delight himself in a long line of descendants, who will perhaps fall into the clutches of Antichrist, when we read that Moses and Samuel preferred other men to their own sons, and did not count as their children those whom they saw to be displeasing to God? When Cicero after divorcing Terentia was requested by Hirtius to marry his sister, he set the matter altogether on one side, and said that he could not possibly devote himself to a wife and to philosophy. Meanwhile that excellent partner, who had herself drunk wisdom at Tully's fountains, married Sallust his enemy, and took for her third husband Messala Corvinus, and thus, as it were, passed through three degrees of eloquence. Socrates had

two wives, Xantippe and Myron, grand-daughter of Aristides. They frequently quarreled, and he was accustomed to banter them for disagreeing about him, he being the ugliest of men, with snub nose, bald forehead, rough-haired, and bandy-legged. At last they planned an attack upon him, and having punished him severely, and put him to flight, vexed him for a long time. On one occasion when he opposed Xantippe; who from above was heaping abuse upon him, the termagant soused him with dirty water, but he only wiped his head and said, "I knew that a shower must follow such thunder as that." Metella, consort of L. Sulla the Fortunate (except in the matter of his wife) was openly unchaste. It was the common talk of Athens, as I learnt in my youthful years when we soon pick up what is bad, and yet Sulla was in the dark, and first got to know the secrets of his household through the abuse of his enemies. Cn. Pompey had an impure wife Mucia, who was surrounded by eunuchs from Pontus and troops of the countrymen of Mithridates. Others thought that he knew all and submitted to it; but a comrade told him during the campaign, and the conqueror of the whole world was dismayed at the sad intelligence. M. Cato, the Censor, had a wife Actoria Paula, a woman of low origin, fond of drink, violent, and (who would believe it?) haughty to Cato. I say this for fear anyone may suppose that in marrying a poor woman he has secured peace. When Philip king of Macedon, against whom Demosthenes thundered in his Philippics, was entering his bed-room as usual, his wife in a passion shut him out. Finding himself excluded he held his tongue, and consoled himself for the insult by reading a tragic poem. Gorgias the Rhetorician recited his excellent treatise on Concord to the Greeks, then at variance among themselves, at Olympia. Whereupon Melanthius his enemy observed: "Here is a man who teaches us concord, and yet could not make concord between himself his wife, and maid-servant, three persons in one house." The truth was that his wife envied the beauty of the girl, and drove the purest of men wild with daily quarrels. Whole tragedies of Euripides are censures on women. Hence Hermione says, "The counsels of evil women have beguiled me." In the semi-barbarous and remote city Leptis it is the custom for a daughter in-law on the second day to beg the loan of a jar from her mother-in-law. The latter at once denies the request, and we see how true was the remark of Terence, ambiguously expressed on purpose—"How is this? do all mothers-in-law hate their daughters-in-law?" We read of a certain Roman noble who, when his friends found fault with him for having divorced a wife, beautiful, chaste, and rich, put out his foot and said to them, "And the shoe before you looks new and elegant, yet no one but myself knows where it pinches." Herodotus tells us that a woman puts off her modesty with her clothes. And our own comic poet thinks the man fortunate who has never been married. Why should I refer to Pasiphaë, Clytemnestra, and Eriphyle, the first of whom, the wife of a king and swimming in pleasure, is said to have lusted for a bull, the second to have killed her: husband for the sake of an adulterer, the third to have betrayed Amphiaraus, and to have preferred a gold necklace to the welfare of her husband. In all the bombast of tragedy and the overthrow of houses, cities, and kingdoms, it is the wives and concubines who stir up strife. Parents take up arms against their children: unspeakable banquets are served: and on account of the rape of one wretched woman Europe and Asia are involved in a ten years' war. We read of some who were divorced the day after they were married, and immediately married again. Both husbands are to blame, both he who was so soon dissatisfied, and he who was so soon pleased. Epicurus the patron of pleasure (though Metrodorus his disciple married Leontia) says that a wise man can seldom marry, because marriage has many drawbacks. And as riches, honors, bodily health, and other things which we call indifferent, are neither good nor bad, but stand as it were midway, and become good and bad according to the use and issue, so wives stand on the border line of good and ill. It is, moreover, a serious matter for a wise man to be in doubt whether he is going to marry a good or a bad woman. Chrysippus ridiculously maintains that a wise man should marry, that he may not outrage Jupiter Gamelius and Genethlius. For upon that principle the Latins would not marry at all, since they have no Jupiter who presides over marriage. But if, as he thinks, the life of men is determined by the names of gods, whoever chooses to sit will offend Jupiter Stator.

49. Aristotle and Plutarch and our Seneca have written treatises on matrimony, out of which we have already made some extracts and now add a few more. "The love of beauty is the forgetting of reason and the near neighbor of madness; a foul blot little in keeping with a sound mind. It confuses counsel, breaks high and generous spirits, draws away men from great thoughts to mean ones; it makes men querulous, ill-tempered, foolhardy, cruelly imperious, servile flatterers, good for nothing, at last not even for love itself. For although in the intensity of passion it burns like a raging fire, it wastes much time through suspicions, tears, and complaints: it begets hatred of itself, and at last hates itself." The course

of love is laid bare in Plato's Phædrus from beginning to end, and Lysias explains all its drawbacks—how it is led not by reason, but by frenzy, and in particular is a harsh jailer over lovely wives. Seneca, too, relates that he knew an accomplished man who before going out used to tie his wife's garter upon his breast, and could not bear to be absent from her for a quarter of an hour; and this pair would never take a drink unless husband and wife alternately put their lips to the cup; and they did other things just as absurd in the extravagant outbursts of their warm but blind affection. Their love was of honorable birth, but it grew out of all proportion. And it makes no difference how honorable may be the cause of a man's insanity. Hence Xystus in his Sentences tells us that "He who too ardently loves his own wife is an adulterer." It is disgraceful to love another man's wife at all, or one's own too much. A wise man ought to love his wife with judgment, not with passion. Let a man govern his voluptuous impulses, and not rush headlong into intercourse. There is nothing blacker than to love a wife as if she were an adulteress. Men who say they have contracted marriage and are bringing up children, for the good of their country and of the race, should at least imitate the brutes, and not destroy their offspring in the womb; nor should they appear in the character of lovers, but of husbands. In some cases marriage has grown out of adultery: and, shameful to relate! men have tried to teach their wives chastity after having taken their chastity away. Marriages of that sort are quickly dissolved when lust is satiated. The first allurement gone, the charm is lost. What shall I say, says Seneca, of the poor men who in numbers are bribed to take the name of husband in order to evade the laws promulgated against bachelors? How can he who is married under such conditions be a guide to morality, teach chastity, and maintain the authority of a husband? It is the saying of a very learned man, that chastity must be preserved at all costs, and that when it is lost all virtue falls to the ground. This holds the primacy of all virtues in woman. This it is that makes up for a wife's poverty, enhances her riches, redeems her deformity, gives grace to her beauty; it makes her act in a way worthy of her forefathers whose blood it does not taint with bastard offspring; of her children, who through it have no need to blush for their mother, or to be in doubt about their father; and above all, of herself, since it defends her from external violation. There is no greater calamity connected with captivity than to be the victim of another's lust. The consulship sheds luster upon men; eloquence gives eternal renown; military glory and a triumph immortalize an obscure family. Many are the spheres ennobled by splendid ability. The virtue of woman is, in a special sense, purity. It was this that made Lucretia the equal of Brutus, if it did not make her his superior, since Brutus learnt from a woman the impossibility of being a slave. It was this that made Cornelia a fit match for Gracchus, and Porcia for a second Brutus. Tanaquil is better known than her husband. His name, like the names of many other kings, is lost in the mists of antiquity. She, through a virtue rare among women, is too deeply rooted in the hearts of all ages for her memory ever to perish. Let my married sisters copy the examples of Theano, Cleobuline, Gorgente, Timoclia, the Claudias and Cornelias; and when they find the Apostle conceding second marriage to depraved women, they will read that before the light of our religion shone upon the world wives of one husband ever held high rank among matrons, that by their hands the sacred rites of Fortuna Muliebris were performed, that a priest or Flamen twice married was unknown, that the high-priests of Athens to this day emasculate themselves by drinking hemlock, and once they have been drawn in to the pontificate, cease to be men.

Book II.

Jerome answers the second, third, and fourth propositions of Jovinianus.

I. (c. 1–4). That those who have become regenerate cannot be overthrown by the devil, Jerome (c. 1) puts it that they cannot be *tempted* by the devil. He quotes 1 John i. 8–ii. 2, as shewing that faithful men can be tempted and sin and need an advocate. The expressions (3) in Heb. vi. as to those who crucify the Son of God afresh do not apply to ordinary sins after baptism, as supposed by Montanus and Novatus. The epistles to the Seven Churches show that the lapsed may return. The Angels, and even our Lord Himself, (4) could be tempted.

II. (c. 5–17). That there is no difference (morally) between one who fasts and one who takes food with thanksgiving. Jovinian has quoted (5) many texts of Scripture to show that God has made animals for men's food. But (6) there are many other uses of animals besides food. And there are many warnings like 1 Cor. vi. 13, as to the danger arising from food. There are among the heathen (7) many instances of abstinence. They recognize (8) the evil of sensual allurements, and often, like Crates the Theban, (9) have cast away what would tempt them; the senses, they teach, (10) should be subject to reason;

and, that (11) except for athletes (Christians do not want to be like Milo of Crotona) bread and water suffice. Horace (12), Xenophon and other eminent Greeks (13), the Essenes and the Brahmans (14), as well as philosophers like Diogenes, testify to the value of abstinence. The Old Testament stories (15) of Esau's pottage, of the lusting of Israel for the flesh-pots of Egypt, and those in the New Testament of Anna, Cornelius, &c., commend abstinence. If some heretics inculcate fasting (16) in such a way as to despise the gifts of God, and weak Christians are not to be judged for their use of flesh, those who seek the higher life (17) will find a help in abstinence.

III. (c. 18–34). The fourth proposition of Jovinianus, that all who are saved will have equal reward, is refuted (19) by the various yields of thirty, sixty, and a hundred fold in the parable of the sower, by (20) the "stars differing in glory" of 1 Cor. xv. 41. It is strange (21) to find the advocate of self-indulgence now claiming equality to the saints. But (22) as there were differences in Ezekiel between cattle and cattle, so in St. Paul between those who built gold or stubble on the one foundation. The differences of gifts (23), of punishments (24), of guilt (25), as in Pilate and the Chief Priests, of the produce of the good seed (26), of the mansions promised in heaven (27–29), of the judgment upon sins both in the church and in Scripture (30–31), of those called at different times to the vineyard (32) are arguments for the diversity of rewards. The parable of the talents (33) holds out as rewards differences of station, and so does the church (34) in its different orders.

Jerome now recapitulates (35) and appeals (36) against the licentious views of Jovinianus, which have already induced many virgins to break their vows; and which, as the new Roman heresy (37), he calls upon the Imperial City (38) to reject.

1. The second proposition of Jovinianus is that the baptized cannot be tempted by the devil. And to escape the imputation of folly in saying this, he adds: "But if any are tempted, it only shows that they were baptized with water, not with the Spirit, as we read was the case with Simon Magus." Hence it is that John says, "Whosoever is begotten of God doeth no sin, because his seed abides in him: and he cannot sin, because he is begotten of God. In this the children of God are manifest, and the children of the Devil." And at the end of the Epistle, "Whosoever is begotten of God sinned not; but his being begotten of God kept him, and the evil one touches him not."

2. This would be a real difficulty and one for ever incapable of solution were it not solved by the witness of John himself, who immediately goes on to say, "My little children, guard yourselves from idols." If everyone that is born of God sinned not, and cannot be tempted by the devil, how is it that he bids them beware of temptation? Again in the same Epistle we read: "If we say that we have no sins, we deceive ourselves, and the truth is not in us. If we confess our sins, he is faithful and just to forgive us our sins, and to cleanse us from all unrighteousness. If we say that we have not sinned, we make him a liar, and his word is not in us." I suppose that John was baptized and was writing to the baptized: I imagine too that all sin is of the devil. Now John confesses himself a sinner, and hopes for forgiveness of sins after baptism. My friend Jovinianus says, "Touch me not, for I am clean." What then? Does the Apostle contradict himself? By no means. In the same passage he gives his reason for thus speaking:

"My little children, these things write I unto you, that ye may not sin. But if any man sin, we have an advocate with the Father, Jesus Christ the righteous: and he is the propitiation for our sins; and not for ours only, but also for the whole world. And hereby know we that we know him, if we keep his commandments. He that saith, I know him, and kept not his commandments, is a liar, and the truth is not in him. But whoso kept his word, in him verily hath the love of God been perfected. Hereby know we that we are in him: he that saith he abides in him ought himself also to walk even as he walked." My reason for telling you, little children, that everyone who is born of God sinned not, is that you may not sin, and that you may know that so long as you sin not you abide in the birth which God has given you. Yea, they who abide in that birth cannot sin. "For what communion hath light with darkness? Or Christ with Belial?" As day is distinct from night, so righteousness and unrighteousness, sin and good works, Christ and Antichrist cannot blend. If we give Christ a lodging-place in our hearts, we banish the devil from thence. If we sin and the devil enter through the gate of sin, Christ will immediately withdraw. Hence David after sinning says: "Restore unto me the joy of thy salvation," that is, the joy which he had lost by sinning. "He who saith, I know him, and kept not his commandments, is a liar, and the truth is not in him." Christ is called the truth: "I am the way, the truth, and the life." In vain do we make our boast in him whose commandments we keep not. To him that knows what is good, and doeth it not, it is sin. "As the body apart from the spirit is dead, even so faith apart from works is dead." And we must not think it a great matter to know the only God, when even devils believe and tremble. "He that saith he abides in him ought himself also to walk even as he walked." Our opponent may choose whichever of the two he likes; we give him his choice. Does he abide in Christ, or not? If he abides, let him then walk as Christ walked. But if there is rashness in professing to copy the virtues of our Lord, he does not abide in Christ, for he does not walk as did Christ. "He did not sin, neither was guile found in his mouth: when he was reviled, he reviled not again, and as a lamb is dumb before its shearer, so opened he not his mouth." To Him came the prince of this world, and found nothing in Him: although He had done no sin, God made Him sin for us. But we, according to the Epistle of James, "all stumble in many things," and "no one is pure from sin, no not if his life be but a day long." For who will boast "that he has a clean heart? or who will be sure that he is pure from sin?" And we are held guilty after the similitude of Adam's transgression. Hence David says, "Behold, I was shapen in iniquity, and in sin did my mother conceive me." And the blessed Job, "Though I be righteous my mouth will speak wickedness, and though I be perfect, I shall be found perverse. If I wash myself with snow water and make my hands never so clean, yet wilt thou plunge me in the ditch and mine own clothes shall abhor me." But that we may not utterly despair and think that if we sin after baptism we cannot be saved, he immediately checks the tendency: "And if any man sin, we have an advocate with the Father, Jesus Christ the righteous, and he is the propitiation for our sins. And not for ours only, but also for the whole world." He addresses this to baptized believers, and he promises them the Lord as an advocate for their offences. He does not say: If you fall into sin, you have an advocate with the Father, Christ, and He is the propitiation for your sins: you might then say that he was addressing those whose baptism had been destitute of the true faith: but what he says is this, "We have an advocate with the Father, Jesus Christ, and he is the propitiation for our sins." And not only for the sins of John and his contemporaries, but for those of the whole world. Now in "the whole world" are included apostles and all the faithful, and a clear proof is established that sin after baptism is possible. It is useless for us to have an advocate Jesus Christ, if sin be impossible.

3. The apostle Peter, to whom it was said, "He that is bathed needed not to wash again," and "Thou art Peter, and upon this rock I will build my Church," through fear of a maid-servant denied Him. Our Lord himself says, "Simon, Simon, behold Satan asked to have you, that he might sift you as wheat. But I made supplication for thee, that thy faith fails not." And in the same place, "Watch and pray, that ye enter not into temptation: the spirit indeed is willing, but the flesh is weak." If you reply that this was said before the Passion, we certainly say after the Passion, in the Lord's prayer, "Forgive us our debts, as we also forgive our debtors; and lead us not into temptation, but deliver us from the evil one." If we do not sin after baptism, why do we ask that we may be forgiven our sins, which were already forgiven in baptism? Why do we pray that we may not enter into temptation, and that we may be delivered from the evil one, if the devil cannot tempt those who are baptized? The case is different if this prayer belongs to the Catechumens, and is not adapted to faithful Christians. Paul, the chosen vessel, chastised his body, and brought it into subjection, lest after preaching to others he himself should be found a reprobate, and he tells that there was given to him "a thorn in the flesh, a messenger of Satan to buffet" him. And to the Corinthians

he writes: "I fear, lest by any means, as the serpent beguiled Eve in his craftiness, your minds should be corrupted from the simplicity that is toward Christ." And elsewhere: "But to whom ye forgive anything, I forgive also: for what I also have forgiven, if I have forgiven anything, for your sakes have I forgiven it in the person of Christ: that no advantage may be gained over us by Satan: for we are not ignorant of his devices." And again: "There hath no temptation taken you, but such as man can bear; but God is faithful, who will not suffer you to be tempted above that ye are able; but will with the temptation make also the way of escape, that ye may be able to endure it." And, "Let him that thinketh he stands, take heed lest he fall." And to the Galatians: "Ye were running well; who did hinder you that ye should not obey the truth?" And elsewhere: "We would fain have come unto you, I Paul once and again; and Satan hindered us." And to the married he says: "Be together again, that Satan tempt you not because of your incontinency." And again: "But I say, walk by the Spirit and ye shall not fulfil the lust of the flesh. For the flesh lusted against the Spirit, and the Spirit against the flesh; for these are contrary the one to the other: that ye may not do the things that ye would." We are a compound of the two, and must endure the strife of the two substances. And to the Ephesians: "Our wrestling is not against flesh and blood, but against the principalities, against the powers, against the world-rulers of this darkness, against the spiritual hosts of wickedness in the heavenly places." Does anyone think that we are safe, and that it is right to fall asleep when once we have been baptized? And so, too, in the epistle to the Hebrews: "For as touching those who were once enlightened and tasted of the heavenly gift, and were made partakers of the Holy Ghost, and tasted the good word of God, and the powers of the age to come, and then fell away, it is impossible to renew them again unto repentance; seeing they crucify to themselves the Son of God afresh, and put him to an open shame." Surely we cannot deny that they have been baptized who have been illuminated, and have tasted the heavenly gift, and have been made partakers of the Holy Spirit, and have tasted the good word of God. But if the baptized cannot sin, how is it now that the Apostle says, "And have fallen away"? Montanus and Novatus would smile at this, for they contend that it is impossible to renew again through repentance those who have crucified to themselves the Son of God, and put Him to an open shame. He therefore corrects this mistake by saying: "But, beloved, we are persuaded better things of you, and things that accompany salvation, though we thus speak; for God is not unrighteous to forget your work and the love which ye shewed towards his name, in that ye ministered unto the Saints, and still do minister." And truly the unrighteousness of God would be great, if He merely punished sin, and did not welcome good works. I have so spoken, says the Apostle, to withdraw you from your sins, and to make you more careful through fear of despair. But, beloved, I am persuaded better things of you, and things that accompany salvation. For it is not accordant with the righteousness of God to forget good works, and the fact that you have ministered and do minister to the Saints for His name's sake, and to remember sins only. The Apostle James also, knowing that the baptized can be tempted, and fall of their own free choice, says: "Blessed is the man that endures temptation: for when he hath been approved, he shall receive the crown of life, which the Lord promised to them that love him." And that we may not think that we are tempted by God, as we read in Genesis Abraham was, he adds: "Let no man say when he is tempted, I am tempted of God: for God cannot be tempted with evil, and He Himself tempted no man. But each man is tempted when he is drawn away by his own lust and enticed. Then the lust, when it hath conceived, bears sin: and the sin, when it is full grown, bringeth forth death." God created us with free will, and we are not forced by necessity either to virtue or to vice. Otherwise, if there be necessity, there is no crown. As in good works it is God who brings them to perfection, for it is not of him that wills, nor of him that runs, but of God that pities and gives us help that we may be able to reach the goal: so in things wicked and sinful, the seeds within us give the impulse, and these are brought to maturity by the devil. When he sees that we are building upon the foundation of Christ, hay, wood, stubble, then he applies the match. Let us then build gold, silver, costly stones, and he will not venture to tempt us: although even thus there is not sure and safe possession. For the lion lurks in ambush to slay the innocent. "Potters' vessels are proved by the furnace, and just men by the trial of tribulation." And in another place it is written: "My son, when thou come to serve the Lord, prepare thyself for temptation." Again, the same James says: "Be ye doers of the word, and not hearers only. For if anyone is a hearer of the word, and not a doer, he is like unto a man beholding his natural face in a mirror: for he beholds himself, and goes away, and straightway forgets what manner of man he was." It was useless to warn them to add works to faith, if they could not sin after baptism. He tells us that "whosoever shall keep the whole law, and yet stumble in one point, he is become guilty of all." Which of us is without sin? "God hath shut up all unto disobedience, that he might have mercy upon all." Peter also says: "The Lord knows how to deliver the godly out of temptation." And concerning false teachers: "These are springs without water, and mists driven by a storm; for whom the blackness of darkness hath been reserved. For, uttering proud words of vanity, they entice in the lusts of the flesh, by lasciviousness, those who had just escaped, and have turned back to error." Does not the Apostle in these words seem to you to have depicted the new party of ignorance? For, as it were, they open the fountains of knowledge and yet have no water: they promise a shower of doctrine like prophetic clouds which have been visited by the truth of God, and are driven by the storms of devils and vices. They speak great things, and their talk is nothing but pride: "But everyone is unclean with God who is lifted up in his own heart." Like those who had just escaped from their sins, they *return* to their own error, and persuade men to luxury, and to the delights of eating and the gratification of the flesh. For whom is not glad to hear them say: "Let us eat and drink, and reign forever"? The wise and prudent they call corrupt, but pay more attention to the honey-tongued. John the apostle, or rather the Savior in the person of John, writes thus to the angel of the Church of Ephesus: "I know thy works and thy toil and patience, and that thou didst bear for my name's sake, and hast not grown weary. But I have this against thee, that thou didst leave thy first love. Remember therefore from whence thou art fallen, and repent, and do the first works; or else I will come to thee, and will move thy candlestick out of its place, except thou repent." Similarly He urges the other churches, Smyrna, Pergamos, Thyatira, Sardis, Philadelphia, Laodicea, to repentance, and threatens them unless they return to the former works. And in Sardis He says He has a few who have not defiled their garments, and they shall walk with Him in white, for they are worthy. But they to whom He says: "Remember from whence thou art fallen"; and, "Behold the devil is about to cast some of you into prison, that ye may be tried"; and, "I know where thou dwellest, even where Satan's throne is"; and, "Remember how thou hast received, and didst hear, and keep it, and repent," and so on, were of course believers, and baptized, who once stood, but fell through sin.

4. I delayed for a little while the production of proofs from the Old Testament, because, wherever the Old Testament is against them they are accustomed to cry out that the Law and the Prophets were until John. But who does not know that under the other dispensation of God all the saints of past times were of equal merit with Christians at the present day? As Abraham in days gone by pleased God in wedlock, so virgins now please him in perpetual virginity. He served the Law and his own times; let us now serve the Gospel and our times, upon whom the ends of the ages have come. David the chosen one, the man after God's own heart, who had performed all His pleasure, and who in a certain psalm had said, "Judge me, O Lord, for I have walked in mine integrity: I have trusted also in the Lord and shall not slide. Examine me, O Lord, and prove me; try my reins and my heart," even he was afterwards tempted by the devil; and repenting of his sin said, "Have mercy upon me, O God, according to thy loving-kindness." He would have a great sin blotted out by great loving-kindness. Solomon, beloved of the Lord, and to whom God had twice revealed Himself, because he loved women forsook the love of God. It is related in the

Book of Days that Manasses the wicked king was restored after the Babylonish captivity to his former rank. And Josiah, a holy man, was slain by the king of Egypt on the plain of Megiddo. Joshua also, the son of Josedech and high-priest, although he was a type of our Savior Who bore our sins, and united to Himself a church of alien birth from among the Gentiles, is nevertheless, according to the letter of Scripture, represented in filthy garments after he attained to the priesthood, and with the devil standing at his right hand; and white raiment is afterwards restored to him. It is needless to tell how Moses and Aaron offended God at the water of strife, and did not enter the land of promise. For the blessed Job relates that even the angels and every creature can sin. "Shall mortal man," he says, "be just before God? Shall a man be spotless in his works? If he puts no trust in his servants, and charges his angels with folly, how much more them that dwell in houses of clay," amongst whom are we, and made of the same clay too. "The life of man is a warfare upon earth." Lucifer fell who was sending to all nations, and he who was nurtured in a paradise of delight as one of the twelve precious stones, was wounded and went down to hell from the mount of God. Hence the Savior says in the Gospel: "I beheld Satan falling as lightning from heaven." If he fell who stood on so sublime a height, who may not fall? If there are falls in heaven, how much more on earth! And yet though Lucifer be fallen (the old serpent after his fall), "his strength is in his loins, and his force is in the muscles of his belly. The great trees are overshadowed by him, and he slept beside the reed, the rush, and the sedge." He is king over all things that are in the waters—that is to say in the seat of pleasure and luxury, of propagation of children, and of the fertilization of the marriage bed. "For who can strip off his outer garment? Who can open the doors of his face? Nations fatten upon him, and the tribes of Phenicia divide him." And lest haply the reader in his secret thought might imagine that those tribes of Phenicia and peoples of Ethiopia only are meant by those to whom the dragon was given for food, we immediately find a reference to those who are crossing the sea of this world, and are hastening to reach the haven of salvation: "His head stands in the ships of the fishermen like an anvil that cannot be wearied: he counted iron as straw, and brass as rotten wood. And all the gold of the sea under him is as mire. He maketh the deep to boil like a pot: he values the sea like a pot of ointment, and the blackness of the deep as a captive. He beholds everything that is high." And my friend Jovinianus thinks he can gain an easy mastery over him. Why speak of holy men and angels, who, being creatures of God, are of course capable of sin? He dared to tempt the Son of God, and though smitten through and through with our Lord's first and second answer, nevertheless raised his head, and when thrice wounded, withdrew only for a time, and deferred rather than removed the temptation. And we flatter ourselves on the ground of our baptism, which though it put away the sins of the past, cannot keep us for the time to come, unless the baptized keep their hearts with all diligence.

5. At length we have arrived at the question of food, and are confronted by our third difficulty. "All things were created to serve for the use of mortal men." And as man, a rational animal, in a sense the owner and tenant of the world, is subject to God, and worships his Creator, so all things living were created either for the food of men, or for clothing, or for tilling the earth, or

conveying the fruits thereof, or to be the companions of man, and hence, because they are man's helpers, they have their name *jumenta*. 'What is man,' says David, 'that thou art mindful of him? And the son of man, that thou visit him? For thou hast made him but little lower than the angels, and crowns him with glory and honor. Thou made him to have dominion over the works of thine hands; thou hast put all things under his feet: all sheep and oxen, yea, and the beasts of the field: the fowl of the air, and the fish of the sea, whatsoever passes through the paths of the seas.' Granted, he says, that the ox was created for ploughing, the horse for riding, the dog for watching, goats for their milk, sheep for their fleeces. What is the use of swine if we may not eat their flesh? of roes, stags, fallow-deer, boars, hares, and such like game? of geese, wild and tame? of wild ducks and fig-peckers? of woodcocks? of coots? of thrushes? Why do hens run about our houses? If they are not eaten, all these creatures were created by God for nothing. But what need is there of argument when Scripture clearly teaches that every moving creature, like herbs and vegetables, were given to us for food, and the Apostle cries aloud 'All things are clean to the clean, and nothing is to be rejected, if it be received with thanksgiving,' and tells us that men will come in the last days, forbidding to marry, and to eat meats, which God created for use? The Lord himself was called by the Pharisees a wine-bibber and a glutton, the friend of publicans and sinners, because he did not decline the invitation of Zacchæus to dinner, and went to the marriage-feast. But it is a different matter if, as you may foolishly contend, he went to the dinner intending to fast, and after the manner of deceivers said, I eat this, not that; I do not drink the wine which I created out of water. He did not make water, but wine, the type of his blood. After the resurrection he ate a fish and part of a honeycomb, not sesame nuts and service-berries. The apostle, Peter, did not wait like a Jew for the stars to peep, but went upon the house-top to dine at the sixth hour. Paul in the ship broke bread, not dried figs. When Timothy's stomach was out of order, he advised him to drink wine, not perry. In abstaining from meats they please their own fancy: as though superstitious Gentiles did not observe the rites of abstinence connected with the Mother of the Gods and with Isis."

6. I will follow in detail the views now expounded, and before I come to Scripture and show by it that fasting is pleasing to God, and chastity accepted by him, I will meet philosophic argument with argument, and will prove that we are not followers of Empedocles and Pythagoras, who on account of their doctrine of the transmigration of souls think nothing which lives and moves should be eaten, and look upon him who fells a fir-tree or an oak as equally guilty with the parricide or the poisoner: but that we worship our Creator Who made all things for the use of man. And as the ox was created for ploughing, the horse for riding, dogs for watching, goats for milk, sheep for their wool: so it was with swine and stags, and roes and hares, and other animals: but the immediate purpose of their creation was not that they might serve for food, but for other uses of men. For if everything that moves and lives was made for food, and prepared for the stomach, let my opponents tell me why elephants, lions, leopards, and wolves were created; why vipers, scorpions, bugs, lice, and fleas; why the vulture, the eagle, the crow, the hawk; why whales, dolphins, seals, and small snails were created. Which of us ever eats

the flesh of a lion, a viper, a vulture, a stork, a kite, or the worms that crawl upon our shores? As then these have their proper uses, so may we say that other beasts, fishes, birds, were created not for eating, but for medicine. In short, to how many uses the flesh of vipers, from which we make our antidotes against poison, may be applied, physicians know well. Ivory dust is an ingredient in many remedies. Hyena's gall restores brightness to the eyes, and its dung and that of dogs cures gangrenous wounds. And (it may seem strange to the reader) Galen asserts in his treatise on Simples, that human dung is of service in a multitude of cases. Naturalists say that snake-skin, boiled in oil, gives wonderful relief in ear-ache. What to the uninitiated seems so useless as a bug? Yet, suppose a leech to have fastened on the throat, as soon as the odor of a bug is inhaled the leech is vomited out, and difficulty in urinating is relieved by the same application. As for the fat of pigs, geese, fowls, and pheasants, how useful they are is told in all medical works, and if you read these books you will see there that the vulture has as many curative properties as it has limbs. Peacock's dung allays the inflammation of gout. Cranes, storks, eagle's gall, hawk's blood, the ostrich, frogs, chameleons, swallow's dung and flesh—in what diseases these are suitable remedies, I could tell if it were my purpose to discuss bodily ailments and their cure. If you think proper you may read Aristotle and Theophrastus in prose, or Marcellus of Side, and our Flavius, who discourse on these subjects in hexameter verse; the second Pliny also, and Dioscorides, and others, both naturalists and physicians, who assign to every herb, every stone, every animal whether reptile, bird, or fish, its own use in the art of which they treat. So then when you ask me why the pig was created, I immediately reply, as if two boys were disputing, by asking you why were vipers and scorpions? You must not judge that anything from the hand of God is superfluous, because there are many beasts and birds which your palate rejects. But this may perhaps look more like contentiousness and pugnacity than truth. Let me tell you therefore that pigs and wild-boars, and stags, and the rest of living creatures were created, that soldiers, athletes, sailors, rhetoricians, miners, and other slaves of hard toil, who need physical strength, might have food: and also those who carry arms and provisions, who wear themselves out with the work of hand or foot, who ply the oar, who need good lungs to shout and speak, who level mountains and sleep out rain or fair. But our religion does not train boxers, athletes, sailors, soldiers, or ditchers, but followers of wisdom, who devote themselves to the worship of God, and know why they were created and are in the world from which they are impatient to depart. Hence also the Apostle says: "When I am weak, then am I strong." And "Though our outward man is decaying, yet our inward man is renewed day by day." And "I have the desire to depart and be with Christ." And, "Make no provision for the flesh to fulfil the lusts thereof." Are all commanded not to have two coats, nor food in their scrip, money in their purse, a staff in the hand, shoes on the feet? or to sell all they possess and give to the poor, and follow Jesus? Of course not: but the command is for those who wish to be perfect. On the contrary John the Baptist lays down one rule for the soldiers, another for the publicans. But the Lord says in the Gospel to him who had boasted of having kept the whole law: "If thou wilt be perfect, go and sell all that thou hast, and give to the poor, and come, follow me." That He might not seem to lay a heavy burden on unwilling shoulders, He sent His hearer away with full power to please himself, saying "If thou wilt be perfect." And so I too say to you: If you wish to be perfect, it is good not to drink wine, and eat flesh. If you wish to be perfect, it is better to enrich the mind than to stuff the body. But if you are an infant and fond of the cooks and their preparations, no one will snatch the dainties out of your mouth. Eat and drink, and, if you like, with Israel rise up and play, and sing "Let us eat and drink, for to-morrow we shall die." Let him eat and drink, who looks for death when he has feasted, and who says with Epicurus, "There is nothing after death, and death itself is nothing." We believe Paul when he says in tones of thunder: "Meats for the belly, and the belly for meats. But God will destroy both them and it."

7. I have quoted these few passages of Scripture to show that we are at one with the philosophers. But who does not know that no universal law of nature regulates the food of all nations, and that each eats those things of which it has abundance? For instance, the Arabians and Saracens, and all the wild tribes of the desert live on camel's milk and flesh: for the camel, to suit the climate and barren soil of those regions, is easily bred and reared. They think it wicked to eat the flesh of swine. Why? Because pigs which fatten on acorns, chestnuts, roots of ferns, and barley, are seldom or never found among them: and if they were found, they would not afford the nourishment of which we spoke just now. The exact opposite is the case with the northern peoples. If you were to force them to eat the flesh of asses and camels, they would think it the same as though they were compelled to devour a wolf or a crow. In Pontus and Phrygia a paterfamilias pays a good price for fat white worms with

blackish heads, which breed in decayed wood. And as with us the woodcock and figpecker, the mullet and scar, are reputed delicacies, so with them it is a luxury to eat the xylophagus. Again, because throughout the glowing wastes of the desert clouds of locusts are found, it is customary with the peoples of the East and of Libya to feed on locusts. John the Baptist proves the truth of this. Compel a Phrygian or a native of Pontus to eat a locust, and he will think it scandalous. Force a Syrian, an African, or Arabian to swallow worms, he will have the same contempt for them as for flies, millepedes, and lizards, although the Syrians are accustomed to eat land-crocodiles, and the Africans even green lizards. In Egypt and Palestine, owing to the scarcity of cattle no one eats beef, or makes the flesh of bulls or oxen, or calves, a portion of their food. Moreover, in my province it is considered a crime to eat veal. Accordingly the Emperor Valens recently promulgated a law throughout the East, prohibiting the killing and eating of calves. He had in view the interests of agriculture, and wished to check the bad practice of the commoner sort of the people who imitated the Jews in devouring the flesh of calves, instead of fowls and sucking pigs. The Nomad tribes, and the Troglodytes, and Scythians, and the barbarous Huns with whom we have recently become acquainted, eat flesh half raw. Moreover the Icthyophagi, a wandering race on the shores of the Red Sea, broil fish on the stones made hot by the sun, and subsist on this poor food. The Sarmatians, the Chuadi, the Vandals, and countless other races, delight in the flesh of horses and wolves. Why should I speak of other nations when I myself, a youth on a visit to Gaul, heard that the Atticoti, a British tribe, eat human flesh, and that although they find herds of swine, and droves of large or small cattle in the woods, it is their custom to cut off the buttocks of the shepherds and the breasts of their women, and to regard them as the greatest delicacies? The Scots have no wives of their own; as though they read Plato's Republic and took Cato for their leader, no man among them has his own wife, but like beasts they indulge their lust to their hearts' content. The Persians, Medes, Indians, and Ethiopians, peoples on a par with Rome itself, have intercourse with mothers and grandmothers, with daughters and granddaughters. The Massagetæ and Derbices think those persons most unhappy who die of sickness—and when parents, kindred, or friends reach old age, they are murdered and devoured. It is thought better that they should be eaten by the people themselves than by the worms. The Tibareni crucify those whom they have loved before when they have grown old. The Hyrcani throw them out half alive to the birds and dogs: the Caspians leave them dead for the same beasts. The Scythians bury alive with the remains of the dead those who were beloved of the deceased. The Bactrians throw their old men to dogs which they rear for the very purpose, and when Stasanor, Alexander's general, wished to correct the practice, he almost lost his province. Force an Egyptian to drink sheep's milk: drive, if you can, a Pelusiote to eat an onion. Almost every city in Egypt venerates its own beasts and monsters, and whatever be the object of worship, that they think inviolable and sacred. Hence it is that their towns also are named after animals Leonto, Cyno, Lyco, Busyris, Thmuis, which is, being interpreted, a *he-goat*. And to make us understand what sort of gods Egypt always welcomed, one of their cities was recently called Antinous after Hadrian's favorite. You see clearly then that not only in eating, but also in burial, in wedlock, and in every department of life, each race follows its own practice and peculiar usages, and takes that for the law of nature which is most familiar to it. But suppose all nations alike ate flesh, and let that be everywhere lawful which the place produces. How does it concern us whose conversation is in heaven? who, as well as Pythagoras and Empedocles and all lovers of wisdom, are not bound to the circumstances of our birth, but of our new birth: who by abstinence subjugates our refractory flesh, eager to follow the allurements of lust? The eating of flesh, and drinking of wine, and fulness of stomach, is the seed-plot of lust. And so the comic poet says, "Venus shivers unless Ceres and Bacchus be with her."

8. Through the five senses, as through open windows, vice has access to the soul. The metropolis and citadel of the mind cannot be taken unless the enemy have previously entered by its doors. The soul is distressed by the disorder they produce, and is led captive by sight, hearing, smell, taste, and touch. If anyone delights in the sports of the circus, or the struggles of athletes, the versatility of actors, the figure of women, in splendid jewels, dress, silver and gold, and other things of the kind, the liberty of the soul is lost through the windows of the eyes, and the prophet's words are fulfilled: "Death is come up into our windows." Again, our sense of hearing is flattered by the tones of various instruments and the modulations of the voice; and whatever enters the ear by the songs of poets and comedians, by the pleasantries and verses of pantomimic actors, weakens the manly fiber of the mind. Then, again, no one but a profligate denies that the profligate and licentious find a delight in sweet odors, different sorts of incense, fragrant balsam, kuphi, oenanthe, and musk, which is nothing but the skin of a

foreign rat. And who does not know that gluttony is the mother of avarice, and, as it were, fetters the heart and keeps it pressed down upon the earth? For the sake of a temporary gratification of the appetite, land and sea are ransacked, and we toil and sweat our lives through, that we may send down our throats honey-wine and costly food. The desire to handle other men's persons, and the burning lust for women, is a passion bordering on insanity. To gratify this sense we languish, grow angry, throw ourselves about with joy, indulge envy, engage in rivalry, are filled with anxiety, and when we have terminated the pleasure with more or less repentance, we once more take fire, and want to do that which we again regret doing. Where, then, that which we may call the thin edge of disturbance, has entered the citadel of the mind through these doors, what will become of its liberty, its endurance, its thought of God, particularly since the sense of touch can picture to itself even bygone pleasures, and through the recollection of vice forces the soul to take part in them, and after a manner to practice what it does not actually commit?

9. At the call of reasoning such as this, many philosophers have forsaken the crowded cities, and their pleasure gardens in the suburbs with well-watered grounds, shady trees, twittering birds, crystal fountains, murmuring brooks, and many charms for eye and ear, lest through luxury and abundance of riches, the firmness of the mind should be enfeebled, and its purity debauched. For there is no good in frequently seeing objects which may one day lead to your captivity, or in making trial of things which you would find it hard to do without. Even the Pythagoreans shunned company of this kind and were wont to dwell in solitary places in the desert. The

Platonists also and Stoics lived in the groves and porticos of temples, that, admonished by the sanctity of their restricted abode, might think of nothing but virtue. Plato, moreover, himself, when Diogenes trampled on his couches with muddy feet (he being a rich man), chose a house called *Academia* at some distance from the city, in a spot not only lonely but unhealthy, so that he might have leisure for philosophy. His object was that by constant anxiety about sickness the assaults of lust might be defeated, and that his disciples might experience no pleasure but that afforded by the things they learned. We have read of some who took out their own eyes lest through sight they might lose the contemplation of philosophy. Hence it was that Crates the famous Theban, after throwing into the sea a considerable weight of gold, exclaimed, "Go to the bottom, ye evil lusts: I will drown you that you may not drown me." But if anyone thinks to enjoy keenly meat and drink in excess, and at the same time to devote himself to philosophy, that is to say, to live in luxury and yet not to be hampered by the vices attendant on luxury, he deceives himself. For if it be the case that even when far distant from them we are frequently caught in the snares of nature, and are compelled to desire those things of which we have a scant supply: what folly it is to think we are free when we are surrounded by the nets of pleasure! We think of what we see, hear, smell, taste, handle, and are led to desire the thing which affords us pleasure. That the mind sees and hears, and that we can neither hear nor see anything unless our senses are fixed upon the objects of sight and hearing, is an old saw. It is difficult, or rather impossible, when we are swimming in luxury and pleasure not to think of what we are doing: and it is an idle pretense which some men put forward that they can take their fill of pleasure with their faith and purity and mental uprightness unimpaired. It is a violation of nature to revel in pleasure, and the Apostle gives a caution against this very thing when he says, "She that giveth herself to pleasure is dead while she lives."

10. The bodily senses are like horses madly racing, but the soul like a charioteer holds the reins. And as horses without a driver go at break-neck speed, so the body if it be not governed by the reasonable soul rushes to its own destruction. The philosophers make use of another illustration of the relations between soul and body; they say the body is a boy, the soul his tutor. Hence the historian tells us "that our soul directs, our body serves. The one we have in common with the gods, the other with the beasts." So then unless the vices of youth and boyhood are regulated by the wisdom of the tutor, every effort and every impulse sets strongly in the direction of wantonness. We might lose four of the senses and yet live,—that is we could do without sight, hearing, smell, and the pleasures of touch. But a human being cannot subsist without tasting food. It follows that reason must be present, that we may take food of such a kind and in such quantities as will not burden the body, or hinder the free movement of the soul: for it is the way with us that we eat, and walk, and sleep, and digest our food, and afterwards in the fulness of blood have to bear the spur of lust. "Wine is a mocker, strong drink a brawler." Whosoever has much to do with these is not wise. And we should not take such food as is difficult of digestion, or such as when eaten will give us reason to complain that we got it and lost it with much effort. The preparation of vegetables, fruit, and pulse is easy, and does not require

the skill of expensive cooks: our bodies are nourished by them with little trouble on our part; and, if taken in moderation, such food is easier to digest, and at less cost, because it does not stimulate the appetite, and therefore is not devoured with avidity. No one has his stomach inflated or overloaded if he eats only one or two dishes, and those inexpensive ones: such a condition comes of pampering the taste with a variety of meats. The smells of the kitchen may induce us to eat, but when hunger is satisfied, they make us their slaves. Hence gorging gives rise to disease: and many persons find relief for the discomfort of gluttony in emetics,—what they disgraced themselves by putting in, they with still greater disgrace put out.

11. Hippocrates in his Aphorisms teaches that stout persons of a coarse habit of body, when once they have attained their full growth, unless the plethora be quickly relieved by blood-letting, develop tendencies to paralysis and the worst forms of disease: they must therefore be bled, that there may be room for fresh growth. For it is not the nature of our bodies to continue in one stay, but go on either to increase or decrease, and no animal can live which is incapable of growth. Whence Galen, a very learned man and the commentator on Hippocrates, says in his exhortation to the practice of medicine that athletes whose whole life and art consists in stuffing cannot live long, nor be healthy: and that their souls enveloped with superfluous blood and fat, and as it were covered with mud, have no refined or heavenly thoughts, but are always intent upon gluttonous and voracious feasting. Diogenes maintains that tyrants do not bring about revolutions in cities, and foment wars civil or foreign for the sake of a simple diet of vegetables and

fruits, but for costly meats and the delicacies of the table. And, strange to say, Epicurus, the defender of pleasure, in all his books speaks of nothing but vegetables and fruits; and he says that we ought to live on cheap food because the preparation of sumptuous banquets of flesh involves great care and suffering, and greater pains attend the search for such delicacies than pleasures the consumption of them. Our bodies need only something to eat and drink. Where there is bread and water, and the like, nature is satisfied. Whatever more there may be does not go to meet the wants of life, but are ministers to vicious pleasure. Eating and drinking does not quench the longing for luxuries, but appeases hunger and thirst. Persons who feed on flesh want also gratifications not found in flesh. But they who adopt a simple diet do not look for flesh. Further, we cannot devote ourselves to wisdom if our thoughts are running on a well-laden table, the supply of which requires an excess of work and anxiety. The wants of nature are soon satisfied: cold and hunger can be banished with simple food and clothing. Hence the Apostle says: "Having food and clothing let us be therewith content." Delicacies and the various dishes of the feast are the nurses of avarice. The soul greatly exults when you are content with little: you have the world beneath your feet, and can exchange all its power, its feasts, and its lusts, the objects for which men rake money together, for common food, and make up for them all with a sack-cloth shirt. Take away the luxurious feasting and the gratification of lust, and no one will want riches to be used either in the belly, or beneath it. The invalid only regains his health by diminishing and carefully selecting his food, *i.e.*, in medical phrase, by adopting a "slender diet." The same food that recovers health, can preserve it, for no one can imagine vegetables to be the cause of disease. And if vegetables do not give the strength of Milo of Crotona—a strength supplied and nourished by meat—what need has a wise man and a Christian philosopher of such strength as is required by athletes and soldiers, and which, if he had it, would only stimulate to vice? Let those persons deem meat according with health who wish to gratify their lust, and who, sunk in filthy pleasure, are always at heat. What a Christian wants is health, but not superfluous strength. And it ought not to disturb us if we find but few supporters; for the pure and temperate are as rare as good and faithful friends, and virtue is always scarce. Study the temperance of Fabricius, or the poverty of Curius, and in a great city you will find few worthy of your imitation. You need not fear that if you do not eat flesh, fowlers and hunters will have learnt their craft in vain.

12. We have read that some who suffered with disease of the joints and with gouty humors recovered their health by proscribing delicacies, and coming down to a simple board and mean food. For they were then free from the worry of managing a house and from unlimited feasting. Horace makes fun of the longing for food which when eaten leaves nothing but regret.

"Scorn pleasure; she but hurts when bought with pain."

And when, in the delightful retirement of the country, by way of satirizing voluptuous men, he described himself as plump and fat, his sportive verse ran thus:

"Pay me a visit if you want to laugh,

You'll find me fat and sleek with well-dress'd hide,

Like any pig from Epicurus' sty."

But even if our food be the most common, we must avoid repletion. For nothing is so destructive to the mind as a full belly, fermenting like a wine vat and giving forth its gases on all sides. What sort of fasting is it, or what refreshment is there after fasting, when we are blown out with yesterday's dinner, and our stomach is made a factory for the closet? We wish to get credit for protracted abstinence, and all the while we devour so much that a day and a night can scarcely digest it. The proper name to give it is not fasting, but rather debauch and rank indigestion.

13. Dicæarchus in his book of Antiquities, describing Greece, relates that under Saturn, that is in the Golden Age, when the ground brought forth all things abundantly, no one ate flesh, but everyone lived on field produce and fruits which the earth bore of itself. Xenophon in eight books narrates the life of Cyrus, King of the Persians, and asserts that they supported life on barley, cress, salt, and black bread. Both the aforesaid Xenophon, Theophrastus, and almost all the Greek writers testify to the frugal diet of the Spartans. Chæremon the Stoic, a man of great eloquence, has a treatise on the life of the ancient priests of Egypt, who, he says, laid aside all worldly business and cares, and were ever in the temple, studying nature and the regulating causes of the heavenly bodies; they never had intercourse with women; they never from the time they began to devote themselves to the divine service set eyes on their kindred and relations, nor even saw their children; they always abstained from

flesh and wine, on account of the light-headedness and dizziness which a small quantity of food caused, and especially to avoid the stimulation of the lustful appetite engendered by this meat and drink. They seldom ate bread, that they might not load the stomach. And whenever they ate it, they mixed pounded hyssop with all that they took, so that the action of its warmth might diminish the weight of the heavier food. They used no oil except with vegetables, and then only in small quantities, to mitigate the unpalatable taste. What need, he says, to speak of birds, when they avoided even eggs and milk as flesh. The one, they said, was liquid flesh, the other was blood with the color changed? Their bed was made of palm-leaves, called by them *baiæ*: a sloping footstool laid upon the ground served for a pillow, and they could go without food for two or three days. The humors of the body which arise from sedentary habits were dried up by reducing their diet to an extreme point.

14. Josephus in the second book of the history of the Jewish captivity, and in the eighteenth book of the Antiquities, and the two treatises against Apion, describes three sects of the Jews, the Pharisees, Sadducees, and Essenes. On the last of these he bestows wondrous praise because they practiced perpetual abstinence from wives, wine, and flesh, and made a second nature of their daily fast. Philo, too, a man of great learning, published a treatise of his own on their mode of life. Neanthes of Cizycus, and Asclepiades of Cyprus, at the time when Pygmalion ruled over the East, relate that the eating of flesh was unknown. Eubulus, also, who wrote the history of Mithras in many volumes, relates that among the Persians there are three kinds of Magi, the first of whom, those of greatest learning and eloquence, take no food

except meal and vegetables. At Eleusis it is customary to abstain from fowls and fish and certain fruits. Bardesanes, a Babylonian, divides the Gymnosophists of India into two classes, the one called Brahmans, the other Samaneans, who are so rigidly self-restrained that they support themselves either with the fruit of trees which grow on the banks of the Ganges, or with common food of rice or flour, and when the king visits them, he is wont to adore them, and thinks the peace of his country depends upon their prayers. Euripides relates that the prophets of Jupiter in Crete abstained not only from flesh, but also from cooked food. Xenocrates the philosopher writes that at Athens out of all the laws of Triptolemus only three precepts remain in the temple of Ceres: respect to parents, reverence for the gods, and abstinence from flesh. Orpheus in his song utterly denounces the eating of flesh. I might speak of the frugality of Pythagoras, Socrates, and Antisthenes to our confusion: but it would be tedious, and would require a work to itself. At all events this is the Antisthenes who, after teaching rhetoric with renown, on hearing Socrates, is related to have said to his disciples, "Go, and seek a master, for I have now found one." He immediately, sold what he had, divided the proceeds among the people, and kept nothing for himself but a small cloak. Of his poverty and toil Xenophon in the Symposium is a witness, and so are his countless treatises, some philosophical, some rhetorical. His most famous follower was the great Diogenes, who was mightier than King Alexander in that he conquered human nature. For Antisthenes would not take a single pupil, and when he could not get rid of the persistent Diogenes he threatened him with a stick if he did not depart. The latter is said to have laid down his head and said, "No stick will be hard enough to prevent me from following you." Satyrus, the biographer of illustrious men, relates that Diogenes to guard himself against the cold, folded his cloak double: his scrip was his pantry: and when aged he carried a stick to support his feeble frame, and was commonly called "Old Hand-to-mouth," because to that very hour he begged and received food from anyone. His home was the gateways and city arcades. And when he wriggled into his tub, he would joke about his movable house that adapted itself to the seasons. For when the weather was cold he used to turn the mouth of the tub towards the south: in summer towards the north; and whatever the direction of the sun might be, that way the palace of Diogenes was turned. He had a wooden dish for drinking; but on one occasion seeing a boy drinking with the hollow of his hand he is related to have dashed the cup to the ground, saying that he did not know nature provided a cup. His virtue and self-restraint were proved even by his death. It is said that, now an old man, he was on his way to the Olympic games, which used to be attended by a great concourse of people from all parts of Greece, when he was overtaken by fever and lay down upon the bank by the road-side. And when his friends wished to place him on a beast or in a conveyance, he did not assent, but crossing to the shade of a tree said, "Go your way, I pray you, and see the games: this night will prove me either conquered or conqueror. If I conquer the fever, I shall go to the games: if the fever conquers me, I shall enter the unseen world." There through the night he lay gasping for breath and did not, as we are told, so much die as banish the fever by death. I have cited the example of only one philosopher, so that our fine, erect, muscular athletes, who hardly make a shadow of a footmark in their swift passage, whose words are in their fists and their reasoning in their heels, who either know nothing of apostolic poverty and the hardness of the cross, or despise it, may at least imitate Gentile moderation.

15. So far I have dealt with the arguments and examples of philosophers. Now I will pass on to the beginning of the human race, that is, to the sphere which belongs to us. I will first point out that Adam received a command in paradise to abstain from one tree though he might eat the other fruit. The blessedness of paradise could not be consecrated without abstinence from food. So long as he fasted, he remained in paradise; he ate, and was cast out; he was no sooner cast out than he married a wife. While he fasted in paradise he continued a virgin: when he filled himself with food in the earth, he bound himself with the tie of marriage. And yet though cast out he did not immediately receive permission to eat flesh; but only the fruits of trees and the produce of the crops, and herbs and vegetables were given him for food, that even when an exile from paradise he might feed not upon flesh which was not to be found in paradise, but upon grain and fruit like that of paradise. But afterwards when God saw that the heart of man from his youth was set on wickedness continually, and that His Spirit could not remain in them because they were flesh, He by the deluge passed sentence on the works of the flesh, and, taking note of the extreme greediness of men, gave them liberty to eat flesh: so that while understanding that all things were lawful for them, they might not greatly desire that which was allowed, lest they should turn a commandment into a cause of transgression. And yet even then, fasting was in part commanded. For, seeing that some animals

are called clean, some unclean, and the unclean animals were taken into Noah's ark by pairs, the clean in uneven numbers (and of course the eating of the unclean was forbidden, otherwise the term unclean would be unmeaning), fasting was in part consecrated: restraint in the use of all was taught by the prohibition of some. Why did Esau lose his birthright? Was it not on account of food? and he could not atone with tears for the impatience of his appetite. The people of Israel cast out from Egypt and on their way to the land of promise, the land flowing with milk and honey, longed for the flesh of Egypt, and the melons and garlic, saying: "Would that we had died by the hand of the Lord in the land of Egypt, when we sat by the flesh pots." And again, "Who shall give us flesh to eat? We remember the fish which we did eat in Egypt for nought; the cucumbers, and the melons, and the leeks, and the onions, and the garlic: but now our soul is dried away: we have nought save this manna to look to."

They despised angels' food, and sighed for the flesh of Egypt. Moses for forty days and forty nights fasted on Mount Sinai, and showed even then that man does not live on bread alone, but on every word of God. He says to the Lord, "the people is full and maketh idols." Moses with empty stomach received the law written with the finger of God. The people that ate and drank and rose up to play fashioned a golden calf, and preferred an Egyptian ox to the majesty of the Lord. The toil of so many days perished through the fulness of a single hour. Moses boldly broke the tables: for he knew that drunkards cannot hear the word of God. "The beloved grew thick, waxed fat, and became sleek: he kicked and forsook the Lord which made him, and departed from the God of his salvation." Hence also it is enjoined in the same Book of

Deuteronomy: "Beware, lest when thou hast eaten and drunk, and hast built goodly houses, and when thy herds and thy flocks multiply, and thy silver and gold is multiplied, then thine heart be lifted up, and thou forget the Lord thy God." In short the people ate and their heart grew thick, lest they should see with their eyes, and hear with their ears, and understand with their heart: so the people well fed and fat-fleshed could not bear the countenance of Moses who fasted, for, to correctly render the Hebrew, it was furnished with horns through his converse with God. And it was not, as some think, to show that there is no difference between virginity and marriage, but to assert his sympathy with severe fasting, that our Lord and Savior when he was transfigured on the Mount revealed Moses and Elias with Himself in glory. Although Moses and Elias were properly types of the Law and the Prophets, as is clearly witnessed by the Gospel: "They spoke of his departure which he was about to accomplish at Jerusalem." For the passion of our Lord is declared not by virginity or marriage, but by the Law and the Prophets. If, however, any persons contentiously maintain that by Moses is signified marriage, by Elias virginity, let me tell them briefly that Moses died and was buried, but Elias was carried off in a chariot of fire and entered on immortality before he approached death. But the second writing of the tables could not be effected without fasting. What was lost by drunkenness was regained by abstinence, a proof that by fasting we can return to paradise, whence, though fulness, we have been expelled. In Exodus we read that the battle was fought against Amalek while Moses prayed, and the whole people fasted until the evening. Joshua, the son of Nun, bade sun and moon stand still, and the victorious army prolonged its fast for more than a day. Saul, as it is written in the first book of Kings, pronounced a curse on him who ate bread before the evening, and until he had avenged himself upon his enemies. So none of his people tasted any food. And all they of the land took food. And so binding was a solemn fast once it was proclaimed to the Lord, that Jonathan, to whom the victory was due, was taken by lot, and could not escape the charge of sinning in ignorance, and his father's hand was raised against him, and the prayers of the people scarce availed to save him. Elijah after the preparation of a forty days fast saw God on Mount Horeb, and heard from Him the words, "What does thou here, Elijah?" There is much more familiarity in this than in the "Where art thou, Adam?" of Genesis. The latter was intended to excite the fears of one who had fed and was lost; the former was affectionately addressed to a fasting servant. When the people were assembled in Mizpeh, Samuel proclaimed a fast, and so strengthened them, and thus made them prevail against the enemy. The attack of the Assyrians was repulsed, and the might of Sennacherib utterly crushed, by the tears and sackcloth of King Hezekiah, and by his humbling himself with fasting. So also the city of Nineveh by fasting excited compassion and turned aside the threatening wrath of the Lord. And Sodom and Gomorrah might have appeased it, had they been willing to repent, and through the aid of fasting gain for themselves tears of repentance. Ahab, the most impious of kings, by fasting and wearing sackcloth, succeeded in escaping the sentence of God, and in deferring the overthrow of his house to the days of his posterity. Hannah, the wife of Elkanah, by fasting won the gift of a son. At Babylon the magicians came into peril, every interpreter of dreams, soothsayer, and diviner was slain. Daniel and the three youths gained a good report by fasting, and although they were fed on pulse, they were fairer and wiser than they who ate the flesh from the king's table. Then it is written that Daniel fasted for three weeks; he ate no pleasant bread; flesh and wine entered not his mouth; he was not anointed with oil; and the angel came to him saying, "Daniel, thou art worthy of compassion." He who in the eyes of God was worthy of compassion, afterwards was an object of terror to the lions in their den. How fair a thing is that which propitiates God, tames lions, terrifies demons! Habakkuk (although we do not find this in the Hebrew Scriptures) was sent to him with the reaper's meal, for by a week's abstinence he had merited so distinguished a server. David, when his son was in danger after his adultery, made confession in ashes and with fasting. He tells us that he ate ashes like bread, and mingled his drink with weeping. And that his knees became weak through fasting. Yet he had certainly heard from Nathan the words, "The Lord also hath put away thy sin." Samson and Samuel drank neither wine nor strong drink, for they were children of promise, and conceived in abstinence and fasting. Aaron and the other priests when about to enter the temple, refrained from all intoxicating drink for fear they should die. Whence we learn that they die who minister in the Church without sobriety. And hence it is a reproach against Israel: "Ye gave my Nazarites wine to drink." Jonadab, the son of Rechab, commanded his sons to drink no wine forever. And when Jeremiah offered them wine to drink, and they of their own accord refused it, the Lord spoke by the prophet, saying: "Because ye have obeyed the commandment of Jonadab your father, Jonadab the son of Rechab shall not want a man to stand before me forever."

On the threshold of the Gospel appears Anna, the daughter of Phanuel, the wife of one husband, and a woman who was always fasting. Long-continued chastity and persistent fasting welcomed a Virgin Lord. His forerunner and herald, John, fed on locusts and wild honey, not on flesh; and the hermits of the desert and the monks in their cells, at first used the same sustenance. But the Lord Himself consecrated His baptism by a forty days' fast, and He taught us that the more violent devils cannot be overcome, except by prayer and fasting. Cornelius the centurion was found worthy through almsgiving and frequent fasts to receive the gift of the Holy Spirit before baptism. The Apostle Paul, after speaking of hunger and thirst, and his other labors, perils from robbers, shipwrecks, loneliness, enumerates frequent fasts. And he advises his disciple Timothy, who had a weak stomach, and was subject to many infirmities, to drink wine in moderation: "Drink no longer water," he says. The fact that he bids him *no longer* drink water shows that he had previously drunk water. The apostle would not have allowed this had not frequent infirmities and bodily pain demanded the concession.

16. The Apostle does indeed blame those who forbade marriage, and commanded to abstain from food, which God created for use with thanksgiving. But he has in view Marcion, and Tatian, and other heretics, who inculcate perpetual abstinence, to destroy, and express their hatred and contempt for, the works of the Creator. But we praise every creature of God, and yet prefer leanness to corpulence, abstinence to luxury, fasting to fulness. "He that labored, labored for himself, and he is eager to his own destruction." And, "From the days of John the Baptist (who fasted and was a virgin) until now

the kingdom of heaven suffered violence, and men of violence take it by force." For we are afraid lest at the coming of the eternal judge we be caught, as in the days of the flood, and at the overthrow of Sodom and Gomorrah, eating and drinking, and marrying, and giving in marriage. For both the flood and the fire from heaven found fulness as well as marriage ready for destruction. Nor need we wonder if the Apostle commands that everything sold in the market be bought and eaten, since with idolaters, and with those who still ate in the temples of the idols meats offered to idols as such, it passed for the highest abstinence to abstain only from food eaten by the Gentiles. And if he says to the Romans: "Let not him that eat set at nought him that eat not: and let not him that eat not judge him that eat," he does not make fasting and fulness of equal merit, but he is speaking against those believers in Christ who were still Judaizing: and he warns Gentile believers, not to offend those by their food who were still too weak in faith. In brief this is clear enough in the sequel: "I know and am persuaded in the Lord Jesus, that nothing is unclean of itself: save that to him who accounted anything to be unclean, to him it is unclean. For if because of meat thy brother is grieved, thou walk no longer in love. Destroy not with thy meat him for whom Christ died. Let not then your good be evil spoken of: for the Kingdom of God is not eating and drinking." And that no one may suppose he is referring to fasting and not to Jewish superstition, he immediately explains, "One man hath faith to eat all things: but he that is weak eat herbs." And again, "One man esteemed one day above another: another esteemed every day alike. Let each man be fully assured in his own mind. He that regarded the day, regarded it unto the Lord: and he that eat, eats unto the Lord, for he giveth God thanks; and he that eat not, unto the Lord he eats not, and giveth God thanks." For they who were still weak in faith and thought some meats clean, some unclean: and supposed there was a difference between one day and another, for example, that the Sabbath, and the New Moons, and the Feast of Tabernacles were holier than other days, were commanded to eat herbs which are indifferently partaken of by all. But such as were of stronger faith believed all meats and all days to be alike.

17. My opponent has dared to maintain that our Lord was called by the Pharisees a wine-bibber and a glutton: and from the fact of His going to marriage feasts and from His not despising the banquets of sinners, I am to infer His wishes respecting ourselves. That Lord, so you suppose, is a glutton who fasted forty days to hallow Christian fasting; who calls them blessed that hunger and thirst; who says that He has food, not that which the disciples surmised, but such as would not perish forever; who forbids us to think of the morrow; who, though He is said to have hungered and thirsted, and to have gone frequently to various meals, except in celebrating the mystery whereby He represented His passion, or in proving the reality of His body is nowhere described as ministering to His appetite; who tells of purple-clad Dives in hell for his feasting, and says that poor Lazarus for his abstinence was in Abraham's bosom; who, when we fast, bids us anoint our head and wash our face, that we fast not to gain glory from men, but praise from the Lord; who did indeed after His resurrection eat part of a broiled fish and of a honey-comb, not to allay hunger and to gratify His palate, but to show the reality of His own body. For whenever He raised anyone from the dead He ordered that

food should be given him to eat, lest the resurrection should be thought a delusion. And this is why Lazarus after his resurrection is described as being at the feast with our Lord. We do not deny that fish and other kinds of flesh, if we choose, may be taken as food; but as we prefer virginity to marriage, so do we esteem fasting and spirituality above meats and full-bloodedness. And if Peter before dinner went to the supper chamber at the sixth hour, a chance fit of hunger does not prejudice fasting. For, if this were so, because our Lord at the sixth hour sat weary on the well of Samaria and wished to drink, all must of necessity, whether they so desire or not, drink at that time. Possibly it was the Sabbath, or the Lord's day, and he hungered at the sixth hour after two or three days' fasting; for I could never believe that the Apostle, if he had eaten a dinner only one day previous and had been blown out with a great meal, would have been hungry by noon next day. But if he did dine the day previous, and was hungry next day before luncheon, I do not think that a man who was so soon hungry ate until he was satisfied. Again, God by the mouth of Isaiah says what fast He did not choose: "In the day of your fast ye find pleasure, and afflict the lowly: ye fast for strife and debate, and to smite with the fist of wickedness. It is not such a fast that I have chosen, saith the Lord." What kind He has chosen He thus teaches: "Deal thy bread to the hungry, and bring the houseless poor into thy house. When thou see the naked cover him, and hide not thyself from thine own flesh." He did not therefore reject fasting, but showed what He would have it to be: for that bodily hunger is not pleasing to God which is made null and void by strife, and plunder, and lust. If God does not desire fasting, how is it that in Leviticus He commands the whole people in the seventh month, on the tenth day of the month, to fast until the evening, and threatens that he who does not afflict his soul shall die and be cut off from his people? How is it that the graves of lust where the people fell in their devotion to flesh remain even to this day in the wilderness? Do we not read that the stupid people gorged themselves with quails until the wrath of God came upon them? Why was the man of God at whose prophecy the hand of King Jeroboam withered, and who ate contrary to the command of God, immediately smitten? Strange that the lion which left the ass safe and sound should not spare the prophet just risen from his meal! He who, while he was fasting, had wrought miracles, no sooner ate a meal than he paid the penalty for the gratification. Joel also cries aloud: "Sanctify a fast, proclaim a time of healing," that it might appear that a fast is sanctified by other works, and that a holy fast avails for the cure of sin. Moreover, just as true virginity is not prejudiced by the counterfeit professions of the virgins of the devil, so neither is true fasting by the periodic fast and perpetual abstinence from certain kinds of food on the part of the worshippers of Isis and Cybele, particularly when a fast from bread is made up for by feasting on flesh. And just as the signs of Moses were imitated by the signs of the Egyptians which were in reality no signs at all, for the rod of Moses swallowed up the rods of the magicians: so when the devil tries to be the rival of God this does not prove that our religion is superstitious, but that we are negligent, since we refuse to do what even men of the world see clearly to be good.

    18. His fourth and last contention is that there are two classes, the sheep and the goats, the just and the unjust: that the just stand on the right hand, the other on

the left: and that to the just the words are spoken: "Come, ye blessed of my Father, and inherit the kingdom prepared for you from the foundation of the world." But that sinners are thus addressed: "Depart from me, ye cursed, into the eternal fire which is prepared for the devil and his angels." That a good tree cannot bring forth evil fruit, nor an evil tree good fruit. Hence it is that the Savior says to the Jews: "Ye are of your father the devil, and the lusts of your father it is your will to do." He quotes the parable of the ten virgins, the wise and the foolish, and shows that the five who had no oil remained outside, but that the other five who had gotten for themselves the light of good works went into the marriage with the bridegroom. He goes back to the flood, and tells us that they who were righteous like Noah were saved, but that the sinners perished all together. We are informed that among the men of Sodom and Gomorrah no difference is made except between the two classes of the good and the bad. The righteous are delivered, the sinners are consumed by the same fire. There is one salvation for those who are released, one destruction for those who stay behind. Lot's wife is a clear warning that we must not deviate a hair's breadth from right. If, however, he says, you object and ask me why the righteous toils in time of peace, or in the midst of persecution, if he is to gain nothing nor have a greater reward, I would assert that he does this, not that he may gain a further reward but that he may not lose what he has already received. In Egypt also the ten plagues fell with equal violence upon all that sinned, and the same darkness hung over master and slave, noble and ignoble, the king and the people. Again at the Red Sea the righteous all passed over, the sinners were all overwhelmed. Six hundred thousand men, besides those who were unfit for war through age or sex, all alike fell in the desert, and two who were alike in righteousness are alike delivered. For forty years all Israel toiled and died alike. As regards food, an homer of manna was the measure for all ages: the clothes of all alike did not wear out: the hair of all alike did not grow, nor the beard increase: the shoes of all lasted the same time. Their feet grew not hard: the food in the mouths of all had the same taste. They went on their way to one resting place with equal toil and equal reward. All Hebrews had the same Passover, the same Feast of Tabernacles, the same Sabbath, the same New Moons. In the seventh, the Sabbatical Year, all prisoners were released without distinction of persons, and in the year of Jubilee all debts were forgiven to all debtors, and he who had sold land returned to the inheritance of his fathers.

19. Then, again, as regards the parable of the sower in the Gospel, we read that the good ground brought forth fruit, some a hundred fold, some sixty fold, and some thirty fold; and, on the other hand, that the bad ground admitted of three degrees of sterility: but Jovinianus makes only two classes, the good soil and the bad. And as in one Gospel our Lord promises the Apostles a hundred fold, in another seven fold, for leaving children and wives, and in the world to come life eternal; and the seven and the hundred mean the same thing: so, too, in the passage before us, the numbers describing the fertility of the soil need not create any difficulty, particularly when the Evangelist Mark gives the inverse order, thirty, sixty, and a hundred. The Lord says, "He that eats my flesh and drinks my blood abides in me, and I in him." As, then, there are not varying degrees of Christ's presence in us, so neither are there degrees of our

abiding in Christ. "Everyone that loveth me will keep my word: and my Father will love him, and we will come unto him, and make our abode with him." He that is righteous, loves Christ: and if a man thus loves, the Father and the Son come to him, and make their abode with him. Now I suppose that when the guest is such as this the host cannot possibly lack anything. And if our Lord says, "In my Father's house are many mansions," His meaning is not that there are different mansions in the kingdom of heaven, but He indicates the number of Churches in the whole world, for though the Church be seven-fold she is but one. "I go," He says, "to prepare *a place* for you," not *places*. If this promise is peculiar to the twelve apostles, then Paul is shut out from that place, and the chosen vessel will be thought superfluous and unworthy. John and James, because they asked more than the others, did not obtain it; and yet their dignity is not diminished, because they were equal to the rest of the apostles. "Know ye not that your bodies are a temple of the Holy Ghost?" A *temple*, He says, not *temples*, in order to show that God dwells in all alike. "Neither for these only do I pray, but for them also that believe on me through their word; as thou, Father, in me, and I in thee, are one, so they may be all one in us. And the glory which thou hast given me I have given unto them. I have loved them, as thou hast loved me. And as we are Father, Son, and Holy Ghost, one God, so may they be one people in themselves, that is, like dear children, partakers of the divine nature." Call the Church what you will, bride, sister, mother, her assembly is but one and never lacks husband, brother, or son. Her faith is one, and she is not defiled by variety of doctrine, nor divided by heresies. She continues a virgin.

Whithersoever the Lamb goes, she follows Him: she alone knows the Song of Christ.

20. "If you tell me," says he, "that one star differed from another star in glory, I reply, that one star does differ from another star; that is, spiritual persons differ from carnal. We love all the members alike, and do not prefer the eye to the finger, nor the finger to the ear: but the loss of any one is attended by the sorrow of all the rest. We all alike come into this world, and we all alike depart from it. There is one Adam of the earth, and another from heaven. The earthly Adam is on the left hand, and will perish: the heavenly Adam is on the right hand, and will be saved. He who says to his brother, '*thou fool,*' and '*raca,*' will be in danger of Gehenna. And the murderer and the adulterer will likewise be sent into Gehenna. In times of persecution some are burnt, some strangled, some beheaded, some flee, or die within the walls of a prison: the struggle varies in kind, but the victors' crown is one. No difference was made between the son who had never left his father, and his brother who was welcomed as a returning penitent. To the laborers of the first hour, the third, the sixth, the ninth, and the eleventh, the same reward of a penny was given, and what may perhaps seem still more strange to you, the first to receive the reward were they who had toiled least in the vineyard."

21. Who is there even of God's elect that would not be disturbed at these and similar passages of Holy Scripture which our crafty opponent, with a perverse ingenuity, twists to the support of his own views? The Apostle John says that many Antichrists had come, and to make no difference between John himself and the lowest penitent is the preaching of a real Antichrist. At the same

time, I am amazed at the portentous forms which Jovinianus, as slippery as a snake and like another Proteus, so rapidly assumes. In sexual intercourse and full feeding he is an Epicurean; in the distribution of rewards and punishments he all at once becomes a Stoic, He exchanges Jerusalem for Citium, Judea for Cyprus, Christ for Zeno. If we may not depart a hair's breadth from virtue, and all sins are equal, and a man who in a fit of hunger steals a piece of bread is no less guilty than he who slays a man: you must, in your turn, be held guilty of the greatest crimes. The case is different if you say that you have no sin, not even the least, and if, although all apostles and prophets and all the saints (as I have maintained in dealing with his second proposition) bewail their sinfulness, you alone boast of your righteousness. But a minute ago you were barefooted: now you not only wear shoes, but decorated ones. Just now you wore a rough coat and a dirty shirt, you were grimy, and haggard, and your hand was horny with toil: now you are clad in linen and silks, and strut like an exquisite in the fashions of the Atrebates and the Laodiceans. Your cheeks are ruddy, your skin sleek, your hair smoothed down in front and behind, your belly protrudes, your shoulders are little mountains, your neck full and so loaded with fat that the half-smothered words can scarce make their escape. Surely in such extremes of dress and mode of life there must be sin on the one side or the other. I will not assert that the sin lies in the food or clothing, but that such fickleness and changing for the worse is almost censurable in itself. And what we censure, is far removed from virtue; and what is far from virtue becomes the property of vice; and what is proved to be vicious is one with sin. Now sin, according to you, is placed on the left hand, and corresponds to the goats. You must, therefore, return to your old habits if you are to be a sheep on the right hand; or, if you perversely repent of your former views and change them for others, whether you like it or not, and although you shave off your beard, you will be reckoned among the goats.

22. But what is the good of calling a one-eyed man Old One-eye, and of showing the inconsistency of an assailant, when we have to refute a whole series of statements? That the sheep and the goats on the right hand and on the left are the two classes of the righteous and the wicked, I do not deny. That a good tree does not bring forth evil fruit, nor an evil one good fruit, no one doubts. The ten virgins also, wise and foolish, we divide into good and bad. We are not ignorant that at the deluge the righteous were delivered, and sinners overwhelmed with the waters. That at Sodom and Gomorrah the just man was rescued, while the sinners were consumed by fire, is clear to everyone. We are also aware that Egypt was stricken with the ten plagues, and that Israel was saved. Even little children in our schools sing how the righteous passed through the Red Sea, and Pharaoh with his host was drowned. That six hundred thousand fell in the desert because they were unbelieving, and that two only entered the land of promise, is taught by Scripture; and so is the rest of your description of the two classes, good and bad, down to the laborers in the vineyard. But what are we to think of your assertion, that because there is a division into good and bad, the good, or the bad it may be, are not distinguished one from another, and that it makes no difference whether one is a ram in the flock or a poor little sheep? whether the sheep have the first or the second fleece? whether the flock is diseased and covered with the

scab, or full of life and vigor? especially when by the authoritative utterances of His own prophet Ezekiel God clearly points out the difference between flock and flock of His rational sheep, saying, "Behold I judge between cattle and cattle, and between the rams and the he-goats, and between the fat cattle and the lean. Because ye have thrust with side and with shoulder, and pushed all the diseased with your horns, until they were scattered abroad." And that we might know what the cattle were, He immediately added: "Ye my flock, the flock of my pasture, are men." Will Paul and that penitent who had lain with his father's wife be on an equality, because the latter repented and was received into the Church: and shall the offender because he is with him on the right hand shine with the same glory as the Apostle? How is it then that tares and wheat grow side by side in the same field until the harvest, that is the end of the world? What is the significance of good and bad fish being contained in the Gospel net? Why, in Noah's ark, the type of the Church, are there different animals with different abodes according to their rank? Why stand the queen upon the Lord's right hand, in raiment of wrought gold, in a vesture of gold? Why had Joseph, representing Christ, a coat of many colors? Why does the Apostle say to the Romans: "According as God had dealt to each man a measure of faith. For even as we have many members in one body, and all the members have not the same office: so we, who are many, are one body in Christ, and severally members one of another. And having gifts differing according to the grace that was given to us, whether prophecy, let us prophesy according to the proportion of our faith; or ministry, let us give ourselves to our ministry; or he that teaches, to his teaching; or he that exhorted, to his exhorting: he that giveth, let him do it with liberality; he that rules, with diligence," and so on. And elsewhere: "One man esteemed one day above another: another esteemed every day alike. Let every man be fully persuaded in his own mind." To the Corinthians he says: "I have planted, Apollos watered: but God gave the increase. So then, neither is he that planted anything, neither he that watered: but God that giveth the increase. Now he that planted and he that watered are one: and every man shall receive his own reward according to his own labor. For we are laborers together with God, ye are God's husbandry, ye are God's building." And again elsewhere: "According to the grace of God which is given unto me, as a wise master-builder I laid a foundation, and another built thereon. But let each man take heed of how he built thereupon. For other foundation can no man lay, than that which is laid, which is Jesus Christ. But if any man built on the foundation, gold, silver, costly stones, wood, hay, stubble: each man's work shall be made manifest: for the day shall reveal it, because it is revealed in fire: and the fire itself shall prove each man's work of what sort it is. If any man's work shall abide which he built thereon, he shall receive a reward. If any man's work shall be burned, he shall suffer loss: but he himself shall be saved; yet so as through fire." If the man whose work is burnt and is to suffer the loss of his labor, while he himself is saved, yet not without proof of fire: it follows that if a man's work remains which he has built upon the foundation, he will be saved without probation by fire, and consequently a difference is established between one degree of salvation and another. Again in another place he says: "Let a man so account of us, as of ministers of Christ, and stewards of the mysteries of God. Here, moreover, it is required in stewards, that a man be found faithful." Would you be assured that between one steward and another there is a great difference (I am not speaking of bad and good, but of the good themselves who stand on the right hand)? then listen to the sequel: "Know ye not that they which minister about the sacrifices, eat of the sacrifices, and they which wait upon the altar have their portion with the altar? Even so did the Lord ordain that they which proclaim the gospel should live of the gospel. But I have used none of these things: and I wrote not these things that it may be so done in my case: for it were good for me rather to die, than that any man should make my glorying void. For if I preach the gospel, I have nothing to glory of; for necessity is laid upon me; for woe is unto me if I preach not the gospel. For if I do this of mine own will, I have a reward: but if not of mine own will, I have a steward-ship entrusted to me. What then is my reward? That, when I preach the gospel, I may make the gospel without charge, so as not to use to the full my right in the gospel. For though I was free from all men, I brought myself under bondage to all, that I might gain the more." You surely cannot say that men commit sin by living by the Gospel, and partaking of the sacrifices. Of course not. The Lord himself made the rule that they who preach the Gospel, should live by the Gospel. But an Apostle who does not abuse this freedom, but labors with his hands that he may not be a burden to anyone, and toils night and day and ministers to his companions of course does this, that for his greater toil he may receive a greater reward.

23. Let us hasten to what remains. "There are diversities of gifts, but the same Spirit. And there are diversities of ministrations, and the same Lord. And there

are diversities of operations, but the same God who worketh all things in all. But to each one is given the manifestation of the Spirit to profit withal." And again: "As the body is one, and hath many members, and all the members of the body, being many, are one body: so also is Christ." But he precludes you from saying that the different members of the one body have the same rank; for he immediately describes the orders of the Church, and says: "And God hath set some in the Church, first, apostles; secondly, prophets; thirdly, teachers; then miracles, then gifts of healings, helps, governments, divers kinds of tongues. Are all apostles? are all prophets? are all teachers? are all workers of miracles? have all gifts of healings? Do all speak with tongues? do all interpret? But desire earnestly the greater gifts. And a still more excellent way show I unto you." And after discoursing more in detail of the graces of charity, he added: "Whether there be prophecies, they shall be done away; whether there be tongues, they shall cease; whether there be knowledge, it shall be done away. For we know in part, and we prophesy in part: but when that which is perfect is come, then that which is in part shall be done away." And afterwards we read: "But now abides faith, hope, love, these three; and the greatest of these is love. Follow after love; yet desire earnestly spiritual gifts, but rather that ye may prophesy." And again: "I would have you all speak with tongues, but rather that ye should prophesy: and greater is he that prophesied than he that Speakes with tongues." And again: "I thank God, I speak with tongues more than you all." Where there are different gifts, and one man is greater, another less, and all are called spiritual, they are all certainly sheep, and they stand on the right hand; but there is a difference between one sheep and another. It is humility that leads the Apostle Paul to say: "I am the least of the apostles, that am not meet to be called an apostle, because I persecuted the church of God. But by the grace of God I am what I am: and his grace which was bestowed upon me was not found vain: but I labored more abundantly than they all: yet not I, but the grace of God which was with me." But the very fact of his thus humbling himself shows the possibility of there being apostles of higher or lower rank, and God is not unjust that He will forget the work of him who is called the chosen vessel of election, and who labored more abundantly than they all, or assign equal rewards to unequal deserts. Afterwards we read, "As in Adam all die, so also in Christ shall all be now alive. But each in his own order." If each is to rise in his own order, it follows that those who rise are of different degrees of merit. "All flesh is not the same flesh; but there is one flesh of men, and another flesh of beasts, and another flesh of birds, and another of fishes. There are also celestial bodies, and bodies terrestrial: but the glory of the celestial is one, and the glory of the terrestrial is another. There is one glory of the sun, and another glory of the moon, and another glory of the stars; for one star differed from another star in glory. So also is the resurrection of the dead." Like a learned commentator, you have explained this passage by saying that the spiritual differs from the carnal. It follows that in heaven there will be both spiritual and carnal persons, and not only will the sheep climb thither, but your goats also. "One star," he says, "differed from another star in glory": this is not the distinction of sheep and goat, but of sheep and sheep, star and star. Lastly, he says, "there is one glory of the sun, and another glory of the moon." But for this, you might maintain that the phrase *one star from another star* covers the whole human race; but he introduces the sun and moon, and you cannot possibly reckon them among the goats. "So," says he, "is also the resurrection of the dead"—the just will shine with the brightness of the sun, and those of the next rank will glow with the splendor of the moon, so that one will be a Lucifer, another an Arcturus, a third an Orion, another Mazzaroth, or some other of the stars whose names are hollowed in the book of Job. "For we all," he says, "must be made manifest before the judgment seat of Christ; that each one may receive the things done in the body, according to what he hath done, whether it be good or bad." And you cannot say that the mode of our manifestation before the judgment-seat of Christ is such that the good receive good things, the bad evil things; for he teaches us in the same epistle that he who soweth sparingly shall reap also sparingly, and he that soweth bountifully shall reap also bountifully. Surely he who sows more and he who sows less are both on the right side. And although they belong to the same class, that of the sower, yet they differ in respect of measure and number. The same Paul, writing to the Ephesians, says: "to the intent that now unto the principalities and the powers in the heavenly places might be made known through the church the manifold wisdom of God." You observe that it is a varied and manifold wisdom of God which is spoken of as existing in the different ranks of the church. And in the same epistle we read, "Unto each one of us was the grace given according to the measure of the grace of Christ": not that Christ's measure varies, but only that so much of His grace is poured out as we can receive.

24. In vain, therefore, do you multiply instances of sheep and goats, of the five wise and five foolish virgins,

St. Jerome

of Egyptians and Israelites, and so forth, because retribution is not in the present, but will be in the future. Hence we find that the day of judgment is promised at the end of all things, because the judgment is not now. For it would be absurd to call the last day the day of judgment, if God were judging at the present time. Now we sail the ship, wrestle, and fight, so that at last we may reach the haven, be crowned, and triumph. But you, with no less adroitness than perversity, make the life of this world illustrate that of the world to come, although we know full well that here unrighteousness prevails, there, righteousness: "until we go into the sanctuary of God, and understand the end of those men." The saint does not die one way, the sinner another. Those who sail the same sea have the same calm and storm. A violent death is not one thing to the robber, another to the martyr. Children are not born one way of adultery and prostitution, in another of pure marriage. Certainly our Lord and the robbers incurred the same penalty of crucifixion. If the judgment of this world and of that which is to come be the same, it follows that they who were here crucified side by side, will also be esteemed of equal rank hereafter. Paul and they who bound him, sailed together, endured the same storm, escaped together to the shore when the ship was broken with the waves. You cannot deny that the prisoner and the keepers were of unequal merit. And what were the circumstances of that same shipwreck of the Apostle and the soldiers? The Apostle Paul afterwards related a vision, and said that they who were with him in the ship had been given to him by the Lord. Are we to suppose that he to whom they were given, and they who were given to him, were of one degree of merit? Ten righteous men can save a sinful city. Lot together with his daughters was delivered from the fire: his sons-in-law would also have been saved, had they been willing to leave the city. Now there was surely a great difference between Lot and his sons-in-law. One city out of the five, Zoar, was saved, and a place which lay under the same sentence as Sodom, Gomorrah, Admah, and Zeboiim, was preserved by the prayers of a holy man. Lot and Zoar were of different merit, but both of them escaped the fire. The robbers who in the absence of David had laid waste Ziklag, and made a prey of the wives and children of the inhabitants were slain on the third day in the plain, but forty men mounted on camels fled. Will you maintain that there was some difference between those who were slain and those who made good their escape? We read in the Gospel that the tower of Siloam fell upon eighteen men who perished in the ruins. Certainly our Savior did not regard them as the only sinners: but they were punished to terrify the rest: it was like scourging a pestilent fellow to teach fools wisdom. If all sinners are punished alike, it is unjust for one to be slain while another is admonished by his comrade's death.

25. You raise the objection that all Israelites had the same measure of manna, an homer, and were alike in respect of dress, and hair, and beard, and shoes; as though we did not all alike partake of the body of Christ. In the Christian mysteries there is one means of sanctification for the master and the servant, the noble and the low-born, for the king and his soldiers, and yet, that which is one varies according to the merits of those who receive it. "Whosoever shall eat or drink unworthily shall be guilty of the body and blood of the Lord." Does it follow that because Judas drank of the same cup as the rest of the apostles, that he and they are of equal merit? But suppose

that we do not choose to receive the sacrament, at all events we all have the same life, breathe the same air, have the same blood in our veins, are fed on the same food. Moreover, if our viands are improved by culinary skill and are made more palatable for the consumer, food of this kind does not satisfy nature, but tickles the appetite. We are all alike subject to hunger, all alike suffer with cold: we alike are shriveled with the frost, or melted with the broiling heat. The sun and the moon, and all the company of the stars, the showers, the whole world run their course for us all alike, and, as the Gospel tells us, the same refreshing rain falls upon all, good and bad, just and unjust. If the present is a picture of the future, then the Sun of Righteousness will rise upon sinners as well as upon the righteous, upon the wicked and the holy, upon the heathen as well as upon Jews and Christians, though the Scripture says, "Unto you that fear the Lord shall the Sun of Righteousness arise." If He will rise to those that fear, He will set to the despisers and the false prophets. The sheep which stand on the right hand will be brought into the kingdom of heaven, the goats will be thrust down to hell. The parable does not contrast the sheep one with another, or on the other hand the goats, but merely makes a difference between sheep and goats. The whole truth is not taught in a single passage: we must always bear in mind the exact point of an illustration. For instance, the ten virgins are not examples of the whole human race, but of the careful and the slothful: the former are ever anticipating the advent of our Lord, the latter abandon themselves to idle slumber without a thought of future judgment. And so at the end of the parable it is said, "Watch, for ye know not the day, nor the hour." If at the deluge Noah was delivered, and the whole world perished, all men were flesh, and therefore were destroyed. You must either say that the sons of Noah and Noah for whose sake they were delivered were of unequal merit, or you must place the accursed Ham in the same rank as his father because he was delivered with him from the flood. At the passion of Christ all wavered, all were unprofitable together: there was none that did good, no not one. Will you therefore dare to say that Peter and the rest of the Apostles who fled denied the Savior in the same sense as Caiaphas and the Pharisees and the people who cried out, "Crucify him, crucify him"? And, to say no more about the Apostles, do you think Annas and Caiaphas, and Judas the traitor guilty of no greater crime than Pilate who was compelled against his will to give sentence against our Lord? The guilt of Judas is proportioned to his former merit, and the greater the guilt, the greater the penalty too. "For the *mighty* shall mightily suffer torment." An evil tree does not bear good fruit, nor a good tree evil fruit. If this be so, tell me how it was that Paul though he was an evil tree and persecuted the Church of Christ, afterwards bore good fruit? And Judas, though he was a good tree and wrought miracles like the other Apostles, afterwards turned traitor and brought forth evil fruit? The truth is that a good tree does not bear evil fruit, nor an evil tree good fruit, so long as they continue in their goodness, or badness. And if we read that every Hebrew keeps the same Passover, and that in the seventh year every prisoner is set free, and that at Jubilee, that is the fiftieth year, every possession returns to its owner, all this refers not to the present, but to the future; for being in bondage during the six days of this world, on the seventh day, the true and eternal Sabbath, we shall be free, at any rate if we wish to be free while still in bondage in the world. If, however, we do not desire it, our ear will be bored in token of our disobedience, and together with our wives and children, whom we preferred to liberty, that is, with the flesh and its works, we shall be in perpetual slavery.

26. As for the parable of the sower which makes both good and bad ground bear a triple crop, and the passage from the apostle in which upon Christ as the foundation one man builds gold, silver, costly stones, another wood, hay, stubble, the meaning is perfectly clear. We know that in a great house there are different vessels, and to wish to contradict so plain a truth would be sheer impudence. Yet that Jovinianus may not triumph in a lie and quote the instance of the apostles by way of discrediting the hundred-fold, sixty-fold, and thirty-fold, let me inform him that in Matthew and Mark a hundred-fold is promised to the apostles who had left all. And I would tell him further, that in the Gospel of Luke we find *much more*, that is πολύ πλείονα, and that there is absolutely no instance in the Gospels of a *hundred* standing for *seven*; and that he is convicted either of forgery, or of ignorance; and that our cause is not prejudiced by the fact that in one Gospel the enumeration begins at a hundred, in another at thirty, since it is a rule with all Scripture, and especially with the older writings, to put the lowest number first and so ascend by degrees to the higher. For instance, suppose one to say that so-and-so lived five and seventy and a hundred years, it does not follow that five and seventy are more than a hundred because they were first mentioned. If you do not on the side of good admit the difference between a hundred, sixty, and thirty, neither will you do so on the side of evil, and the seed which fell by the wayside, upon the rock,

and among thorns, will be equally faulty. But if the former three, or the latter three, on the side of good, or on the side of evil respectively, are one and the same, it was foolish instead of speaking of two things to enumerate six kinds, and all the more because according to the account of the parable in Matthew, Mark, and Luke, the Savior always added: "He that hath ears to hear, let him hear." Where there is no deep inner meaning, it is useless to draw our attention to the mystic sense.

27. You give it as your opinion that, since the Father and the Son make their abode with the faithful, and since Christ is their guest, nothing is lacking. I suppose, however, that Christ's abiding with the Corinthians was one thing, with the Ephesians another: it was one thing, I say, for Him to abide with those whom Paul blamed for many sins, another for Him to dwell with those to whom the apostle revealed mysteries hidden from the beginning of the world; one thing for Him to be in Titus and Timothy, another in Paul. Certainly amongst them that have been born of women, there has not arisen a greater than John the Baptist. But the term greater implies others who are less. And "he who is least in the kingdom of heaven is greater than he." You see then that in heaven one is greatest and another is least, and that among the angels and the invisible creation there is a manifold and infinite diversity. Why do the apostles say: "Lord, increase our faith," if there is one measure for all? And why did our Lord rebuke His disciple, saying: "O thou of little faith, wherefore didst thou doubt?" In Jeremiah also we read concerning the future kingdom: "Behold, the days come, saith the Lord, that I will make a new covenant with the house of Israel, and with the house of Judah not according to the covenant that I made with their

fathers." And so on after: "I will put my law in their inward parts, and in their heart will I write it; and I will be their God and they shall be my people: and they shall teach no more every man his neighbor, and every man his brother, saying, Know the Lord: for they shall all know me, from the least of them unto the greatest of them." The context of this passage clearly shows that the prophet is describing the future kingdom, and how can there possibly be in it a least or greatest, if all are to be equal? The secret is disclosed in the Gospel: "Whosoever shall do and teach, he shall be called great in the kingdom of heaven: but whosoever shall teach, and not do, shall be least." The Savior taught us at a feast to take the lowest place, lest, when one greater than us came, we should be thrust with disgrace from the higher place. If we cannot fall, but only raise ourselves by penitence, what is the meaning of the ladder at Bethel, on which the angels come from heaven to earth and descend as well as ascend? Surely while on that ladder they are reckoned among the sheep and stand on the right hand. There are angels who descend from heaven; but Jovinianus is sure that they retain their inheritance.

28. But when Jovinianus supposes that the many mansions in our Father's house are churches scattered throughout the world, who can refrain from laughing; since Scripture plainly teaches in John's Gospel that our Lord was discoursing not of the number of the churches, but of the heavenly mansions, and the eternal tabernacles for which the prophet longed? "In my Father's house," He says, "are many mansions: if it were not so, I would have told you; for I go to prepare a place for you. And if I go and prepare a place for you I will come again, and will receive you unto myself, that where I am, there ye may be

also." The place and the mansions which Christ says He would prepare for the apostles are of course in the Father's house, that is, in the kingdom of heaven, not on earth, where for the present He was leading the apostles. And at the same time regard must be had to the sense of Scripture: "I might tell you," He says, "that I go to prepare a place for you, if there were not many mansions in my Father's house, that is to say, if each individual did not prepare for himself a mansion through his own works rather than receive it through the bounty of God. The preparation is therefore not mine, but yours." This view is supported by the fact that it profited Judas nothing to have a place prepared, since he lost it by his own fault. And we must interpret in the same way what our Lord says to the sons of Zebedee, one of whom wished to sit on His left hand, the other on His right: "My cup indeed ye shall drink: but to sit on my right hand, and on my left hand, is not mine to give, but it is for them for whom it hath been prepared of my Father." It is not the Son's to give; how then is it the Father's to prepare? There are, He says, prepared in heaven, many different mansions, destined for many different virtues, and they will be awarded not to persons, but to persons' works. In vain therefore do you ask of me what rests with yourselves, a reward which my Father has prepared for those whose virtues will entitle them to rise to such dignity. Again when He says: "I will come again, and will receive you unto myself: that where I am, there ye may be also," He is speaking especially to the apostles, concerning whom it is elsewhere written, "That as I and thou, Father, are one, so they also may be one in us," inasmuch as they have believed, have been perfected, and can say, "the Lord is my portion." If, however, there are *not* many mansions, how is it taught in the Old Testament correspondingly with the New, that the chief priest has one rank, the priests another, the Levites another, the doorkeepers another, the sacristans another? How is it that in the book of Ezekiel, where a description is given of the future Church and of the heavenly Jerusalem, the priests who have sinned are degraded to the rank of sacristans and doorkeepers, and although they are in the temple of God, that is on the right hand, they are not among the rams, but among the poorest of the sheep? How again is it that in the river which flows from the temple, and replenishes the salt sea, and gives new life to everything, we read there are many kinds of fish? Why do we read that in the kingdom of heaven there are Archangels, Angels, Thrones, Dominions, Powers, Cherubim and Seraphim, and every name which is named, not only in this present world, but also that which is to come? A difference of name is meaningless where there is not a difference of rank. An Archangel is of course an Archangel to other inferior angels, and Powers, and Dominions have other spheres over which they exercise authority. This is what we find in heaven and in the administration of God. You must not therefore smile and sneer at us, as is your wont, for making a graduated series of emperors, prefects and counts, tribunes and centurions, companies, and all the other steps in the service.

29. It is mere trifling to quote the passage: "Know ye not that your bodies are a temple of the Holy Ghost," for it is customary in Holy Scripture to speak of a single object as though it were many, and of many as though they were one. And Jovinianus himself should know that even in a temple there are many divisions—the outer and the inner courts, the vestibules, the holy place, and the Holy of Holies. There are also in a temple kitchens,

pantries, oil-cellars, and cupboards for the vessels. And so in the temple of our body there are different degrees of merit. God does not dwell in all alike, nor does He impart Himself to all in the same degree. A portion of the spirit of Moses was taken and given to the seventy elders. I suppose there is a difference between the abundance of the river, and that of the rivulets. Elijah's spirit was given in double measure to Elisha, and thus double grace wrought greater miracles. Elijah while living restored a dead man to life; Elisha after death did the same. Elijah invoked famine on the people; Elisha in a single day put the enemy's forces in the power of the city which they besieged. No doubt the words, "Know ye not that your bodies are a temple of the Holy Ghost," refer to the whole assembly of the faithful, who, joined together, make up the one body of Christ. But the question now is, who in the body is worthy to be the feet of Christ, and who the head? who is His eye, and who His hand?—a distinction indicated by the two women in the Gospel, the penitent and the holy woman, one of whom held His feet, the other His head. Some authorities, however, think there was only one woman, and that she who began at His feet gradually advanced to His head. Jovinianus further urges against us our Lord's words, "I pray not for these only, but also for those who shall believe on me through their word: that as I, Father, in thee and thou in me are one, so they all may be one in us," and reminds us that the whole Christian people is one in God, and, as His well-beloved sons, are "partakers of the divine nature." We have already said, and the truth must now be inculcated more in detail, that we are not one in the Father and the Son according to nature, but according to grace. For the essence of the human soul and the essence of God are not the same, as the Manicheans constantly assert. But, says our Lord: "Thou hast loved them as thou hast loved me." You see, then, that we are privileged to partake of His essence, not in the realm of nature, but of grace, and the reason why we are beloved of the Father is that He has loved the Son; and the members are loved, those namely of the body. "For as many as received Christ, to them gave He power to become sons of God, even to them that believe on His name: which were born not of blood, nor of the will of the flesh, nor of the will of man, but of God." The Word was made flesh that we might pass from the flesh into the Word. The Word did not cease to be what He had been; nor did the human nature lose that which it was by birth. The glory was increased, the nature was not changed. Do you ask how we are made one body with Christ? Your creator shall be your instructor: "He that eats my flesh and drinks my blood abides in me, and I in him. As the living Father sent me, and I live because of the Father, so he that eats me, he also shall live because of me. This is the bread which came down out of heaven." But the Evangelist John, who had drunk in wisdom from the breast of Christ, agrees herewith, and says: "Hereby know we that we abide in him, and he in us, because he hath given us of his Spirit. Whosoever shall confess that Jesus is the Son of God, God abides in him, and he in God." If you believe in Christ, as the apostles believed, you shall be made one body with them in Christ. But, if it is rash for you to claim for yourself a faith and works like theirs when you have not the same faith and works, you cannot have the same place.

30. You repeat the words bride, sister, mother, and affirm that all these are titles of the one Church and names applied to all believers. The fact goes against you.

For if the Church admits but one rank, and has not many members in one body, what necessity is there for calling her bride, sister, mother? It must be that she is the bride of some, the sister of others, the mother of others. All indeed stand on the right hand, but one stands as a bridegroom, another as a brother, a third as a son. "My little children" says the Apostle, "of whom I am again in travail until Christ be formed in you." Do you think that the children who are being born and the apostle who is in travail are of equal rank? And the folly of your contention that we love all the members alike, and do not prefer the eye to the finger, nor the hand to the ear, but that if one be lost all mourn, is proved by the lesson which the apostle teaches the Corinthians: "Some members are more honorable, others excite the sense of shame: and those parts to which shame attaches are clothed with more abundant honor; whereas our comely parts have no need of our care." Do you think that the mouth and the belly, the eyes and the outlets of the body are to be classed together as of equal merit? "The lamp of thy body," he says, "is thine eye. If thine eye be blinded, thy whole body is in darkness." If you cut off a finger, or the tip of the ear, there is indeed pain, but the loss is not so great, nor is the disfigurement attended by so much pain as it would be were you to take out the eyes, mutilate the nose, or saw through a bone. Some members we can dispense with and yet live: without others life is an impossibility. Some offences are light, some heavy. It is one thing to owe ten thousand talents, another to owe a farthing. We shall have to give account of the idle word no less than of adultery; but it is not the same thing to be put to the blush, and to be put upon the rack, to grow red in the face and to ensure lasting torment. Do you think I am merely expressing my own views? Hear what the Apostle John says: "He who knows that his brother sinned a sin not unto death, let him ask, and he shall give him life, even to him that sinned not unto death. But he that hath sinned unto death, who shall pray for him?" You observe that if we entreat for smaller offences, we obtain pardon: if for greater ones, it is difficult to obtain our request: and that there is a great difference between sins. And so with respect to the people of Israel who had sinned a sin unto death, it is said to Jeremiah: "Pray not thou for this people, neither entreat for them, and do not withstand me, for I will not hear thee." Moreover, if it be true that we all alike enter the world and all alike leave it, and this is a precedent for the world to come, it follows that whether righteous or sinners we shall all be equally esteemed by God, because the conditions of our birth and death are now the same. And if you contend that there are two Adams, the one of the earth, the other from heaven; and that they who were in the earthly Adam stand on the left hand, those who were in the heavenly are on the right hand, before we go further, let me ask you a question concerning two brothers: Was Esau in the earthly Adam, or in the heavenly? No one doubts that you will reply, he was in the earthly. In which was Jacob? Without hesitation you will say, in the heavenly. How then was he in the heavenly when Christ had not yet come in the flesh—Christ who is called the second Adam from heaven? You must either reckon all before the incarnation of Christ in the old Adam, and even the just in the man from the earth, and then they will be on the left among your goats; or, if it be impious to give Isaac the same place as Ishmael, Jacob as Esau, the saints as sinners, the last Adam will date from the time when Christ was born of a Virgin, and your argument from the two Adams will not benefit your sheep and goats, because we have proved that in the first Adam there were both sheep and goats, and that of those who were in one and the same man, some stood on the right hand of God, others on the left: "For from Adam even until Moses death reigned over all, even over them that had not sinned after the likeness of Adam's transgression."

31. As regards your attempt to show that railing and murder, the use of the expression *raca* and adultery, the idle word and godlessness, are rewarded with the same punishment, I have already given you my reply, and will now briefly repeat it. You must either deny that you are a sinner if you are not to be in danger of Gehenna: or, if you are a sinner you will be sent to hell for even a light offence: "The mouth that lieth," says one, "kills the soul." I suspect that you, like other men, have occasionally told a lie: for all men are liars, that God alone may be true, and that He may be justified in His words, and may prevail when He judges. It follows either that you will not be a man lest you be found a liar: or if you are a man and are consequently a liar, you will be punished with parricides and adulterers. For you admit no difference between sins, and the gratitude of those whom you raise from the mire and set on high will not equal the rage against you of those whom for the trifling offences of daily life you have thrust into utter darkness. And if it be so that in a persecution one is stifled, another beheaded, another flees, or the fourth dies within the walls of a prison, and one crown of victory awaits various kinds of struggle, the fact tells in our favor. For in martyrdom it is the will, which gives occasion to the death, that is crowned. My duty is to resist the frenzy of the heathen, and not deny the Lord. It

rests with them either to behead, or to burn, or to shut up in prison, or enforce various other penalties. But if I escape, and die in solitude, there will not at my death be the same crown for me as for them, because the confession of Christ will not have been to me as to them the cause of death. As for your remark that absolutely no difference was made between the brother who had always been with his father, and him who was afterwards welcomed as a penitent, I am willing to add, if you like, that the one drachma which was lost and was found was put with the others, and that the one sheep which the good shepherd, leaving the ninety and nine, sought and brought back, made up the full tale of a hundred. But it is one thing to be a penitent, and with tears sue for pardon, another to be always with the father. And so both the shepherd and the father say by the mouth of Ezekiel to the sheep that was carried back, and to the son that was lost, "And I will establish my covenant with thee; and thou shalt know that I am the Lord: that thou mayest remember, and be confounded, and never open thy mouth ever more, because of thy shame, when I have forgiven thee all that thou hast done." That penitents may have their due it is enough for them to feel shame instead of all other punishment. Hence in another place it is said to them, "Then shall ye remember your evil ways, and all the crimes wherewith ye were defiled, and ye shall loathe yourselves in your own sight for all the wickedness that ye have done; and ye shall know that I am the Lord, when I shall have done you good for my name's sake, and not according to your evil ways, nor according to your evil doings." The son, moreover, was reproved by his father for envying his brother's deliverance, and for being tormented by jealousy while the angels in heaven were rejoicing. The parallel, however, is not to be drawn between the merits of the two sons (one of whom was temperate, the other a prodigal) and those of the whole human race, but the characters depicted are either Jews and Christians, or saints and penitents. In the lifetime of Bishop Damasus I dedicated to him a small treatise upon this parable.

32. And if a penny was given to all the laborers, those of the first, the third, the sixth, the ninth, and the eleventh hours, and they came first for the reward who were the last to work in the vineyard, even here the persons described do not belong to one time or one age, but from the beginning of the world to the end of it there are different calls and a special meaning attaches to each. Abel and Seth were called at the first hour: Enoch and Noah at the third: Abraham, Isaac, and Jacob at the sixth: Moses and the prophets at the ninth: at the eleventh the Gentiles, to whom the recompense was first given because they believed on the crucified Lord, and inasmuch as it was hard for them to believe they earned a great reward. Many kings and prophets have desired to see the things that we see, and have not seen them. But the one penny does not represent one reward, but one life, and one deliverance from Gehenna. And as by the favor of the sovereign those guilty of various crimes are released from prison, and each one, according to his toil and exertions, is in this or that condition of life, so too the penny, as it were by the favor of our Sovereign, is the discharge from prison of us all by baptism. Now our work is, according to our different virtues, to prepare for ourselves a different future.

33. So far I have replied to the separate portions of his argument; I shall now address myself to the general

question. Our Lord says to his disciples, "Whosoever would become great among you, let him be least of all." If we are all to be equal in heaven, in vain do we humble ourselves here that we may be greater there. Of the two debtors who owed, one five hundred pence, the other fifty, he to whom most was forgiven loved most. And so the Savior says, "I say to you, her sins which are many are forgiven her, for she hath loved much. But to whom little is forgiven, the same loveth little." He who loves little, and has little forgiven, he will of course be of inferior rank. The householder when he set out delivered to his servants his goods, to one five talents, to another two, to another one, to each according to his ability. Just as in another Gospel it is written that a nobleman setting out for a far country to receive for himself a kingdom and return, called the servants, and gave them each a sum of money, with which one gained ten pounds, another five, and they, each according to his ability and the gain he had made, received ten or five cities. But one who had received a talent, or a pound, buried it in the ground, or tied it up in a napkin, and kept it until his master's return. Our first thought is that if, according to the modern Zeno, the righteous do not toil in hope of reward, but to avoid the loss of what they already have, he who buried his pound or talent that he might not lose it, did no wrong, and the caution of him who kept his money is worthy of more praise than the fruitless toil of those who wore themselves out and yet received no reward for their labor. Then observe that the very talent which was taken from the timid or negligent servant, was not given to him who had the smaller profit, but to him who had gained the most, that is, to him who had been placed over ten cities. If difference of rank is not constituted by the difference in number, why did our Lord say, "He gave to everyone according to his ability"? If the gain of five talents and ten talents is the same, why were not ten cities given to him who gained the least, and five to him who gained the most? But that our Lord is not satisfied with what we have, but always desires more, He himself shows by saying, "Wherefore didst thou not give my money to the money-changers, that so when I came I might have received it with usury?" The Apostle Paul understood this, and forgetting those things which were behind, reached forward to those things which were in front, that is, he made daily progress, and did not keep the grace given to him carefully wrapped up in a napkin, but his spirit, like the capital of a keen man of business, was renewed from day to day, and if he were not always growing larger, he thought himself growing less. Six cities of refuge are mentioned in the law, provided for fugitives who were involuntary homicides, and the cities themselves belonged to the priests. I should like to ask whether you would put those fugitives among your goats, or among our sheep. If they were goats, they would be slain like other homicides, and would not enter the cities of God's ministers. If you say they were sheep, they will not possibly be such sheep as can enjoy full liberty and feed without fear of wolves. And it will be plain to you that sheep indeed they are, but wandering sheep: that they are on the right hand, but do not stand there: they flee until the High Priest dies and descending into hell liberates their souls. The Gibeonites met the children of Israel, and although other nations were slaughtered, they were kept for hewers of wood and drawers of water. And of such value were they in God's eyes, that the family of Saul was destroyed for the wrong done to them. Where would you put them? Among the goats? But they were not slain, and they were avenged by the determination of God. Among the sheep? But holy Scripture says they were not of the same merit as the Israelites. You see then that they do indeed stand on the right hand, but are of a far inferior grade. Jonathan came between David, the holy man, and Saul, the worst of kings, and we can neither place him among the kids because he was worthy of a prophet's love, nor amongst the rams lest we make him equal to David, and particularly when we know that he was slain. He will, therefore, be among the sheep, but low down. And just as in the case of David and Jonathan, you will be bound to recognize differences between sheep and sheep. "That servant, which knew his lord's will, and made not ready, nor did according to his will, shall be beaten with many stripes; but he that knew not, and did things worthy of stripes, shall be beaten with few stripes. And to whomsoever much is given, of him shall much be required: and to whom they commit much, of him will they ask the more." Lo! more or less is committed to different servants, and according to the nature of the trust, as well as of the sin, is the number of stripes inflicted.

    34. The whole account of the land of Judah and of the tribes is typical of the church in heaven. Let us read Joshua the son of Nun, or the concluding portions of Ezekiel, and we shall see that the historical division of the land as related by the one finds a counterpart in the spiritual and heavenly promises of the other. What is the meaning of the seven and eight steps in the description of the temple? or again, what significance attaches to the fact that in the Psalter, after being taught the mystic alphabet by the one hundred and eighteenth psalm we arrive by fifteen steps at the point where we can sing: "Behold, now

bless the Lord, all ye servants of the Lord: ye who stand in the house of the Lord, in the courts of the house of our God." Why did two tribes and a half dwell on the other side of Jordan, a district abounding in cattle, while the remaining nine tribes and a half either drove out the old inhabitants from their possessions, or dwelt with them? Why did the tribe of Levi receive no portion in the land, but have the Lord for their portion? And how is it that of the priests and Levites, themselves, the high priest alone entered the Holy of Holies where were the cherubim and the mercy-seat? Why did the other priests wear linen raiment only, and not have their clothing of wrought gold, blue, scarlet, purple, and fine cloth? The priests and Levites of the lower order took care of the oxen and wains: those of the higher order carried the ark of the Lord on their shoulders. If you do away with the gradations of the tabernacle, the temple, the Church, if, to use a common military phrase, all upon the right hand are to be "up to the same standard," bishops are to no purpose, priests in vain, deacons useless. Why do virgins persevere? widows toil? Why do married women practice continence? Let us all sin, and when once we have repented, we shall be on the same footing as the apostles.

35. But now we have just sighted land: the foaming billows have been rolling mountain high: our ship has been borne aloft, or has rushed headlong into the depths beneath: little by little the haven opens to the view of the weary and exhausted sailors. We have discussed the married, widows, and virgins. We have preferred virginity to widowhood, widowhood to marriage. The passage of the apostle, in which he treats questions of this kind, has been expounded, and particular objections have been met. We also took a survey of secular literature, and inquired

what was thought of virgins, and what of those who had one husband; and by way of contrast we pointed out the cares which sometimes attend wedlock. Then we passed to the second division, in which our opponent denies the possibility of sinning to those who have been baptized with complete faith. And we showed that God alone is faultless, and every creature is at fault, not because all have sinned, but because all may sin, and those who stand have cause to fear when they see the fall of men like themselves. In the third place we came to fasting, and inasmuch as our opponent's argument fell under two heads, and he appealed either to philosophy, or to Holy Scripture, we also furnished a several reply. In the fourth, that is the last section, the sheep and goats on the right hand and the left, the righteous and the wicked, were distributed into two classes, the intention being to show that there is no difference between one just man and another, or between one sinner and another. To prove the point Jovinianus had accumulated countless instances from Scripture which apparently favored his view, and this contention we rebutted both by arguments and illustrations from Scripture, and pulverized Zeno's old opinion no less with common sense than with the words of inspiration.

36. I must in conclusion say a few words to our modern Epicurus wantoning in his gardens with his favorites of both sexes. On your side are the fat and the sleek in their festal attire. If I may mock like Socrates, add if you please, all swine and dogs, and, since you like flesh so well, vultures too, eagles, hawks, and owls. We shall never be afraid of the host of Aristippus. If ever I see a fine fellow, or a man who is no stranger to the curling irons, with his hair nicely done and his cheeks all aglow,

he belongs to your herd, or rather grunts in concert with your pigs. To our flock belong the sad, the pale, the meanly clad, who, like strangers in this world, though their tongues are silent, yet speak by their dress and bearing. "Woe is me," say they, "that my sojourning is prolonged! that I dwell among the tents of Kedar!" that is to say, in the darkness of this world, for the light shineth in the darkness, and the darkness comprehended it not. Boast not of having many disciples. The Son of God taught in Judea, and only twelve apostles followed Him. "I have trodden the wine-press alone," He says, "and of the peoples there was no man with me." At the passion He was left alone, and even Peter's fidelity to Him wavered: on the other hand all the people applauded the doctrine of the Pharisees, saying, "Crucify him, crucify him. We have no king but Cæsar," that is in effect, we follow vice, not virtue; Epicurus, not Christ; Jovinianus, not the Apostle Paul. If many assent to your views, that only indicates voluptuousness; for they do not so much approve your utterances, as favor their own vices. In our crowded thoroughfares a false prophet may be seen any day stick in hand belaboring the fools about him, and knocking out the teeth of those who offend him, and yet he never lacks constant followers. And do you regard it as a mark of great wisdom if you have a following of many pigs, whom you are feeding to make pork for hell? Since you published your views, and set the mark of your approval on baths in which the sexes bathe together, the impatience which once threw over burning lust the semblance of a robe of modesty has been laid bare and exposed. What was once hidden is now open to the gaze of all. You have revealed your disciples, such as they are, not made them. One result of your teaching is that sin is no longer even repented of. Your virgins whom, with a depth of wisdom never found before in speech or writing, you have taught the apostle's maxim that it is better to marry than to burn, have turned secret adulterers into acknowledged husbands. It was not the apostle, the chosen vessel, who gave this advice; it was Virgil's widow:

"She calls it wedlock; thus she veils her fault."

37. About four hundred years have passed since the preaching of Christ flashed upon the world, and during that time in which His robe has been torn by countless heresies, almost the whole body of error has been derived from the Chaldæan, Syriac, and Greek languages. Basilides, the master of licentiousness and the grossest sensuality, after the lapse of so many years, and like a second Euphorbus, was changed by transmigration into Jovinian, so that the Latin tongue might have a heresy of its own. Was there no other province in the whole world to receive the gospel of pleasure, and into which the serpent might insinuate itself, except that which was founded by the teaching of Peter, upon the rock Christ? Idol temples had fallen before the standard of the Cross and the severity of the Gospel: now on the contrary lust and gluttony endeavor to overthrow the solid structure of the Cross. And so God says by Isaiah, "O my people, they which bless you cause you to err, and trouble the paths of your feet." Also by Jeremiah, "Flee out of the midst of Babylon, and save every man his life, and believe not the false prophets which say, Peace, peace, and there is no peace;" who are always repeating, "The temple of the Lord, the temple of the Lord." "Thy prophets have seen for thee false and foolish things; they

have not laid bare thine iniquity that they might call thee to repentance: who devour God's people like bread: they have not called upon God." Jeremiah announced the captivity and was stoned by the people. Hananiah, the son of Azzur, broke the bars of wood for the present, but was preparing bars of iron for the future. False prophets always promise pleasant things, and please for a time. Truth is bitter, and they who preach it are filled with bitterness. For with the unleavened bread of sincerity and truth the Lord's Passover is kept, and it is eaten with bitter herbs. Admirable are your utterances and worthy of the ears of the bride of Christ standing in the midst of her virgins, and widows, and celibates! (their very name is derived from the fact that they who abstain from intercourse are fit for heaven). This is what you say: "Fast seldom, marry often. You cannot do the work of marriage unless you take mead, and flesh, and *solid food*. For lust strength is required. Flesh is soon spent and enervated. You need not be afraid of fornication. He who has been once baptized into Christ cannot fall, for he has the consolation of marriage to slake his lust. And if you do fall, repentance will restore you, and you who were hypocrites at baptism may have a firm faith in your repentance. Be not disturbed by the thought of a difference between the righteous and the penitent, and do not imagine that pardon even gives a lower place; rather believe that it takes away your crown. For there is one reward: he who stands on the right hand shall enter into the kingdom of heaven." Through counsels such as these your swine-herds are richer than our shepherds, and the he-goats draw after them many of the other sex: "They were as fed horses: they were mad after women": they no sooner see a woman than they neigh after her, and, shame to say! find scriptural authority for the consolation of their incontinence. But the very women, unhappy creatures! though they deserve no pity, who chant the words of their instructor (for what does God require of them but to become mothers?), have lost not only their chastity, but all sense of shame, and defend their licentious practices with an access of impudence. You have, moreover, in your army many subalterns, you have your guardsmen and your skirmishers at the outposts, the round-bellied, the well-dressed, the exquisites, and noisy orators, to defend you with tooth and nail. The noble make way for you, the wealthy print kisses on your face. For unless you had come, the drunkard and the glutton could not have entered paradise. All honor to your virtue, or rather to your vices! You have in your camp, even amazons with uncovered breasts, bare arms and knees, who challenge the men who come against them to a battle of lust. Your household is a large one, and so in your aviaries not only turtle-doves, but hoopoes are fed, which may wing their flight over the whole field of rank debauchery. Pull me to pieces and scatter me to the winds: tax me with what offences you please: accuse me of luxurious and delicate living: you would like me better if I were guilty, for I should belong to your herd.

38. But I will now address myself to you, great Rome, who with the confession of Christ have blotted out the blasphemy written on your forehead. Mighty city, mistress-city of the world, city of the Apostle's praises, shew the meaning of your name. *Rome* is either *strength* in Greek, or *height* in Hebrew. Lose not the excellence your name implies: let virtue lift you up on high, let not voluptuousness bring you low. By repentance, as the history of Nineveh proves, you may escape the curse

wherewith the Savior threatened you in the Apocalypse. Beware of the name of Jovinianus. It is derived from that of an idol. The Capitol is in ruins: the temples of Jove with their ceremonies have perished. Why should his name and vices flourish now in the midst of you, when even in the time of Numa Pompilius, even under the sway of kings, your ancestors gave a heartier welcome to the self-restraint of Pythagoras than they did under the consuls to the debauchery of Epicurus?

Against Vigilantius.
───────────────────

Introduction.

Full details respecting Vigilantius, against whom this treatise, the result of a single night's labor, is directed, may be found in a work on "Vigilantius and His Times," published in 1844 by Dr. Gilly, canon of Durham. It will perhaps, however, assist the reader if we briefly remark that he was born about 370, at Calagurris, near Convenæ (Comminges), which was a station on the Roman road from Aquitaine to Spain. His father was probably the keeper of the inn, and Vigilantius appears to have been brought up to his father's business. He was of a studious character, and Sulpicius Severus, the ecclesiastical historian, who had estates in those parts, took him into his service, and, possibly, made him manager of his estates. Having been ordained he was introduced to Jerome (then living at Bethlehem, in 395) through Paulinus of Nola, who was the friend of Sulpicius Severus. After staying with Jerome for a considerable time he begged to be dismissed, and left in great haste without giving any reason. Returning to Gaul, he settled in his native country. Jerome hearing that he was spreading reports of him as favoring the views of Origen, and in other ways defaming him and his friends, wrote him a sharp letter of rebuke (Letter LXI.). The work of Vigilantius which drew from Jerome the following treatise was written in the year a.d. 406; not "hastily, under provocation such as he may have felt in leaving Bethlehem." but after the lapse of six or seven years. The points against which he argued as being superstitious are: (1) the reverence paid to the relics of holy men by carrying them round the church in costly vessels or silken wrappings to be kissed, and the prayers offered to the dead; (2) the late watchings at the basilicas of the martyrs, with their attendant scandals, the burning of numerous tapers. alleged miracles, etc.; (3) the sending of alms to Jerusalem, which, Vigilantius urged, had better be spent among the poor in each separate diocese, and the monkish vow of poverty; (4) the exaggerated estimate of virginity.

The bishop of the diocese, Exsuperius of Toulouse, was strongly in favor of the views of Vigilantius, and they began to spread widely. Complaints having reached Jerome through the presbyter Riparius, he at once expressed his indignation, and offered to answer in detail if the work of Vigilantius were sent to him. In 406 he received it through Sisinnius, who was bearing alms to the East. It has been truly said that this treatise has less of reason and more of abuse than any other which Jerome wrote. But in spite of this the author was followed by the chief ecclesiastics of the day, and the practices impugned by Vigilantius prevailed almost unchecked till the sixteenth century.

1. The world has given birth to many monsters; in Isaiah we read of centaurs and sirens, screech-owls and

pelicans. Job, in mystic language, describes Leviathan and Behemoth; Cerberus and the birds of Stymphalus, the Erymanthian boar and the Nemean lion, the Chimæra and the many-headed Hydra, are told of in poetic fables. Virgil describes Cacus. Spain has produced Geryon, with his three bodies. Gaul alone has had no monsters, but has ever been rich in men of courage and great eloquence. All at once Vigilantius, or, more correctly, *Dormitantius*, has arisen, animated by an unclean spirit, to fight against the Spirit of Christ, and to deny that religious reverence is to be paid to the tombs of the martyrs. Vigils, he says, are to be condemned; Alleluia must never be sung except at Easter; continence is a heresy; chastity a hot-bed of lust. And as Euphorbus is said to have been born again in the person of Pythagoras, so in this fellow the corrupt mind of Jovinianus has arisen; so that in him, no less than in his predecessor, we are bound to meet the snares of the devil. The words may be justly applied to him: "Seed of evildoers, prepare thy children for the slaughter because of the sins of thy father." Jovinianus, condemned by the authority of the Church of Rome, amidst pheasants and swine's flesh, breathed out, or rather belched out his spirit. And now this tavern-keeper of Calagurris, who, according to the name of his native village is a Quintilian, only dumb instead of eloquent, is mixing water with the wine. According to the trick which he knows of old, he is trying to blend his perfidious poison with the Catholic faith; he assails virginity and hates chastity; he revels with worldlings and declaims against the fasts of the saints; he plays the philosopher over his cups, and soothes himself with the sweet strains of psalmody, while he smacks his lips over his cheese-cakes; nor could he deign to listen to the songs of David and Jeduthun, and Asaph and the sons of Core, except at the banqueting table. This I have poured forth with more grief than amusement, for I cannot restrain myself and turn a deaf ear to the wrongs inflicted on apostles and martyrs.

2. Shameful to relate, there are bishops who are said to be associated with him in his wickedness—if at least they are to be called bishops—who ordain no deacons but such as have been previously married; who credit no celibate with chastity—nay, rather, who show clearly what measure of holiness of life they can claim by indulging in evil suspicions of all men, and, unless the candidates for ordination appear before them with pregnant wives, and infants wailing in the arms of their mothers, will not administer to them Christ's ordinance. What are the Churches of the East to do? What is to become of the Egyptian Churches and those belonging to the Apostolic Seat, which accept for the ministry only men who are virgins, or those who practice continency, or, if married, abandon their conjugal rights? Such is the teaching of Dormitantius, who throws the reins upon the neck of lust, and by his encouragement doubles the natural heat of the flesh, which in youth is mostly at boiling point, or rather slakes it by intercourse with women; so that there is nothing to separate us from swine, nothing wherein we differ from the brute creation, or from horses, respecting which it is written: "They were toward women like raging horses; everyone neighed after his neighbor's wife." This is that which the Holy Spirit says by the mouth of David: "Be ye not like horse and mule which have no understanding." And again respecting Dormitantius and his friends: "Bind the jaws of them who draw not near unto thee with bit and bridle."

3. But it is now time for us to adduce his own words and answer him in detail. For, possibly, in his malice, he may choose once more to misrepresent me, and say that I have trumped up a case for the sake of showing off my rhetorical and declamatory powers in combating it, like the letter which I wrote to Gaul, relating to a mother and daughter who were at variance. This little treatise, which I now dictate, is due to the reverend presbyters Riparius and Desiderius, who write that their parishes have been defiled by being in his neighborhood, and have sent me, by our brother Sisinnius, the books which he vomited forth in a drunken fit. They also declare that some persons are found who, from their inclination to his vices, assent to his blasphemies. He is a barbarian both in speech and knowledge. His style is rude. He cannot defend even the truth; but, for the sake of laymen, and poor women, laden with sins, ever learning and never coming to a knowledge of the truth, I will spend upon his melancholy trifles a single night's labor, otherwise I shall seem to have treated with contempt the letters of the reverend persons who have entreated me to undertake the task.

4. He certainly well represents his race. Sprung from a set of brigands and persons collected together from all quarters (I mean those whom Cn. Pompey, after the conquest of Spain, when he was hastening to return for his triumph, brought down from the Pyrenees and gathered together into one town, whence the name of the city Convenæ), he has carried on their brigand practices by his attack upon the Church of God. Like his ancestors the Vectones, the Arrabaci, and the Celtiberians, he makes his raids upon the churches of Gaul, not carrying the standard of the cross, but, on the contrary, the ensign

of the devil. Pompey did just the same in the East. After overcoming the Cilician and Isaurian pirates and brigands, he founded a city, bearing his own name, between Cilicia and Isauria. That city, however, to this day, observes the ordinances of its ancestors, and no Dormitantius has arisen in it; but Gaul supports a native foe, and sees seated in the Church a man who has lost his head and who ought to be put in the strait-jacket which Hippocrates recommended. Among other blasphemies, he may be heard to say, "What need is there for you not only to pay such honor, not to say adoration, to the thing, whatever it may be, which you carry about in a little vessel and worship?" And again, in the same book, "Why do you kiss and adore a bit of powder wrapped up in a cloth?" And again, in the same book, "Under the cloak of religion we see what is all but a heathen ceremony introduced into the churches: while the sun is still shining, heaps of tapers are lighted, and everywhere a paltry bit of powder, wrapped up in a costly cloth, is kissed and worshipped. Great honor do men of this sort pay to the blessed martyrs, who, they think, are to be made glorious by trumpery tapers, when the Lamb who is in the midst of the throne, with all the brightness of His majesty, gives them light?"

5. Madman, who in the world ever adored the martyrs? who ever thought man was God? Did not Paul and Barnabas, when the people of Lycaonia thought them to be Jupiter and Mercury, and would have offered sacrifices to them, rend their clothes and declare they were men? Not that they were not better than Jupiter and Mercury, who were but men long ago dead, but because, under the mistaken ideas of the Gentiles, the honor due to God was being paid to them. And we read the same

respecting Peter, who, when Cornelius wished to adore him, raised him by the hand, and said, "Stand up, for I also am a man." And have you the audacity to speak of "the mysterious something or other which you carry about in a little vessel and worship?" I want to know what it is that you call "something or other." Tell us more clearly (that there may be no restraint on your blasphemy) what you mean by the phrase "a bit of powder wrapped up in a costly cloth in a tiny vessel." It is nothing less than the relics of the martyrs which he is vexed to see covered with a costly veil, and not bound up with rags or haircloth, or thrown on the midden, so that Vigilantius alone in his drunken slumber may be worshipped. Are we, therefore guilty of sacrilege when we enter the basilicas of the Apostles? Was the Emperor Constantius I. guilty of sacrilege when he transferred the sacred relics of Andrew, Luke, and Timothy to Constantinople? In their presence the demons cry out, and the devils who dwell in Vigilantius confess that they feel the influence of the saints. And at the present day is the Emperor Arcadius guilty of sacrilege, who after so long a time has conveyed the bones of the blessed Samuel from Judea to Thrace? Are all the bishops to be considered not only sacrilegious, but silly into the bargain, because they carried that most worthless thing, dust and ashes, wrapped in silk in golden vessel? Are the people of all the Churches fools, because they went to meet the sacred relics, and welcomed them with as much joy as if they beheld a living prophet in the midst of them, so that there was one great swarm of people from Palestine to Chalcedon with one voice reechoing the praises of Christ? They were forsooth, adoring Samuel and not Christ, whose Levite and prophet Samuel was. You show mistrust because you think only of the dead body, and therefore blaspheme. Read the Gospel— "The God of Abraham, the God of Isaac, the God of Jacob: He is not the God of the dead, but of the living." If then they are alive, they are not, to use your expression, kept in honorable confinement.

6. For you say that the souls of Apostles and martyrs have their abode either in the bosom of Abraham, or in the place of refreshment, or under the altar of God, and that they cannot leave their own tombs, and be present where they will. They are, it seems, of senatorial rank, and are not subjected to the worst kind of prison and the society of murderers, but are kept apart in liberal and honorable custody in the isles of the blessed and the Elysian fields. Will you lay down the law for God? Will you put the Apostles into chains? So that to the day of judgment they are to be kept in confinement, and are not with their Lord, although it is written concerning them, "They follow the Lamb, whithersoever he goes." If the Lamb is present everywhere, the same must be believed respecting those who are with the Lamb. And while the devil and the demons wander through the whole world, and with only too great speed present themselves everywhere; are martyrs, after the shedding of their blood, to be kept out of sight shut up in a coffin, from whence they cannot escape? You say, in your pamphlet, that so long as we are alive we can pray for one another; but once we die, the prayer of no person for another can be heard, and all the more because the martyrs, though they cry for the avenging of their blood, have never been able to obtain their request. If Apostles and martyrs while still in the body can pray for others, when they ought still to be anxious for themselves, how much more must they do so when once they have won their crowns, overcome, and

triumphed? A single man, Moses, oft wins pardon from God for six hundred thousand armed men; and Stephen, the follower of his Lord and the first Christian martyr, entreats pardon for his persecutors; and when once they have entered on their life with Christ, shall they have less power than before? The Apostle Paul says that two hundred and seventy-six souls were given to him in the ship; and when, after his dissolution, he has begun to be with Christ, must he shut his mouth, and be unable to say a word for those who throughout the whole world have believed in his Gospel? Shall Vigilantius the live dog be better than Paul the dead lion? I should be right in saying so after Ecclesiastes, if I admitted that Paul is dead in spirit. The truth is that the saints are not called dead, but are said to be asleep. Wherefore Lazarus, who was about to rise again, is said to have slept. And the Apostle forbids the Thessalonians to be sorry for those who were asleep. As for you, when wide awake you are asleep, and asleep when you write, and you bring before me an apocryphal book which, under the name of Esdras, is read by you and those of your feather, and in this book it is written that after death no one dares pray for others. I have never read the book: for what need is there to take up what the Church does not receive? It can hardly be your intention to confront me with Balsamus, and Barbelus, and the Thesaurus of Manichæus, and the ludicrous name of Leusiboras; though possibly because you live at the foot of the Pyrenees, and border on Iberia, you follow the incredible marvels of the ancient heretic Basilides and his so-called knowledge, which is mere ignorance, and set forth what is condemned by the authority of the whole world. I say this because in your short treatise you quote Solomon as if he were on your side, though Solomon never wrote the words in question at all; so that, as you have a second Esdras you may have a second Solomon. And, if you like, you may read the imaginary revelations of all the patriarchs and prophets, and, when you have learned them, you may sing them among the women in their weaving-shops, or rather order them to be read in your taverns, the more easily by these melancholy ditties to stimulate the ignorant mob to replenish their cups.

7. As to the question of tapers, however, we do not, as you in vain misrepresent us, light them in the daytime, but by their solace we would cheer the darkness of the night, and watch for the dawn, lest we should be blind like you and sleep in darkness. And if some persons, being ignorant and simple minded laymen, or, at all events, religious women—of whom we can truly say, "I allow that they have a zeal for God, but not according to knowledge"—adopt the practice in honor of the martyrs, what harm is thereby done to you? Once upon a time even the Apostles pleaded that the ointment was wasted, but they were rebuked by the voice of the Lord. Christ did not need the ointment, nor do martyrs need the light of tapers; and yet that woman poured out the ointment in honor of Christ, and her heart's devotion was accepted. All those who light these tapers have their reward according to their faith, as the Apostle says: "Let everyone abound in his own meaning." Do you call men of this sort idolaters? I do not deny, that all of us who believe in Christ have passed from the error of idolatry. For we are not born Christians, but become Christians by being born again. And because we formerly worshipped idols, does it follow that we ought not now to worship God lest we seem to pay like honor to Him and to idols? In the one case respect was paid to idols, and therefore the ceremony

is to be abhorred; in the other the martyrs are venerated, and the same ceremony is therefore to be allowed. Throughout the whole Eastern Church, even when there are no relics of the martyrs, whenever the Gospel is to be read the candles are lighted, although the dawn may be reddening the sky, not of course to scatter the darkness, but by way of evidencing our joy. And accordingly the virgins in the Gospel always have their lamps lighted. And the Apostles are told to have their loins girded, and their lamps burning in their hands. And of John Baptist we read, "He was the lamp that burns and shineth"; so that, under the figure of corporeal light, that light is represented of which we read in the Psalter, "Thy word is a lamp unto my feet, O Lord, and a light unto my paths."

8. Does the bishop of Rome do wrong when he offers sacrifices to the Lord over the venerable bones of the dead men Peter and Paul, as we should say, but according to you, over a worthless bit of dust, and judges their tombs worthy to be Christ's altars? And not only is the bishop of one city in error, but the bishops of the whole world, who, despite the tavern-keeper Vigilantius, enter the basilicas of the dead, in which "a worthless bit of dust and ashes lies wrapped up in a cloth," defiled and defiling all else. Thus, according to you, the sacred buildings are like the sepulchers of the Pharisees, whitened without, while within they have filthy remains, and are full of foul smells and uncleanliness. And then he dares to expectorate his filth upon the subject and to say: "Is it the case that the souls of the martyrs love their ashes, and hover round them, and are always present, lest haply if anyone come to pray and they were absent, they could not hear?" Oh, monster, who ought to be banished to the ends of the earth! do you laugh at the relics of the

martyrs, and in company with Eunomius, the father of this heresy, slander the Churches of Christ? Are you not afraid of being in such company, and of speaking against us the same things which he utters against the Church? For all his followers refuse to enter the basilicas of Apostles and martyrs, so that, forsooth, they may worship the dead Eunomius, whose books they consider are of more authority than the Gospels; and they believe that the light of truth was in him just as other heretics maintain that the Paraclete came into Montanus, and say that Manichæus himself was the Paraclete. You cannot find an occasion of boasting even in supposing that you are the inventor of a new kind of wickedness, for your heresy long ago broke out against the Church. It found, however, an opponent in Tertullian, a very learned man, who wrote a famous treatise which he called most correctly *Scorpiacum*, because, as the scorpion bends itself like a bow to inflict its wound, so what was formerly called the heresy of Cain pours poison into the body of the Church; it has slept or rather been buried for a long time, but has been now awakened by Dormitantius. I am surprised you do not tell us that there must upon no account be martyrdoms, inasmuch as God, who does not ask for the blood of goats and bulls, much less requires the blood of men. This is what you say, or rather, even if you do not say it, you are taken as meaning to assert it. For in maintaining that the relics of the martyrs are to be trodden under foot, you forbid the shedding of their blood as being worthy of no honor.

9. Respecting vigils and the frequent keeping of night-watches in the basilicas of the martyrs, I have given a brief reply in another letter which, about two years ago, I wrote to the reverend presbyter Riparius. You argue that

they ought to be abjured, lest we seem to be often keeping Easter, and appear not to observe the customary yearly vigils. If so, then sacrifices should not be offered to Christ on the Lord's day lest we frequently keep the Easter of our Lord's Resurrection, and introduce the custom of having many Easters instead of one. We must not, however, impute to pious men the faults and errors of youths and worthless women such as are often detected at night. It is true that, even at the Easter vigils, something of the kind usually comes to light; but the faults of a few form no argument against religion in general, and such persons, without keeping vigil, can go wrong either in their own houses or in those of other people. The treachery of Judas did not annul the loyalty of the Apostles. And if others keep vigil badly, our vigils are not thereby to be stopped; nay, rather let those who sleep to gratify their lust be compelled to watch that they may preserve their chastity. For if a thing once done be good, it cannot be bad if often done; and if there is some fault to be avoided, the blame lies not in its being done often, but in its being done at all. And so we should not watch at Easter-tide for fear that adulterers may satisfy their long pent-up desires, or that the wife may find an opportunity for sinning without having the key turned against her by her husband. The occasions which seldom recur are those which are most eagerly longed for.

10. I cannot traverse all the topics embraced in the letters of the reverend presbyters; I will adduce a few points from the tracts of Vigilantius. He argues against the signs and miracles which are wrought in the basilicas of the martyrs, and says that they are of service to the unbelieving, not to believers, as though the question now were for whose advantage they occur, not by what power.

Granted that signs belong to the faithless, who, because they would not obey the word and doctrine, are brought to believe by means of signs. Even our Lord wrought signs for the unbelieving, and yet our Lord's signs are not on that account to be impugned, because those people were faithless, but must be worthy of greater admiration because they were so powerful that they subdued even the hardest hearts, and compelled men to believe. And so I will not have you tell me that signs are for the unbelieving; but answer my question—how is it that poor worthless dust and ashes are associated with this wondrous power of signs and miracles? I see, I see, most unfortunate of mortals, why you are so sad and what causes your fear. That unclean spirit who forces you to write these things has often been tortured by this worthless dust, aye, and is being tortured at this moment, and though in your case he conceals his wounds, in others he makes confession. You will hardly follow the heathen and impious Porphyry and Eunomius, and pretend that these are the tricks of the demons, and that they do not really cry out, but feign their torments. Let me give you my advice: go to the basilicas of the martyrs, and some day you will be cleansed; you will find there many in like case with yourself, and will be set on fire, not by the martyrs' tapers which offend you, but by invisible flames; and you will then confess what you now deny, and will freely proclaim your name—that you who speak in the person of Vigilantius are really either Mercury, for greedy of gain was he; or Nocturnus, who, according to Plautus's "Amphitryon," slept while Jupiter, two nights together, had his adulterous connection with Alcmena, and thus begat the mighty Hercules; or at all events Father Bacchus, of drunken fame, with the tankard hanging from his shoulder, with his ever ruby face, foaming lips, and unbridled brawling.

11. Once, when a sudden earthquake in this province in the middle of the night awoke us all out of our sleep, you, the most prudent and the wisest of men, began to pray without putting your clothes on, and recalled to our minds the story of Adam and Eve in Paradise; they, indeed, when their eyes were opened were ashamed, for they saw that they were naked, and covered their shame with the leaves of trees; but you, who were stripped alike of your shirt and of your faith, in the sudden terror which overwhelmed you, and with the fumes of your last night's booze still hanging about you, showed your wisdom by exposing your nakedness in only too evident a manner to the eyes of the brethren. Such are the adversaries of the Church; these are the leaders who fight against the blood of the martyrs; here is a specimen of the orators who thunder against the Apostles, or, rather, such are the mad dogs which bark at the disciples of Christ.

12. I confess my own fear, for possibly it may be thought to spring from superstition. When I have been angry, or have had evil thoughts in my mind, or some phantom of the night has beguiled me, I do not dare to enter the basilicas of the martyrs, I shudder all over in body and soul. You may smile, perhaps, and deride this as on a level with the wild fancies of weak women. If it be so, I am not ashamed of having a faith like that of those who were the first to see the risen Lord; who were sent to the Apostles; who, in the person of the mother of our Lord and Savior, were commended to the holy Apostles. Belch out your shame, if you will, with men of the world, I will fast with women; yea, with religious men whose looks witness to their chastity, and who, with the cheek pale

from prolonged abstinence, show forth the chastity of Christ.

13. Something, also, appears to be troubling you. You are afraid that, if continence, sobriety, and fasting strike root among the people of Gaul, your taverns will not pay, and you will be unable to keep up through the night your diabolical vigils and drunken revels. Moreover, I have learnt from those same letters that, in defiance of the authority of Paul, nay, rather of Peter, John, and James, who gave the right hand of fellowship to Paul and Barnabas, and commanded them to remember the poor, you forbid any pecuniary relief to be sent to Jerusalem for the benefit of the saints. Now, if I reply to this, you will immediately give tongue and cry out that I am pleading my own cause. You, forsooth, were so generous to the whole community that if you had not come to Jerusalem, and lavished your own money or that of your patrons, we should all be on the verge of starvation. I say what the blessed Apostle Paul says in nearly all his Epistles; and he makes it a rule for the Churches of the Gentiles that, on the first day of the week, that is, on the Lord's day, contributions should be made by everyone which should be sent up to Jerusalem for the relief of the saints, and that either by his own disciples, or by those whom they should themselves approve; and if it were thought fit, he would himself either send, or take what was collected. Also in the Acts of the Apostles, when speaking to the governor Felix, he says, "After many years I went up to Jerusalem to bring alms to my nation and offerings, and to perform my vows, amidst which they found me purified in the temple." Might he not have distributed in some other part of the world, and in the infant Churches which he was training in his own faith, the gifts he had received from

others? But he longed to give to the poor of the holy places who, abandoning their own little possessions for the sake of Christ, turned with their whole heart to the service of the Lord. It would take too long now if I purposed to repeat all the passages from the whole range of his Epistles in which he advocates and urges with all his heart that money be sent to Jerusalem and to the holy places for the faithful; not to gratify avarice, but to give relief; not to accumulate wealth, but to support the weakness of the poor body, and to stave off cold and hunger. And this custom continues in Judea to the present day, not only among us, but also among the Hebrews, so that they who meditate in the law of the Lord, day and night, and have no father upon earth except the Lord alone, may be cherished by the aid of the synagogues and of the whole world; that there may be equality—not that some may be refreshed while others are in distress, but that the abundance of some may support the need of others.

14. You will reply that everyone can do this in his own country, and that there will never be wanting poor who ought to be supported with the resources of the Church. And we do not deny that doles should be distributed to all poor people, even to Jews and Samaritans, if the means will allow. But the Apostle teaches that alms should be given to all, indeed, especially, however, to those who are of the household of faith. And respecting these the Savior said in the Gospel, "Make to yourselves friends of the mammon of unrighteousness, who may receive you into everlasting habitations." What! Can those poor creatures, with their rags and filth, lorded over, as they are, by raging lust, can they who own nothing, now or hereafter, have eternal

habitations? No doubt it is not the poor simply, but the poor in spirit, who are called blessed; those of whom it is written, "Blessed is he who gives his mind to the poor and needy; the Lord shall deliver him in the evil day." But the fact is, in supporting the poor of the common people, what is needed is not mind, but money. In the case of the saintly poor the mind has blessed exercises, since you give to one who receives with a blush, and when he has received is grieved, that while sowing spiritual things he must reap your carnal things. As for his argument that they who keep what they have, and distribute among the poor, little by little, the increase of their property, act more wisely than they who sell their possessions, and once for all give all away, not I but the Lord shall make answer: "If thou wilt be perfect, go sell all that thou hast and give to the poor, and come, follow Me." He speaks to him who wishes to be perfect, who, with the Apostles, leaves father, ship, and net. The man whom you approve stands in the second or third rank; yet we welcome him provided it be understood that the first is to be preferred to the second, and the second to the third.

15. Let me add that our monks are not to be deterred from their resolution by you with your viper's tongue and savage bite. Your argument respecting them runs thus: If all men were to seclude themselves and live in solitude, who is there to frequent the churches? Who will remain to win those engaged in secular pursuits? Who will be able to urge sinners to virtuous conduct? Similarly, if all were as silly as you, who could be wise? And, to follow out your argument, virginity would not deserve our approbation. For if all were virgins, we should have no marriages; the race would perish; infants would not cry in their cradles; midwives would lose their

pay and turn beggars; and Dormitantius, all alone and shriveled up with cold, would lie awake in his bed. The truth is, virtue is a rare thing and not eagerly sought after by the many. Would that all were as the few of whom it is said: "Many are called, few are chosen." The prison would be empty. But, indeed, a monk's function is not to teach, but to lament; to mourn either for himself or for the world, and with terror to anticipate our Lord's advent. Knowing his own weakness and the frailty of the vessel which he carries, he is afraid of stumbling, lest he strike against something, and it fall and be broken. Hence he shuns the sight of women, and particularly of young women, and so far chastens himself as to dread even what is safe.

16. Why, you will say, go to the desert? The reason is plain: That I may not hear or see you; that I may not be disturbed by your madness; that I may not be engaged in conflict with you; that the eye of the harlot nay not lead me captive: that beauty may not lead me to unlawful embraces. You will reply: "This is not to fight, but to run away. Stand in line of battle, put on your armor and resist your foes, so that, having overcome, you may wear the crown." I confess my weakness. I would not fight in the hope of victory, lest some time or other I lose the victory. If I flee, I avoid the sword; if I stand, I must either overcome or fall. But what need is there for me to let go certainties and follow after uncertainties? Either with my shield or with my feet I must shun death. You who fight may either be overcome or may overcome. I who fly do not overcome, inasmuch as I fly; but I fly to make sure that I may not be overcome. There is no safety in sleep with a serpent beside you. Possibly he will not bite me, yet it is possible that after a time he may bite me.

We call women mothers who are no older than sisters and daughters, and we do not blush to cloak our vices with the names of piety. What business has a monk in the women's cells? What is the meaning of secret conversation and looks which shun the presence of witnesses? Holy love has no restless desire. Moreover, what we have said respecting lust we must apply to avarice, and to all vices which are avoided by solitude. We therefore keep clear of the crowded cities, that we may not be compelled to do what we are urged to do, not so much by nature as by choice.

17. At the request of the reverend presbyters, as I have said, I have devoted to the dictation of these remarks the labor of a single night, for my brother Sisinnius is hastening his departure for Egypt, where he has relief to give to the saints, and is impatient to be gone. If it were not so, however, the subject itself was so openly blasphemous as to call for the indignation of a writer rather than a multitude of proofs. But if Dormitantius wakes up that he may again abuse me, and if he thinks fit to disparage me with that same blasphemous mouth with which he pulls to pieces Apostles and martyrs, I will spend upon him something more than this short lucubration. I will keep vigil for a whole night in his behalf and in behalf of his companions, whether they be disciples or masters, who think no man to be worthy of Christ's ministry unless he is married and his wife is seen to be with child.

To Pammachius Against John of Jerusalem.

Introduction.

The letter against John of Jerusalem was written about the year 398 or 399, and was a product of the Origenistic controversy. Its immediate occasion was the visit of Epiphanius, bishop of Salamis in Cyprus, at Jerusalem, in 394. The bishop preached, in the Church of the Resurrection (§11), a pointed sermon against Origenism, which was thought to be so directly aimed at John that the latter sent his archdeacon to remonstrate with the preacher (§14). After many unseemly scenes, Epiphanius advised Jerome and his friends to separate from their bishop (§39). But how were they to have the ministrations of the Church? This difficulty was surmounted by Epiphanius, who took Jerome's brother to the monastery which he had founded at Ad, in the diocese of Eleutheropolis, and there ordained him against his will, even using force to overcome his opposition (Jerome, Letter LI. 1). Epiphanius attempted to defend his action (Jerome, Letter LI. 2), but John, after some time, appealed to Alexandria against Jerome and his supporters as schismatics. The bishop, Theophilus, at once took the side of John: but a letter, written by his emissary Isidore and intended for John, fell into the hands of Jerome (§37). The letter showed that Isidore was coming as a mere partisan of John, and Jerome, therefore, treated both it and the bearer with secret contempt. The dispute was thus prolonged for about four years, and, after some attempts at reconciliation, and the exhibition of much bitterness, amounting to the practical excommunication of Jerome and his friends, the dispute was stopped, perhaps by Theophilus, perhaps through the influence of Melania. The letter written to Pammachius at Rome, in 397 or 398, against John, was abruptly broken off, and it is almost certain that it was never published during Jerome's lifetime. Jerome afterwards had so much influence with Theophilus that we find him interceding for John, who had fallen under the Pontiff's displeasure (Letter LXXXVI. 1).

The date of this treatise is the subject of controversy. In §1 Jerome says that he wrote "after three years," that is, three years from the visit of Epiphanius to Jerusalem, which was in 394. This would give the date 397. At §14, also, he says that Epiphanius had been brooding over his wrongs for three years. Another note of time is found in the words of §43, that John had "lately" sought to obtain a sentence of exile against Jerome from "that wild beast who threatened the necks of the whole world," that is, the Prefect Rufinus, who died at the end of 395. All these statements point to the year 397. On the other hand, at §17, he speaks of his "Commentaries" on Ecclesiastes and Ephesians as having been written "about (*ferme*) ten years ago"; and the preface to Ecclesiastes says that he had read Ecclesiastes with Blesilla at Rome "about (*ferme*) five years ago," consequently, fifteen years before the writing of this treatise. Blesilla's death was in 384. The reading of Ecclesiastes may, therefore, have been in 383. And the fifteen years would bring us to 398. Also, at §41, Jerome says, addressing John. "You seem to have slept for thirteen years," implying that it was for thirteen years that the state of things complained of by John had existed, that is, the presence of the monks in his diocese, or, at least, their leaving their own dioceses. Jerome left Antioch, the diocese of his ordination, at the end of 385 or beginning of 386; these thirteen years, therefore, bring us to 399, the date adopted by Vallarsi. There is, however, an intimation in "Pallad. Hist. Laus.," c. 117, that Melania, the friend of Rufinus, gave assistance in the matter of "the schism of nearly 400 monks who followed Paulinus," which is admitted to relate to the schism at Bethlehem, caused by the question of the ordination of Paulinianus. We know that Melania and Rufinus left Jerusalem early in 397, and that, before their departure, Jerome and Rufinus were reconciled. It would, therefore, seem most probable that the treatise, which is written with so much animosity against John, Rufinus's fellow-worker, and contains invidious allusions to Rufinus himself (§11, "your friends, who grin like dogs and turn up their noses," Jerome's constant description of Rufinus), was written before the reconciliation of Rufinus and Jerome, that is, in the end of 386 or the beginning of 387, and that it was broken off and kept unpublished because the situation had changed. Vallarsi places it in 399. He quotes the passages which make for the later date, but strangely omits the more definite statements which make for the earlier. It should be added that the letter of Jerome (LXXXII.) to Theophilus is evidently written at the same time, and under the same feelings, as this treatise. and, if the arguments above given are valid, that letter must be placed in 397, not in 399, as stated in the note prefixed to it. The short letter (LXXXVI.) to Theophilus is, in that case, probably to be placed in 398 or 399, rather than 401, as there stated.

The treatise is a letter to Pammachius, who had been disturbed by the complaints of Bishop John to Siricius, bishop of Rome, against Jerome. Jerome begins (1) by pleading necessity for his attack on the bishop. Epiphanius has accused him of heresy (2). Let him answer plainly (3), for it is pride alone (4) which prevents this. It is said that John's letter of explanation or apology was approved by Theophilus (5); but it did not touch the point, that is, the accusation of Origenism. Only three points are treated (6), and Epiphanius adduced eight—namely (7) Origen's opinions (i.) that the Son does not see the Father; (ii.) that souls are confined in earthly bodies, as in a prison; (iii.) that the devil may be saved; (iv.) that the skins with which God clothed Adam and Eve were human bodies; (v.) that the body in the resurrection will be without sex; (vi.) that the descriptions of Paradise are allegorical: trees meaning angels, and rivers the heavenly virtues; (vii) that the waters above and below the firmament are angels and devils; (viii.) that the image of God was altogether lost at the Fall. John, instead of answering on the first head, merely expressed his faith in the Trinity (8, 9), and all through tries to make out (10) that the question between him and Epiphanius relates merely to the ordination of Paulinianus. Jerome then relates the extraordinary scenes of the altercation between Epiphanius and John (11–14). He then turns to the Origenistic notions that angels are cast down into human souls (15, 16), that the spirits of men pass into the heavenly bodies (17) and that the souls of men had a previous existence (18), and pass up and down in the scale of creation (19, 20). John, instead of answering on these points, contents himself with protesting against Manichæism (21.) Jerome presses him on the question of the origin of souls (22), pronouncing rashly for creationism. He then passes to the question of the state of the body after the resurrection (23), asserting the restoration of the *flesh* as it now is (24–27), both in the case of Christ (28) and in our own, adducing testimonies from the Old Testament (29–32), and discussing the appearances of our Lord after His resurrection (34–36). He then passes to a detailed examination of John's letter or "Apology" to Theophilus (37), quoting its words, and telling the story of the mission of Isidore (37, 38), and the attempts of the Count Archelaus to make peace (39). The ordination of Paulinianus, on which John lays stress, is a subterfuge (40, 41). The schism is due to the heretical tendencies of the bishop, who is everywhere denounced by Epiphanius (42, 43).

The letter is, throughout, violent and contemptuous in its tone, with an arrogant assumption that the writer is in possession of the whole truth on the difficult subject on which he writes, and that he has a right to demand from his bishop a confession of faith on each point on which he chooses to catechize him. Its importance lies in the fact that it, to a large extent, fixed the belief of churchmen on the points it deals with, and the mode of dealing with supposed heresy, for more than a thousand years.

1. If, according to the Apostle Paul, we cannot pray as we feel, and speech does not express the thoughts of our own minds, how much more dangerous is it to judge of another man's heart, and to trace and explain the meaning of the particular words and expressions which he uses? The nature of man is prone to mercy, and in considering another's sin, everyone commiserates himself. Accordingly, if you blame one who offends in word, a man will say it was only simplicity; if you tax a man with craft, he to whom you speak will not admit that there is anything more in it than ignorance, so that he may avoid the suspicion of malice. And it will thus come to pass that you, the accuser, are made a slanderer, and the censured party is regarded, not as a heretic, but merely as a man without culture. You know, Pammachius, you

know that it is not enmity or the lust of glory which leads me to engage in this work, but that I have been stimulated by your letters and that I act out of the fervor of my faith; and, if possible, I would have all understand that I cannot be blamed for impatience and rashness, seeing that I speak only after the lapse of three years. In fact, if you had not told me that the minds of many are troubled at the "Apology" which I am about to discuss, and are tossing to and fro on a sea of doubt, I had determined to persist in silence.

2. So away with Novatus, who would not hold out a hand to the erring! Perish Montanus and his mad women! Montanus, who would hurl the fallen into the abyss that they may never rise again. Every day we all sin and make some slip or other. Being then merciful to ourselves, we are not rigorous towards others; nay, rather, we pray and beseech him either to simply tell us our own faults, or to openly defend those of other men. I dislike ambiguities; I dislike to be told what is capable of two meanings. Let us contemplate with unveiled face the glory of the Lord. Once upon a time the people of Israel halted between two opinions. But, said Elias, which is by interpretation *the strong one of the Lord,* "How long halt ye between two opinions? If the Lord be God, go after him; but if Baal, follow him." And the Lord himself says concerning the Jews, "the strange children lied unto me; the strange children became feeble, and limped out of their by-paths." If there really is no ground for suspecting him of heresy (as I wish and believe), why does he not speak out my opinion in my own words? He calls it simplicity; I interpret it as artfulness. He wishes to convince me that his belief is sound; let his speech, then, also be sound. And, indeed, if the ambiguity attached to a

single word, or a single statement, or two or three, I could be indulgent on the score of ignorance; nor would I judge what is obscure or doubtful by the standard of what is certain and clear. But, as things are, this "simplicity" is nothing but a platform trick, like walking on tiptoe over eggs or standing corn; there is doubt and suspicion everywhere. You might suppose he was not writing an exposition of the faith, but was writing a disputation on some imaginary theme. What he is now so keen upon, we learnt long ago in the schools. He puts on our own armor to fight against us. Even if his faith be correct, and he speaks with circumspection and reserve, his extreme care rouses my suspicions. "He that walketh uprightly, walketh boldly." It is folly to bear a bad name for nothing. A charge is brought against him of which he is not conscious. Let him confidently deny the charge which hangs upon a single word, and freely turn the tables against his adversary. Let the one exhibit the same boldness in repelling the charge which the other shows in advancing it. And when he has said all that he wishes and purposes to say, and such things as are above suspicion, if his opponent persists in slander, let him try conclusions in open court. I wish no one to sit still under an imputation of heresy, lest, if he say nothing, his want of openness be interpreted, amongst those who are not aware of his innocence, as the consciousness of guilt, although there is no need to demand the presence of a man and to reduce him to silence when you have his letters in your possession.

  3. We all know what he wrote to you, what charge he brought against you, wherein (as you maintain) he has slandered you. Answer the points, one by one; follow the footsteps of this letter; leave not a single jot or tittle of the

slander unnoticed. For if you are careless, and accidentally pass over any thing as I believe you on your oath to have done, he will immediately cry out: "Now, now, you have got the worst of it, the whole thing turns upon this." Words do not sound the same in the ears of friends and enemies. An enemy looks for a knot even in a bulrush; a friend judges even crooked to be straight. It is a saying of secular writers that lovers are blind in their judgments, though, perhaps, you are too busy with the sacred books to pay any attention to such literature. You should never boast of what your friends think of you. That is true testimony which comes from the lips of foes. On the contrary, if a friend speaks in your behalf he will be considered not as a witness but a judge or a partisan. This is the sort of thing your enemies will say, who perhaps give no credit to you, and only wish to vex you. But I, whom you say you have never willingly injured, yet whose name you are always bound to bandy about in your letters, advise you either to openly proclaim the faith of the Church, or to speak as you believe. For that cautious mincing and weighing of words may, no doubt, deceive the unlearned; but a careful hearer and reader will quickly detect the snare, and will show in open daylight the subterranean mines by which truth is overthrown. The Arians (no one knows more about them than you) for a long time pretended that they condemned the *Homoousion* on account of the offence it gave, and they besmeared poisonous error with honeyed words. But at last the snake uncoiled itself, and its deadly head, which lay concealed under all its folds, was pierced by the sword of the Spirit. The Church, as you know, welcomes penitents, and is so overwhelmed by the multitude of sinners that it is forced, in the interests of the misguided flocks, to be lenient to the wounds of the shepherds. Ancient and modern heresy observes the same rule—the people hear one thing, the priests preach another.

4. And first, before I translate and insert in this book the letter which you wrote to Bishop Theophilus, and show you that I understand your excessive care and circumspection, I should like a word of expostulation with you. What is the meaning of this towering arrogance which makes you refuse to reply to those who question you respecting the faith? How is it that you regard almost as public enemies the vast multitude of brethren, and the bands of monks, who refuse to communicate with you in Palestine? The Son of God, for the sake of one sick sheep, leaving the ninety and nine on the mountains, endured the buffeting, the cross, the scourge; He took up the burden, and patiently carried on His shoulders to heaven the voluptuous woman that was a sinner. Is it for you to act the "most reverend father in God," the fastidious prelate; to stand apart in your wealth and wisdom, in your grandeur and your learning; to frown superciliously upon your fellow servants, and scarce vouchsafe a glance to those who have been redeemed with the blood of your Lord? Is this what you have learnt from the Apostles' precept to be "ready always to give answer to every man that asked you a reason concerning the hope that is in you"? Suppose we do, as you pretend, seek occasion, and that, under the pretext of zeal for the faith, we are sowing strife, framing a schism, and fomenting quarrels. Then take away the occasion from those who wish for an occasion; so that having given satisfaction on the point of faith, and solved all the difficulties in which you are involved, you may show clearly to all that the dispute is not one of doctrine, but of order. But perhaps when

questioned concerning the faith, you say that it is from wise forethought that you hold your tongue, so that it may not be said that you have proved yourself a heretic—in as much as you make satisfaction to your accusers. If that be so, then men ought not to refute any charges of which they are accused, lest, having denied them, they may be held to be guilty. The accusations of the laity, deacons, and presbyters, are, I suppose, beneath your notice. For you can, as you are perpetually boasting, make a thousand clerics in an hour. But you have to answer Epiphanius, our father in God, who, in the letters which he sent, openly calls you a heretic. Certainly you are not his superior in respect of years, of learning, of his exemplary life, or of the judgment of the whole world. If it is a question of age, you are a young man writing to an old one. If it is one of knowledge, you are a person not so very accomplished writing to a learned man, although your partisans maintain that you are a more finished speaker than Demosthenes, more sharp-witted than Chrysippus, wiser than Plato, and perhaps have persuaded you that they are right. As regards his life and devotion to the faith, I will say no more, that I may not seem to be seeking to wound you. At the time when the whole East (except our fathers in God Athanasius and Paulinus) was overrun by the Arian and Eunomian heresies; when you did not hold communion with the Westerns; then, in the very worst of the exile which made them confessors, he, though a simple convent priest, gained the ear of Eutychius, and afterwards as bishop of Cyprus was unmolested by Valens. For he was always so highly venerated that heretics on the throne thought it would redound to their own disgrace if they persecuted such a man. Write therefore to him. Answer his letter. So let the rest understand your purpose and judge of your eloquence and wisdom; do not keep all your accomplishments to yourself. Why, when you are challenged in one quarter, do you turn your arms towards another? A question is put to you in Palestine, your answer is given in Egypt. When some are bleareyed, you anoint the eyes of others who are not affected. If you tell another what is meant to give us satisfaction, such action springs entirely from pride; if you tell him what we do not ask for, it is entirely uncalled for.

5. But you say, "the bishop of Alexandria approved of my letter." What did he approve of? Your correct utterances against Arius, Photinus, and Manichæus. For who, at this time of day, accuses you of being an Arian? Who now fastens on you the guilt of Photinus and Manichæus? Those faults were long ago corrected, those enemies were shattered. You were not so foolish as to openly defend a heresy which you knew was offensive to the whole Church. You knew that if you had done this, you must have been immediately removed, and your heart was upon the pleasures of your episcopal throne. You so tuned your expressions as to neither displease the simple, nor offend your own incontestably marked by deceit and slipperiness; what, then, are we to do with the remaining five, with regard to which, because no opportunity was afforded for ambiguity, supporters. You wrote well, but nothing to the purpose. How was the bishop of Alexandria to know of what you were accused, or what things they were of which a confession was demanded from you? You ought to have set forth in detail the charges brought against you, and then have met them one by one. There is an old story which tells how a certain man, who, when he was speaking fluently, was carried

along by a torrent of words, without touching the question before the court, and thus drew the wise remark from the judge, "Excellent! excellent! but to what purpose is all this excellence?" Quacks have but one lotion for all affections of the eyes. He who is accused of many things, and in dissipating the charges passes over some, confesses all that he omits to mention. Did you not reply to the letter of Epiphanius, and yourself choose the points for refutation? No doubt, in replying, you rested on the axiom, that no man is so brave as to put the sword to his own throat. Choose which alternative you like. You shall have your choice: you either replied to the letter of Epiphanius, or you did not. If you did reply, why did you take no notice of the most important, and the most numerous, of the charges brought against you? If you did not reply, what becomes of your "Apology," of which you boast amongst the simple, and which you are scattering broadcast amongst those who do not understand the matter?

6. The questions for you to answer were arranged, as I shall presently show, under eight heads. You touch only three, and pass on. As regards the rest, you maintain a magnificent silence. If you had with perfect frankness replied to seven, I should still cling to the charge which remained; and what you said nothing about, that I should hold to be the truth. But as things are, you have caught the wolf by the ears; you can neither hold fast, nor dare let go. With a sort of careless security and an air of abstraction, you skim over and touch the surface of three in which there is nothing or but little of importance. And your procedure is so dark and close that you confess more by your silence than you rebut by your arguments. Everyone has the right forthwith to say to you, "If the light that is in

thee be darkness, how great is the darkness." Even in answering three little questions, respecting which you seemed to say something, you are not clear from suspicion and from blame, but your replies are and you were therefore unable to cheat your hearers, you preferred to maintain unbroken silence rather than openly confess what had been covered in obscurity?

7. The questions relate to the passages in the Περὶ Ἀρχῶν. The first is this, "for as it is unfitting to say that the Son can see the Father, so neither is it meet to think that the Holy Spirit can see the Son." The second point is the statement that souls are tied up in the body as in a prison; and that before man was made in Paradise they dwelt amongst rational creatures in the heavens. Wherefore, afterwards to console itself, the soul says in the Psalms, "Before I was humbled, I went wrong"; and "Return, my soul, to thy rest"; and "Lead my soul out of prison"; and similarly elsewhere. Thirdly, he says that both the devil and demons will some time or other repent, and ultimately reign with the saints. Fourthly, he interprets the coats of skin, with which Adam and Eve were clothed after their fall and ejection from Paradise, to be human bodies, and we are to suppose of course that previously, in Paradise, they had neither flesh, sinews, nor bones. Fifthly, he most openly denies the resurrection of the flesh and the bodily structure, and the distinction of senses, both in his explanation of the first Psalm, and in many other of his treatises. Sixthly, he so allegorizes Paradise as to destroy historical truth, understanding angels instead of trees, heavenly virtues instead of rivers, and he overthrows all that is contained in the history of Paradise by his figurative interpretation. Seventhly, he thinks that the waters which are said in Scripture to be

above the heavens are holy and supernal essences, while those which are above the earth and beneath the earth are, on the contrary, demoniacal essences. The eighth is Origen's cavil that the image and likeness of God, in which man was created, was lost, and was no longer in man after he was expelled from Paradise.

8. These are the arrows with which you are pierced; these the weapons with which throughout the whole letter you are wounded; or I should rather say Epiphanius throws himself as a suppliant at your knees, and casts his hoary locks beneath your feet, and, for a time laying aside his episcopal dignity, prays for your salvation in words such as these: "Grant to me and to yourself the favor of your salvation; save yourself, as it is written, from this crooked generation, and forsake the heresy of Origen, and all heresies, dearly beloved." And lower down, "In the defence of heresy you kindle hatred against me, and destroy that love which I had towards you; insomuch that you would make us even repent of holding communion with you who so resolutely defend the errors and doctrines of Origen." Tell me, prince of arguers, to which, out of the eight sections, you have replied. For the present, I say nothing of the rest. Take the first blasphemy—that the Son cannot see the Father, nor the Holy Spirit the Son. By what weapons of yours has it been pierced? the answer we get is, "We believe that the Holy and Adorable Trinity are of the same substance; that they are co-eternal, and of the same glory and Godhead, and we anathematize those who say that there is any greatness, smallness, inequality, or aught that is visible in the Godhead of the Trinity. But as we say the Father is incorporeal, invisible, and eternal; so we say the Son and Holy Spirit are incorporeal, invisible, and eternal." If you

did not say this, you would not hold to the Church. I do not ask whether there was not a time when you refused to say this. I will not discuss the question, whether you were fond of those who preached such doctrines; on whose side you were when, for expressing those sentiments, they underwent banishment; or who the man was that, when the presbyter Theo preached in the Church that the Holy Spirit is God, closed his ears, and excitedly rushed out of doors that he might not so much as hear the impiety. I recognize a man, as one may say, as one of the faithful, even though his repentance comes late. That unhappy man Prætextatus, who died after he had been chosen consul, a profane person and an idolater, was wont in sport to say to blessed Pope Damascus, "Make me bishop of Rome, and I will at once be a Christian." Why do you, with many words and intricate periods, take the trouble to show me that you are not an Arian? Either deny that the accused said what is imputed to him, or, if he did give utterance to such sentiments, condemn him for so speaking. You have still to learn how intense is the zeal of the orthodox. Listen to the Apostle: "If I or an angel from heaven bring you another gospel than that we have declared, let him be anathema." You would extenuate the fault and hide the name of the guilty party: as though everything were right and no one were accused of blasphemy, you frame, in artificial language, an uncalled-for profession of your faith. Speak out at once, and let your letter thus begin: "Let him be accursed who has dared to write such things." Pure faith is impatient of delay. As soon as the scorpion appears, he must be crushed under foot. David, who was proved to be a man after God's own heart, says: "Do not I hate those that hate thee, O Lord, and did not I pine away over thine enemies?

I hated them with a perfect hatred." Had I heard my father, or mother, or brother say such things against my Master Christ, I would have broken their blasphemous jaws like those of a mad dog, and my hand should have been amongst the first lifted up against them. They who said to father and mother, "We know you not," these men fulfilled the will of the Lord. He that loveth father or mother more than Christ, is not worthy of Him.

9. It is alleged that your master, whom you call a Catholic, and whom you resolutely defend, said, "the Son sees not the Father, and the Holy Spirit sees not the Son." And you tell me that the Father is invisible, the Son invisible, the Holy Ghost invisible, as though the angels, both cherubim and seraphim, were not also, in accordance with their nature, invisible to our eyes. David was certainly in doubt even as regards the appearance of the heavens: "I shall see," he says, "the heavens, the works of Thy fingers." I shall see, not I see. I shall see when with unveiled face I shall behold the glory of the Lord: but now we see in part, and we know in part. The question is whether the Son sees the Father, and you say, "The Father is invisible." It is disputed whether the Holy Spirit sees the Son, and you answer, "The Son is invisible." The point at issue is, whether the Trinity have mutually the vision of one another; human ears cannot endure such blasphemy, and you say the Trinity is invisible. You wander in the realms of praise in all other directions; you spend your eloquence on things which no one wants to hear about. You put your hearer off the scent, to avoid telling us what we ask for. But granted that all this is superfluous. We make you a present of the fact that you are not an Arian; nay, even more, that you never have been. We allow that in the explanation of the first section

no suspicion rests upon you, and that all that you said was frank and free from error. We speak to you with equal frankness. Did our father in God, Epiphanius, accuse you of being an Arian? Did he fasten upon you the heresy of Eunomius, the *Godless*, or that of Aerius? The point of the whole letter is that you follow the erroneous doctrines of Origen, and are associated with others in this heresy. Why, when a question is put to you on one point, do you give an answer about another; and, as if you were speaking to fools, hide the charges contained in the letters, and tell us what you said in the church in the presence of Epiphanius? A confession of faith is demanded of you, and you inflict upon us your very eloquent dissertations. I beseech my readers to remember the judgment seat of the Lord, and as you know that you must be judged for the judgment you give, favor neither me nor my opponent, and consider not the persons of the arguers, but the case itself. Let us then continue what we began.

    10. You write in your letter that, before Paulinianus was made a presbyter, the pope Epiphanius never took you to task in connection with Origen's errors. To begin with, this is doubtful, and I have to consider which of the two men I should believe. He says that he did object, you deny it; he brings forward witnesses, you will not listen to them when they are produced; he even relates that another besides yourself was arraigned by him: you refuse to admit this in the case of either; he sends a letter to you by one of his clergy, and demands an answer: you are silent, dare not open your lips, and, challenged in Palestine, speak at Alexandria. Which of you is to be believed is not for me to say. I suppose that you yourself would not, in the face of so distinguished a

man, venture to claim truth for yourself, and impute falsehood to him. But it is possible that each speaks from his own point of view. I will call a witness against you, and that witness is yourself. For if there were no dispute about doctrines, if you had not roused the anger of an old man, if he had given you no reply, what need was there for you, who do not excel in gifts of speech, to discuss in a single sermon in the church the whole circle of doctrine—the Trinity, the assumption of our Lord's body, the cross, hell, the nature of angels, the condition of souls, the Savior's resurrection and our own, and this as taking place on this earth (topics perhaps omitted in your manuscript) in the presence of the masses, in the presence, too, of a man of such distinction? and to speak with such perfect assurance and to gallop through it all without stopping to draw breath? What shall we say of the ancient writers of the Church, who were scarcely able to explain single difficulties in many volumes? What of the vessel of election, the Gospel trumpet, the roaring of our lion, the thunderer of the Gentiles, the river of Christian eloquence, who, when confronted by the mystery concealed from ages and generations, and by the depth of the riches of the wisdom and knowledge of God, rather marvels at it than discusses it? What of Isaiah, who pointed beforehand to the Virgin? That single thing was too much for him, and he says, "Who shall declare his generation?" In our age a poor manikin has been found, who, with one turn of the tongue, and a brilliancy exceeding that of the sun, discourses on all ecclesiastical questions. If no one asked you for the display, and everything was quiet, you were foolish to enter voluntarily upon so hazardous a discussion. If, on the other hand, the object of your speaking was the satisfaction you owed to the faith, it follows that the cause of strife was not the ordination of a priest, who, it is certain, was ordained long after. You have deceived only those who were not on the spot, and your letters flatter the ears of strangers only.

11. We were present (we know the whole case) when the bishop Epiphanius spoke against Origen in your church, and he was the ostensible, you the real object of attack. You and your crew grinned like dogs, drew in your nostrils, scratched your heads, nodded to one another, and talked of the "silly old man." Did you not, in front of the Lord's tomb, send your archdeacon to tell him to cease discussing such matters? What bishop ever gave such a command to one of his own presbyters in the presence of the people? When you were going from the Church of the Resurrection to the Church of the Holy Cross, and a crowd of all ages, and both sexes, was flowing to meet him, presenting to him their little ones, kissing his feet, plucking the fringes of his garments, and when he could not stir a step forward, and could hardly stand against the waves of the surging crowd, were not you so tortured by envy as to exclaim against "the vainglorious old man"? And you were not ashamed to tell him to his face that his stopping was of set purpose and design. Pray recall that day when the people who had been called together were kept waiting until the seventh hour by the mere hope of hearing Epiphanius, and the subject of the harangue you then delivered. You spoke, forsooth, with indignant rage against the Anthropomorphites, who, with rustic simplicity, think that God has actually the members of which we read in Scripture; and showed by your eyes, hands, and every gesture that you had the old man in view, and wished him to be suspected of that most foolish

heresy. When through sheer fatigue, with dry month, head thrown back, and quivering lips, to the satisfaction of the whole people, who had longed for the end, you at last wound up, how did the crazy and "silly old man" treat you? He rose to indicate that he would say a few words, and after saluting the assembly with voice and hand proceeded thus: "All that has been said by one who is my brother in the episcopate, but my son in point of years, against the heresy of the Anthropomorphites, has been well and faithfully spoken, and my voice, too, condemns that heresy. But it is fair that, as we condemn this heresy so we should also condemn the perverse doctrines of Origen." You cannot, I think, have forgotten what a burst of laughter, what shouts of applause ensued. This is what you call in your letter his speaking to the people anything he chose, no matter what it might be. He, forsooth, was mad because he contradicted you in your own kingdom. "Anything he chose, no matter what." Either give him praise, or blame. Why, here as well as elsewhere, do you move with so uncertain a step? If what he said was good, why not openly proclaim it? if evil, why not boldly censure it? And yet, let us note with what wisdom, modesty, and humility this pillar of truth and faith, who dares to say that so illustrious a man speaks to the people what he chooses, alludes to himself. "One day I was speaking in his presence; and, taking occasion from some words in the lesson for the day, I expressed, in his hearing and in that of the whole Church, such views respecting the faith and all the doctrines of the Church as by the grace of God I unceasingly teach in the Church, and in my catechetical lectures."

12. What, I ask, is the meaning of this effrontery and bombast? All philosophers and orators attack Gorgias

of Leontini for daring openly to pledge himself to answer any question which any person might choose to put to him. If the honor of the priesthood and respect for your title did not restrain me, and if I did not know what the Apostle says, "I wist not, brethren, that he was the high priest: for it is written, Thou shalt not speak evil of the ruler of thy people," how loudly and indignantly might I complain of what you relate! You, on the contrary, disparage the dignity of your title by the contempt which you throw, both in word and deed, on one who is almost the father of the whole episcopate, and a monument of the sanctity of former days. You say that on a certain day, when something in the lesson for the day stirred you up, you made a discourse in his hearing, and in that of the whole Church, concerning the faith and all the doctrines of the Church. After this we cannot but wonder at the weakness of Demosthenes; for we are told that he spent a long time in elaborating his splendid oration against Æschines. We are quite mistaken in looking up to Tully; for his merit, according to Cornelius Nepos, who was present, was nothing but this, that he delivered his famous defence of the seditious tribune Cornelius, almost word for word as it was published. Behold a Lysias and a Gracchus raised up for us! or, to name one of more modern days, Quintus Aterius, the man who had all his powers at hand like a stock of ready money, so that he needed someone to tell him when to stop, and of whom Cæsar Augustus said very well, "Our friend Quintus must have the break put on."

13. Is there any man in his right senses who would declare that in a single sermon he had discussed the faith and all the doctrines of the Church? Pray show me what that lesson is which is so seasoned with the whole savor

of Scripture that its occurrence in the service induced you to enter the arena and put your wit to the hazard. And if you had not been overwhelmed by the torrent of your eloquence, you might have been convinced that it was impossible for you to speak upon the whole circle of doctrines without any deliberation. But how stands the case? You promise one thing and present another. Our custom is, for the space of forty days, to deliver public lectures to those who are to be baptized on the doctrine of the Holy and Adorable Trinity. If the lesson for the day stimulated you to discuss all doctrines in a single hour, what necessity was there to repeat the instruction of the previous forty days? But if you meant to recapitulate what you had been saying during the whole of Lent, how could one lesson on a certain day "stir you up" to speak of all these doctrines? But even here his language is ambiguous; for possibly he took occasion, from the particular lesson, to go over summarily what he was accustomed to deliver in church to the candidates for baptism during the forty days of Lent. For it is eloquence all the same whether a few things are said in many words, or many things in few words. There is another permissible meaning, that, as soon as the one lesson gave him the spur, he was fired with such oratorical zeal that for forty days he never ceased speaking. But, then, even the easy-going old man, who was hanging upon his lips, and longing to know what he had never heard before, must have almost fallen from his seat asleep. However, we must put up with it; perhaps this, also, is a case of the simplicity which we know to be his manner.

14. Let us quote the rest, in which, after the labyrinths of his perplexing discussion, he expresses himself by no means ambiguously but openly, and thus

concludes his wonderful homilies: "When we had thus spoken in his presence, and when out of the extreme honor which we paid him we invited him to speak after us, he praised our preaching, and said that he marveled at it, and declared to all that it was the Catholic faith." The extreme honor you paid him is evidenced by the extreme insults offered to him, when through the archdeacon you bade him be silent, and loudly proclaimed that it was the love of praise which made him linger among the crowd. The present is the key to the past. For three whole years from that time he has brooded in silence over the wrongs he suffered, and, spurning all personal strife, has only asked for a more correct expression of your faith. You, with your endless resources, and making a profit out of the religion of the whole world, have been sending those very dignified envoys of yours hither and thither, and have been trying to awake the old man out of his sleep that he might answer you. And in truth it was right that as you had conferred such signal honor upon him he should praise your utterances, particularly such as were *ex tempore*. But as men have a way of sometimes praising what they do not approve, and of nourishing another's folly by meaningless commendation, he not only praised your utterances, but praised and marveled at them as well; and what is more, to magnify the marvel, he declared to the whole people that they were in harmony with the Catholic faith. Whether he really said all this, we ourselves are witnesses. The fact is, he came to us half dead with dismay at your words, and saying that he had been too precipitate in communicating with you. And further, when he was much entreated by the whole monastery to return to you from Bethlehem, and was unable to resist the entreaties of so many, he did indeed return in the evening, but only to escape again at midnight. His letters to the pope Siricius prove the same thing, and if you read them you will see clearly in what sense he marveled at your utterances and acknowledged them Catholic. But we are threshing chaff, and have spent many words in refuting gratuitous nonsense and old wives' fables.

15. Let us pass on to the second point. Here, as though there were nothing for his consideration, he vapors, and vents himself unconcernedly, pretending to be asleep, so that he may lull his readers also into slumber. "But we were speaking of the other matters pertaining to the faith, that is to say, that all things visible and invisible, the heavenly powers and terrestrial creatures have one and the same creator, even God, that is, the Holy Trinity, as the blessed David says, 'By the word of the Lord were the heavens established, and all the host of them by the breath of His mouth'; and the creation of man is a simple proof of the same; for it was God Himself who took slime from the earth, and through the grace of His own inspiration bestowed on it a reasonable soul, and one endowed with free will; not a part of His own nature (as some impiously teach), but His own workmanship. And concerning the holy angels, the belief of Christians similarly follows Holy Scripture, which says of God, "Who maketh His angels spirits, and His ministers a flaming fire." Holy Scripture does not allow us to believe that their nature is unchangeable, for it says, "And angels which kept not their own principality, but left their proper habitation, He hath kept in everlasting bonds under darkness unto the judgment of the great day"; we know, therefore, that they have changed, and having lost their own dignity and glory have become more like demons. But that the souls of men

are caused by the fall of the angels, or by their conversion, we never believed, nor have we so taught (God forbid!), and we confess that the view is at variance with the teaching of the Church."

16. We want to know whether souls, before man was made in paradise, and Adam was fashioned out of the earth, were among reasonable creatures; whether they had their own rank, lived, continued, subsisted; and whether the doctrine of Origen is true, who said that all reasonable creatures, incorporeal and invisible, if they grow remiss, little by little sink to a lower level, and, according to the character of the places to which they descend, take to themselves bodies. (For instance, that they may be at first ethereal, afterward aërial.) And that when they reach the neighborhood of earth they are invested with grossest bodies, and last of all are tied to human flesh; and that the demons themselves who, of their own choice, together with their leader the devil, have forsaken the service of God, if they begin to amend a little, are clothed with human flesh, so that, when they have undergone a process of repentance after the resurrection, and after passing through the same circuit by which they reached the flesh, they may return to proximity to God, being released even from aërial and ethereal bodies; and that then every knee will bow to God, of things in heaven, and things on earth, and things under the earth, and that God may be all to all. When these are the real questions, why do you pass over the points at issue, and, leaving the arena, fix yourself in the region of remote and utterly irrelevant discussion?

17. You believe that one God made all creatures, visible and invisible. Arius, who says that all things were created through the Son, would also confess this. If you had been accused of holding Marcion's heresy, which

introduces two Gods, the one the God of goodness, the other of justice, and asserts that the former is the Creator of things invisible, the latter of things visible, your answer would have been well adapted to satisfy me on a question of that sort. You believe it is the Trinity which creates the universe. Arians and Semi-Arians deny that, blasphemously maintaining that the Holy Spirit is not the Creator, but is Himself created. But who now lays it to your charge that you are an Arian? You say that the souls of men are not a part of the nature of God, as though you were now called a Manichean by Epiphanius. You protest against those who assert that souls are made out of angels, and say that their nature, in its fall, becomes the substance of humanity. Don't conceal what you know, nor feign a simplicity which you do not possess. Origen never said that souls are made out of angels, since he teaches that the term *angels* describe an office, not a nature. For in his book Περὶ Ἀρχῶν he says that angels, and thrones, and dominions, powers and rulers of the world, and of darkness, and every name which is named, not only in this world, but in that which is to come, become the souls of those bodies which they have taken on either through their own desire or for the sake of their appointed duties; that the sun also, himself, and the moon, and the company of all the stars, are the souls of what were once reasonable and incorporeal creatures; and that though now subject to vanity, that is to say, to fiery bodies which we, in our ignorance and inexperience, call luminaries of the world, they shall be delivered from the bondage of corruption and brought to the liberty of the glory of the sons of God. Wherefore every creature groaned and travailed in pain together. And the Apostle laments, saying, "Wretched man that I am! who shall deliver me from the body of this death?" This is not the time to controvert this doctrine, which is partly heathen, and partly Platonic. About ten years ago in my "Commentary" on Ecclesiastes, and in my explanation of the Epistle to the Ephesians, I think my own views were made clear to thoughtful men.

18. I now beg you, whose eloquence is so exuberant, and who expound the truth concerning all topics in the course of one sermon, to give an answer to your interrogators in concise and clear terms. When God formed man out of slime, and through the grace of His own inspiration gave him a soul, had that soul previously existed and subsisted which was afterwards bestowed by the inspiration of God, and where was it? or did it gain its capacity both to exist and to live from the power of God, on the sixth day, when the body was formed out of the slime? You are silent regarding this, and pretend you do not know what is wanted, and busy yourself with irrelevant questions. You leave Origen untouched, and rave against the absurdities of Marcion, Apollinaris, Eunomius, Manichæus, and the other heretics. You are asked for a hand and you put out a foot, and all the while covertly insinuate the doctrine to which you hold. You speak smooth things to plain men like us, but in such a way as in no degree to displease those of your own party.

19. You say that demons rather than souls are made out of angels, as though you did not know that, according to Origen, the demons themselves are souls belonging to aerial bodies, and, after being demons, destined to become human souls if they repent. You write that the angels are mutable; and, under cover of a pious opinion, introduce an impiety by maintaining that, after the lapse of many ages, souls are produced not from the angels, but from whatever it was into which the angels

were first changed. I wish to make my meaning clearer; suppose a person of the rank of tribune to be degraded through his own misconduct, and to pass through the several steps of the cavalry service until he becomes a private, does he all at once cease to be a tribune and become a recruit? No; but he is first colonel, then, successively, major officer of two hundred, captain, commissary, patrol, trooper, and, lastly, a recruit; and although our tribune eventually becomes a common soldier, still he did not pass from the rank of tribune to that of recruit, but to that of colonel. Origen uses Jacob's ladder to teach that reasonable creatures by slow degrees sink to the lowest step, that is to flesh and blood; and that it is impossible for anyone to be suddenly precipitated from number one hundred to number one without reaching the last by passing through the successive numbers, as in descending the rounds of a ladder; and that they change their bodies as often as they change their resting-places in going from heaven to earth. These are the tricks and artifices by which you make us out to be "Pelusiots" and "beasts of burden" and "animal men" who do "not receive the things pertaining to the Spirit." You are the "people of Jerusalem," and can make a mock even of the angels. But your mysteries are being dragged into the light, and your doctrine, which is a mere conglomerate of heathen fables, is publicly exposed in the ears of Christians. What you so much admire is what we long ago despised when we found it in Plato. And we despised it because we received the foolishness of Christ. And we received the foolishness of Christ because the weakness of God is wiser than men. And is it not a shame for us, who are Christians and priests of God, to entangle ourselves in words of doubtful meaning, as though we were merely jesting; to keep our phrases balanced between two meanings, in a way which deceives the speaker himself more than his hearers?

20. One of your company, when pressed by me to say what he thought concerning the soul, whether it had existed before the flesh, or not, replied that soul and body had existed together. I knew the man was a heretic, and was seeking to entangle me in my speech. At last I caught him saying that the soul gained that name from the time when it began to animate a body, whereas it was formerly called a demon, or angel of Satan, or spirit of fornication, or, on the other hand, dominion, power, agent of the spirit, or messenger. Well, but if the soul existed before Adam was made in Paradise (in any rank and condition), and lived and acted (for we cannot think that what is incorporeal and eternal is dull and torpid like a dormouse), there must have been some precedent cause to account for the soul, which at first had no body, being afterwards invested with a body. And if it is natural to the soul to be without a body, it must be contrary to nature for it to be in a body. If it is contrary to nature to be in a body, it follows that the resurrection of the body is contrary to nature. But the resurrection will not be contrary to nature; therefore, according to you, the body, which is contrary to nature, when it rises again will be without a soul.

21. You say that the soul is not of the essence of God. Well! This is what we might expect, for you condemn the impious Manichæus, to make mention of whose name is pollution. You say that angels are not turned into souls. I agree to some extent, although I know what meaning you give to the words. But, now that we have learnt what you deny, we wish to know what you

believe. "Having taken slime of the earth," you say, "God fashioned man, and through the grace of His own inbreathing bestowed upon him a rational soul, and through the grace of free will, not a portion of His own divine nature (as some impiously maintain), but His own handiwork." See how he goes out of his way to be eloquent about what we did not ask for. We know that God fashioned man out of the earth; we are aware that He breathed into his face, and man became a living soul; we are not ignorant that the soul is characterized by reason and free choice, and we know that it is the workmanship of God. No one doubts that Manichæus errs in saying that the soul is the essence of God. I now ask: When was that soul made, which is the work of God, which is distinguished by free will and reason, and is not of the essence of the Creator? Was it made at the same time that man was made out of the slime, and the breath of life was breathed into his face? Or, having previously existed, and having associated with reasonable and incorporeal creatures as well as lived, was it afterwards gifted with the inbreathing of God? Here you are silent; here you feign a rustic simplicity, and make scriptural words a cloak for unscriptural tenets. Where you affirm what no one wants to know, that the soul is not a part of God's own nature (as some impiously maintain), you ought rather to have declared (and this is what we all want to know) that it is not that which previously existed, which He had before created, which had long dwelt among rational, incorporeal, and invisible creatures. You say none of these things; you bring forward Manichæus, and keep Origen out of sight, and, just as when children ask for something to eat their nursemaids put them off with some little joke, so you direct the thoughts of us poor rustics to other matters, so that we may be taken up with the fresh character on the stage, and may not ask for what we want.

22. But suppose the fact to be that you merely omit this, and that your simplicity does not mean something you are shrewd enough to conceal. Having once begun to speak of the soul, and to deduce arguments on such an important topic from man's first creation, why do you leave the discussion in mid-air, and suddenly pass to the angels, and the conditions under which the body of our Lord existed? Why do you pass by such a vast slough of difficulty, and leave us to stick in the mire? If the inbreathing of God (a view for which you have no liking, and a point which you now leave unsettled) is the creating of the human soul; whence had Eve her soul, seeing that God did not breathe into her face? But I will not dwell upon Eve, since she, as a type of the Church, was made out of one of her husband's ribs, and ought not, after so many ages, to be subjected to the calumnies of her descendants. I ask whence Cain and Abel, who were the firstborn of our first parents, had their souls? And the whole human race downwards, what, are we to think, was the origin of their souls? Did they come by propagation, like brute beasts? So that, as body springs from body, so soul from soul. Or is it the case that rational creatures, longing for bodily existence, sink by degrees to earth, and at last are tied even to human bodies? Surely (as the Church teaches in accordance with the Savior's words, "My Father worketh hitherto and I work"; and the passage in Isaiah, "Who maketh the spirit of man in him"; and in the Psalms, "Who fashioned one by one the hearts of them") God is daily making souls—He, with whom to will is to do, and who never ceases to be a Creator. I

know what you are accustomed to say in opposition to this, and how you confront us with adultery and incest. But the dispute about these is a tedious one, and would exceed the narrow limits of the time at our disposal. The same argument may be retorted upon you, and whatever seems unworthy in the Creator of the present dispensation is again not unworthy, since it is His gift. Birth from adultery imputes no blame to the child, but to the father. As in the case of seeds, the earth which cherishes does not sin, nor the seed which is thrown into the furrows, nor the heat and moisture, under whose influence the grain bursts into bud, but some man, as for example, the thief and robber, who, by fraud and violence, plucks up the seed: so in the begetting of men, the womb, which corresponds to the earth, receives its own, and nourishes what it has received, and then gives a body to that which it nourishes, and divides into the several members the body it has formed. And among those secret recesses of the belly the hand of God is always working, and there is the same Creator of body and soul. Do not despise the goodness of your Maker, who fashioned you and made you as He chose. He Himself is the virtue of God and the wisdom of God, who, in the womb of the Virgin, built a house for Himself. Jephthah, who is reckoned by the Apostle among the saints, is the son of a harlot. But listen: Esau, born of Rebecca had Isaac, a "hairy man," both in mind and body, like good wheat, degenerates into darnel and wild oats; because the cause of vice and virtue does not lie in the seed, but in the will of him who is born. If it is an offence to be born with a human body, how is it that Isaac, Samson, John Baptist, are the children of promise? You see, I trust, what it is to have the courage of one's convictions. Suppose I am wrong, I openly say what I think. Do you, then, likewise either freely profess our opinions, or firmly maintain your own. Do not set yourself in my line of battle, so that, by feigning simplicity, you may be safe, and may be able, when you choose, to stab your opponent in the back. It is impossible for me, at the present moment, to write a book against the opinions of Origen. If Christ gives us life, we will devote another work to them. The point now is, whether the accused has answered the questions put to him, and whether his reply be clear and open.

23. Let us pass from this to the most notorious point, that relating to the resurrection of the flesh and of the body; and here, my reader, I would admonish you that you may know I speak under a sense of fear and of the judgment of God, and that you ought so to hear. For, if the pure faith is to be found in his exposition, and there is no suspicion of unfaithfulness, I am not so foolish as to seek an occasion of accusing him, and while I wish to censure another for his fault be myself censured as a slanderer. I will ask you, therefore, to read what follows on the resurrection of the flesh; and, having read it, if it satisfies you (I know it is well calculated to please the ignorant), suspend your judgment, wait a while, refrain from expressing an opinion until I have finished my reply; and if after that it satisfies you, then you shall fix on us the brand of slander. "His passion also on the cross, His death and burial, which was the saving of the world, and His resurrection in a true and not an imaginary sense, we confess; and that being the firstborn from the dead, He conveyed to heaven the first fruits of our bodily substance which, after being laid in the tomb, He raised to life, thus giving us the hope of resurrection in the resurrection of His own body; wherefore we all hope so to rise from the

dead, as He rose again; not in any foreign and strange bodies, which are but phantom shapes assumed for the moment; but as He Himself rose again in that body which was laid in the holy sepulcher at our very doors, so we, in the very bodies with which we are now clothed, and in which we are now buried, hope to rise again for the same reason and by the same command. For the bodies which, as the Apostle says, are sown in corruption, shall rise in incorruption; being sown in dishonor, they shall rise in glory. 'It is sown an animal body, it shall rise a spiritual body'; and of them the Savior said in his teaching: 'For they who shall be worthy of that world, and of the resurrection from the dead, shall neither marry nor be given in marriage, for they can die no more, but shall be as the angels of God, since they are the sons of the resurrection.'"

24. Again, in another part of his letter, that is, towards the end of his own homilies, that he might cheat the ear of the ignorant, he makes a grand parade and noise about the Resurrection, but in ambiguous and balanced language. He says: "We have not omitted the second glorious advent of our Lord Jesus Christ, who shall come in His own glory to judge the quick and the dead; for He shall awake all the dead, and cause them to stand before His own judgment-seat; and shall render to every one according to what he has done in the body, whether it be good or bad; for every one shall either be crowned in the body because he lived a pure and righteous life, or be condemned, because he was the slave alike of pleasure and iniquity." What we read in the Gospel, that at the end of the world, if it were possible, even the elect are to be seduced, we see verified in this passage. The ignorant crowd hears of the dead and buried, hears of the

resurrection of the dead in a true and not an imaginary sense, hears that the first fruits of our bodily substance in our Lord's body have reached the heavenly regions, hears that we shall rise again not in foreign and strange bodies, which are mere phantom shapes, but, as our Lord rose in the body which lay amongst us in the holy sepulcher, so we also in the very bodies with which we are now clothed and buried shall rise again in the day of judgment. And that no one might think this too little, he adds in the last section: "And He shall render to every one according to what he did in the body, whether it were good or bad: for every one shall either be crowned in the body for his pure and righteous life, or shall be condemned, because he was the slave of pleasure and iniquity." Hearing these things the ignorant crowd suspects no artifice, no snares in all this noise about the dead, the burial of the body, and the resurrection. It believes things are as they are said to be. For there is more devotion in the ears of the people than in the priest's heart.

25. Again and again, my reader, I admonish you to be patient, and to learn what I also have learnt through patience; and yet, before I take the veil off the dragon's face, and briefly explain Origen's views respecting the resurrection (for you cannot know the efficacy of the antidote unless you see clearly what the poison is), I beg you to read his statements with caution, and to go over them again and again. Mark well that, though he nine times speaks of the resurrection of the body, he has not once introduced the resurrection of the flesh, and you may fairly suspect that he left it out on purpose. Well, Origen says in several places, and especially in his fourth book "Of the Resurrection," and in the "Exposition of the First Psalm," and in the "Miscellanies," that there is a double

error common in the Church, in which both we and the heretics are implicated: "We, in our simplicity and fondness for the flesh, say that the same bones, and blood, and flesh, in a word, limbs and features, and the whole bodily structure, rise again at the last day: so that, forsooth, we shall walk with our feet, work with our hands, see with our eyes, hear with our ears, and carry about with us a belly never satisfied, and a stomach which digests our food. Consequently, believing this, we say that we must eat, drink, perform the offices of nature, marry wives, beget children. For what is the use of organs of generation, if there is to be no marriage? For what purpose are teeth, if the food is not to be masticated? What is the good of a belly and of meats, if, according to the Apostle, both it and they are to be destroyed? And the same Apostle again exclaims, 'Flesh and blood shall not inherit the Kingdom of God, nor shall corruption inherit incorruption.'" This, according to him, is what we in our rustic innocence maintain. But as for the heretics, amongst whom are Marcion, Apelles, Valentinus, Manes (a synonym for Mania), he says that they utterly deny the resurrection of the flesh and of the body, and allow salvation only to the soul, and hold that it is futile for us to say that we shall rise after the pattern of our Lord, since our Lord also Himself rose again in a phantom body, and not only His resurrection, but His very nativity was *docetic* or imaginary; that is, more apparent than real. Origen himself is dissatisfied with both opinions. He says that he shuns both errors, that of the flesh, which our party maintain, and that of the phantoms, maintained by the heretics, because both sides go to the opposite extremes, some wishing to be the same that they have been, others denying altogether the resurrection of the body. "There are four elements," he says, "known to philosophers and physicians: earth, water, air, and fire, and out of these all things and human bodies are compacted. We find earth in flesh, air in the breath, water in the moisture of the body, fire in its heat. When, then, the soul, at the command of God, lets go this perishing and feeble body, little by little all things return to their parent substances: flesh is again absorbed into the earth, the breath is mingled with the air, the moisture returns to the depths, the heat escapes to the ether. And as if you throw into the sea a pint of milk and wine, and wish again to separate what is mixed together, although the wine and milk which you threw in is not lost, and yet it is impossible to keep separate what was poured out; so the substance of flesh and blood does not perish, indeed, so far as concerns the original matter, yet they cannot again become the former structure, nor can they be altogether the same that they were." Observe that when such things are said, the firmness of the flesh, the fluidity of the blood, the density of the sinews, the interlacing of the veins, and the hardness of the bones is denied.

26. "For another reason," he says, "we confess the resurrection of our bodies, those which have been laid in the grave and have turned to dust; Paul's body will be that of Paul, Peter's that of Peter, and each will have his own; for it is not right that souls should sin in one body and be tormented in another, nor is it worthy of the Righteous Judge that one body should shed its blood for Christ and another be crowned." Who, hearing this, would think he denied the resurrection of the flesh? "And," he says, "every seed has its own law of being inherent in it by the gift of God, the Creator, which law contains in embryonic form the future growth. The bulky tree, with its trunk,

boughs, fruit, leaves, is not seen in the seed, but nevertheless exists in the seed by implication or, according to the Greek expression, by the *spermatikos logos*. There is within the grain of corn a marrow, or vein, which, when it has been dissolved in the earth, attracts to itself the surrounding materials, and rises again in the shape of stalk, leaves, and ear; and thus, while it is one thing when it dies, it is another thing when it rises from the dead; for in the grain of wheat, roots, stalk, leaves, ears, trunk are as yet unseparated. In the same manner, in human bodies, according to the law of their being, certain original principles remain which ensure their resurrection, and a sort of marrow, that is a seed-plot of the dead, is fostered in the bosom of the earth. But when the day of judgment shall have come, and at the voice of the archangel, and the sound of the last trumpet, the earth shall totter, immediately the seeds will be instinct with life, and in a moment of time will cause the dead to burst into life; yet the flesh which they will reconstitute will not be the same flesh, nor will it be in the old forms. To give you the assurance that we speak the truth, let me quote the words of the Apostle: 'But someone says, How shall the dead rise? and with what body will they come? Thou fool, that which thou sows, thou sows not that body which shall be, but a bare grain, it may be of wheat, or the seed of a vine and a tree.' And as we have already made the grain of wheat, and to some extent the planting of trees, the subject of our reasoning, let us now take the grape-stone as an example. It is a mere granule, so small that you can scarcely hold it between your two fingers. Where are the roots? where the tortuous interlacing of roots, of trunk and off-shoots? Where the shade of the leaves, and the lovely clusters teeming with coming wine? What you have in your fingers is parched and scarcely discernible; nevertheless, in that dry granule, by the power of God and the secret law of propagation, the foaming new wine must have its origin. You will allow all this in the case of a tree; will you not admit such things to be possible in the case of a man? The plant which perishes is thus decked with beauty; why should we think that man, who abides, will receive back his former meanness? Do you demand that there should be flesh, bones, blood, limbs, so that you must have the barber to cut your hair, that your nose may run, your nails must be trimmed, your lower parts may gender filth or minister to lust? If you introduce these foolish and gross notions, you forget what is told us of the flesh, namely, that in it we cannot please God, and that it is an enemy; you forget, also, what is told us of the resurrection of the dead: 'It is sown in corruption, it shall rise in incorruption. It is sown in dishonor, it shall rise in glory. It is sown in weakness, it shall rise in power. It is sown a natural body, it shall rise a spiritual body.' Now we see with our eyes, hear with our ears, act with our hands, walk with our feet. But in that spiritual body we shall be all sight, all hearing, all action, all movement. The Lord shall transfigure the body of our humiliation and fashion it according to His own glorious body. In saying *transfigure* he affirms *identity* with the members which we now have. But a *different* body, spiritual and ethereal, is promised to us, which is neither tangible, nor perceptible to the eye, nor ponderable; and the change it undergoes will be suitable to the difference in its future abode. Otherwise, if there is to be the same flesh and if our bodies are to be the same, there will again be males and females, there will again be marriage; men will have the shaggy eyebrow and the flowing beard; women will have their smooth cheeks and narrow chests, and their bodies must adapt themselves to conception and parturition. Even tiny infants will rise again; old men will also rise; the former to be nursed, the latter to be supported by the staff. And, simple ones, be not deceived by the resurrection of our Lord, because He showed His side and His hands, stood on the shore, went for a walk with Cleophas, and said that He had flesh and bones. That body, because it was not born of the seed of man and the pleasure of the flesh, has its peculiar prerogatives. He ate and drank after His resurrection, and appeared in clothing, and allowed Himself to be touched, that He might make His doubting Apostles believe in His resurrection. But still He does not fail to manifest the nature of an aërial and spiritual body. For He enters when the doors are shut, and in the breaking of bread vanishes out of sight. Does it follow then that after our resurrection we shall eat and drink, and perform the offices of nature? If so, what becomes of the promise, 'The mortal must put on immortality.'"

27. Here we have the complete explanation of the fact that in your exposition of the faith, to deceive the ears of the ignorant, you nine times make mention of the body, and not even once of the flesh, and all the while men think that you confess the body of flesh, and that the flesh is identical with the body. If it is the same as the body, it means nothing different. I say this, for I know your answer: "I thought the body was the same as the flesh; I spoke with all simplicity." Why do you not rather call it flesh to signify the body, and speak indifferently at one time of the flesh, at another of the body, that the body may be shown to consist of flesh, and the flesh to be the body. But believe me, your silence is not the silence of

simplicity. For flesh is defined one way, the body another; all flesh is body, but not everybody is flesh. Flesh is properly what is comprised in blood, veins, bones, and sinews. Although the body is also called flesh, yet sometimes it is designated ethereal or aërial, because it is not subject to touch and sight; and yet it is frequently both visible and tangible. A wall is a body, but is not flesh; a stone is a body, but it is not said to be flesh. Wherefore the Apostle calls some bodies celestial, some terrestrial. A celestial body is that of the sun, moon, stars; a terrestrial body is that of fire, air, water, and the rest, which bodies being inanimate are known as consisting of material elements. You see we understand your subtleties, and publish abroad the mysteries which you utter in the bedchamber and amongst the perfect, mysteries which may not reach the ears of outsiders. You smile, and with hand uplifted and a snap of the fingers retort, "All the glory of the king's daughter is within." And, "The king led me into his bedchamber." It is clear why you spoke of the resurrection of the body and not of that of the flesh; of course it was that we in our ignorance might think that when body was spoken of flesh was meant; while yet the perfect would understand that, when body was spoken of, flesh was denied. Lastly, the Apostle, in his Epistle to the Colossians, wishing to show that the body of Christ was made of flesh, and was not spiritual, aërial, attenuated, said significantly, "And you, when you were some time alienated from Christ and enemies of His spirit in evil works, He has reconciled in the body of His flesh through death." And again in the same Epistle: "In whom ye were circumcised with a circumcision made without hands in the putting off of the body of the flesh." If by body is meant flesh only, and the word is not ambiguous, nor capable of diverse significations, it was quite superfluous to use both expressions—*bodily* and *of flesh*—as though body did not imply flesh.

28. In the symbol of our faith and hope, which was delivered by the Apostles, and is not written with paper and ink, but on fleshy tables of the heart, after the confession of the Trinity and the unity of the Church, the whole symbol of Christian dogma concludes with the resurrection of the flesh. You dwell so exclusively upon the subject of the body, harping upon it in your discourse, repeating first the body, and secondly the body, and again the body, and nine times over the body, that you do not even once name the flesh; whereas they always speak of the flesh, but say nothing of the body. I would have you know that we see through what you craftily add, and with wise precaution seek to conceal. For you make use of the same passages to prove the reality of the resurrection by means of which Origen denies it; you support questionable positions with doubtful arguments, and thus raise a storm which in a moment overthrows the settled fabric of faith. You quote the words, "It is sown an animal body: it shall rise a spiritual body." "For they shall neither marry, nor be given in marriage, but shall be as the angels in heaven." What other instances would you take if you were denying the resurrection? You intend to confess the resurrection of the flesh, you say, in a real and not an imaginary sense. After the remarks with which you smooth things over to the ears of the ignorant, to the effect that we rise again with the very bodies with which we died and were buried, why do you not go on and speak thus: "The Lord after His resurrection showed the prints of the nails in His hands, pointed to the wound of the spear in His side, and when the Apostles doubted because

they thought they saw a phantom, gave them reply, 'Handle Me and see, for a spirit hath not flesh and blood as ye see Me have'; and specially to Thomas, 'Put thy finger into My hands, and thy hand into My side, and be not faithless, but believing.' Similarly after the resurrection we shall have the same members which we now use, the same flesh and blood and bones, for it is not the nature of these which is condemned in Holy Scripture, but their works. Then again, it is written in Genesis: 'My Spirit shall not abide in those men, because they are flesh.' And the Apostle Paul, speaking of the corrupt doctrine and works of the Jews, says: 'I rested not in flesh and blood.' And to the Saints, who, of course, were in the flesh, he says: 'But ye are not in the flesh, but in the spirit, if the Spirit of God dwells in you.' For by denying that they were in the flesh who clearly were in the flesh, he condemned not the substance of the flesh but its sins."

29. The true confession of the resurrection declares that the flesh will be glorious, but without destroying its reality. And when the Apostle says, "This is corruptible and mortal," his words denote *this very body,* that is to say, the flesh which was then seen. But when he adds that it puts on incorruption and immortality, he does not say that that which is put on, that is the clothing, does away with the body which it adorns in glory, but that it makes that body glorious, which before lacked glory; so that the more worthless robe of mortality and weakness being laid aside, we may be clothed with the gold of immortality, and, so to speak, with the blessedness of strength as well as virtue; since we wish not to be stripped of the flesh, but to put on over it the vesture of glory, and desire to be clothed upon with our house, which is from heaven, that mortality may be swallowed up by life.

Certainly, no one is clothed upon who was not previously clothed. Accordingly, our Lord was not so transfigured on the mountain that He lost His hands and feet and other members, and suddenly began to roll along in a round shape like that of the sun or a ball; but the same members glowed with the brightness of the sun and blinded the eyes of the Apostles. Hence, also, His garments were changed, but so as to become white and glistening, not aërial, for I suppose you do not intend to maintain that His clothes also were spiritual. The Evangelist adds that His face shone like the sun; but when mention is made of His face, I reckon that His other members were beheld as well. Enoch was translated in the flesh; Elias was carried up to heaven in the flesh. They are not dead, they are inhabitants of Paradise, and even there retain the members with which they were rapt away and translated. What we aim at in fasting, they have through fellowship with God. They feed on heavenly bread, and are satisfied with every word of God, having Him as their food who is also their Lord. Listen to the Savior saying: "And my flesh rests in hope." And elsewhere, "His flesh saw not corruption." And again, "All flesh shall see the salvation of God." And must you be forever making the body a twofold thing? Rather quote the vision of Ezekiel, who joins bones to bones and brings them forth from their sepulchers, and then, making them to stand on their feet, binds them together with flesh and sinews, and clothes them with skin.

30. Listen to those words of thunder which fall from Job, the vanquisher of torments, who, as he scrapes away the filth of his decaying flesh with a potsherd, solaces his miseries with the hope and the reality of the resurrection: "Oh, that," he says, "my words were written!

Oh, that they were inscribed in a book with an iron pen, and on a sheet of lead, that they were graven in the rock forever! For I know that my Redeemer lives, and that in the last day I shall rise from the earth, and again be clothed with my skin, and in my flesh shall see God, Whom I shall see for myself, and my eyes shall behold, and not another. This my hope is laid up in my bosom." What can be clearer than this prophecy? No one since the days of Christ speaks so openly concerning the resurrection as he did before Christ. He wishes his words to last forever; and that they might never be obliterated by age, he would have them inscribed on a sheet of lead, and graven on the rock. He hopes for a resurrection; nay, rather he knew and saw that Christ, his Redeemer, was alive, and at the last day would rise again from the earth. The Lord had not yet died, and the athlete of the Church saw his Redeemer rising from the grave. When he says, "And I shall again be clothed with my skin, and in my flesh see God," I suppose he does not speak as if he loved his flesh, for it was decaying and putrifying before his eyes; but in the confidence of rising again, and through the consolation of the future, he makes light of his present misery. Again he says: "I shall be clothed with my skin." What mention do we find here of an ethereal body? What of an aërial body, like to breath and wind? Where there is skin and flesh, where there are bones and sinews, and blood and veins, there assuredly is fleshy tissue and distinction of sex. "And in my flesh," he says, "I shall see God." When all flesh shall see the salvation of God, and Jesus as God, then I, also, shall see the Redeemer and Savior, and my God. But I shall see him in that flesh which now tortures me, which now melts away for pain. Therefore, in my flesh shall I behold God, because by His own resurrection He has healed all my infirmities." Does it not seem to you that Job was then writing against Origen, and was holding a controversy similar to ours against the heretics, for the reality of the flesh in which he underwent tortures? For he could not bear to think that all his sufferings would be in vain; while the flesh he actually bore was tortured as flesh indeed, it would be some other and spiritual kind of flesh that would rise again. Wherefore he presses home and emphasizes the truth, and puts a stop to all that might lie hid in an artful confession, by speaking out plainly: "Whom I shall see for myself and my eyes shall behold and not another." If he is not to rise again in his own sex, if he is not to have the same members which were then lying on the dunghill, if he does not open the same eyes to see God with which he was then looking at the worms, where will Job then be? You do away with what constituted Job, and give me the hollow phrase, *Job shall rise again;* it is as if you were to order a ship to be restored after shipwreck, and then were to refuse each particular thing of which a ship is made.

31. I will speak freely, and although you screw your mouths, pull your hair, stamp your feet, and take up stones like the Jews, I will openly confess the faith of the Church. The reality of a resurrection without flesh and bones, without blood and members, is unintelligible. Where there are flesh and bones, where there are blood and members, there must of necessity be diversity of sex. Where there is diversity of sex, there John is John, Mary is Mary. You need not fear the marriage of those who, even before death, lived in their own sex without discharging the functions of sex. When it is said, "In that day they shall neither marry, nor be given in marriage," the words refer to those who can marry, and yet will not

do so. For no one says of the angels, "They shall not marry, nor be given in marriage." I never heard of a marriage being celebrated among the spiritual virtues in heaven: but where there is sex, there you have man and woman. Hence it is that, although you were reluctant, you were compelled by the truth to confess that, "A man must either be crowned in the body because he lived a pure and upright life, or be condemned in the body, because he was the slave of pleasure and iniquity." Substitute *flesh* for *body*, and you have not denied the existence of male and female. Who can have any glory from a life of chastity if we have no sex which would make unchastity possible? Whoever crowned a stone for continuing a virgin? Likeness to the angels is promised us, that is, the blessedness of their angelic existence without flesh and sex will be bestowed on us in our flesh and with our sex. I am simple enough so to believe, and so know how to confess that sex can exist without the functions of the senses; that it is thus that men rise, and that it is thus that they are made equal to the angels. Nor will the resurrection of the members all at once seem superfluous, because they are to have no office, since, while we are still in this life, we strive not to perform the works of the members. Moreover, likeness to the angels does not imply a changing of men into angels, but their growth in immortality and glory.

32. But as for the arguments drawn from boys, and infants, and old men, and meats, and excrements, which you employ against the Church, they are not your own; they flow from a heathen source. For the heathen mock us with the same. You say you are a Christian; lay aside the weapons of the heathen. It is for them to learn from you to confess the resurrection of the dead, not for you to learn

from them to deny it. Or if you belong to the enemy's camp, show yourself openly as an adversary, that you may share the wounds we inflict on the heathen. I will allow you your jest about the necessity of nursemaids to stop the infants from crying; of the decrepit old men, who, you fear, would be shriveled with winter's cold. I will admit also that the barbers have learnt their craft for nothing, for do we not know that the people of Israel for forty years experienced no growth of either nails or hair; and, still more, their clothes were not worn out, nor did their shoes wax old? Enoch and Elias, concerning whom we spoke a while ago, abide all this time in the same state in which they were carried away. They have teeth, belly, organs of generation, and yet have no need of meats, or wives. Why do you slander the power of God, who can from that *marrow* and *seedplot* of which you speak, not only produce flesh from flesh, but also make one body from another; and change water, that is worthless flesh, into the precious wine of an aërial body? the same power by which He created all things out of nothing can give back what has existed, because it is a much smaller thing to restore what has been, than to make what never was. Do you wonder that there is a resurrection from the condition of infancy and old age to that of mature manhood, seeing that a perfect man was made out of the slime of the earth without having gone through successive stages of growth? A rib is changed into a woman; and by the third mode of creating man, the poor elements of our birth which put us to the blush are changed into flesh, bound together by the members, run into veins, harden into bones. There is a fourth sort of human generation of which I can tell you. "The Holy Spirit shall come upon thee, and the power of the Highest shall overshadow thee.

Wherefore that holy thing which shall be born of thee shall be called the Son of God." Adam was created one way, Eve another, Abel another, the man Jesus Christ another. And yet, different as are all these beginnings, the nature of man remains one and the same.

33. If I wished to prove the resurrection of the flesh and of all the members, and to give the meaning of the several passages, many books would be required; but the matter in hand does not call for this. For I purposed not to reply to Origen in every detail, but to disclose the mysteries of your insincere "Apology." I have, however, tarried long in maintaining the opposite to your position, and am afraid that, in my eagerness to expose fraud, I may leave a stumbling-block in the way of the reader. I will, therefore, mass together the evidence, and glance at the proofs in passing, so that we may bring all the weight of Scripture to bear upon your poisonous argument. He who has not a wedding garment, and has not kept that command, "Let your garments be always white," is bound hand and foot that he may not recline at the banquet, or sit on a throne, or stand at the right hand of God; he is sent to Gehenna, where there is weeping and gnashing of teeth. "The hairs of your head are numbered." If the hairs, I suppose the teeth would be more easily numbered. But there is no object in numbering them if they are someday to perish. "The hour will come in which all who are in the tombs shall hear the voice of the Son of God, and shall come forth." They shall hear with ears, come forth with feet. This Lazarus had already done. They shall, moreover, come forth from the tombs; that is, they who had been laid in the tombs, the dead, shall come, and shall rise again from their graves. For the dew which God gives is healing to their bones. Then shall be fulfilled what God

says by the prophet, "Go, my people, into thy closets for a little while, until mine anger pass." The closets signify the graves, out of which that, of course, is brought forth which had been laid therein. And they shall come out of the graves like young mules free from the halter. Their heart shall rejoice, and their bones shall rise like the sun; all flesh shall come into the presence of the Lord, and He shall command the fishes of the sea; and they shall give up the bones which they had eaten; and He shall bring joint to joint, and bone to bone; and they who slept in the dust of the earth shall arise, some to life eternal, others to shame and everlasting confusion. Then shall the just see the punishment and tortures of the wicked, for their worm shall not die, and their fire shall not be extinguished, and they shall be beheld by all flesh. As many of us, therefore, as have this hope, as we have yielded our members servants to uncleanness, and to iniquity unto iniquity, so let us yield them servants to righteousness unto holiness, that we may rise from the dead and walk in newness of life. As also the life of the Lord Jesus is manifested in our mortal body, so also He who raised up Jesus Christ from the dead shall quicken our mortal bodies on account of His Spirit Who dwelleth in us. For it is right that as we have always borne about the putting to death of Christ in our body, so the life, also, of Jesus, should be manifested in our mortal body, that is, in our flesh, which is mortal according to nature, but eternal according to grace. Stephen also saw Jesus standing on the right hand of the Father, and the hand of Moses became snowy white, and was afterwards restored to its original color. There was still a hand, though the two states were different. The potter in Jeremiah, whose vessel, which he had made, was broken through the roughness of the stone, restored from the same lump and from the same clay that which had fallen to pieces; and, if we look at the word *resurrection* itself, it does not mean that one thing is destroyed, another raised up; and the addition of the word *dead,* points to our own flesh, for that which in man dies, that is also brought to life. The wounded man on the road to Jericho is taken to the inn with all his limbs complete, and the stripes of his offences are healed with immortality.

34. Even the graves were opened at our Lord's passion when the sun fled, the earth trembled, and many of the bodies of the saints arose, and were seen in the holy city. "Who is this," says Isaiah, "that cometh up from Edom, with shining raiment from Bozrah, so beautiful in his glistening robe?" Edom is by interpretation either *earthy* or *bloody;* Bosor either *flesh,* or *in tribulation.* In few words he shows the whole mystery of the resurrection, that is, both the reality of the flesh and the growth in glory. And the meaning is: Who is he that cometh up from the earth, cometh up from blood? According to the prophecy of Jacob, He has bound His foal to the vine, and has trodden the wine-press alone, and His garments are red with new wine from Bosor, that is from flesh, or from the tribulation of the world: for He Himself has conquered the world. And, therefore, His garments are red and shining, because He is beauteous in form more than the sons of men, and on account of the glory of His triumph they have been changed into a white robe; and then, in truth, as concerns Christ's flesh, were fulfilled the words, "Who is this that cometh up all in white, leaning upon her beloved?" And that which is written in the same book: "My beloved is white and ruddy." These men are his true followers who have not defiled their garments with women, for they have

continued virgins, who have made themselves eunuchs for the kingdom of heaven's sake. And so they shall be in white clothing. Then shall the saying of our Lord appear perfectly realized: "All that my Father has given me, I shall not lose aught thereof, but I will raise it up again at the last day;" the whole of His humanity, forsooth, which He had taken upon Him in its entirety at His birth. Then shall the sheep which was lost, and was wandering in the lower world, be carried whole on the Savior's shoulders, and the sheep which was sick with sin shall be supported by the mercy of the Judge. Then shall they see him who pierced Him, who shouted, "Crucify Him, crucify Him." Again and again shall they beat their breasts, they and their women, those women to whom our Lord said, as He carried His cross, "Ye daughters of Jerusalem, weep not for me but weep for yourselves, and for your children." Then shall be fulfilled the prophecy of the angels, who said to the stupefied Apostles, "Ye men of Galilee, why stand ye looking with astonishment into heaven? This Jesus who is taken from you into heaven, shall come in like manner as ye have seen Him go into heaven." But what are we to think of a man saying that our Lord ate with the Apostles for forty days after His resurrection in order that they might not think Him to be a phantom, and then asserting that it was a phantom which did this very thing, which ate and which was seen by many in the flesh. That which was seen is either real, or false. If it is real, it follows that He really ate, and really had members. But if it is false, how could He be willing to give false impressions in order to prove the truth of His resurrection? For no one proves what is true by means of what is false. You will say, are we then going to eat after our resurrection? I know not. Scripture does not tell us;

and yet, if the question be asked, I do not think we shall eat. For I have read that the kingdom of God is not meat and drink, while it promises such things as eye hath not seen, nor ear heard, nor have entered into the heart of man. Moses fasted forty days and forty nights. Human nature does not allow of this, but what is impossible with men is not impossible with God. Just as, in foretelling the future, it matters not whether a person announces what will take place after ten years or after a hundred, since the knowledge of futurity is all one; so he who can fast for forty days and yet live,—not, indeed, that he can of himself fast, but that he lives by the power of God,—will also be able to live forever without food and drink. Why did our Lord eat a honeycomb? To prove the resurrection: not to give your palate the pleasure of tasting honey. He asked for a fish broiled on the coals that He might confirm the doubting Apostles, who did not dare approach Him because they thought they saw not a body, but a spirit. The daughter of the ruler of the synagogue was raised to life and took food. Lazarus, who had been four days dead, rose again, and comes before us at a dinner; not because he was accustomed to eat in the lower world, but because a case which presented such difficulties challenged the believer's criticism. As He showed them real hands and a real side, so He really ate with His disciples; really walked with Cleophas; conversed with men with a real tongue; really reclined at supper; with real hands took bread, blessed and brake it, and was offering it to them. And as for His suddenly vanishing out of their sight, that is the power of God, not of a shadowy phantom. Besides, even before His resurrection, when they had led Him out from Nazareth that they might cast Him down headlong from the brow of the hill, He passed through the midst of them, that is, escaped out of their hands. Can we follow Marcion, and say that because, when He was held fast, He escaped in a manner contrary to nature, therefore His birth must have been only apparent? Has not the Lord a privilege which is conceded to magicians? It is related of Apollonius of Tyana that, when standing in court before Domitian, he all at once disappeared. Do not put the power of the Lord on a level with the tricks of magicians, so that He may appear to have been what He was not, and may be thought to have eaten without teeth, walked without feet, broken bread without hands, spoken without a tongue, and showed a side which had no ribs.

35. And how was it, you will say, that they did not recognize Him on the road if He had the same body which He had before? Let me recall what Scripture says: "Their eyes were holden, that they might not know Him." And again, "Their eyes were opened, and they knew Him." Was He one person when He was not known, and another when He was known? He was surely one and the same. Whether, therefore, they knew Him, or not, depended on their sight; it did not depend upon Him Who was seen; and yet it did depend on Him in this sense, that He held their eyes that they might not know Him. Lastly, that you may see that the mistake which held them was not to be attributed to the Lord's body, but to the fact that their eyes were closed, we are told: "Their eyes were opened, and they knew Him." Wherefore, also, Mary Magdalene so long as she did not recognize Jesus, and sought the living among the dead, thought He was the gardener. Afterwards she recognized Him and then she called Him Lord. After His resurrection Jesus was standing on the shore, His disciples were in the ship. When the others did not know

Him, the disciple whom Jesus loved said to Peter, "It is the Lord." For virginity is the first to recognize a virgin body. He was the same, yet was not seen alike by all as the same. And immediately it is added, "And no one durst ask Him, Who art Thou? for they knew that He was the Lord." No one durst, because they knew that He was God. They ate with Him at dinner because they saw He was a man and had flesh; not that He was one person as God, another as man: but, being one and the same Son of God, He was known as man, adored as God. I suppose I must now air my philosophy, and say that our senses are not to be relied on, and especially sight. A Carneades must be awaked from the dead to tell us the truth—that an oar seems broken in the water, porticos afar off look more magnificent, the angles of towers seem rounded in the distance, that the backs of pigeons change their colors with every movement. When Rhoda announced Peter, and told the Apostles, they did not believe that he had escaped, on account of the greatness of the danger, but suspected it was a phantom. Moreover, in passing through closed doors, He exhibited the same power as in vanishing out of sight. Lynceus, as fable relates, used to see through a wall. Could not the Lord enter when the doors were shut, unless He were a phantom? Eagles and vultures perceive dead bodies across the sea. Shall not the Savior see His Apostles without opening the door? Tell me, sharpest of disputants, which is greater, to hang the vast weight of the earth on nothing, and to balance it on the changing surface of the waves; or that God should pass through a closed door, and the creature yield to the Creator? You allow the greater; you object to the less. Peter walked upon the waters with his heavy and solid body. The soft water does not yield: his faith doubts a little, and immediately his body understands its own nature; that we may know that it was not his body that walked on the water, but his faith.

36. I pray you, who use such elaborate arguments against the resurrection, let us have some simple talk together. Do you believe that our Lord really rose again in the same body in which He died and was buried, or do you not believe it? If you believe it, why do you make propositions which lead to the denial of the resurrection? If you do not believe, you who thus try to deceive the minds of the ignorant, and parade the word resurrection, though you mean nothing by it, listen to me. Not long ago, a certain disciple of Marcion said: "Woe to him who rises again with this flesh and these bones!" Our heart at once with joy replied, "We are buried together, and we shall rise together with Christ through baptism." "Do you speak of the resurrection of the soul, or of the flesh?" I answered, "Not that of the soul alone, but that of the flesh, which, together with the soul, is born again in the laver. And how shall that perish which has been born again in Christ?" "Because it is written," said he, "'Flesh and blood shall not inherit the kingdom of God.'" "I intreat you to mind what is said—'Flesh and blood shall not inherit the kingdom of God.'" "It is said that they shall not rise again." "Not at all, but only 'they shall not inherit the kingdom.'" "How so?" "'Because' it follows, 'neither shall corruption inherit incorruption.' So long then as they remain mere flesh and blood, they shall not inherit the kingdom of God. But when the corruptible shall have put on incorruption, and the mortal shall have put on immortality, and the clay of the flesh shall have been made into a vessel, then that flesh which was formerly kept down by a heavy weight upon the earth, when once it

has received the wings of the spirit—wings which imply its change, not its destruction—shall fly with fresh glory to heaven; and then shall be fulfilled that which is written, 'Death is swallowed up in victory. Where, O death, is thy boasting? O death, where is thy sting?'"

37. Reversing the order, we have given our answer respecting the state of souls and the resurrection of the flesh; and, leaving out the opening portions of the letter, we have confined ourselves to the refutation of this most remarkable treatise. For we preferred to speak of the things of God rather than of our own wrongs. "If one man sin against another, they shall pray for him to the Lord. But if he sins against God, who shall pray for him?" In these days, on the contrary, we make it our first business to pursue with undying hate those who have injured us—to those who blaspheme God we indulgently hold out the hand. John writes to Bishop Theophilus an apology, of which the introduction runs thus: "You, indeed, as a man of God, adorned with apostolic grace, have upon you the care of all the Churches, especially of that which is at Jerusalem, though you yourself are distracted with countless anxieties for the Church of God, which is under you." This is barefaced adulation, and an attempt to concentrate authority in the hands of an individual. You, who ask for ecclesiastical rules, and make use of the canons of the Council of Nicæa, and claim authority over clerics who belong to another diocese and are actually living with their own bishop, answer my question, What has Palestine to do with the bishop of Alexandria? Unless I am deceived, it is decreed in those canons that Cæsarea is the metropolis of Palestine, and Antioch of the whole of the East. You ought therefore either to appeal to the bishop of Cæsarea, with whom you know that we have

St. Jerome

communion while we disdain to communicate with you, or, if judgment were to be sought at a distance, letters ought rather to be addressed to Antioch. But I know why you were unwilling to send to Cæsarea, or to Antioch. You knew what to flee from, what to avoid. You preferred to assail with your complaints ears that were preoccupied rather than pay due honor to your metropolitan. And I do not say this because I have anything to blame in the mission itself, except certain partialities which beget suspicion, but because you ought rather to clear yourself in the actual presence of your questioners. You begin with the words, "You have sent a most devoted servant of God, the presbyter Isidore, a man of influence no less from the dignity of his very gait and dress than from that of his divine understanding, to heal those whose souls are grievously sick; would that they had any sense of their illness! A man of God sends a man of God." No difference is made between a priest and a bishop; the same dignity belongs to the sender and the sent; this is lame enough; the ship, as the saying goes, is wrecked in harbor. That Isidore, whom you extol to the sky by your praises, lies under the same imputation of heresy at Alexandria as you at Jerusalem; wherefore he appears to have come to you not as an envoy, but as a confederate. Besides, the letters in his own handwriting, which, three months before the sending of the embassy, had been sent to us through an error in the address, were delivered to the presbyter Vincentius, and to this day they are in his keeping. In these letters the writer encourages the leader of his army to plant his foot firmly upon the rock of the faith, and not to be terrified by our Jeremiads. He promises, before we had any suspicion of his mission, that he will come to Jerusalem, and that on his arrival the ranks of his adversaries will be instantly crushed. And amongst the rest he uses these words: "As smoke vanishes in the air, and wax melts beside the fire, so shall they be scattered who are forever resisting the faith of the Church, and are now through simple men endeavoring to disturb that faith."

38. I ask you, my reader, what does a man, who writes these things before he comes, appear to you to be? An adversary, or an envoy? This is the man whom we may, indeed, call most pious, or most religious, and, to give the exact equivalent of the word, one devoted to the worship of God. This is the man of divine understanding, so influential, and of such dignity in gait and dress, that, like a spiritual Hippocrates, he is able by his presence to relieve the sickness of our souls, provided, however, we are willing to submit to his treatment. If such is his medicine, let him heal himself, since he is accustomed to heal others. To us, that divine understanding of his is folly for the sake of Christ. We willingly remain in the sickness of our simplicity, rather than, by using your eye-salve, learn an impious abuse of sight. Next come the words: "The excellent intentions of your Holiness compel our prayers to the Lord night and day; and, as though those intentions were already perfectly realized, we offer our prayers to Him in the holy places, that He may give you a perfect reward, and bestow on you the crown of life." You do right in giving thanks; for, if Isidore had not come you would not now have found in the whole of Palestine such a faithful associate. If he had not brought you the aid he had promised beforehand, you would find yourself surrounded by a crowd of rustics incapable of understanding your wisdom. This very apology of which we are now speaking was dictated in the presence and, to

a great extent, with the assistance of Isidore, so that the same person both composed the letter and carried it to its destination.

39. Your letter goes on to relate that "though he had come hither and had had three separate interviews with us, and had applied to the matter the healing language no less of your divine wisdom than of his own understanding, he found that he could be of no use to any one, nor could anyone be of use to him." The fact is that he who is said to have had "three separate interviews with us," so that in his coming he might maintain the mystic number, and who talked to us about the command issued by Bishop Theophilus, did not choose to deliver the letters sent to us by him. And when we said: If you are an envoy, produce your credentials; if you have no letters, how can you prove to us that you are an envoy? He replied that he had, indeed, letters to us but he had been adjured by the bishop of Jerusalem not to give them to us. You see here the true envoy consistent with his proper character; you see how impartial he shows himself to both sides, that he may make peace, and exclude the suspicion of favoring either party. At all events, he had come without a plaster, and had not the physician's instruments at his command, and therefore his medicine was of no avail. "Jerome and those associated with him," you continue, "both secretly, and in the presence of all, again and again and with the attestation of an oath, satisfied him that they never had any doubts of our orthodoxy, saying: We have now just the same feeling toward him, as regards matters of faith, that we had when we used to communicate with him." See what dogmatic agreement can do. Isidore, in order that he might make such a report as this, is taken into close fellowship, and is spoken of as a man of God, and a

most devout priest, a man of influence, of holy and venerable gait, and of divine understanding, the Hippocrates of the Christians. I, a poor wretch, hiding away in solitude, suddenly cut off by this mighty pontiff, have lost the name of priest. This "Jerome," then, with his ragged herd and shabby following, did he dare to give any answer to Isidore and his thunderbolts? Of course not; and doubtless for no other motive than fear that the envoy would never yield, and might overwhelm them by his presence and gigantic stature. "Not once, nor thrice, but again and again they swore that they knew the individual in question to be orthodox, and that they had never suspected him of heresy." What undisguised and shameless lying! A witness borne by a man to himself! Such witness as is not believed even in the mouth of a Cato, for in the mouth of two or three witnesses shall every word be established. Was there ever a word said, or a message sent to you, to the effect that, without being satisfied as to your orthodoxy, we would endure communion with you? When, through the instrumentality of the Count Archelaus, a most accomplished as well as a most Christian man, who tried to negotiate a peace between us, a place had been appointed where we were to meet, was not one of the first things postulated that the faith should form the basis of future agreement? He promised to come. Easter was approaching; a great multitude of monks had assembled; you were expected at the appointed place; what to do you did not know. All at once you sent word that someone or other was sick, you could not come that day. Is it a stage-player or a bishop who thus speaks? Suppose what you said was true, to suit the pleasure of one feeble woman who fears that she may have a headache, or may feel sick, or haste a pain in the stomach, while you are away, do you neglect the interests of the Church? Do you despise so many men, Christians and monks assembled together? We were unwilling to give occasion for breaking off the negotiation; we saw through the artifice of your procrastination, and sought to overcome the wrong you did us by patience. Archelaus wrote again, advising him that he was staying on for two days, in case he should be willing to come. But he was busy; his dear little woman had not ceased to vomit, he could not bestow a thought upon us until she should have escaped from her nausea. Well, after two months, at last the long-looked-for Isidore arrived, and what he heard from us was not as you pretend, a testimony in your behalf, but the reason why we demanded satisfaction. For when he raised the point, "Why, if he were a heretic, did you communicate with him?" he was answered by us all that we communicated without any suspicion of his heresy; but that, after he had been summoned by the Most Reverend Epiphanius, both by word and by letter, and had disdained to answer, documents were addressed to the monks by Epiphanius himself, to the effect that, unless he gave satisfaction respecting the faith, no one should rashly communicate with him. The letters are in our hands; there can be no doubt about the matter. This, then, was the reply made by the whole body of the brethren: not, as you maintain, that you were not a heretic, because at a former time you were not said to be one. For upon that showing, a man must be said not to be sick, because previous to his sickness he was in good health.

40. To proceed with the letter. "But when the ordination of Paulinianus, and the others associated with him, was brought forward, they began to feel that they themselves were in the wrong. For the sake of charity and

concord every concession was made to them, and the only point insisted on was that, though they had been ordained contrary to the rules, yet they should be subject to the authority of the Church of God, that they should not rend it, and set up an authority of their own. But they, not agreeing to this, began to raise questions concerning the faith; and thus they made it evident to all that if the presbyter Jerome and his friends were not accused, they had no charge to bring against us, but that they only betook themselves to doctrinal questions because, when charges of error and misconduct were brought against them, they were utterly unable to reply to us on matters of that sort, or to give any satisfactory explanation of their wrong-doing: not that they had any hope that we could be convicted of heresy, but they were striving to injure our reputation."

41. No one must blame the translator for this verbiage: the Greek is the same. Meanwhile I rejoice that whereas I thought I was beheaded I find my presbyterial head on my shoulders again. He says that we are utterly incapable of conviction, and he draws back from the encounter. If the cause of discord is not due to discussions about the faith, but springs from the ordination of Paulinianus, is it not the extreme of folly to give occasion to those who seek occasion by refusing to answer? Confess the faith; but do it so as to answer the question put to you, that it may be clear to all that the dispute is not one of faith, but of order. For so long as you are silent when questioned concerning the faith, your adversary has a right to say to you: "The matter is not one of order but of faith." If it is a question of order, you act foolishly in saying nothing when questioned concerning the faith. If it is one of faith, it is foolish of you to make a pretext of the

question of order. Moreover, when you say your aim was that they might be subject to the Church, that they might not rend it, nor set up an authority of their own; who they are of whom you speak I do not well understand. If you are speaking of me and the presbyter Vincentius, you have been asleep long enough, if you only wake up now, after thirteen years, to say these things. For the reason why I forsook Antioch and he Constantinople, both famous cities, was, not that we might praise your popular eloquence, but that, in the country and in solitude, we might weep over the sins of our youth, and draw down upon us the mercy of Christ. But if Paulinianus is the subject of your remarks, he, as you see, is subject to his bishop, and lives at Cyprus: he sometimes comes to visit us, not as one of your clergy, but as another's, his, namely, by whom he was ordained. But if he wished even to stay here, and to live a quiet, solitary life sharing our exile, what does he owe you except the respect which we owe to all bishops? Suppose that he had been ordained by you; he would only tell you the same that I, a poor wretch of a man, told Bishop Paulinus of blessed memory. "Did I ask to be ordained by you?" I said. "If in bestowing the rank of presbyter you do not strip us of the monastic state, you can bestow or withhold ordination as you think best. But if your intention in giving the name presbyter was to take from me that for which I forsook the world, I must still claim to be what I always was; you have suffered no loss by ordaining me."

42. "That they might not rend the Church," he says, "and set up an authority of their own." Who rends the Church? Do we, who as a complete household at Bethlehem communicate in the Church? Or is it you, who either being orthodox refuse through pride to speak

concerning the faith, or else being heterodox are the real render of the Church? Do we rend the Church, who, a few months ago, about the day of Pentecost, when the sun was darkened and all the world dreaded the immediate coming of the Judge, presented forty candidates of different ages and sexes to your presbyter for baptism? There were certainly five presbyters in the monastery who had the right to baptize; but they were unwilling to do anything to move you to anger, for fear you might make this a pretext for reticence concerning the faith. Is it not you, on the contrary, who rend the Church, you who commanded your presbyters at Bethlehem not to give baptism to our candidates at Easter, so that we sent them to Diospolis to the Confessor and Bishop Dionysius for baptism? Are we said to rend the Church, who, outside our cells, hold no position in the Church? Or do not you rather rend the Church, who issue an order to your clergy that if anyone says Paulinianus was consecrated presbyter by Epiphanius, he is to be forbidden to enter the Church. Ever since that time to this day we can only look from without on the cave of the Savior, and, while heretics enter, we stand afar off and sigh.

43. Are we schismatics? Is not he the schismatic who refuses a habitation to the living, a grave to the dead, and demands the exile of his brethren? Who was it that set at our throats, with special fury, that wild beast who constantly menaced the throats of the whole world? Who is it that permits the rain to beat upon the bones of the saints, and their harmless ashes, up to the present hour? These are the endearments with which the good shepherd invites us to reconciliation, and at the same time accuses us of setting up an authority of our own—us who are united in communion and charity with all the bishops, so

long, at least, as they are orthodox. Do you yourself constitute the Church, and is whosoever offends you shut out from Christ? If we defend our own authority—prove that we have a bishop in your diocese. The reason that we have not had communion with you is the question of faith; answer our questions, and it will become one of order.

44. "They," you go on, "also take advantage of other letters which they say Epiphanius wrote to them. But he, too shall give account for all his doings before the judgment seat of Christ, where great and small shall be judged without respect of persons. Still, how can they rely on his letter which he wrote only because we took him to task on the matter of the unlawful ordination of Paulinianus and his associates; as in the opening of that very letter he intimates?" What, I ask, is the meaning of this blindness? how is it that he is immersed, as the saying goes, in Cimmerian darkness? He says that we make a pretext, and that we have no letters from Epiphanius against him, and he immediately adds, "How can they rely on his letter, which he only wrote because he was taken to task by us, in the matter of the unlawful ordination of Paulinianus and his associates; as in the opening of that very letter he intimates?" We have no such letter! And what letter then is that, which in its opening sentence speaks of Paulinianus? There is something in the body of the letter of which you are afraid to make mention. Well! He was taken to task, you say, by you because of the age of Paulinianus. But you yourself ordain a man presbyter, and send him out as an envoy and a colleague. You have the boldness falsely to call Paulinianus a boy, and then to send out your own boy presbyter. You likewise take Theoseca, a deacon of the church of Thiria, and make him presbyter, and put

weapons into his hands against us, and make a misuse of his eloquence for our injury. You alone are at liberty to trample on the rights of the Church; whatever you do, is the standard of teaching; and you do not blush to challenge Epiphanius to stand with you before the judgment seat of Christ. The sequel of this passage is to the following effect: he throws it in the teeth of Epiphanius that he was the partner of his table and an inmate of his house, and declares that they never had any talk together concerning the views of Origen, and he supports what he says with the attestation of an oath, saying: "He never showed, as God is witness, that he had even the suspicion that our faith was not correct?" I am unwilling to answer and argue acrimoniously, lest I seem to be convicting a bishop of perjury. There are several letters of Epiphanius in our possession. One to John himself, others to the bishops of Palestine, and one of recent date to the pontiff of Rome; and in these he speaks of himself as impugning his views in the presence of many, and says that he was not thought worthy of a reply, "and the whole Monastery," he says, "is witness to what we in our insignificance assert."

Against the Pelagians:

Dialogue Between Atticus, a Catholic, and Critobulus, a Heretic.

The anti-Pelagian Dialogue is the last of Jerome's controversial works, having been written in the year 417, within three years of his death. It shows no lack of his old vigor, though perhaps something of the prolixity induced by old age. He looks at the subject more calmly than those of the previous treatises, mainly because it lay somewhat outside the track of his own thoughts. He was induced to interest himself in it by his increasing regard for Augustin, and by the coming of the young Spaniard, Orosius, in 414, from Augustin to sit at his feet. Pelagius also had come to Palestine, and, after an investigation of his tenets, at a small council at Jerusalem, in 415, presided over by Bishop John, and a second, at Diospolis in 416, had been admitted to communion. Jerome appears to have taken no part in these proceedings, and having been at peace with Bishop John for nearly twenty years, was no doubt unwilling to act against him. But he had come to look upon Pelagius as infected with the heretical "impiety," which he looked upon (i. 28) as far worse than moral evil; and connected him, as we see from his letter to Ctesiphon (CXXXIII.), with Origenism and Rufinus; and he brings his great knowledge of Scripture to bear upon the controversy. He quotes a work of Pelagius, though giving only the headings, and the numbers of the chapters, up to 100 (i. 26–32); and, though at times his conviction appears weak, and there are passages (i.5, ii. 6–30, iii. 1) which give occasion to the observation that he really, if unconsciously, inclined to the views of Pelagius, and that he is a "Synergist," not, like Augustin, a thorough predestinarian, the Dialogue, as a whole, is clear and forms a substantial contribution to our knowledge. Although its tone is less violent than that of his ascetic treatises, it appears to have stirred up the strongest animosity against him. The adherents of Pelagius attacked and burned the monasteries of Bethlehem, and Jerome himself only escaped by taking refuge in a tower. His sufferings, and the interference of Pope Innocentius in his behalf, may be seen by referring to Letters CXXXV.–CXXXVII., with the introductory notes prefixed to them.

The following is a summary of the argument: Atticus, the Augustinian, at once (c. 1) introduces the question: Do you affirm that, as Pelagius affirms, men can live without sin? Yes, says the Pelagian Critobulus, but I do not add, as is imputed to us, "without the grace of God." Indeed, the fact that we have a free will is from grace. Yes, replies Atticus, but what is this grace? Is it only our original nature, or is it needed in every act. In every act, is the reply (2); yet one would hardly say that we cannot mend a pen without grace (3), for, if so, where is our free will? But, says Atticus (5), the Scriptures speak of our need of God's aid in everything. In that case, says Critobulus, the promised reward must be given not to us but to God, Who works in us. Reverting then to the first point stated, Atticus asks, does the possibility of sinlessness extend to single acts, or to the whole life? Certainly to the whole as well as the part, is the answer. But we wish, or will to be sinless; why then are we not actually sinless? Because (8) we do not exert our will to the full. But (9) no one has ever lived without sin. Still, says the Pelagian, God commands us to be perfect, and he does not command impossibilities. Job, Zacharias, and Elizabeth are represented as perfectly righteous. No, it is answered (12), faults are attributed to each of them. John says, "He that is born of God sinned not" (13); yet, "If we say we have no sin we deceive ourselves." The Apostles, though told to be perfect (14) were not perfect: and St. Paul says (14a), "I count not myself to have apprehended." Men are called just and perfect only in comparison of others (16), or because of general subjection to the will of God (18), or according to their special characteristics (19), as we may speak of a bishop as excellent in his office, though he may not fulfil the ideal of the pastoral epistles (22).

The discussion now turns to the words of Pelagius' book. "All are ruled by their own will" (27). No; for Christ says, "I came not to do My own will." "The wicked shall not be spared in the judgment." But we must distinguish between the impious or heretics who will be destroyed (28) and Christian sinners who will be forgiven. Some of his sayings contradict each other or are trifling (29, 30). "The kingdom of heaven is promised in the Old Testament." Yes, but more fully in the New. Returning to the first thesis, "That a man can be without sin if he wills it," the Pelagian says, If things, like desires which arise spontaneously and have no issue, are reckoned blamable, we charge the sin on our Maker; to which it is only answered that, though we cannot understand God's ways, we must not arraign His justice. In the rest of the book, Atticus alone speaks, going through the Old Testament, and showing that each of the saints falls into some sin, which, though done in ignorance or half-consciousness, yet brings condemnation with it.

Prologue.

1. After writing the letter to Ctesiphon, in which I replied to the questions propounded, I received frequent expostulations from the brethren, who wanted to know why I any longer delayed the promised work in which I undertook to answer all the subtleties of the preachers of

Impassibility. For everyone knows what was the contention of the Stoics and Peripatetics, that is, the old Academy, some of them asserted that the πάθη, which we may call *emotions,* such as sorrow, joy, hope, fear, can be thoroughly eradicated from the minds of men; others that their power can be broken, that they can be governed and restrained, as unmanageable horses are held in check by peculiar kinds of bits. Their views have been explained by Tully in the "Tusculan Disputations," and Origen in his "Stromata" endeavors to blend them with ecclesiastical truth. I pass over Manichæus, Priscillianus, Evagrius of Ibora, Jovinianus, and the heretics found throughout almost the whole of Syria, who, by a perversion of the import of their name, are commonly called *Massalians,* in Greek, *Euchites,* all of whom hold that it is possible for human virtue and human knowledge to attain perfection, and arrive, I will not say merely at a likeness to, but an equality with God; and who go the length of asserting that, when once they have reached the height of perfection, even sins of thought and ignorance are impossible for them. And although in my former letter addressed to Ctesiphon and aimed at their errors, so far as time permitted, I touched upon a few points in the book which I am now endeavoring to hammer out, I shall adhere to the method of Socrates. What can be said on both sides shall be stated; and the truth will thus be clear when both sides express their opinions. Origen is peculiar in maintaining on the one hand that it is impossible for human nature to pass through life without sin, and on the other, that it is possible for a man, when he turns to better things, to become so strong that he sins no more.

2. I shall add a few words in answer to those who say that I am writing this work because I am inflamed

with envy. I have never spared heretics, and I have done my best to make the enemies of the Church my own. Helvidius wrote against the perpetual virginity of Saint Mary. Was it envy that led me to answer him, whom I had never seen in the flesh? Jovinianus, whose heresy is now being fanned into flame, and who disturbed the faith of Rome in my absence, was so devoid of gifts of utterance, and had such a pestilent style that he was a fitter object for pity than for envy. So far as I could, I answered him also. Rufinus did all in his power to circulate the blasphemies of Origen and the treatise "On First Principles" (Περὶ Ἀρχῶν), not in one city, but throughout the whole world. He even published the first book of Eusebius' "Apology for Origen" under the name of Pamphilus the martyr, and, as though Origen had not said enough, vomited forth a fresh volume on his behalf. Am I to be accused of envy because I answered him? and was his eloquence such a rushing torrent as to deter me through fear from writing or dictating anything in reply? Palladius, no better than a villainous slave, tried to impart energy to the same heresy, and to excite against me fresh prejudice on account of my translation of the Hebrew. Was I envious of such distinguished ability and nobility? Even now the mystery of iniquity worketh, and everyone chatters about his views: yet I, it seems, am the only one who is filled with envy at the glory of all the rest; I am so poor a creature that I envy even those who do not deserve envy. And so, to prove to all that I do not hate the men but their errors, and that I do not wish to vilify any one, but rather lament the misfortune of men who are deceived by knowledge falsely so-called, I have made use of the names of Atticus and Critobulus in order to express our own views and those of our opponents. The truth is that all we who hold the Catholic faith, wish and long that, while the heresy is condemned, the men may be reformed. At all events, if they will continue in error, the blame does not attach to us who have written, but to them, since they have preferred a lie to the truth. And one short answer to our calumniators, whose curses fall upon their own heads, is this, that the Manichean doctrine condemns the nature of man, destroys free will, and does away with the help of God. And again, that it is manifest madness for man to speak of himself as being what God alone is. Let us so walk along the royal road that we turn neither to the right hand nor to the left; and let us always believe that the eagerness of our wills is governed by the help of God. Should anyone cry out that he is slandered and boast that he thinks with us; he will then show that he assents to the true faith, when he openly and sincerely condemns the opposite views. Otherwise his case will be that described by the prophet: "And yet for all this her treacherous sister Judah hath not returned unto me with her whole heart, but feignedly." It is a smaller sin to follow evil which you think is good, than not to venture to defend what you know for certain is good. If we cannot endure threats, injustice, poverty, how shall we overcome the flames of Babylon? Let us not lose by hollow peace what we have preserved by war. I should be sorry to allow my fears to teach me faithlessness, when Christ has put the true faith in the power of my choice.

Book I.

1. Atticus. I hear, Critobulus, that you have written that man can be without sin, if he chooses; and that the commandments of God are easy. Tell me, is it true?

Critobulus. It is true, Atticus; but our rivals do not take the words in the sense I attached to them.

A. Are they then so ambiguous as to give rise to a difference as to their meaning? I do not ask for an answer to two questions at once. You laid down two propositions; the one, that man can be without sin, if he chooses: the other, that God's commandments are easy. Although, therefore, they were uttered together, let them be discussed separately, so that, while our faith appears to be one, no strife may arise through our misunderstanding each other.

C. I said, Atticus, that man can be without sin, if he chooses; not, as some maliciously make us say, without the grace of God (the very thought is impiety), but simply that he can, if he chooses; the aid of the grace of God being presupposed.

A. Is God, then, the author of your evil works?

C. By no means. But if there is any good in me, it is brought to perfection through His impulse and assistance.

A. My question does not refer to natural constitution, but to action. For who doubts that God is the Creator of all things? I wish you would tell me this: the good you do, is it yours or God's?

C. It is mine and God's: I work and He assists.

A. How is it then that everybody thinks you do away with the grace of God, and maintain that all our actions proceed from our own will?

C. I am surprised, Atticus, at your asking me for the why and wherefore of other people's mistakes, and wanting to know what I did not write, when what I did write is perfectly clear. I said that man can be without sin, if he chooses. Did I add, *without the grace of God?*

A. No; but the fact that you added nothing implies your denial of the need of grace.

C. Nay, rather, the fact that I have not denied grace should be regarded as tantamount to an assertion of it. It is unjust to suppose we deny whatever we do not assert.

A. You admit then that man can be sinless, if he chooses, but with the grace of God.

C. I not only admit it, but freely proclaim it.

A. So then he who does away with the grace of God is in error.

C. Just so. Or rather, he ought to be thought impious, seeing that all things are governed by the pleasure of God, and that we owe our existence and the faculty of individual choice and desire to the goodness of God, the Creator. For that we have free will, and according to our own choice incline to good or evil, is part of His grace who made us what we are, in His own image and likeness.

2. A. No one doubts, Critobulus, that all things depend on the judgment of Him Who is Creator of all, and that whatever we have ought to be attributed to His goodness. But I should like to know respecting this faculty, which you attribute to the grace of God, whether you reckon it as part of the gift bestowed in our creation, or suppose it energetic in our separate actions, so that we avail ourselves of its assistance continually; or is it the case that, having been once for all created and endowed with free will, we do what we choose by our own choice or strength? For I know that very many of your party refer all things to the grace of God in such a sense that they understand the power of the will to be a gift not of a particular, but of a general character, that is to say, one

which is bestowed not at each separate moment, but once for all at creation.

C. It is not as you affirm; but I maintain both positions, that it is by the grace of God we were created such as we are, and also that in our several actions we are supported by His aid.

A. We are agreed, then, that in good works, besides our own power of choice, we lean on the help of God; in evil works we are prompted by the devil.

C. Quite so; there is no difference of opinion on that point.

A. They are wrong, then, who strip us of the help of God in our separate actions. The Psalmist sings: "Except the Lord build the house, they labor in vain who build it. Except the Lord keep the city, the watchman wakes but in vain;" and there are similar passages. But these men endeavor by perverse, or rather ridiculous interpretations, to twist his words to a different meaning.

3. C. Am I bound to contradict others when you have my own answer?

A. Your answer to what effect? That they are right, or wrong?

C. What necessity compels me to set my opinion against other men's?

A. You are bound by the rules of discussion, and by respect for truth. Do you not know that every assertion either affirms, or denies, and that what is affirmed or denied ought to be reckoned among good or bad things? You must, therefore, admit, and no thanks to you, that the statement to which my question relates is either a good thing or a bad.

C. If in particular actions we must have the help of God, does it follow that we are unable to make a pen, or mend it when it is made? Can we not fashion the letters, be silent or speak, sit, stand, walk or run, eat or fast, weep or laugh, and so on, without God's assistance?

A. From my point of view it is clearly impossible.

C. How then have we free will, and how can we guard the grace of God towards us, if we cannot do even these things without God?

4. A. The bestowal of the grace of free will is not such as to do away with the support of God in particular actions.

C. The help of God is not made of no account; inasmuch as creatures are preserved through the grace of free will once for all given to them. For if without God, and except He assist me in every action, I can do nothing. He can neither with justice crown me for my good deeds, nor punish me for my evil ones, but in each case He will either receive His own or will condemn the assistants He gave.

A. Tell me, then, plainly, why you do away with the grace of God. For whatever you destroy in the parts you must of necessity deny in the whole.

C. I do not deny grace when I assert that I was so created by God, that by the grace of God it was put within the power of my choice either to do a thing or not to do it.

A. So God falls asleep over our good actions, when once the faculty of free will has been given; and we need not pray to Him to assist us in our separate actions, since it depends upon our own choice and will either to do a thing if we choose, or not to do it if we do not choose.

5. C. As in the case of other creatures, the conditions of elicit creation are observed; so, when once the power of free will was granted, everything was left to our own choice.

A. It follows, as I said, that I ought not to beg the assistance of God in the details of conduct, because I consider it was given once for all.

C. If He co-operates with me in everything the result is no longer mine, but His Who assists, or rather works in and with me; and all the more because I can do nothing without Him.

A. Have you not read, pray, "that it is not of him that wills, nor of him that runs, but of God that showed mercy!" From this we understand that to will and to run is ours, but the carrying into effect our willing and running pertains to the mercy of God, and is so effected that on the one hand in willing and running free will is preserved; and on the other, in consummating our willing and running, everything is left to the power of God. Of course, I ought now to adduce the frequent testimony of Scripture to show that in the details of conduct the saints intreat the help of God, and in their several actions desire to have Him for their helper and protector. Read through the Psalter, and all the utterances of the saints, and you will find their actions never unaccompanied by prayer to God. And this is a clear proof that you either deny the grace which you banish from the parts of life; or if you concede its presence in the parts, a concession plainly much against your will, you must have come over to the views of us who preserve free will for man, but so limit it that we do not deny the assistance of God in each action.

6. C. That is a sophistical conclusion and a mere display of logical skill. No one can strip me of the power of free will; otherwise, if God were really my helper in what I do, the reward would not be due to me, but to Him who wrought in me.

A. Make the most of your free will; arm your tongue against God, and therein prove yourself free, if you will, to blaspheme. But to go a step farther, there is no doubt as to your sentiments, and the delusions of your profession have become as clear as day. Now, let us turn back to the starting-point of our discussion. You said just now that, granted God's assistance, man may be sinless if he chooses. Tell me, please, for how long? Forever, or only for a short time?

C. Your question is unnecessary. If I say for a short time, forever will none the less be implied. For whatever you allow for a short time, you will admit may last forever.

A. I do not quite understand your meaning.

C. Are you so senseless that you do not recognize plain facts?

7. A. I am not ashamed of my ignorance. And both sides ought to be well agreed on a definition of the subject of dispute.

C. I maintain this: he who can keep himself from sin one day, may do so another day: if he can on two, he may on three; if on three, on thirty: and so on for three hundred, or three thousand, or as long as ever he chooses to do so.

A. Say then at once that a man may be without sin forever, if he chooses. Can we do anything we like?

C. Certainly not, for I cannot do all I should like; but all I say is this, that a man can be without sin, if he chooses.

A. Be so good as to tell me this: do you think I am a man or a beast?

C. If I had any doubt as to whether you were a man, or a beast, I should confess myself to be the latter.

A. If then, as you say, I am a man, how is it that when I wish and earnestly desire not to sin, I do transgress?

C. Because your choice is imperfect. If you really wished not to sin, you really would not.

A. Well then, you who accuse me of not having a real desire, are you free from sin because you have a real desire?

C. As though I were talking of myself whom I admit to be a sinner, and not of the few exceptional ones, if any, who have resolved not to sin.

8. A. Still, I who question, and you who answer, both consider ourselves sinners.

C. But we are capable of not being so, if we please.

A. I said I did not wish to sin, and no doubt your feeling is the same. How is it then that what we both wish we can neither do?

C. Because we do not wish perfectly.

A. Show me any of our ancestors who had a perfect will and the power in perfection.

C. That is not easy. And when I say that a man may be without sin if he chooses, I do not contend that there ever have been such; I only maintain the abstract possibility—if he chooses. For *possibility of being* is one thing, and is expressed in Greek by τῇ δυνάμει (possibility); *being* is another, the equivalent for which is τῇ ἐνεργείᾳ 139· (actuality). I can be a physician; but meanwhile I am not. I can be an artisan; but I have not yet learnt a trade. So, whatever I am able to be, though I am not that yet, I shall be if I choose.

9. A. Art is one thing, that which is above art is another. Medical skill, craftsmanship, and so on, are

found in many persons; but to be always without sin is a characteristic of the Divine power only. Therefore, either give me an instance of those who were forever without sin; or, if you cannot find one, confess your impotence, lay aside bombast, and do not mock the ears of fools with this *being* and *possibility of being* of yours. For who will grant that a man can do what no man was ever able to do? You have not learnt even the rudiments of logic. For if a man is able, he is no longer unable. Either grant that someone was able to do what you maintain was possible to be done; or if no one has had this power, you must, though against your will, be held to this position, that no one is able to effect what yet you profess to be possible. That was the point at issue between the powerful logicians, Diodorus and Chrysippus, in their discussion of possibility. Diodorus says that alone can possibly happen which is either true or will be true. And whatever will be, that, he says, must of necessity happen. But whatever will not be, that cannot possibly happen. Chrysippus, however, says that things which will not be might happen; for instance, this pearl might be broken, even though it never will. They, therefore, who say that a man can be without sin if he chooses, will not be able to prove the truth of the assertion, unless they show that it will come to pass. But whereas the whole future is uncertain, and especially such things as have never occurred, it is clear that they say something will be which will not be. And Ecclesiastes supports this decision: "All that shall be, has already been in former ages."

10. C. Pray answer this question: has God given possible or impossible commands?

A. I see your drift. But I must discuss it later on, that we may not, by confusing different questions, leave our audience in a fog. I admit that God has given possible commands, for otherwise He would Himself be the author of injustice, were He to demand the doing of what cannot possibly be done. Reserving this until later, finish your argument that a man can be without sin, if he chooses. You will either give instances of such ability, or, if no one has had the power, you will clearly confess that a man cannot avoid sin always.

C. Since you press me to give what I am not bound to give, consider what our Lord says, "That it is easier for a camel to go through a needle's eye, than for a rich man to enter into the kingdom of heaven." And yet he said a thing might possibly happen, which never has happened. For no camel has ever gone through a needle's eye.

A. I am surprised at a prudent man submitting evidence which goes against himself. For the passage in question does not speak of a possibility, but one impossibility is compared with another. As a camel cannot go through a needle's eye, so neither will a rich man enter the kingdom of heaven. Or, if you should be able to show that a rich man does enter the kingdom of heaven, it follows, also, that a camel goes through a needle's eye. You must not instance Abraham and other rich men, about whom we read in the Old Testament, who, although they were rich, entered the kingdom of heaven; for, by spending their riches on good works, they ceased to be rich; nay, rather, inasmuch as they were rich, not for themselves, but for others, they ought to be called God's stewards rather than rich men. But we must seek evangelical perfection, according to which there is the command, "If thou wilt be perfect, go and sell all that thou hast, and give to the poor, and come, follow Me."

11. C. You are caught unawares in your own snare.

A. How so?

C. You quote our Lord's utterance to the effect that a man can be perfect. For when He says, "If thou wilt be perfect, sell all that thou hast, and give to the poor, and come, follow Me," He shows that a man, if he chooses, and if he does what is commanded, can be perfect?

A. You have given me such a terrible blow that I am almost dazed. But yet the very words you quote, "If thou wilt be perfect," were spoken to one who could not, or rather would not, and, therefore, could not; show me now, as you promised, someone who would and could.

C. Why am I compelled to produce instances of perfection, when it is clear from what the Savior said to one, and through one to all, "If thou wilt be perfect" that it is possible for men to be perfect?

A. That is a mere shuffle. You still stick fast in the mire. For, either, if a thing is possible, it has occurred at some time or other; or, if it never has happened, grant that it is impossible.

12. C. Why do I any longer delay? You must be vanquished by the authority or Scripture. To pass over other passages, you must be silenced by the two in which we read the praises of Job, and of Zacharias and Elizabeth. For, unless I am deceived, it is thus written in the book of Job: "There was a man in the land of Uz, whose name was Job; and that man was perfect and upright, a true worshipper of God, and one who kept himself from every evil thing." And again: "Who is he that reproved one that is righteous and free from sin, and Speakes words without knowledge?" Also, in the Gospel according to Luke, we read: "There was in the days of

Herod, king of Judea, a certain priest named Zacharias, of the course of Abijah: and he had a wife of the daughters of Aaron, and her name was Elizabeth. And they were both righteous before God, walking in all the commandments and ordinances of the Lord blameless." If a true worshipper of God is also without spot and without offence, and if those who walked in all the ordinances of the Lord are righteous before God, I suppose they are free from sin, and lack nothing that pertains to righteousness.

A. You have cited passages which have been detached not only from the rest of Scripture, but from the books in which they occur. For even Job, after he was stricken with the plague, is convicted of having spoken many things against the ruling of God, and to have summoned Him to the bar: "Would that a man stood with God in the judgment as a son of man stands with his fellow." And again: "Oh that I had one to hear me! that the Almighty might hear my desire, and that the judge would himself write a book!" And again: "Though I be righteous, mine own mouth shall condemn me: though I be perfect, it shall prove me perverse. If I wash myself with snow-water, and make my hands never so clean, Thou hast dyed me again and again with filth. Mine own clothes have abhorred me." And of Zacharias it is written, that when the angel promised the birth of a son, he said: "Whereby shall I know this? for I am an old man, and my wife well stricken in years." For which answer he was at once condemned to silence: "Thou shalt be silent, and not able to speak, until the day that these things shall come to pass, because thou believe not my words, which shall be fulfilled in their season." From this it is clear that men are called righteous, and said to be without fault; but that, if negligence comes over them, they may fall; and that a man always occupies a middle place, so that he may slip from the height of virtue into vice, or may rise from vice to virtue; and that he is never safe, but must dread shipwreck even in fair weather; and, therefore, that a man cannot be without sin. Solomon says, "There is not a righteous man upon earth that doeth good and sinned not"; and likewise in the book of Kings: "There is no man that sinned not." So, also, the blessed David says: "Who can understand his errors? Cleanse Thou me from hidden faults, and keep back Thy servant from presumptuous sins." And again: "Enter not into judgment with Thy servant, for in Thy sight shall no man living be justified." Holy Scripture is full of passages to the same effect.

13. C. But what answer will you give to the famous declaration of John the Evangelist: "We know that whosoever is begotten of God sinned not; but the begetting of God kept him, and the evil one touches him not. We know that we are of God, and the whole world lieth in the evil one?"

A. I will requite like with like, and will show that, according to you, the little epistle of the Evangelist contradicts itself. For, if whosoever is begotten of God sinned not because His seed abides in him, and he cannot sin, because he is born of God, how is it that the writer says in the same place: "If we say that we have no sin, we deceive ourselves, and the truth is not in us?" You cannot explain. You hesitate and are confused. Listen to the same Evangelist telling us that "If we confess our sins, he is faithful and just to forgive us our sins, and to cleanse us from all unrighteousness." We are then righteous when we confess that we are sinners, and our righteousness depends not upon our own merits, but on the mercy of God, as the Holy Scripture says, "The righteous man accused himself when he begins to speak," and elsewhere, "Tell thy sins that thou mayest be justified." "God hath shut up all under sin, that He may have mercy upon all." And the highest righteousness of man is this—whatever virtue he may be able to acquire, not to think it his own, but the gift of God. He then who is born of God does not sin, so long as the seed of God remains in him, and he cannot sin, because he is born of God. But seeing that, while the householder slept, an enemy sowed tares, and that when we know not, a Sower by night scatters in the Lord's field darnel and wild oats among the good corn, this parable of the householder in the Gospel should excite our fears. He cleanses his floor, and gathers the wheat into his garner, but leaves the chaff to be scattered by the winds, or burned by the fire. And so we read in Jeremiah, "What is the chaff to the wheat? saith the Lord." The chaff, moreover, is separated from the wheat at the end of the world, a proof that, while we are in the mortal body, chaff is mixed with the wheat. But if you object, and ask why did the Apostle say, "and he cannot sin, because he is born of God," I reply by asking you what becomes of the reward of his choice? For if a man does not sin because he cannot sin, free will is destroyed, and goodness cannot possibly be due to his efforts, but must be part of a nature unreceptive of evil.

14. C. The task I set you just now was an easy one by way of practice for something more difficult. What have you to say to my next argument? Clever as you are, all your skill will not avail to overthrow it. I shall first quote from the Old Testament, then from the New. Moses is the chief figure in the Old Testament, our Lord and Savior in the New. Moses says to the people, "Be perfect in the sight of the Lord your God." And the Savior bids

the Apostles "Be perfect as your heavenly Father is perfect." Now it was either possible for the hearers to do what Moses and the Lord commanded, or, if it be impossible, the fault does not lie with them who cannot obey, but with Him who gave impossible commands.

A. This passage to the ignorant, and to those who are unaccustomed to meditate on Holy Scripture, and who neither know nor use it, does appear at first sight to favor your opinion. But when you look into it, the difficulty soon disappears. And when you compare passages of Scripture with others, that the Holy Spirit may not seem to contradict Himself with changing place and time, according to what is written, "Deep calleth unto deep at the noise of thy water spouts," the truth will show itself, that is, that Christ did give a possible command when He said: "Be ye perfect as your heavenly Father is perfect," and yet that the Apostles were not perfect.

C. I am not talking of what the Apostles did, but of what Christ commanded. And the fault does not lie with the giver of the command, but with the hearers of it, because we cannot admit the justice of him who commands without conceding the possibility of doing what is commanded.

A. Good! Don't tell me then that a man can be without sin if he chooses, but that a man can be what the Apostles were not.

C. Do you think me fool enough to dare say such a thing?

A. Although you do not say it in so many words, however reluctant you may be to admit the fact, it follows by natural sequence from your proposition. For if a man can be without sin, and it is clear the Apostles were not without sin, a man can be higher than the Apostles: to say nothing of patriarchs and prophets whose righteousness under the law was not perfect, as the Apostle says, "For all have sinned, and fall short of the glory of God: being justified freely by His grace through the redemption that is in Christ Jesus: whom God set forth to be a propitiator."

14a. C. This way of arguing is intricate and brings the simplicity which becomes the Church into the tangled thickets of philosophy. What has Paul to do with Aristotle? or Peter with Plato? For as the latter was the prince of philosophers, so was the former chief of the Apostles: on him the Lord's Church was firmly founded, and neither rushing flood nor storm can shake it.

A. Now you are rhetorical, and while you taunt me with philosophy, you yourself cross over to the camp of the orators. But listen to what your same favorite orator says: "Let us have no more commonplaces: we get them at home."

C. There is no eloquence in this, no bombast like that of the orators, who might be defined as persons whose object is to persuade, and who frame their language accordingly. We are seeking unadulterated truth, and use unsophisticated language. Either the Lord did not give impossible commands, so that they are to blame who did not do what was possible; or, if what is commanded cannot be done, then not they who do not things impossible are convicted of unrighteousness, but He Who commanded things impossible, and that is an impious statement.

A. I see you are much more disturbed than is your wont; so I will not ply you with arguments. But let me briefly ask what you think of the well-known passage of the Apostle when he wrote to the Philippians: "Not that I have already obtained, or am already made perfect: but I press on, if so be that I may apprehend that for which also I was apprehended by Christ Jesus. Brethren, I count not myself to have yet apprehended: but one thing I do; forgetting the things which are behind, and stretching forward to the things which are before, I press on towards the goal unto the prize of the high calling of God in Christ Jesus. Let us, therefore, as many as be perfect, be thus minded: and if in anything ye are otherwise minded, even this shall God reveal unto you," and so on; no doubt you know the rest, which, in my desire to be brief, I omit. He says that he had not yet apprehended, and was by no means perfect; but, like an archer, aimed his arrows at the mark set up (more expressively called σκοπός in Greek), lest the shaft, turning to one side or the other, might show the unskillfulness of the archer. He further declares that he always forgot the past, and ever stretched forward to the things in front, thus teaching that no heed should be paid to the past, but the future earnestly desired; so that what to-day he thought perfect, while he was stretching forward to better things and things in front, to-morrow proves to have been imperfect. And thus at every step, never standing still, but always running, he shows that to be imperfect which we men thought perfect, and teaches that our only perfection and true righteousness is that which is measured by the excellence of God. "I press on towards the goal," he says, "unto the prize of the high calling of God in Christ Jesus." Oh, blessed Apostle Paul, pardon me, a poor creature who confesses my faults, if I venture to ask a question. You say that you had not yet obtained, nor yet apprehended, nor were yet perfect, and that you always forgot the things behind, and stretched forward to the things in front, if by any means you might have part in the resurrection of the dead, and win the prize of your high calling. How, then, is it that you immediately add, "As many therefore as are perfect are thus minded"? (or, let us be thus minded, for the copies vary). And what mind is it that we have, or are to have? that we are perfect? that we have apprehended that which we have not apprehended, received what we have not received, are perfect who are not yet perfect? What mind then have we, or rather what mind ought we to have who are not perfect? To confess that we are imperfect, and have not yet apprehended, nor yet obtained, this is true wisdom in man: know thyself to be imperfect; and, if I may so speak, the perfection of all who are righteous, so long as they are in the flesh, is imperfect. Hence we read in Proverbs: "To understand true righteousness." For if there were not also a false righteousness, the righteousness of God would never be called true. The Apostle continues: "and if ye are otherwise minded, God will also reveal that to you." This sounds strange to my ears. He who but just now said, "Not that I have already obtained, or am already perfect"; the chosen vessel, who was so confident of Christ's dwelling in him that he dared to say "Do ye seek a proof of Christ that Speakes in me? "and yet plainly confessed that he was not perfect; he now gives to the multitude what he denied to himself in particular, he unites himself with the rest and says, "As many of us as are perfect, let us be thus minded." But why he said this, he explains presently. Let us, he means, who wish to be perfect according to the poor measure of human frailty, think this, that we have not yet obtained, nor yet apprehended, nor are yet perfect, and inasmuch as we are not yet perfect, and, perhaps, think otherwise than true and perfect perfection requires, if we are minded otherwise than is dictated by the full knowledge of God, God will also reveal this to us, so that we may pray with David and say, "Open Thou mine eyes that I may behold wondrous things out of Thy law."

15. All this makes it clear that in Holy Scripture there are two sorts of perfection, two of righteousness, and two of fear. The first is that perfection, and incomparable truth, and perfect righteousness and fear, which is the beginning of wisdom, and which we must measure by the excellence of God; the second, which is within the range not only of men, but of every creature, and is not inconsistent with our frailty, as we read in the Psalms: "In Thy sight shall no man living be justified," is that righteousness which is said to be perfect, not in comparison with God, but as recognized by God. Job, and Zacharias, and Elizabeth, were called righteous, in respect of that righteousness which might someday turn to unrighteousness, and not in respect of that which is incapable of change, concerning which it is said, "I am God, and change not." And this is that which the Apostle elsewhere writes: "That which hath been made glorious hath not been made glorious in this respect, by reason of the glory that surpasses"; because, that is, the righteousness of the law, in comparison of the grace of the Gospel, does not seem to be righteousness at all. "For if," he says, that which passes away was with glory, much more that which remained is in glory. And again, "We know in part, and we prophesy in part; but when that which is perfect is come, that which is in part shall be done away." And, "For now we see in a mirror, darkly; but then face to face: now I know in part; but then shall I know even as also I have been known." And in the Psalms, "Such knowledge is too wonderful for me; it is high, I cannot attain unto it." And again, "When I thought

how I might know this, it was too painful for me; until I went into the sanctuary of God, and considered their latter end." And in the same place, "I was as a beast before thee: nevertheless I am continually with thee." And Jeremiah says, "Every man is become brutish and without knowledge." And to return to the Apostle Paul, "The foolishness of God is wiser than men." And much besides, which I omit for brevity's sake.

16. C. My dear Atticus, your speech is really a clever feat of memory. But the labor you have spent in mustering this host of authorities is to my advantage. For I do not any more than you compare man with God, but with other men, in comparison with whom he who takes the trouble can be perfect. And so, when we say that man, if he chooses, can be without sin, the standard is the measure of man, not the majesty of God, in comparison with Whom no creature can be perfect.

A. Critobulus, I am obliged to you for reminding me of the fact. For it is just my own view that no creature can be perfect in respect of true and finished righteousness. But that one differs from another, and that one man's righteousness is not the same as another's, no one doubts; nor again that one may be greater or less than another, and yet that, relatively to their own status and capacity, men may be called righteous who are not righteous when compared with others. For instance, the Apostle Paul, the chosen vessel who labored more than all the Apostles, was, I suppose, righteous when he wrote to Timothy, "I have fought the good fight, I have finished the course, I have kept the faith: henceforth there is laid up for me the crown of righteousness, which the Lord, the righteous judge, shall give to me at that day: and not only to me, but also to all them that love His appearing."

Timothy, his disciple and imitator, whom he taught the rules of action and the limits of virtue, was also righteous. Are we to think there was one and the same righteousness in them both, and that he had not more merit who labored more than all? "In my Father's house are many mansions." I suppose there are also different degrees of merit. "One star differed from another star in glory," and in the one body of the Church there are different members. The sun has its own splendor, the moon tempers the darkness of the night; and the five heavenly bodies which are called planets traverse the sky in different tracks and with different degrees of luminousness. There are countless other stars whose movements we trace in the firmament. Each has its own brightness, and though each in respect of its own is perfect, yet, in comparison with one of greater magnitude, it lacks perfection. In the body also with its different members, the eye has one function, the hand another, the foot another. Whence the Apostle says, "The eye cannot say to the hand, I have no need of thee: or again the head to the feet, I have no need of you. Are all Apostles? are all prophets? are all teachers? are all workers of miracles? have all gifts of healing? do all speak with tongues? do all interpret? But desire earnestly the greater gifts. But all these worketh the one and the same Spirit, dividing to each one severally even as He will." And here mark carefully that he does not say, as each member desires, but as the Spirit Himself will. For the vessel cannot say to him that makes it, "Why dost thou make me thus or thus? Hath not the potter a right over the clay, from the same lump to make one part a vessel unto honor, and another unto dishonor?" And so in close sequence he added, "Desire earnestly the greater gifts," so that, by the exercise of faith and diligence, we may win something in addition to other gifts, and may be superior to those who, compared with us, are in the second or third class. In a great house there are different vessels, some of gold, some of silver, brass, iron, wood. And yet while in its kind a vessel of brass is perfect, in comparison with one of silver it is called imperfect, and again one of silver, compared with one of gold, is inferior. And thus, when compared with one another, all things are imperfect and perfect. In a field of good soil, and from one sowing, there springs a crop thirty-fold, sixty-fold, or a hundred-fold. The very numbers show that there is disparity in the parts of the produce, and yet in its own kind each is perfect. Elizabeth and Zacharias, whom you adduce and with whom you cover yourself as with an impenetrable shield, may teach us how far they are beneath the holiness of blessed Mary, the Lord's Mother, who, conscious that God was dwelling in her, proclaims without reserve, "Behold, from henceforth all generations shall call me blessed. For He that is mighty hath done to me great things; and holy is His name. And His mercy is unto generations and generations of them that fear Him: He hath showed strength with His arm." Where, observe, she says she is blessed not by her own merit and virtue, but by the mercy of God dwelling in her. And John himself, a greater than whom has not arisen among the sons of men, is better than his parents. For not only does our Lord compare him with men, but with angels also. And yet he, who was greater on earth than all other men, is said to be less than the least in the kingdom of heaven.

17. Need we be surprised that, when saints are compared, some are better, some worse, since the same holds good in the comparison of sins? To Jerusalem,

pierced and wounded with many sins, it is said, "Sodom is justified by thee." It is not because Sodom, which has sunk forever into ashes, is just in herself, that it is said by Ezekiel, "Sodom shall be restored to her former estate"; but that, in comparison with the more accursed Jerusalem, she appears just. For Jerusalem killed the Son of God; Sodom through fulness of bread and excessive luxury carried her lust beyond all bounds. The publican in the Gospel who smote upon his breast as though it were a magazine of the worst thoughts, and, conscious of his offences, dared not lift up his eyes, is justified rather than the proud Pharisee. And Thamar in the guise of a harlot deceived Judah, and in the estimation of this man himself who was deceived, was worthy of the words, "Thamar is more righteous than I." All this goes to prove that not only in comparison with Divine majesty are men far from perfection, but also when compared with angels, and other men who have climbed the heights of virtue. You may be superior to someone whom you have shown to be imperfect, and yet be outstripped by another; and consequently may not have true perfection, which, if it be perfect, is absolute.

18. C. How is it then, Atticus, that the Divine Word urges us to perfection?

A. I have already explained that in proportion to our strength each one, with all his power, must stretch forward, if by any means he may attain to, and apprehend the reward of his high calling. In short Almighty God, to whom, as the Apostle teaches, the Son must in accordance with the dispensation of the Incarnation be subjected, that "God may be all in all," clearly shows that all things are by no means subject to Himself. Hence the prophet anticipates his own final subjection, saying, "Shall not my soul be subject to God alone? for of Him cometh my salvation." And because in the body of the Church Christ is the head, and some of the members still resist, the body does not appear to be subject even to the head. For if one member suffers, all the members suffer with it, and the whole body is tortured by the pain in one member. My meaning may be more clearly expressed thus. So long as we have the treasure in earthen vessels, and are clothed with frail flesh, or rather with mortal and corruptible flesh, we think ourselves fortunate if, in single virtues and separate portions of virtue, we are subject to God. But when this mortal shall have put on immortality, and this corruptible shall have put on incorruption, and death shall be swallowed up in the victory of Christ, then will God be all in all: and so there will not be merely wisdom in Solomon, sweetness in David, zeal in Elias and Phinees, faith in Abraham, perfect love in Peter, to whom it was said, "Simon, son of John, loves thou me?" zeal for preaching in the chosen vessel, and two or three virtues each in others, but God will be wholly in all, and the company of the saints will rejoice in the whole band of virtues, and God will be all in all.

19. C. Do I understand you to say that no saint, so long as he is in this poor body, can have all virtues?

A. Just so, because now we prophesy in part, and know in part. It is impossible for all things to be in all men, for no son of man is immortal.

C. How is it, then, that we read that he who has one virtue appears to have all?

A. By partaking of them, not possessing them, for individuals must excel in particular virtues. But I confess I don't know where to find what you say you have read.

C. Are you not aware that the philosophers take that view?

A. The philosophers may, but the Apostles do not. I heed not what Aristotle, but what Paul, teaches.

C. Pray does not James the Apostle write that he who stumbles in one point is guilty of all?

A. The passage is its own interpreter. James did not say, as a starting-point for the discussion, he who prefers a rich man to a poor man in honor is guilty of adultery or murder. That is a delusion of the Stoics who maintain the equality of sins. But he proceeds thus: "He who said, Thou shalt not commit adultery, said also, Thou shalt not kill: but although thou dost not kill, yet, if thou commit adultery, thou art become a transgressor of the law." Light offences are compared with light ones, and heavy offences with heavy ones. A fault that deserves the rod must not be avenged with the sword; nor must a crime worthy of the sword, be checked with the rod.

C. Suppose it true that no saint has all the virtues: you will surely grant that within the range of his ability, if a man do what he can, he is perfect.

A. Do you not remember what I said before?

C. What was it?

A. That a man is perfect in respect of what he has done, imperfect in respect of what he could not do.

C. But as he is perfect in respect of what he has done, because he willed to do it, so in respect of that which constitutes him imperfect, because he has not done it, he might have been perfect, had he willed to do it.

A. Who does not wish to do what is perfect? Or who does not long to grow vigorously in all virtue? If you look for all virtues in each individual, you do away with the distinctions of things, and the difference of graces, and the variety of the work of the Creator, whose prophet cries aloud in the sacred song: "In wisdom hast thou made them all." Lucifer may be indignant because he has not the brightness of the moon. The moon may dispute over her eclipses and ceaseless toil, and ask why she must traverse every month the yearly orbit of the sun. The sun may complain and want to know what he has done that he travels more slowly than the moon. And we poor creatures may demand to know why it is that we were made men and not angels; although your teacher, *the Ancient*, the fountain from which these streams flow, asserts that all rational creatures were created equal and started fairly, like charioteers, either to succumb halfway, or to pass on rapidly and reach the wished for goal. Elephants, with their huge bulk, and griffins, might discuss their ponderous frames and ask why they must go on four feet, while flies, midges, and other creatures like them have six feet under their tiny wings, and there are some creeping things which have such an abundance of feet that the keenest vision cannot follow their countless and simultaneous movements. Marcion and all the heretics who denied the Creator's works might speak thus. Your principle goes so far that while its adherents attack particular points, they are laying hands on God; they are asking why He only is God, why He envies the creatures, and why they are not all endowed with the same power and importance. You would not say so much (for you are not mad enough to openly fight against God), yet this is your meaning in other words, when you give man an attribute of God, and make him to be without sin like God Himself. Hence the Apostle, with his voice of thunder, says, concerning different graces: "There are diversities of gifts, but the same spirit; and differences of ministrations, but the same Lord; and there are diversities of workings, but the same God, Who worketh all things in all."

20. C. You push this one particular point too far in seeking to convince me that a man cannot have all excellences at the same time. As though God were guilty of envy, or unable to bestow upon His image and likeness a correspondence in all things to his Creator.

A. Is it I or you who go too far? You revive questions already settled, and do not understand that likeness is one thing, equality another; that the former is a painting, the latter, reality. A real horse courses over the plains; the painted one with his chariot does not leave the wall. The Arians do not allow to the Son of God what you give to every man. Some do not dare to confess the perfect humanity of Christ, lest they should be compelled to accept the belief that He had the sins of a man as though the Creator were unequal to the act of creating, and the title Son of Man were co-extensive with the title Son of God. So either set me something else to answer, or lay aside pride and give glory to God.

C. You forget a former answer of yours, and have been so busy forging your chain of argument, and careering through the wide fields of Scripture, like a horse that has slipped its bridle, that you have not said a single word about the main point. Your forgetfulness is a pretext for escaping the necessity of a reply. It was foolish in me to concede to you for the nonce what you asked, and to suppose that you would voluntarily give up what you had received, and would not need a reminder to make you pay what you owed.

A. If I mistake not, it was the question of possible commands of which I deferred the answer. Pray proceed as you think best.

21. C. The commands which God has given are either possible or impossible. If possible, it is in our power to do them, if we choose. If impossible, we cannot be held guilty for omitting duties which it is not given us to fulfill. Hence it results that, whether God has given possible or impossible commands, a man can be without sin if he chooses.

A. I beg your patient attention, for what we seek is not victory over an opponent, but the triumph of truth over falsehood. God has put within the power of mankind all arts, for we see that a vast number of men have mastered them. To pass over those which the Greeks call βάναυσοι, as we may say, the manual arts, I will instance grammar, rhetoric, the three sorts of philosophy—physics, ethics, logic—geometry also, and astronomy, astrology, arithmetic, music, which are also parts of philosophy; medicine, too, in its threefold division—theory, investigation, practice; a knowledge of law in general and of particular enactments. Which of us, however clever he may be, will be able to understand them all, when the most eloquent of orators, discussing rhetoric and jurisprudence, said: "A few may excel in one, in both no one can." You see, then, that God has commanded what is possible, and yet, that no one can by nature attain to what is possible. Similarly he has given different rules and various virtues, all of which we cannot possess at the same time. Hence it happens that a virtue which in one person takes the chief place, or is found in perfection, in another is but partial; and yet, he is not to blame who has not all excellence, nor is he condemned for lacking that which he has not; but he is justified through what he does possess. The Apostle described the character of a bishop when he wrote to Timothy, "The bishop, therefore, must be without reproach, the husband of one wife, temperate, modest, orderly, given to hospitality, apt to teach; no brawler, no striker; but gentle, not contentious, no lover of money; one that rules well his own house, having his children in subjection with all modesty." And again, "Not a novice, lest, being puffed up, he fall into the condemnation of the devil. Moreover, he must have good testimony from them that are without, lest he fall into reproach and the snare of the devil." Writing also to his disciple Titus, he briefly points out what sort of bishops he ought to ordain: "For this cause left I thee in Crete, that thou shouldest set in order the things that were wanting, and appoint elders in every city, as I gave thee charge; if any man is blameless, the husband of one wife, having children that believe, who are not accused of riot or unruly. For the bishop must be blameless (or free from accusation, for so much is conveyed by the original) as God's steward; not self-willed, not soon angry, no brawler, no striker, not greedy of filthy lucre; but given to hospitality, kind, modest, just, holy, temperate; holding to the faithful word which is according to the teaching, that he may be able both to exhort in the sound doctrine, and to convict the gainsayers." I will not now say anything of the various rules relating to different persons, but will confine myself to the commands connected with the bishop.

22. God certainly wishes bishops or priests to be such as the chosen vessel teaches they should be. As to the first qualification it is seldom or never that one is found *without reproach;* for who is it that has not some

fault, like a mole or a wart on a lovely body? If the Apostle himself says of Peter that he did not tread a straight path in the truth of the Gospel, and was so far to blame that even Barnabas was led away into the same dissimulation, who will be indignant if that is denied to him which the chief of the Apostles had not? Then, supposing you find one, "the husband of one wife, sober-minded, orderly, given to hospitality," the next attribute—διδακτικόν , *apt to teach*, not merely as the Latin renders the word, *apt to be taught*—you will hardly find in company with the other virtues. A bishop or priest that is a brawler, or a striker, or a lover of money, the Apostle rejects, and in his stead would have one gentle, not contentious, free from avarice, one that rules well his own house, and what is very hard, one who has his children in subjection with all modesty, whether they be children of the flesh or children of the faith. "With all modesty," he says. It is not enough for him to have his own modesty unless it be enhanced by the modesty of his children, companions, and servants, as David says, "He that walketh in a perfect way, he shall minister unto me." Let us consider, also, the emphasis laid on modesty by the addition of the words "having his children in subjection with all modesty." Not only in deed but in word and gesture must he hold aloof from immodesty, lest perchance the experience of Eli be his. Eli certainly rebuked his sons, saying, "Nay, my sons, nay; it is not a good report which I hear of you." He chided them, and yet was punished, because he should not have chided, but cast them off. What will he do who rejoices at vice or lacks the courage to correct it? Who fears his own conscience, and therefore pretends to be ignorant of what is in everybody's mouth? The next point is that the bishop must be free from accusation, that he have a good report from them who are without, that no reproaches of opponents be levelled at him, and that they who dislike his doctrine may be pleased with his life. I suppose it would not be easy to find all this, and particularly one "able to resist the gain-sayers," to check and overcome erroneous opinions. He wishes no novice to be ordained bishop, and yet in our time we see the youthful novice sought after as though he represented the highest righteousness. If baptism immediately made a man righteous, and full of all righteousness, it was of course idle for the Apostle to repel a novice; but baptism annuls old sins, does not bestow new virtues; it looses from prison, and promises rewards to the released if he will work. Seldom or never, I say, is there a man who has all the virtues which a bishop should have. And yet if a bishop lacked one or two of the virtues in the list, it does not follow that he can no longer be called righteous, nor will he be condemned for his deficiencies, but will be crowned for what he has. For to have all and lack nothing is the virtue of Him "Who did no sin; neither was guile found in His mouth; Who, when He was reviled, reviled not again;" Who, confident in the consciousness of virtue, said, "Behold the prince of this world comes, and finds nothing in me;" "Who, being in the form of God, thought it not robbery to be on an equality with God, but emptied Himself, taking the form of a servant, and became obedient unto death, even the death of the cross. Wherefore God gave Him the name which is above every name, that at the name of Jesus every knee should bow, of things in heaven, and things on earth, and things under the earth." If, then, in the person of a single bishop you will either not find at all, or with difficulty, even a few of the things commanded, how will you deal with the mass of men in general who are bound to fulfil all the commandments?

23. Let us reason from things bodily to things spiritual. One man is swift-footed, but not strong-handed. That man's movements are slow, but he stands firm in battle. This man has a fine face, but a harsh voice: another is repulsive to look at, but sings sweetly and melodiously. There we see a man of great ability, but equally poor memory; here is another whose memory serves him, but whose wits are slow. In the very discussions with which when we were boys we amused ourselves, all the disputants are not on a level, either in introducing a subject, or in narrative, or in digressions, or wealth of illustration, and charm of peroration, but their various oratorical efforts exhibit different degrees of merit. Of churchmen I will say more. Many discourse well upon the Gospels, but in explaining an Apostle's meaning are unequal to themselves. Others, although most acute in the New Testament are dumb in the Psalms and the Old Testament. I quite agree with Virgil—*Non omnia possumus omnes;* and seldom or never is the rich man found who in the abundance of his wealth has everything in equal proportions. That God has given possible commands, I admit no less than you. But it is not for each one of us to make all these possible virtues our own, not because our nature is weak, for that is a slander upon God, but because our hearts and minds grow weary and cannot keep all virtues simultaneously and perpetually. And if you blame the Creator for having made you subject to weariness and failure, I shall reply, your censure would be still more severe if you thought proper to accuse Him of not having made you God. But you will say, if I have

not the power, no sin attaches to me. You have sinned because you have not done what another could do. And again, he in comparison with whom you are inferior will be a sinner in respect of some other virtue, relatively to you or to another person; and thus it happens that whoever is thought to be first, is inferior to him who is his superior in some other particular.

24. C. If it is impossible for man to be without sin, what does the Apostle Jude mean by writing, "Now unto Him that is able to keep you without sin, and to set you before the presence of His glory without blemish"? This is clear proof that it is possible to keep a man without sin and without blemish.

A. You do not understand the passage. We are not told that a man can be without sin, which is your view, but that God, if He chooses, can keep a man free from sin, and of His mercy guard him so that he may be without blemish. And I say that all things are possible with God; but that everything which a man desires is not possible to him, and especially, an attribute which belongs to no created thing you ever read of.

C. I do not say that a man is without sin, which, perhaps, appears to you to be possible; but that he may be, if he chooses. For actuality is one thing, possibility another. In the actual we look for an instance; possibility implies that our power to act is real.

A. You are trifling, and forget the proverb, "Don't do what is done." You keep turning in the same mire, and only make more dirt. I shall, therefore, tell you, what is clear to all, that you are trying to establish a thing that is not, never was, and, perhaps, never will be. To employ your own words, and show the folly and inconsistency of your argument, I say that you are maintaining an impossible possibility. For your proposition, that a man can be without sin if he chooses, is either true or false. If it be true, show me who the man is; if it be false, whatever is false can never happen. But let us have no more of these notions. Hissed off the stage, and no longer daring to appear in public, they should stay on the bookshelves, and not let themselves be heard.

25. Let us proceed to other matters. And here I must speak uninterruptedly, so far, at least, as is consistent with giving you an opportunity of refuting me, or asking any question you think fit.

C. I will listen patiently, though I cannot say gladly. The ability of your reasoning will strike me all the more, while I am amazed at its falsity.

A. Whether what I am going to say is true or false, you will be able to judge when you have heard it.

C. Follow your own method. I am resolved, if I am unable to answer, to hold my tongue rather than assent to a lie.

A. What difference does it make whether I defeat you speaking or silent, and, as it is in the story of Proteus, catch you asleep or awake?

C. When you have said what you like, you shall hear what you will certainly not like. For though truth may be put to hard shifts it cannot be subdued.

A. I want to sift your opinions a little, that your followers may know what an inspired genius you are. You say, "It is impossible for any but those who have the knowledge of the law to be without sin"; and you, consequently, shut out from righteousness a large number of Christians, and, preacher of sinlessness though you are, declare nearly all to be sinners. For how many Christians have that knowledge of the law which you can find but seldom, or hardly at all, in many doctors of the Church? But your liberality is so great that, in order to stand well with your Amazons, you have elsewhere written, "Even women ought to have a knowledge of the law," although the Apostle preaches that women ought to keep silence in the churches, and if they want to know anything consult their husbands at home. And you are not content with having given your cohort a knowledge of Scripture, but you must delight yourself with their songs and canticles, for you have a heading to the effect that "Women also should sing unto God." Who does not know that women should sing in the privacy of their own rooms, away from the company of men and the crowded congregation? But you allow what is not lawful, and the consequence is, that, with the support of their master, they make an open show of that which should be done with modesty, and with no eye to witness.

26. You go on to say, "The servant of God should utter from his lips no bitterness, but ever that which is sweet and pleasant"; and as though a servant of God were one thing, a doctor and priest of the Church another, forgetting what was previously laid down, you say in another heading, "A priest or doctor ought to watch the actions of all, and confidently rebuke sinners, lest he be responsible for them and their blood be required at his hands." And, not satisfied with saying it once, you repeat it, and inculcate that, "A priest or doctor should flatter no one, but boldly rebuke all, lest he destroy both himself and those who hear him." Is there so little harmony in one and the same work that you do not know what you have previously said? For if the servant of God ought to utter no bitterness from his mouth, but always that which is sweet and pleasant, it follows either that a priest and

doctor will not be servants of God who ought to confidently rebuke sinners, and flatter no one, but boldly reprove all: or, if a priest and a doctor are not only servants of God, but have the chief place among His servants, it is idle to reserve smooth and pleasant speeches for the servants of God, for these are characteristic of heretics and of them who wish to deceive; as the Apostle says, "They that are such serve not our Lord Christ but their own belly, and by their smooth and fair speech they beguile the hearts of the innocent." Flattery is always insidious, crafty, and smooth. And the flatterer is well described by the philosophers as "*a pleasant enemy.*" Truth is bitter, of gloomy visage and wrinkled brow, and distasteful to those who are rebuked. Hence the Apostle says, "Am I become your enemy, because I tell you the truth?" And the comic poet tells us that "Obsequiousness is the mother of friendship, truth of enmity." Wherefore we also eat the Passover with bitter herbs, and the chosen vessel teaches that the Passover should be kept with truth and sincerity. Let truth in our case be plain speaking, and bitterness will instantly follow.

27. In another place you maintain that "All are governed by their own free choice." What Christian can bear to hear this? For if not one, nor a few, nor many, but all of us are governed by our own free choice, what becomes of the help of God? And how do you explain the text, "A man's goings are ordered by the Lord"? And "A man's way is not in himself"; and "No one can receive anything, unless it be given him from above"; and elsewhere, "What hast thou which thou didst not receive? But if thou didst receive it, why dost thou glory as if thou hadst not received it?" Our Lord and Savior says: "I am come down from heaven not to do Mine own will, but the

will of the Father who sent Me." And in another place, "Father, if it be possible, let this cup pass from Me; nevertheless not My will, but Thine be done." And in the Lord's prayer, "Thy will be done as in heaven, so on earth." How is it that you are so rash as to do away with all God's help? Elsewhere, you make a vain attempt to append the words "not without the grace of God"; but in what sense you would have them understood is clear from this passage, for you do not admit His grace in separate actions, but connect it with our creation, the gift of the law, and the power of free will.

28. The argument of the next section is, "In the day of judgment, no mercy will be shown to the unjust and to sinners, but they must be consumed in eternal fire." Who can bear this, and suffer you to prohibit the mercy of God, and to sit in judgment on the sentence of the Judge before the day of judgment, so that, if He wished to show mercy to the unjust and the sinners, He must not, because you have given your veto? For you say it is written in the one hundred and fourth Psalm, "Let sinners cease to be in the earth, and the wicked be no more." And in Isaiah, "The wicked and sinners shall be burned up together, and they who forsake God shall be consumed." Do you not know that mercy is sometimes blended with the threatening of God? He does not say that they must be burnt with eternal fires, but let them cease to be in the earth, and the wicked be no more. For it is one thing for them to desist from sin and wickedness, another for them to perish forever and be burnt in eternal fire. And as for the passage which you quote from Isaiah, "Sinners and the wicked shall be burned up together," he does not add forever. "And they who forsake God shall be consumed." This properly refers to heretics, who leave the straight

path of the faith, and shall be consumed if they will not return to the Lord whom they have forsaken. And the same sentence is ready for you if you neglect to turn to better things. Again, is it not marvelous temerity to couple the wicked and sinners with the impious, for the distinction between them is great? Every impious person is wicked and a sinner; but we cannot conversely say every sinner and wicked person is also impious, for impiety properly belongs to those who have not the knowledge of God, or, if they have once had it, lose it by transgression. But the wounds of sin and wickedness, like faults in general, admit of healing. Hence, it is written, "Many are the scourges of the sinner"; it is not said that he is eternally destroyed. And through all the scourging and torture the faults of Israel are corrected, "For whom the Lord loveth He chastened, and scourges every son whom He receives." It is one thing to smite with the affection of a teacher and a parent; another to be madly cruel towards adversaries. Wherefore, we sing in the first Psalm, "The impious do not rise in the judgment," for they are already sentenced to destruction; "nor sinners in the counsel of the just." To lose the glory of the resurrection is a different thing from perishing forever. "The hour cometh," he says, "In which all that are in the tombs shall hear His voice, and shall come forth: they that have done good unto the resurrection of life, and they that have done ill unto the resurrection of judgment." And so the Apostle, in the same sense, because in the same Spirit, says to the Romans, "As many as have sinned without law shall also perish without law; and as many as have sinned under law, shall be judged by law." The man without law is the unbeliever who will perish forever. Under the law is the sinner who believes in God, and who will be judged by the law, and will not perish. If the wicked and sinners are to be burned with everlasting fire, are you not afraid of the sentence you pass on yourself, seeing that you admit you are wicked and a sinner, while still you argue that a man is not without sin, but that he may be. It follows that the only person who can be saved is an individual who never existed, does not exist, and perhaps never will, and that all our predecessors of whom we read must perish. Take your own case. You are puffed up with all the pride of Cato, and have Milo's giant shoulders; but is it not amazing temerity for you, who are a sinner, to take the name of a teacher? If you are righteous, and, with a false humility, say you are a sinner, we may be surprised, but we shall rejoice at having so unique a treasure, and at reckoning amongst our friends a personage unknown to patriarch, prophet, and Apostle. And if Origen does maintain that no rational creatures ought to be lost, and allows repentance to the devil, what is that to us, who say that the devil and his attendants, and all impious persons and transgressors, perish eternally, and that Christians, if they be overtaken by sin, must be saved after they have been punished?

29. Besides all this you add two chapters which contradict one another, and which, if true, would effectually close your mouth. "Except a man have learned, he cannot be acquainted with wisdom and understand the Scriptures." And again, "He that has not been taught, ought not to assume that he knows the law." You must, then, either produce the master from whom you learned, if you are lawfully to claim the knowledge of the law; or, if your master is a person who never learned from anyone else, and taught you what he did nor know himself, it follows that you are not acting rightly in

claiming a knowledge of Scripture, when you have not been taught, and in starting as a master before you have been a disciple. And yet, perhaps, with your customary humility, you make your boast that the Lord Himself, Who teaches all knowledge, was your master, and that, like Moses in the cloud and darkness, face to face, you hear the words of God, and so, with the halo round your head, take the lead of us. And even this is not enough, but all at once you turn Stoic, and thunder in our ears Zeno's proud maxims. "A Christian ought to be so patient that if anyone wished to take his property he would let it go with joy." Is it not enough for us patiently to lose what we have, without returning thanks to him who ill-treats and plunders us, and sending after him all blessings? The Gospel teaches that to him who would go to law with us, and by strife and litigation take away our coat, we must give our cloak also. It does not enjoin the giving of thanks and joy at the loss of our property. What I say is this, not that there is any enormity in your view, but that everywhere you are prone to exaggeration, and indulge in ambitious flights. This is why you add that "The bravery of dress and ornament is an enemy of God." What enmity, I should like to know, is there towards God if my tunic is cleaner than usual, or if the bishop, priest, or deacon, or any other ecclesiastics, at the offering of the sacrifices walk in white? Beware, ye clergy; beware, ye monks; widows and virgins, you are in peril unless the people see you begrimed with dirt, and clad in rags. I say nothing of lay-men, who proclaim open war and enmity against God if they wear costly and elegant apparel.

30. Let us hear the rest. "We must love our enemies as we do our neighbors"; and immediately, falling into a deep slumber, you lay down this

proposition: "We must never believe an enemy." Not a word is needed from me to show the contradiction here. You will say that both propositions are found in Scripture, but you do not observe the particular connection in which the passages occur. I am told to love my enemies and pray for my persecutors. Am I bidden to love them as though they were my neighbors, kindred, and friends, and to make no difference between a rival and a relative? If I love my enemies as my neighbors, what more affection can I show to my friends? If you had maintained this position, you ought to have taken care not to contradict yourself by saying that we must never believe an enemy. But even the law teaches us how an enemy should be loved. If an enemy's beast be fallen, we must raise it up. And the Apostle tells us, "If thine enemy hunger, feed him; if he thirst, give him drink. For by so doing thou shalt heap coals of fire upon his head," not by way of curse and condemnation, as most people think, but to chasten and bring him to repentance, so that, overcome by kindness, and melted by the warmth of love, he may no longer be an enemy.

31. Your next point is that "the kingdom of heaven is promised even in the Old Testament," and you adduce evidence from the Apocrypha, although it is clear that the kingdom of heaven was first preached under the Gospel by John the Baptist, and our Lord and Savior, and the Apostles. Read the Gospels. John the Baptist cries in the desert, "Repent, for the kingdom of heaven is at hand"; and concerning the Savior it is written, "From that time He began to preach and to say, Repent, for the kingdom of heaven is at hand." And again, "Jesus went round about the towns and villages, teaching in their synagogues, and preaching the kingdom of God." And He commanded His

Apostles to "go and preach, saying, the kingdom of heaven is at hand." But you call us Manicheans because we prefer the Gospel to the law, and say that in the latter we have the shadow, in the former, the substance, and you do not see that your foolishness goes hand in hand with impudence. It is one thing to condemn the law, as Manichæus did; it is another to prefer the Gospel to the law, for this is in accordance with apostolic teaching. In the law the servants of the Lord speak, in the Gospel the Lord Himself; in the former are the promises, in the latter their fulfilment; there are the beginnings, here is perfection; in the law the foundations of works are laid; in the Gospel the edifice is crowned with the top-stone of faith and grace. I have mentioned this to show the character of the teaching given by our distinguished professor.

32. The hundredth heading runs thus: "A man can be without sin, and easily keep the commandments of God if he chooses," as to which enough has already been said. And although he professes to imitate, or rather complete the work of the blessed martyr Cyprian in the treatise which the latter wrote to Quirinus, he does not perceive that he has said just the opposite in the work under discussion. Cyprian, in the fifty-fourth heading of the third book, lays it down that no one is free from stain and without sin, and he immediately gives proofs, among them the passage in Job, "Who is cleansed from uncleanness? Not he who has lived but one day upon the earth." And in the fifty-first Psalm, "Behold I was shapen in iniquity, and in sin did my mother conceive me." And in the Epistle of John, "If we say that we have no sin, we deceive ourselves, and the truth is not in us." You, on the other hand, maintain that "A man can be without sin," and

that you may give your words the semblance of truth, you immediately add, "And easily keep the commandments of God, if he chooses," and yet they have been seldom or never kept by anyone. Now, if they were easy, they ought to have been kept by all. But if, to concede you a point, at rare intervals someone may be found able to keep them, it is clear that what is rare is difficult. And by way of supplementing this and displaying the greatness of your own virtues (we are to believe, forsooth, that you bring forth the sentiment out of the treasure of a good conscience), you have a heading to the effect that: "We ought not to commit even light offences." And for fear some one might think you had not explained in the work the meaning of *light,* you add that, "We must not even think an evil thought," forgetting the words, "Who understands his offences? Clear thou me from hidden faults, and keep back thy servant from presumptuous sins, O Lord." You should have known that the Church admits even failures through ignorance and sins of mere thought to be offences; so much so that she bids sacrifices be offered for errors, and the high priest who makes intercession for the whole people previously offers victims for himself. Now, if he were not himself righteous, he would never be commanded to offer for others. Nor, again, would he offer for himself if he were free from sins of ignorance. If I were to attempt to show that error and ignorance is sin, I must roam at large over the wide fields of Scripture.

  33. C. Pray have you not read that "He who looks upon a woman to lust after her hath committed adultery with her already in his heart?" It seems that not only are the look and the allurements to vice reckoned as sin, but whatever it be to which we give assent. For either we can

avoid an evil thought, and consequently may be free from sin; or, if we cannot avoid it, that is not reckoned as sin which cannot be avoided.

A. Your argument is ingenious, but you do not see that it goes against Holy Scripture, which declares that even ignorance is not without sin. Hence it was that Job offered sacrifices for his sons, lest, perchance, they had unwittingly sinned in thought. And if, when one is cutting wood, the axe-head flies from the handle and kills a man, the owner is commanded to go to one of the cities of refuge and stay there until the high priest dies; that is to say, until he is redeemed by the Savior's blood, either in the baptistery, or in penitence which is a copy of the grace of baptism, through the ineffable mercy of the Savior, who would not have any one perish, nor delights in the death of sinners, but would rather that they should be converted and live.

C. It is surely strange justice to hold me guilty of a sin of error of which my conscience does not accuse itself. I am not aware that I have sinned, and am I to pay the penalty for an offence of which I am ignorant? What more can I do, if I sin voluntarily?

A. Do you expect me to explain the purposes and plans of God? The Book of Wisdom gives an answer to your foolish question: "Look not into things above thee, and search not things too mighty for thee." And elsewhere, "Make not thyself overwise, and argue not more than is fitting." And in the same place, "In wisdom and simplicity of heart seek God." You will perhaps deny the authority of this book; listen then to the Apostle blowing the Gospel trumpet: "O the depth of the riches both of the wisdom and knowledge of God! how unsearchable are His judgments, and His ways past

Introduction to and the Treatises of St. Jerome

tracing out! For whom hath known the mind of the Lord? or who hath been His counsellor?" Your questions are such as he elsewhere describes: "But foolish and ignorant questioning avoid, knowing that they gender strife." And in Ecclesiastes (a book concerning which there can be no doubt) we read, "I said, I will be wise, but it was far from me. That which is exceeding deep, who can find it out?" You ask me to tell you why the potter makes one vessel to honor, another to dishonor, and will not be satisfied with Paul, who replies on behalf of his Lord, "O man, who art thou that replies against God?"

The remainder of this book is occupied by a series of quotations from the Old Testament, designed to show that it is not only the outer and conscious act which is reckoned sinful, but the opposition to the Divine will, which is often implicit and half-conscious. Occasionally, also, the speaker shows how the texts quoted enforce the argument which he has before used, that men may be spoken of as righteous in a general sense, yet by no means free from sins of thought or desire, if not of act.

The passages quoted are:

Gen. viii. 21. I will not curse the ground....for the mind of man is set on evil from his youth.

xvii. 17, xviii. 12. Abraham and Sarah laughing at the promise.

xxxvii. 35. Jacob's excessive grief.

Exod. xxi. 12, 13. The guilt of one who slays another unawares.

Lev. iv. 2, 27. Offerings for sins of ignorance.

v. 3. Offerings for ceremonial uncleanness.

ix. 1. Offerings for Aaron at his consecration.

xii. 6. Offerings for women after childbirth.

xiv. 1, 6, xvi. 6, xii. 7. Offerings for the leper.

xv. 31, xvi. 2, 5. Offerings for the people on the day of atonement.

xxii. 14. Eating the hallowed things ignorantly; compared with 1 Cor. xi. 27, 28, of careless participation in Sacrament.

Numbers vi. 1. Offerings for the Nazarite.

xiv. 7, vii. 28, 29. Offerings for imploring God's Mercy.

xxviii. 15, 22, xxix. 5, v. 11, 17. Offerings at the feast.

Numbers xxxv. 13. The cities of refuge provided for manslayers.

Deut. ix. 6, xviii. 13. Israel warned not to boast of righteousness.

xviii. 9–12, v. 14, 15. Perfection used only of avoiding idolatry.

xxii. 8. The housetop without a parapet makes a man guilty.

xxiii. 2. Defilement from unconscious personal acts.

Josh. vii. 12. The people made guilty by the sin of Achan.

xi. 19, 20. The racial guilt of the Canaanites.

1 Sam. xiv. 27. Jonathan made guilty by tasting the honey.

xvi. 6. The Lord sees the heart, not the outward appearance.

2 Sam. iv. 11. Ishbosheth spoken of as righteous.

vi. 7, 8. Uzzah smitten for carelessness.

2 Sam. xxiv. 10. David's numbering the people.

1 Kings viii. 46. Solomon's Prayer—There is none that sinned not.

xiv. 5. The prophet detecting the motive of Jeroboam's wife.

2 Kings iv. 27. Elijah seeing the Shunamite's heart.

1 Chron. ii. 32. Sept. Half-prophets.

Habakkuk iii. 1. Vulgate. A prayer "for sins of ignorance" ("upon Shigionoth"), supposed to be in recognition of over-boldness in i. 2–4.

Ezek. xlvi. 20. The sacrifice of Ezekiel's restored temple.

Jer. x. 23. The way of man not in himself.

xvii. 9. The heart deceitful.

Prov. xiv. 12. A way that seemed right to a man.

xix. 21. Many devices in a man's heart.

xx. 9. Who can say, I have a clean heart?

17. Who will boast that he is clean?

Eccl. vii. 16. The heart of a man is full of wickedness.

Book II.

This book can hardly be said to form part of a dialogue. It is rather an argument from Scripture to prove the point of the Augustinian arguer, Atticus. From the fourth chapter onwards it consists, like the last five chapters of Book I., of a chain of Scripture texts, taken from the New Testament and the Prophets, to show the universality of sin, and thus to refute the Pelagian assertion that a man can be without sin if he wills. We shall, therefore, give, as in the previous case, a list of the texts and the first words of them, only giving Jerome's words where he introduces some original remark of his own, or some noteworthy comment.

St. Jerome

The Pelagian begins by reiterating the dilemma: If the commandments are given to be obeyed, then man can be without sin; if he is, by his creation, such that he must be a sinner, then God, not he, is the author of sin. To the argument that sacrifices are enjoined for sins of ignorance, he replies by appealing from the Old Testament to the New, which leads to a discussion (2, 3) on St. Paul's description of the conflict with sin, in Romans vii. Paul, it is argued, speaks not as a sinner, but as a *man*, and thus confesses the sinfulness of humanity. That men may be without ingrained vice is possible; that they can be without sin is not. This leads the Augustinian, Atticus, resuming his list of testimonies, to the fact that, though men are found who are righteous as avoiding wickedness (κακία), yet none is without sin (ἀναμάρτητος).

In Psalm xxxii. 5. One who speaks of himself as "holy," yet confesses his transgression.

Prov. xxiv. 16. Explains this, "The righteous falls, but sins again."

xviii. 17, LXX. and Vulgate. A righteous man accuses himself when he begins to speak.

Ps. lviii. 3. Sinners are estranged from the womb; that is, either, as St. Paul says (Rom. v. 14), they sin "after the similitude of Adam"; or, "when Christ, as the firstborn, opened the virgin's womb" (Exod. xiii. 2). The heretics refused to acknowledge the mystery, which was prefigured by the Eastern door of the Temple (Ezek. xliv. 2), which closed again when once the High Priest had gone through it.

Job iv. 17–21. Shall mortal man be just with God?

vii. 1. The life of man is temptation.

20, 21. If I have sinned, what can I do?

ix. 15, 16. If I were righteous, he would not hear me.

29–31. If I wash myself with snow water, etc.

x. 15. If I be righteous, etc.

xiv. 4, 5. Who will be free from uncleanliness? Not one.

Prov. xvi. 26, LXX. Man toiled in sorrow.

Job xl. 4. What shall I answer thee?

Prov. xx. 9. "Who will boast that he has a clean heart?" which shows at least that the commandments are not easy, as Pelagius says they are.

1 John v. 3. "His commandments are not grievous," and

Matt. xi. 30. "My yoke is easy," are true only in comparison with Judaism, and should be compared with

Acts xv. 10. A yoke …which neither our fathers nor we are able to bear.

James iv. 11. "Thou judges the law," that is, if you say that the condemnation of sins of ignorance is unreasonable. That we all sin in such ways is evident from

James i. 20. "The wrath of man worketh not the righteousness of God." But anger is constantly condemned as in

Prov. xv. 1, LXX. "Wrath destroys even wise men."

Eph. iv. 26. Let not the sun go down upon your wrath.

Matt. v. 22. He who is angry…shall be in danger of council.

Eccles. xi. 19. "I am the most foolish of all men." This is said by Christ in the person of humanity. So

Ps. lxix. 5. "God, Thou knowest my foolishness." But

1 Cor. i. 25. The foolishness of God is wiser than men.

Ecclus. i. 18. "In much wisdom is much grief," shows the wise man's sense of imperfection. So

viii. 7. "I hated my life," and

14. "There be righteous men unto whom it happened according to the work of the wicked;" that is, God sees evil where we do not.

17. "However much a man may labor, yet he shall not find it;" and

ix. 2, 3. There is one event to all. The heart...is full of evil.

x. 1. "Dead flies cause the ointment to stink;" That is, almost everyone is defiled by heresy or other faults.

1 Pet. ii. 17, 18. Judgement must begin at the house of God.

6. There are four emotions which agitate mankind, two relating to the present, two to the future; two to good, and two to evil. There is sorrow, called in Greek λύπη, and joy, in Greek χαρά or ἡδονή, although many translate the latter word by *voluptas,* pleasure; the one of which is referred to evil, the other to good. And we go too far if we rejoice over such things as we ought not, as, for example, riches, power, distinctions, the bad fortune of enemies, or their death; or, on the other hand, if we are tortured with grief on account of present evils, adversity, exile, poverty, weakness, and the death of kindred, all of which is forbidden by the Apostle. And again, if we covet those things which we consider good, inheritance, distinctions, unvaried prosperity, bodily health, and the like, in the

possession of which we rejoice and find enjoyment; or if we fear those things which we deem adverse. Now, according to the Stoics, Zeno that is to say and Chrysippus, it is possible for a perfect man to be free from these emotions; according to the Peripatetics, it is difficult and even impossible, an opinion which has the constant support of all Scripture. Hence Josephus, the historian of the Maccabees, said that the emotions can be subdued and governed, not extirpated, and Cicero's five books of "Tusculan Disputations" are full of these discussions. According to the Apostle, the weakness of the body and spiritual hosts of wickedness in the heavenly places fight against us. And the same writer tells us that the works of the flesh and the works of the spirit are manifest, and these are contrary the one to the other, so that we do not the things that we would. If we do not what we would, but what we would not, how can you say that a man can be without sin if he chooses? You see that neither an Apostle, nor any believer can perform what he wishes. "Love covered a multitude of sins," not so much sins of the past as sins of the present, that we may not sin anymore while the love of God abides in us. Wherefore it is said concerning the woman that was a sinner, "Her sins which are many are forgiven her, for she loved much." And this shows us that the doing what we wish does not depend merely upon our own power, but upon the assistance which God in His mercy gives to our will.

7. The quotations from Scripture are now continued:

In 1 John i. 5, John i. 7, 8, Matt. v. 14, Christ and the Apostles are called the Light of the world. The world therefore is darkness.

1 Tim. vi. 16. God only hath immortality and is "only wise"; yet others, like the Prince of Tyre (Ezek. xxviii. 3), are wise derivatively. So we are pure, but only by grace. Thus

1 John i. 7. The blood of Christ cleanses us.

Job xxv. 5, 6. The stars are not pure in his sight.

Gal. ii. 16. "By the law no flesh shall be justified;" but

Rom. iii. 1, 24, 28, 30. Being justified freely through His grace, etc.

vi. 14. Not under the law, but under grace.

ix. 16. Not of him that wills, but of God which shows mercy.

ix. 30–32. The Gentiles…attained to the righteousness by faith.

x. 2. Christ is the end of the law to everyone that believeth.

8. The Apostle confesses his need of this grace for his work.

1 Cor. i. 1–3. Grace to you from God.

7, 8. That ye come behind in no gift—that no flesh may glory in His sight.

1 Cor. iii. 6–10. Paul planted…but God gave the increase.

18, 19. If any man thinketh himself to be wise, let him become a fool.

iv. 4. I know nothing against myself, yet I am not hereby justified.

7. What have ye that ye did not receive?

19. I will come to you, *if the Lord will.*

9. The Apostle shows also his need of grace himself.

1 Cor. xv. 9, 10. By the grace of God I am what I am, etc.

2 Cor. iii. 4–6. Our sufficiency is of God.

Gal. ii. 16. We have believed that we might, be justified by faith.

ii. 21. If righteousness come by the law, Christ is dead for nought.

iii. 10, 13. Christ hath redeemed us from the curse of the law.

24. The law our teacher to bring us to Christ.

v. 4. Ye are severed from Christ, ye that would be justified by the law.

10.

Phil. ii. 13. It is God that worketh in you.

2 Thess. iii. 3. The Lord is faithful, He shall establish you.

1 Tim. vi. 20, 21. O Timothy, guard that which is committed unto thee.

Tit. iii. 4–7. The kindness and mercy of God our Savior saved us.

11. We now turn to the Gospels "and supplement the flickering flame of the Apostolic light with the brightness of the lamp of Christ."

Matt. v. 22. "Every man who is angry…shall be in danger of the council." Which of us is not here condemned?

23, 24. "First be reconciled to thy brother." Who is there that finds this command easy?

37. "Let your speech be Yea, yea, Nay, nay." Who has ever kept this commandment?

The Psalmist says Ps. cxvi. 11. All men are liars.

12.

Matt. vi. 34. "Be not anxious for to-morrow." Do you fulfil this?

vii. 14. "Narrow is the gate which leadeth to life." How can you say that the commandments are easy?

Luke ix. 58. "The Son of Man hath not where to lay His head." This is interpreted by

Is. xxviii. 12. "Receive him that is weary, and this is my rest;" and

Is. lxvi. 1, 2. "On whom shall I rest but on him that is humble?" Christ finds few on whom to rest. How then can His commands be said to be easy?

Matt. ix. 12, 13. "I came not to call the righteous." "They that are whole need not the physician." Had the world not been full of sin, Christ would not have come. So

Ps. xii. 1. Help, Lord, for the godly man ceased.

xiv. 1, 3. They are corrupt...none doeth good.

Matt. x. 9. "Get you no gold...nor shoes." Who has fulfilled this? Not even the Apostles, for

Acts xii. 8. The angel bids Peter to bind on his sandals.

13.

Matt. x. 22–34. Describes the persecutions of Christ's followers, and gives the command to take up the cross. Are these easy?

xiv. 31. Even Peter's faith fails, and he begins to sink.

xv. 19, 20. Out of the heart came evil thoughts, etc.

xvi. 25. Whosoever will lose his life will find it.

xviii. 7. "Woe to the man through whom stumbling cometh." But

James iii. 2. In many things we all stumble or err.

Phil. ii. 21. All seek their own.

Matt. xix. 21. The young lawyer had kept all the law, yet failed.

xxiii. 26–28. The woes on the Pharisees fall in their measure upon all.

14.

Matt. xxvi. 39. "Not as I will, but as Thou wilt." Yet Critobulus says, by his own will he can do right.

Mark xiv. 37. "Could ye not watch with me one hour?" They *could* not.

vi. 5. He could do no mighty works because of their unbelief.

vii. 24. "He went into the borders of Tyre and Sidon." If Christ could not do as he wished, how can we?

ix. 5. Peter's request at the Transfiguration shows his ignorance.

xiii. 32. Even the Son knows not all things; how then can we?

xiv. 35. If it be possible. How can you say it is possible every hour to avoid sin?

15.

Mark xvi. 14. Even the Apostles showed unbelief and hardness of heart.

1 John v. 19. The world lieth in the evil one.

Luke i. 20. Even Zacharias disbelieved God's message.

Matt. xvii. 15. The disciples could not relieve the lunatic, because of unbelief.

Mark iv. 34. The disciple's dispute about precedence.

Luke ix. 54. James and John show a vindictive spirit.

xiv. 26, 27. The commands to forsake all and take up the cross are not easy.

xvi. 15. That which is exalted among men is abomination in the sight of God.

xvii. 1. It is impossible but that occasions of stumbling should come.

xvii. 6. The Apostles' faith was not even like a grain of mustard seed.

James iii. 2.

Matt. xvii. 19.

16.

Luke xviii. 1. We are always to pray. This shows our weakness.

27. Who, then, can be saved? It is possible, but to God only.

xxii. 24. The contest for precedence at the last supper.

31, 32. Peter's faith almost overcome by Satan.

Luke xxii. 43. Even Christ in his agony needs an angel to strengthen Him.

46. Pray that ye enter not into temptation.

17.

John v. 30. Even Christ says, "I cannot do anything by myself"; and

vii. 10. Was irresolute about going up to the Feast of Tabernacles.

19. None of you doeth the law.

viii. 3. None of the accusers of the woman taken in adultery were without sin. Christ wrote their names in the earth (Jerem. xvii. 13).

x. 8. All who came (not who were sent; Jerem. xiv. 15) before Christ were robbers.

xvii. 12. I kept them—they did not keep themselves.

Acts xv. 39. Paul and Barnabas quarreled.

xvi. 6, 7. They were forbidden to preach where they chose.

18. Even the Apostles, with their full light, show their dependence on grace.

Acts xvii. 30. The times before Christ were times of ignorance.

1 Cor. iv. 19. I will come *if the Lord will.*

James ii. 10. To stumble in one point is to be guilty of all.

iii. 2. In many things we all stumble.

8. The tongue is a deadly poison.

19.

James iv. 1. Wars arise from our lust. David indeed said,

Ps. xxvi. 2. "Examine me and prove me," etc. This self-confidence led to his fall.

li. 1. Have mercy on me, O God.

lxxx. 5. "Thou feed us with the bread of tears." Similarly

Ps. xxx. 6, 7. I said I shall never be moved...Thou didst hide Thy face.

xxxii. 5. I said I will confess my sin,

xxxvii. 5, 6. *He* shall make thy righteousness as the light.

39. The salvation of the righteous *is of the Lord.*

xxxviii. 7. There is no soundness in my flesh.

Rom. vii. 18. In my flesh dwelleth no good thing.

Ps. xxxviii. 8. Vulgate. My loins are filled with deceits.

xxxix. 5. He hath made our days as handbreadths.

lxix. 5. My sins are not hid from thee.

lxxvii. 2. My soul refused to be comforted.

10. This is the changing of the right hand of the Most High.

20.

Ps. lxxxix. 2. Mercy shall be *built up* forever.

xci. 6. From "the thing that walketh in darkness" who can be free? For

xi. 2. "The wicked bend their bow"—an image of the heretics.

xcii. 14. Those that are planted in the house of the Lord shall flourish.

ciii. 8, 10. The Lord is full of compassion.

2 Sam. viii. 13, 14. David receives the promises with the humble confession of his weakness. "Is this the law of man, O God?"

xvi. 10. He humbles himself under Abishai's violence and Shimei's curse.

xvii. 14. And is delivered only by God's confounding the counsel of Ahithophel.

1 Kings xiv. 8. It was God who gave Jeroboam the kingdom.

21.

1 Kings xv. 11. Asa, though a good man, was faulty.

xix. 4. Elijah fled from Jezebel.

Ps. cxviii. 6. The Lord is my keeper.

2 Chron. xvii. 3. Jehoshaphat prospers because the Lord is with him. Yet

xix. 2. He is rebuked for joining with Ahab.

2 Chron. xxii. 9. Ahaziah received burial among kings because descended from righteous Jehoshaphat.

2 Kings xviii. 3, 4, 7. Hezekiah did great things, but only through the Lord's help.

14. He gave the consecrated gold to the king of Assyria.

22. Even the best kings of Judah were imperfect.

2 Kings xx. 1, 5. Hezekiah wept when death was at hand, and recovered through special mercy.

13, 17. But he sinned in receiving the Babylonian envoys.

2 Chron. xxxii. 26. He fell by the lifting up of his heart.

xxxiv. 2. Josiah was a righteous man; yet

22, 23. He needed the aid of Huldah; and

xxxv. 22. He was slain through not heeding God's warning; and

23. The prophets also are weak and sinful.

Lam. iv. 20. Jeremiah lamented his fall.

Numb. xx. 10, 12. Moses is punished for his sin at Meribah. This is the meaning of Ps. cxli. 6. Vulgate. Their judges were swallowed up, joined to the Rock, etc.

Hosea ii. 19. God in mercy forgives Israel's unfaithfulness.

xi. 9. "I will not enter into the city." Only the Holy One is not joined to the mass of ungodliness.

Amos vi. 13. We turn righteousness into wormwood.

Jonah i. 14. The sailors confess that God is just in raising the storm.

Micah vii. 2. The godly man is perished from the earth, etc.

vi. 8. The command of justice, mercy, and a humble walk with God is only possible to humble faith, for

Ps. cxl. 6. "The wicked walk on every side," and James iv. 6. God giveth grace to the humble.

24.

Habakkuk iii. 16. Let rottenness enter into my bones, if only I may rest, etc.

Zech. iii. 1. Joshua is represented as clothed in filthy garments, and is freed through God's mercy.

But Jovinian's heir says "I am quite free from sin, I have no filthy garments, I am governed by my own will, I am greater than an Apostle. The Apostle does what he would not, and what he would he does not; but I do what I will, and what I would not I do not: the kingdom of heaven has been prepared for me, or rather I have by my virtuous life prepared it for myself. Adam was subject to punishment, and so are others who think themselves guilty after the similitude of Adam's transgressions; I and my crew alone have nothing to fear. Other men shut up in their cells and who never see women, because, poor creatures! they do not listen to my words, are tormented with desire: crowds of women may surround me, I feel no stirring of concupiscence. For to me may be applied the words, 'Holy stones are rolled upon the ground,' and the reason why I am insensible to the attraction of sin is that in the power of free will I carry Christ's trophy about with me." But let us listen to God proclaiming by the mouth of Isaiah: "O my people, they which call thee happy cause thee to err, and destroy the way of thy paths." Who is the greatest subverter of the people of God—he who, relying on the power of free choice, despises the help of the Creator, and is satisfied with following his own will, or he who dreads to be judged by the details of the Lord's commandments? To men of this sort, God says, "Woe unto you that are wise in your own eyes, and prudent in your own sight." Isaiah, if we follow the Hebrew, laments and says, "Woe is me because I have been silent, because I am a man of unclean lips: and I dwell in the midst of a people of unclean lips, for mine eyes have seen the Lord of Hosts." He for his meritorious and virtuous life enjoyed the sight of God, and conscious of his sins confessed that he had unclean lips. Not that he had said anything repugnant to the will of God, but because, either from fear, or from a deep sense of shame, he had been silent, and had not reproved the errors of the people so freely as a prophet should. When do we sinners rebuke offenders, we who flatter wealth and accept the persons of sinners for the sake of filthy lucre? for we shall hardly say that we speak with perfect frankness to men of whose assistance we stand in need. Suppose that we do not such things as they, suppose we keep ourselves from every form of sin; to refrain from speaking the truth is certainly sin. In the Septuagint, however, we do not find the words "because I have been silent," but "because I was pricked," that is with the consciousness of sin; and thus the words of the prophet are fulfilled. "My life was turned into misery while I was pierced by the thorn." He was pricked by the thorn of sin: you are decked with the flowers of virtue. "The moon shall be ashamed, and the sun confounded, when the Lord shall punish the host of heaven on high." This is explained by another passage. "Even the stars are unclean in His sight," and again, "He charged His angels with folly." The moon is ashamed, the sun is confounded, and the sky covered with sackcloth, and shall we fearlessly and joyously, as though we were free from all sin, face the majesty of the Judge, when the mountains shall melt away, that is, all who are lifted up by pride, and all the host of the heavens, whether they be stars, or angelic powers, when the heavens shall be rolled together as a scroll, and all their host shall fade away like leaves?

The argument is now carried on mostly by the quotation of passages from the prophets:

25.

Is. xxxiv. 5. "My sword hath drunk its fill in the heavens. It will come down in Edom."

How much more is there wrath against sin on earth! Edom means blood, which cannot inherit the kingdom (1 Cor. xv. 50).

xlv. 9. Woe unto him who strives with his Maker.

liii. 6. We have all gone astray like sheep.

Ezek. xvi. 14. Jerusalem is perfect in beauty; yet

Ezek. xvi. 60, 61. Her salvation is not of merit but of mercy.

Nahum i. 3. Though he cleanse, yet will he not make thee innocent.

1 Cor. xv. 9. I am not worthy—because I persecuted.

Ezek. xx. 43, 44. When pardoned, Jerusalem will still remember her sin.

Let us confess with shame that these are the utterances of men who have already won their reward; sinners upon earth, and still in our frail and mortal bodies let us adopt the language of the saints in heaven who have even been endowed with incorruption and immortality. "And ye say the way of the Lord is not equal, when your ways are not equal." It is Pharisaic pride to attribute to the injustice of the Creator sins which are due to our own will, and to slander His righteousness. The sons of Zadok, the priests of the spiritual temple, that is the Church, go not out to the people in their ministerial robes, lest by human intercourse they may lose their holiness and be defiled. And do you suppose that you, in the thick of the throng, and an ordinary individual, are pure?

26. Let us hastily run through the prophet Jeremiah:

Jerem. v. 1, 2. Is there any that doeth justly, etc.

vii. 21, 22. God rejects the sacrifices, because of the worshippers' evil lives.

xiii. 23. Can the Ethiopian change his skin?

27.

Jerem. xvii. 14. "Heal me, O Lord." Otherwise Jeremiah could only say, as in the text next quoted,

xx. 14, 17, 18. Cursed be the day wherein I was born, etc.

xxiii. 23. Am I a God at hand, etc. So conscious is he of God's power.

xxiv. 6, 7. God, not they themselves, will plant them, etc.

xxvi. 21–24. Jeremiah needed the help of Ahikam. How much more do we need that of God.

28.

Jerem. xxxi. 34. The promise of the new covenant.

xxxii. 30. The children of Israel have perpetually done evil.

xxxvii. 18, 19. Yet Jeremiah himself trembled before Zedekiah.

Jerem. xxx. 10, 11. Fear not, O Jacob, for *I am with thee.*

29.

Amos vi. 14. "We have taken us horns by our own strength." These are the boasts of heretics. But

Is. xvi. 6. His strength (Moab's) is by no means according to his arrogance.

Jerem. i. 7, 20. Men's sin will only be abolished because God is gracious to them. If you will abandon your assertions of natural ability, I will concede that your whole contention stands good, but only by the gift of God.

Lam. iii. 26–42. It is good that a man should quietly wait for the salvation of the Lord.

30.

Dan. iv. 17. The Most High rules in the kingdom of men.

Ps. cxiii. 7, 8. He raises up the poor out of the dust.

Is. xl. 17. He doeth what He will in heaven and in earth.

The words of 2 Maccabees v. 17, which say that Antiochus Epiphanes had power to overthrow the Temple, "because of the multitude of sins," are quoted in connection with the confessions of Daniel.

Dan. ix. 5. "We have sinned and dealt perversely," which is shown by

20. "While I was yet praying," etc., to be a personal, not only a national confession.

24. The prophecy of the seventy weeks shows that the prophet looked to God alone for the establishment of righteousness.

So then, until that end shall come, and this corruptible and mortal shall put on incorruption and immortality, we must be liable to sin; not, as you falsely say, owing to the fault of our nature and creation, but through the frailty and fickleness of human will, which varies from moment to moment; because God alone changes not. You ask in what respects Abel, Enoch, Joshua the son of Nun, or Elisha, and the rest of the saints have sinned. There is no need to look for a knot in a bulrush; I freely confess I do not know; and I only wish that, when sins are manifest, I might still be silent. "I know nothing against myself," says St. Paul, "yet am I not hereby justified." "Man looks on the outward appearance, but the Lord looks on the heart." Before Him no man is justified. And so Paul says confidently, "All have sinned, and come short of the glory of God"; and "God hath shut up all under sin that He may have mercy upon all"; and similarly in other passages which we have repeated again and again.

Book III.

1. Critob. I am charmed with the exuberance of your eloquence, but at the same time I would remind you that, "In the multitude of words there wanted not transgression." And how does it bear upon the question before us? You will surely admit that those who have received Christian baptism are without sin. And that being free from sin they are righteous. And that once they are righteous, they can, if they take care, preserve their righteousness, and so through life avoid all sin.

Attic. Do you not blush to follow the opinion of Jovinian, which has been exploded and condemned? For he relies upon just the same proofs and arguments as you do; nay, rather, you are all eagerness for his inventions, and desire to preach in the East what was formerly condemned at Rome, and not long ago in Africa. Read then the reply which was given to him, and you will there find the answer to yourself. For in the discussion of doctrines and disputed points, we must have regard not to persons but to things. And yet let me tell you that baptism condones past offences, and does not preserve righteousness in the time to come; the keeping of that is dependent on toil and industry, as well as earnestness, and above all on the mercy of God. It is ours to ask, to Him it belongs to bestow what we ask; ours to begin, His it is to finish; ours to offer what we can, His to fulfil what we cannot perform. "For except the Lord build the house, they labor in vain that build it. Except the Lord keep the city, the watchman wakes but in vain." Wherefore the Apostle bids us so run that we may attain. All indeed run, but one receives the crown. And in the Psalm it is written, "O Lord, thou hast crowned us with thy favor as with a shield." For our victory is won and the crown of our victory is gained by His protection and through His shield; and here we run that hereafter we may attain; there he shall receive the crown who in this world has proved the conqueror. And when we have been baptized we are told, "Behold thou art made whole; sin no more lest a worse thing happen unto thee." And again, "Know ye not that ye are a temple of God, and that the Spirit of God dwelleth in you? If any man profanes the temple of God, him shall God destroy." And in another place, "The Lord is with you so long as ye are with Him: if ye forsake Him, He will also forsake you." Where is the man, do you suppose, in whom as in a shrine and sanctuary the purity of Christ is permanent, and in whose case the serenity of the temple is saddened by no cloud of sin? We cannot always have the same countenance, though the philosophers falsely boast that this was the experience of Socrates; how much less can our minds be always the same! As men have many expressions of countenance, so also do the feelings of their hearts vary. If it were possible for us to be always immersed in the waters of baptism, sins would fly over our heads and leave us untouched.

The Holy Spirit would protect us. But the enemy assails us, and when conquered does not depart, but is ever lying in ambush, that he may secretly shoot the upright in heart.

2. In the Gospel according to the Hebrews, which is written in the Chaldee and Syrian language, but in Hebrew characters, and is used by the Nazarenes to this day (I mean the Gospel according to the Apostles, or, as is generally maintained, the Gospel according to Matthew, a copy of which is in the library at Cæsarea), we find, "Behold, the mother of our Lord and His brethren said to Him, John Baptist baptizes for the remission of sins; let us go and be baptized by him. But He said to them, what sin have I committed that I should go and be baptized by him? Unless, haply, the very words which I have said are only ignorance." And in the same volume, "If thy brother sin against thee in word, and make amends to thee, receive him seven times in a day." Simon, His disciple, said to Him, "Seven times in a day?" The Lord answered and said to him, "I say unto thee until seventy times seven." Even the prophets, after they were anointed with the Holy Spirit, were guilty of sinful words. Ignatius, an apostolic man and a martyr, boldly writes, "The Lord chose Apostles who were sinners above all men." It is of their speedy conversion that the Psalmist sings, "Their infirmities were multiplied; afterwards they made haste." If you do not allow the authority of this evidence, at least admit its antiquity, and see what has been the opinion of all good churchmen. Suppose a person who has been baptized to have been carried off by death either immediately, or on the very day of his baptism, and I will generously concede that he neither thought nor said anything whereby, through error and ignorance, he fell into sin. Does it follow that he will, therefore, be without

sin, because he appears not to have overcome, but to have avoided sin? Is not the true reason rather that by the mercy of God he was released from the prison of sins and departed to the Lord? We also say this, that God can do what He wills; and that man of himself and by his own will cannot, as you maintain, be without sin. If he can, it is idle for you now to add the word grace, for, with such a power, he has no need of it. If, however, he cannot avoid sin without the grace of God, it is folly for you to attribute to him an ability which he does not possess. For whatever depends upon another's will, is not in the power of him whose ability you assert, but of him whose aid is clearly indispensable.

3. C. What do you mean by this perversity, or, rather, senseless contention? Will you not grant me even so much—that when a man leaves the waters of baptism he is free from sin?

A. Either I fail to express my meaning clearly, or you are slow of apprehension.

C. How so?

A. Remember both what you maintained and also what I say. You argued that a man can be free from sin if he chooses. I reply that it is an impossibility; not that we are to think that a man is not free from sin immediately after baptism, but that that time of sinlessness is by no means to be referred to human ability, but to the grace of God. Do not, therefore, claim the power for man, and I will admit the fact. For how can a man be able who is not able of himself? Or what is that sinlessness which is conditioned by the immediate death of the body? Should the man's life be prolonged, he will certainly be liable to sins and to ignorance.

C. Your logic stops my mouth. You do not speak with Christian simplicity, but entangle me in some fine distinctions between being and ability to be.

A. Is it I who plays these tricks with words? The article came from your own workshop.

For you say, not that a man is free from sin, but that he is able to be; I, on the other hand, will grant what you deny, that a man is free from sin by the grace of God, and yet will maintain that he is not able of himself.

C. It is useless to give commandments if we cannot keep them.

A. No one doubts that God commanded things possible. But because men do not what they might, therefore the whole world is subject to the judgment of God, and needs His mercy. On the other hand, if you can produce a man who has fulfilled the whole law, you will certainly be able to show that there is a man who does not need the mercy of God. For everything which can happen must either take place in the past, the present, or the future. As to your assertion that a man can be without sin if he chooses, show that it has happened in the past, or at all events that it does happen at the present day; the future will reveal itself. If, however, you can point to no one who either is, or has been, altogether free from sin, it remains for us to confine our discussion to the future. Meanwhile, you are vanquished and a captive as regards two out of three periods of time, the past and the present. If anyone hereafter shall be greater than patriarchs, prophets, apostles, inasmuch as he is without sin, then you may perhaps be able to convince future generations as to their time.

4. C. Talk as you like, argue as you please, you will never wrest from me free will, which God bestowed

once for all, nor will you be able to deprive me of what God has given, the ability if I have the will.

A. By way of example let us take one proof: "I have found David, the Son of Jesse, a man after Mine own heart, who shall do all My will." There is no doubt that David was a holy man, and yet he who was chosen that he might do all God's will is blamed for certain actions. Of course it was possible for him who was chosen for the purpose to do all God's will. Nor is God to blame Who beforehand spoke of his doing all His will as commanded, but blame does attach to him who did not what was foretold. For God did not say that He had found a man who would unfailingly do His bidding and fulfil His will, but only one who would do all His will. And we, too, say that a man can avoid sinning, if he chooses, according to his local and temporal circumstances and physical weakness, so long as his mind is set upon righteousness and the string is well stretched upon the lyre. But if a man grows a little remiss it is with him as with the boatman pulling against the stream, who finds that, if he slackens but for a moment, the craft glides back and he is carried by the flowing waters whither he would not. Such is the state of man; if we are a little careless we learn our weakness, and find that our power is limited. Do you suppose that the Apostle Paul, when he wrote "the coat (or cloak) that I left at Troas with Carpus, bring when thou come, and the books, especially the parchments," was thinking of heavenly mysteries, and not of those things which are required for daily life and to satisfy our bodily necessities? Find me a man who is never hungry, thirsty, or cold, who knows nothing of pain, or fever, or the torture of strangury, and I will grant you that a man can think of nothing but virtue. When the Apostle was struck by the servant, he delivered himself thus against the High Priest who commanded the blow to be given: "God shall strike thee, thou whited wall." We miss the patience of the Savior Who was led as a lamb to the slaughter, and opened not His mouth, but mercifully said to the smiter, "If I have spoken evil, bear witness of the evil; but if well, why smites thou Me?" We do not disparage the Apostle, but declare the glory of God Who suffered in the flesh and overcame the evil inflicted on the flesh and the weakness of the flesh—to say nothing of what the Apostle says elsewhere:5297"Alexander, the coppersmith, did me much evil; the Lord, the righteous Judge, will recompense him in that day."

5. C. I have been longing to say something, but have checked the words as they were bursting from my lips. You compel me to say it.

A. Who hinders you from saying what you think? Either what you are going to say is good—and you ought not to deprive us of what is good—or it is bad, and, therefore, it is not regard for us, but shame that keeps you silent.

C. I will say, I will say after all, what I think. Your whole argument tends to this: You accuse nature, and blame God for creating man such as he is.

A. Is this what you wished, and yet did not wish, to say? Pray speak out, so that all may have the benefit of your wisdom. Are you censuring God because he made man to be man? Let the angels also complain because they are angels. Let every creature discuss the question, Why it is as it was created? and not what the Creator could have made it. I must now amuse myself with the rhetorical exercises of childhood, and passing from the gnat and the ant to cherubim and seraphim, inquire why each was not created with a happier lot. And when I reach the exalted powers, I will argue the point: Why God alone is only God, and did not make all things gods? For, according to you, He will either be unable to do so, or will be guilty of envy. Censure Him, and demand why He allows the devil to be in this world, and carry off the crown when you have won the victory.

C. I am not so senseless as to complain of the existence of the devil, through whose malice death entered into the world; but what grieves me is this: that dignitaries of the Church, and those who usurp the title of master, destroy free will; and once that is destroyed, the way is open for the Manicheans.

A. Am I the destroyer of free will because, throughout the discussion, my single aim has been to maintain the omnipotence of God as well as free will?

C. How can you have free will, and yet say that man can do nothing without God's assistance?

A. If he is to be blamed who couples free will and God's help, it follows that we ought to praise him who does away with God's help.

C. I am not making God's help unnecessary, for to His grace we owe all our ability; but I and those who think with me keep both within their own bounds. To God's grace we assign the gift of the power of free choice; to our own will, the doing, or the not doing, of a thing; and thus rewards and punishments for doing or not doing can be maintained.

6. A. You seem to me to be lost in forgetfulness, and to be going over the lines of argument already traversed as though not a word had been previously said. For, by this long discussion, it has been established that the Lord, by the same grace wherewith He bestowed upon

us free choice, assists and supports us in our individual actions.

C. Why, then, does He crown and praise what He has Himself wrought in us?

A. That is to say, our will which offered all it could, the toil which strove in action, and the humility which ever looked to the help of God.

C. So, then, if we have not done what He commanded, either God was willing to assist us, or He was not. If He was willing and did assist us, and yet we have not done what we wished, then He, and not we, has been overcome. But if He would not help, the man is not to be blamed who wished to do His will, but God, who was able to help, but would not.

A. Do you not see that your dilemma has landed you in a deep abyss of blasphemy? Whichever way you take it, God is either weak or malevolent, and He is not so much praised because He is the author of good and gives His help, as abused for not restraining evil. Blame Him, then, because He allows the existence of the devil, and has suffered, and still suffers, evil to be done in the world. This is what Marcion asks, and the whole pack of heretics who mutilate the Old Testament, and have mostly spun an argument something like this: Either God knew that man, placed in Paradise, would transgress His command, or He did not know. If He knew, man is not to blame, who could not avoid God's foreknowledge, but He Who created him such that he could not escape the knowledge of God. If He did not know, in stripping Him of foreknowledge you also take away His divinity. Upon the same showing God will be deserving of blame for choosing Saul, who was to prove one of the worst of kings. And the Savior must be convicted either of ignorance, or of unrighteousness,

St. Jerome

inasmuch as He said in the Gospel, "Did I not choose you the twelve, and one of you is a devil?" Ask Him why He chose Judas, a traitor? Why He entrusted to him the bag when He knew that he was a thief? Shall I tell you the reason? God judges the present, not the future. He does not make use of His foreknowledge to condemn a man though He knows that he will hereafter displease Him; but such is His goodness and unspeakable mercy that He chooses a man who, He perceives, will meanwhile be good, and who, He knows, will turn out badly, thus giving him the opportunity of being converted and of repenting. This is the Apostle's meaning when he says, "Dost thou not know that the goodness of God leadeth thee to repentance? but after thy hardness and impenitent heart treasures up for thyself wrath in the day of wrath and revelation of the righteous judgment of God, Who will render to every man according to his works." For Adam did not sin because God knew that he would do so; but God inasmuch as He is God, foreknew what Adam would do of his own free choice. You may as well accuse God of falsehood because He said by the mouth of Jonah: "Yet three days, and Nineveh shall be overthrown." But God will reply by the mouth of Jeremiah, "At what instant I shall speak concerning a nation, and concerning a kingdom, to pluck up, and to break down, and to destroy it; if that nation, concerning which I have spoken, turn from their evil, I will repent of the evil that I thought to do unto them. And at what instant I shall speak concerning a nation, and concerning a kingdom, to build and to plant it; if it does evil in my sight, that it obey not my voice, then I will repent of the good, wherewith I said I would benefit them." Jonah, on a certain occasion, was indignant because, at God's command, he had spoken falsely; but his sorrow was proved to be ill founded, since he would rather speak truth and have a countless multitude perish, than speak falsely and have them saved. His position was thus illustrated: "Thou grieves over the ivy (or gourd), for the which thou hast not labored, neither made it grow, which came up in a night, and perished in a night; and should not I have pity on Nineveh, that great city, wherein are more than six score thousand persons that cannot discern between their right hand and their left hand?" If there was so vast a number of children and simple folk, whom you will never be able to prove sinners, what shall we say of those inhabitants of both sexes who were at different periods of life? According to Philo, and the wisest of philosophers, Plato (so the "Timæus" tells us), in passing from infancy to decrepit old age, we go through seven stages, which so gradually and so gently follow one another that we are quite insensible of the change.

C. The drift of your whole argument is this—what the Greeks call αὐτέξουσιον, and we free will, you admit in terms, but in effect destroy. For you make God the author of sin, in asserting that man can of himself do nothing, but that he must have the help of God to Whom is imputed all we do. But we say that, whether a man does good or evil, it is imputed to him on account of the faculty of free choice, inasmuch as he did what he chose, and not to Him Who once for all gave him free choice.

A. Your shuffling is to no purpose; you are caught in the snares of truth. For upon this showing, even if He does not Himself assist, according to you He will be the author of evil, because He might have prevented it and did not. It is an old maxim that if a man can deliver another from death and does not, he is a homicide.

C. I withdraw and yield the point; you have won; provided, however, that victory is the subverting of the truth by specious words, that is to say, not by truth, but by falsehood. For I might make answer to you in the Apostle's words, "Though I be rude in speech, yet not in knowledge." When you speak, your rhetorical tricks are too much for me, and I seem to agree with you; but when you stop speaking, it all goes out of my head, and I see quite clearly that your argument does not flow from the fountains of truth and Christian simplicity, but rests on the labored subtleties of the philosophers.

A. Do you wish me, then, once more to resort to the evidence of Scripture? If so, what becomes of the boast of your disciples that no one can answer your arguments or solve the questions you raise?

C. I not only wish, but am eager that you should do so. Show me any place in Holy Scripture where we find that, the power of free choice being lost, a man does what of himself he either would not, or could not do.

8. A. We must use the words of Scripture not as you propose, but as truth and reason demand. Jacob says in his prayer, "If the Lord God will be with me, and will keep me in this way that I go, and will give me bread to eat, and raiment to put on, so that I come again to my father's house in peace, then shall the Lord be my God, and this stone, which I have set up for a token, shall be God's house; and of all that Thou shalt give me I will surely give the tenth unto Thee." He did not say, If thou preserve my free choice, and I gain by my toil food and raiment, and return to my father's house. He refers everything to the will of God, that he may be found worthy to receive that for which he prays. On Jacob's return from Mesopotamia an army of angels met him,

who are called God's camp. He afterwards contended with an angel in the form of a man, and was strengthened by God; whereupon, instead of Jacob, the *supplanter,* he received the name, *the most upright of God.* For he would not have dared to return to his cruel brother unless he had been strengthened and secured by the Lord's help. In the sequel we read, "The sun rose upon him after he passed over Phanuel," which is, being interpreted, *the face of God.* Hence Moses also says, "I have seen the Lord face to face, and my life is preserved," not by any natural quality—but by the condescension of God, Who had mercy. So then the Sun of Righteousness rises upon us when God makes His face to shine upon us and gives us strength. Joseph in Egypt was shut up in prison, and we next hear that the keeper of the prison, believing in his fidelity, committed everything to his hand. And the reason is given: "Because the Lord was with him: and whatsoever he did, the Lord made it to prosper." Wherefore, also, dreams were suggested to Pharaoh's attendants, and Pharaoh had one which none could interpret, that so Joseph might be released, and his father and brethren fed, and Egypt saved in the time of famine. Moreover, God said to Israel, in a vision of the night, "I am the God of thy fathers; fear not to go down into Egypt; for I will make of thee there a great nation, and I will go down with thee into Egypt; and I will also surely bring thee up again, and Joseph shall put his hand upon thine eyes." Where in this passage do we find the power of free choice? Is not the whole circumstance that he ventured to go to his son, and entrust himself to a nation that knew not the Lord, due to the help of the God of his fathers? The people was released from Egypt with a strong hand and an outstretched arm; not the hand of Moses and

Aaron, but of Him who set the people free by signs and wonders, and at last smote the firstborn of Egypt, so that they who at first were persistent in keeping the people, eagerly urged them to depart. Solomon says, "Trust in the Lord with all thine heart, and lean not upon thine own understanding: in all thy ways acknowledge Him, and He shall direct thy paths." Understand what He says—that we must not trust in our wisdom, but in the Lord alone, by Whom the steps of a man are directed. Lastly, we are bidden to show Him our ways, and make them known, for they are not made straight by our own labor, but by His assistance and mercy. And so it is written, "Make my way right before Thy face," so that what is right to Thee may seem also right to me. Solomon says the same—"Commit thy works unto the Lord, and thy thoughts shall be established." Our thoughts are then established when we commit all we do to the Lord our helper, resting it, as it were, upon the firm and solid rock, and attribute everything to Him.

9. The Apostle Paul, rapidly recounting the benefits of God, ended with the words, "And who is sufficient for these things?" Wherefore, also, in another place he says, "Such confidence have we through Christ to Godward; not that we are sufficient of ourselves to think anything as of ourselves; but our sufficiency is from God; Who also made us sufficient as ministers of a new covenant; not of the letter but of the spirit; for the letter killed, but the spirit giveth life." Do we still dare to pride ourselves on free will, and to abuse the benefits of God to the dishonor of the giver? Whereas the same chosen vessel openly writes, "We have this treasure in earthen vessels, that the exceeding greatness of the power may be of God, and not from ourselves." Therefore, also, in

another place, checking the impudence of the heretics, he says, "He that glories, let him glory in the Lord. For not he that commended himself is approved, but whom the Lord commended." And again, "In nothing was I behind the very chiefest Apostles, though I be nothing." Peter, disturbed by the greatness of the miracles he witnessed, said to the Lord, "Depart from me, for I am a sinful man." And the Lord said to His disciples, "I am the vine and ye are the branches: He that abides in Me and I in him, the same bears much fruit, for apart from Me ye can do nothing." Just as the vine branches and shoots immediately decay when they are severed from the parent stem, so all the strength of men fades and perishes, if it be bereft of the help of God. "No one," He says, "can come unto Me except the Father Who sent Me draw him." When He says, "No one can come unto Me," He shatters the pride of free will; because, even if a man will to go to Christ, except that be realized which follows—"unless My heavenly Father draw him"—desire is to no purpose, and effort is in vain. At the same time it is to be noted that he who is drawn does not run freely, but is led along either because he holds back and is sluggish, or because he is reluctant to go.

10. Now, how can a man who cannot by his own strength and labor come to Jesus, at the same time avoid all sins? and avoid them perpetually, and claim for himself a name which belongs to the might of God? For if He and I are both without sin, what difference is there between me and God? One more proof only I will adduce, that I may not weary you and my hearers. Sleep was removed from the eyes of Ahasuerus, whom the Seventy call Artaxerxes, that he might turn over the memoirs of his faithful ministers and come upon Mordecai, by whose

evidence he was delivered from a conspiracy; and that thus Esther might be more acceptable, and the whole people of the Jews escape imminent death. There is no doubt that the mighty sovereign to whom belonged the whole East, from India to the North and to Ethiopia, after feasting sumptuously on delicacies gathered from every part of the world would have desired to sleep, and to take his rest, and to gratify his free choice of sleep, had not the Lord, the provider of all good things, hindered the course of nature, so that in defiance of nature the tyrant's cruelty might be overcome. If I were to attempt to produce all the instances in Holy Writ, I should be tedious. All that the saints say is a prayer to God; their whole prayer and supplication a strong wrestling for the pity of God, so that we, who by our own strength and zeal cannot be saved, may be preserved by His mercy. But when we are concerned with grace and mercy, free will is in part void; in part, I say, for so much as this depends upon it, that we wish and desire, and give assent to the course we choose. But it depends on God whether we have the power in His strength and with His help to perform what we desire, and to bring to affect our toil and effort.

11. C. I simply said that we find the help of God not in our several actions, but in the grace of creation and of the law, that free will might not be destroyed. But there are many of us who maintain that all we do is done with the help of God.

A. Whoever says that must leave your party. Either, then, say the same yourself and join our side, or, if you refuse, you will be just as much our enemy as those who do not hold our views.

C. I shall be on your side if you speak my sentiments, or rather you will be on mine if you do not contradict them. You admit health of body, and deny health of the soul, which is stronger than the body. For sin is to the soul what disease or a wound is to the body. If then you admit that a man may be healthy so far as he is flesh, why do you not say he may be healthy so far as he is spirit?

    A. I will follow in the line you point out,
                      "and you to-day
Shall ne'er escape; where'r you call, I come."

    C. I am ready to listen.

    A. And I to speak to deaf ears. I will therefore reply to your argument. Made up of soul and body, we have the nature of both substances. As the body is said to be healthy if it is troubled with no weakness, so the soul is free from fault if it is unshaken and undisturbed. And yet, although the body may be healthy, sound, and active, with all the faculties in their full vigor, yet it suffers much from infirmities at more or less frequent intervals, and, however strong it may be, is sometimes distressed by various humors; so the soul, bearing the onset of thoughts and agitations, even though it escape shipwreck, does not sail without danger, and remembering its weakness, is always anxious about death, according as it is written, "What man is he that shall live and not see death?"—death, which threatens all mortal men, not through the decay of nature, but through the death of sin, according to the prophet's words, "The soul that sinned, it shall die." Besides, we know that Enoch and Elias have not yet seen this death which is common to man and the brutes. Show me a body which is never sick, or which after sickness is ever safe and sound, and I will show you a soul which never sinned, and after acquiring virtues will never again sin. The thing is impossible, and all the more when we remember that vice borders on virtue, and that, if you deviate ever so little, you will either go astray or fall over a precipice. How small is the interval between obstinacy and perseverance, miserliness and frugality, liberality and extravagance, wisdom and craft, intrepidity and rashness, caution and timidity! some of which are classed as good, others as bad. And the same applies to bodies. If you take precautions against biliousness, the phlegm increases. If you dry up the humors too quickly, the blood becomes heated and vitiated with bile, and a sallow hue spreads over the countenance. Without question, however much we may exercise all the care of the physician, and regulate our diet, and be free from indigestion and whatever fosters disease, the causes of which are in some cases hidden from us and known to God alone, we shiver with cold, or burn with fever, or howl with colic, and implore the help of the true physician, our Savior, and say with the Apostles, "Master, save us, we perish."

12. C. Granted that no one could avoid all sin in boyhood, youth, and early manhood; can you deny that very many righteous and holy men, after falling into vice, have heartily devoted themselves to the acquisition of virtue and through these have escaped sin?

A. This is what I told you at the beginning—that it rests with ourselves either to sin or not to sin, and to put the hand either to good or evil; and thus free will is preserved, but according to circumstances, time, and the state of human frailty; we maintain, however, that perpetual freedom from sin is reserved for God only, and for Him Who being the Word was made flesh without incurring the defects and the sins of the flesh. And, because I am able to avoid sin for a short time, you cannot logically infer that I am able to do so continually. Can I fast, watch, walk, sing, sit, sleep perpetually?

C. Why then in Holy Scripture are we stimulated to aim at perfect righteousness? For example: "Blessed are the pure in heart, for they shall see God," and "Blessed are the undefiled in the way, who walk in the law of the Lord." And God says to Abraham, "I am thy God, be thou pleasing in My sight, and be thou without spot, or blame, and I will make My covenant between Me and thee, and will multiply thee exceedingly." If that is impossible which Scripture testifies, it was useless to command it to be done.

A. You play upon Scripture until you wear a question threadbare, and remind me of the platform tricks of a conjurer who assumes a variety of characters, and is now Mars, next moment Venus; so that he who was at first all sternness and ferocity is dissolved into feminine softness. For the objection you now raise with an air of novelty—"Blessed are the pure in heart," "Blessed are the undefiled in the way," and "Be without spot," and so forth—is refuted when the Apostle replies, "We know in part, and we prophesy in part," and, "Now we see through a mirror darkly, but when that which is perfect is come, that which is in part shall be done away." And therefore we have but the shadow and likeness of the pure heart, which hereafter is destined to see God, and, free from spot or stain, to live with Abraham. However great the patriarch, prophet, or Apostle may be, it is said to them, in the words of our Lord and Savior, "If ye being evil, know how to give good gifts unto your children, how much more shall your Father Which is in heaven give good things to them which ask Him?" Then again even Abraham, to whom it was said, "Be thou without spot and

St. Jerome

blame," in the consciousness of his frailty fell upon his face to the earth. And when God had spoken to Him, saying, "Thy wife Sarai shall no longer be called Sarai, but Sara shall her name be, and I will give thee a son by her, and I will bless him and he shall become a great nation, and kings of nations shall spring from him," the narrative at once proceeds to say, "Abraham fell upon his face, and laughed, and said in his heart, Shall a child be born unto him that is an hundred years old? and shall Sarah, that is ninety years old, bear?" And Abraham said unto God, "Oh, that Ishmael might live before thee!" And God said, "Nay, but Sarah thy wife shall bear thee a son, and thou shalt call his name Isaac," and so on. He certainly had heard the words of God, "I am thy God, be thou pleasing in My sight, and without spot"; why then did he not believe what God promised, and why did he laugh in his heart, thinking that he escaped the notice of God, and not daring to laugh openly? Moreover he gives the reasons for his unbelief, and says, "How is it possible for a man that is a hundred years old to beget a son of a wife that is ninety years old?" "Oh, that Ishmael might live before thee," he says. "Ishmael whom thou once give me. I do not ask a hard thing, I am content with the blessing I have received." God convinced him by a mysterious reply. He said, "Yea." The meaning is, that shall come to pass which you think shall not be. Your wife Sara shall bear you a son, and before she conceives, before he is born, I will give the boy a name. For, from your error in secretly laughing, your son shall be called Isaac, that is *laughter*. But if you think that God is seen by those who are pure in heart in this world, why did Moses, who had previously said, "I have seen the Lord face to face, and my life is preserved," afterwards entreat that he might see him distinctly? And because he said that he had seen God, the Lord told him, "Thou canst not see My face. For man shall not see My face, and live." Wherefore also the Apostle calls Him the only invisible God, Who dwells in light unapproachable, and Whom no man hath seen, nor can see. And the Evangelist John in holy accents testifies, saying, "No man hath at any time seen God. The only begotten Son Who is in the bosom of the Father, He hath declared Him." He Who sees, also declares, not how great He is Who is seen, nor how much He knows Who declares; but as much as the capacity of mortals can receive.

13. And whereas you think he is blessed who is undefiled in the way, and walks in His law, you must interpret the former clause by the latter. From the many proofs I have adduced you have learnt that no one has been able to fulfil the law. And if the Apostle, in comparison with the grace of Christ, reckoned those things as filth which formerly, under the law, he counted gain, so that he might win Christ, how much more certain ought we to be that the reason why the grace of Christ and of the Gospel has been added is that, under the law, no one could be justified? Now if, under the law, no one is justified, how is he perfectly undefiled in the way who is still walking and hastening to reach the goal? Surely, he who is in the course, and who is advancing on the road, is inferior to him who has reached his journey's end. If, then, he is undefiled and perfect who is still walking in the way and advancing in the law, what more shall he have who has arrived at the end of life and of the law? Hence the Apostle, speaking of our Lord, says that, at the end of the world, when all virtues shall receive their consummation, He will present His holy Church to

Himself without spot or wrinkle, and yet you think that Church perfect, while yet in the flesh, which is subject to death and decay. You deserve to be told, with the Corinthians, "Ye are already perfect, ye are already made rich: ye reign without us, and I would that ye did reign, that we might also reign with you"—since true and stainless perfection belongs to the inhabitants of heaven, and is reserved for that day when the bridegroom shall say to the bride, "Thou art all fair, my love; and there is no spot in thee." And in this sense we must understand the words: "That ye may be blameless and harmless, as children of God, without blemish"; for He did not say *ye are,* but *may be.* He is contemplating the future, not stating a case pertaining to the present; so that here is toil and effort, in that other world the rewards of labor and of virtue. Lastly, John writes: "Beloved, we are sons of God, and it is not yet made manifest what we shall be. We know that when He shall be manifested, we shall be like Him: for we shall see Him even as He is." Although, then, we are sons of God, yet likeness to God, and the true contemplation of God, is promised us then, when He shall appear in His majesty.

14. From this swelling pride springs the audacity in prayer which marks the directions in your letter to a certain widow as to how the saints ought to pray. "He," you say, "rightly lifts up his hands to God; he pours out supplications with a good conscience who can say, 'Thou knowest, Lord, how holy, how innocent, how pure from all deceit, wrong, and robbery are the hands which I spread out unto Thee; how righteous, how spotless, and free from all falsehood are the lips with which I pour forth my prayers unto Thee, that Thou mayest pity me.'" Is this the prayer of a Christian, or of a proud Pharisee like him

who says in the Gospel, "God, I thank Thee that I am not as other men are, robbers, unjust, adulterers, or even as this publican: I fast twice in the week, I give tithes of all that I possess." Yet he merely thanks God because, by His mercy, he is not as other men: he execrates sin, and does not claim his righteousness as his own. But you say, "Now Thou knowest how holy, how innocent, how pure from all deceit, wrong, and robbery are the hands which I spread out before Thee." He says that he fasts twice in the week, that he may afflict his vicious and wanton flesh, and he gives tithes of all his substance. For "the ransom of a man's life is his riches." You join the devil in boasting, "I will ascend above the stars, I will place my throne in heaven, and I will be like the Most High." David says, "My loins are filled with illusions"; and "My wounds stink and are corrupt because of my foolishness"; and "Enter not into judgment with Thy servant"; and "In Thy sight no man living shall be justified." You boast that you are holy, innocent, and pure, and spread out clean hands unto God. And you are not satisfied with glorying in all your works, unless you say that you are pure from all sins of speech; and you tell us how righteous, how spotless, how free from all falsehood your lips are. The Psalmist sings, "Every man is a liar"; and this is supported by apostolical authority: "That God may be true," says St. Paul, "and every man a liar"; and yet you have lips righteous, spotless, and free from all falsehood. Isaiah laments, saying, "Woe is me! for I am undone, because I am a man of unclean lips, and I dwell in the midst of a people of unclean lips"; and afterwards one of the seraphim brings a hot coal, taken with the tongs, to purify the prophet's lips, for he was not, according to the tenor of your words, arrogant, but he confessed his own faults.

Just as we read in the Psalms, "What shall be due unto thee, and what shall be done more unto thee in respect of a deceitful tongue? Sharp arrows of the mighty, with coals that make desolate." And after all this swelling with pride, and boastfulness in prayer, and confidence in your holiness, like one fool trying to persuade another, you finish with the words "These lips with which I pour out my supplication that Thou mayest have pity on me." If you are holy, if you are innocent, if you are cleansed from all defilement, if you have sinned neither in word nor deed—although James says, "He who offends not in word is a perfect man," and "No one can curb his tongue"—how is it that you sue for mercy? so that, forsooth, you bewail yourself, and pour out prayers because you are holy, pure, and innocent, a man of stainless lips, free from all falsehood, and endowed with a power like that of God. Christ prayed thus on the cross: "My God, my God, why hast Thou forsaken Me? Why art Thou so far from helping Me?" And, again, "Father, into Thy hands I commend My spirit," and "Father, forgive them, for they know not what they do." And this is He, who, returning thanks for us, had said, "I confess to Thee, O Father, Lord of heaven and earth."

15. Our Lord so instructed His Apostles that, daily at the sacrifice of His body, believers make bold to say, "Our Father, Which art in Heaven, hallowed be Thy name"; they earnestly desire the name of God, which in itself is holy, to be hallowed in themselves; you say, "Thou knowest, Lord, how holy, how innocent, and how pure are my hands." Then they say: "Thy Kingdom come," anticipating the hope of the future kingdom, so that, when Christ reigns, sin may by no means reign in their mortal body, and to this they couple the words, "Thy

will be done in earth as it is in Heaven"; so that human weakness may imitate the angels, and the will of our Lord may be fulfilled on earth; you say, "A man can, if he chooses, be free from all sin." The Apostles prayed for the daily bread, or the bread better than all food, which was to come, so that they might be worthy to receive the body of Christ; and you are led by your excess of holiness and well-established righteousness to boldly claim the heavenly gifts. Next comes, "Forgive us our debts, as we also forgive our debtors." No sooner do they rise from the baptismal font, and by being born again and incorporated into our Lord and Savior thus fulfil what is written of them, "Blessed are they whose iniquities are forgiven and whose sins are covered," than at the first communion of the body of Christ they say, "Forgive us our debts," though these debts had been forgiven them at their confession of Christ; but you in your arrogant pride boast of the cleanness of your holy hands and of the purity of your speech. However thorough the conversion of a man may be, and however perfect his possession of virtue after a time of sins and failings, can such persons be as free from fault as they who are just leaving the font of Christ? And yet these latter are commanded to say, "Forgive us our debts, as we also forgive our debtors"; not in the spirit of a false humility, but because they are afraid of human frailty and dread their own conscience. They say, "Lead us not into temptation"; you and Jovinian unite in saying that those who with a full faith have been baptized cannot be further tempted or sin. Lastly, they add, "But deliver us from the evil one." Why do they beg from the Lord what they have already by the power of free will? Oh, man, now thou hast been made clean in the laver, and of thee it is said, "Who is this that cometh up all white, leaning upon her beloved?" The bride, therefore, is washed, yet she cannot keep her purity, unless she be supported by the Lord. How is it that you long to be set free by the mercy of God, you who but a little while ago were released from your sins? The only explanation is the principle by which we maintain that, when we have done all, we must confess we are unprofitable.

16. So then your prayer outdoes the pride of the Pharisee, and you are condemned when compared with the Publican. He, standing afar off, did not dare to lift up his eyes unto Heaven, but smote upon his breast, saying, "God be merciful unto me a sinner." And on this is based our Lord's declaration, "I say unto you this man went down to his house justified rather than the other. For everyone that exalted himself shall be abased, and he that humbled himself shall be exalted." The Apostles are humbled that they may be exalted. Your disciples are lifted up that they may fall. In your flattery of the widow previously mentioned you are not ashamed to say that piety such as is found on earth, and truth which is everywhere a stranger, had made their home with her in preference to all others. You do not recollect the familiar words, "O my people, they which call thee blessed cause thee to err, and destroy the paths of thy feet"; and you expressly praise her and say, "Happy beyond all thought are you! how blessed! if righteousness, which is believed to be now nowhere but in Heaven, is found with you alone on earth." Is this teaching or slaying? Is it raising from earth, or casting down from heaven, to attribute that to a poor creature of a woman, which angels would not dare arrogate to themselves? If piety, truth, and righteousness are found on earth nowhere but in one woman, where shall we find your righteous followers,

who, you boast, are sinless on earth? These two chapters on prayer and praise you and your disciples are wont to swear are none of yours, and yet your brilliant style is so clearly seen in them, and the elegance of your Ciceronian diction is so marked that, although you strut about with the slow pace of a tortoise, you have not the courage to acknowledge what you teach in private and expose for sale. Happy man! whose books no one writes out but your own disciples, so that whatever appears to be unacceptable, you may contend is not your own but someone else's work. And where is the man with ability enough to imitate the charm of your language?

17. C. I can put it off no longer; my patience is completely overcome by your iniquitous words. Tell me, pray, what sin have little infants committed. Neither the consciousness of wrong nor ignorance can be imputed to those who, according to the prophet Jonah, know not their right hand from their left. They cannot sin, and they can perish; their knees are too weak to walk, they utter inarticulate cries; we laugh at their attempts to speak; and, all the while, poor unfortunates! the torments of eternal misery are prepared for them.

A. Ah! now that your disciples have turned masters you begin to be fluent, not to say eloquent. Antony, an excellent orator, whose praises Tully loudly proclaims, says that he had seen many fluent men, but so far never an eloquent speaker; so don't amuse me with flowers of oratory which have not grown in your own garden, and with which the ears of inexperience and of boyhood are wont to be tickled, but plainly tell me what you think.

C. What I say is this—you must at least allow that they have no sin who cannot sin.

A. I will allow it, if they have been baptized into Christ; and if you will not then immediately bind me to agree with your opinion that a man can be without sin if he chooses; for they neither have the power nor the will; but they are free from all sin through the grace of God, which they received in their baptism.

C. You force me to make an invidious remark and ask, Why, what sin have they committed? that you may immediately have me stoned in some popular tumult. You have not the power to kill me, but you certainly have the will.

A. He slays a heretic who allows him to be a heretic. But when we rebuke him we give him life; you may die to your heresy, and live to the Catholic faith.

C. If you know us to be heretics, why do you not accuse us?

A. Because the Apostle teaches me to avoid a heretic after the first and second admonition, not to accuse him. The Apostle knew that such a one is perverse and self-condemned. Besides, it would be the height of folly to make my faith depend on another man's judgment. For supposing someone were to call you a Catholic, am I to immediately give assent? Whoever defends you, and says that you rightly hold your perverse opinions, does not succeed in rescuing you from infamy, but charges himself with perfidy. Your numerous supporters will never prove you to be a Catholic, but will show that you are a heretic. But I would have such opinions as these suppressed by ecclesiastical authority; otherwise we shall be in the case of those who show some dreadful picture to a crying child. May the fear of God grant us this—to despise all other fears. Therefore, either defend your opinions, or abandon what you are unable to defend. Whoever may be called in to defend you must be enrolled as a partisan, not as a patron.

18. C. Tell me, pray, and rid me of all doubts, why little children are baptized.

A. That their sins may be forgiven them in baptism.

C. What sin are they guilty of? How can anyone be set free who is not bound?

A. You ask me! The Gospel trumpet will reply, the teacher of the Gentiles, the golden vessel shining throughout the world: "Death reigned from Adam even unto Moses: even over those who did not sin after the likeness of the transgression of Adam, who is a figure of Him that was to come." And if you object that some are spoken of who did not sin, you must understand that they did not sin in the same way as Adam did by transgressing God's command in Paradise. But all men are held liable either on account of their ancient forefather Adam, or on their own account. He that is an infant is released in baptism from the chain which bound his father. He who is old enough to have discernment is set free from the chain of his own or another's sin by the blood of Christ. You must not think me a heretic because I take this view, for the blessed martyr Cyprian, whose rival you boast of being in the classification of Scripture proofs, in the epistle addressed to Bishop Fidus on the Baptism of Infants speaks thus: "Moreover, if even the worst offenders, and those who previous to baptism sin much against God, once they believe have the gift of remission of sins, and no one is kept from baptism and from grace, how much more ought not an infant to be kept from baptism seeing that, being only just born, he has committed no sin? He has only, being born according to the flesh among Adam's sons, incurred the taint of ancient death by his first birth. And he is the more easily admitted to remission of sins because of the very fact that not his own sins but those of another are remitted to him. And so, dearest brother, it was our decision in council that no one ought to be kept by us from baptism and from the grace of God, Who is merciful to all, and kind, and good. And whereas this rule ought to be observed and kept with reference to all, bear in mind that it ought so much the more to be observed with regard to infants themselves and those just born, for they have the greater claims on our assistance in order to obtain Divine mercy, because their cries and tears from the very birth are one perpetual prayer."

19. That holy man and eloquent bishop Augustin not long ago wrote to Marcellinus (the same that was afterwards, though innocent, put to death by heretics on the pretext of his taking part in the tyranny of Heraclian) two treatises on infant baptism, in opposition to your heresy which maintains that infants are baptized not for remission of sins, but for admission to the kingdom of heaven, according as it is written in the Gospel, "Except a man be born again of water and of the Spirit, he cannot enter into the kingdom of heaven." He addressed a third, moreover, to the same Marcellinus, against those who say as do you, that a man can be free from sin, if he chooses, without the help of God. And, recently, a fourth to Hilary against this doctrine of yours, which is full of perversity. And he is said to have others on the anvil with special regard to you, which have not yet come to hand. Wherefore, I think I must abandon my task, for fear Horace's words may be thrown at me, "Don't carry firewood into a forest." For we must either say the same

as he does, and that would be superfluous; or, if we wished to say something fresh, we should find our best points anticipated by that splendid genius. One thing I will say and so end my discourse, that you ought either to give us a new creed, so that, after baptizing children into the name of the Father, Son, and Holy Spirit, you may baptize them into the kingdom of heaven; or, if you have one baptism both for infants and for persons of mature age, it follows that infants also should be baptized for the remission of sins after the likeness of the transgression of Adam. But if you think the remission of another's sins implies injustice, and that he has no need of it who could not sin, cross over to Origen, your special favorite, who says that ancient offences committed long before in the heavens are loosed in baptism. You will then be not only led by his authority in other matters, but will be following his error in this also.

Find this and other great works of the early Church Fathers at lighthousechristianpublishing.com.

Our Father who art in heaven, hallowed be thy name.
Thy kingdom come, Thy will be done, on earth as it is in heaven.
Give us this day our daily bread and forgive us our trespasses as we forgive those who trespass against us.
And lead us not into temptation, but deliver us from evil, for Thine is the kingdom, the power and the glory. Forever and ever.

Amen

St. Jerome

Hail Mary full of grace, the Lord is with thee. Blessed art thou amongst women and blessed is the fruit of thy womb Jesus. Holy Mary mother of God, pray for us sinners, now and the hour of our death.

www.ingramcontent.com/pod-product-compliance
Lightning Source LLC
Chambersburg PA
CBHW052129070526
44585CB00017B/1753